"This deeply researched and lucidly written volume illumines the life of one of the most important but least examined figures in the early history of American (and world) evangelicalism. The continuities between Mears's multiple contributions and the far more heralded career of Billy Graham, for example, are simply astonishing. Migliazzo writes with empathetic yet not uncritical engagement. He provides a wonderful addition to our understanding of American religious history in general, and to the history of women in the formation of evangelicalism in particular."

— GRANT WACKER
author of *One Soul at a Time: The Story of Billy Graham*

"Historians have long recognized that Christianity in America has been strengthened, if not sustained, by women. Yet, when it comes to twentieth-century evangelicalism, most of the stories we tell focus on strong male characters. Arlin Migliazzo joins a growing number of scholars who are trying to correct this narrative. He has convinced me that all future accounts of modern evangelicalism must place a California Sunday school teacher at the center. This well-researched and accessible biography of Henrietta Mears is a game-changer."

— JOHN FEA
author of *Believe Me: The Evangelical Road to Donald Trump*

"We have long needed a scholarly biography of Henrietta Mears, one of the most influential women—and educators—in modern American evangelicalism. Migliazzo has given us one that is readable, chock-full of detail, and centered on Mears's passion for Christian education. As director of a wildly popular ministry at First Presbyterian Church of Hollywood, she built bridges connecting leading conservative Protestants both to each other and to the wider culture. Mears thus emerges as one of the chief architects of today's evangelical church."

— ANDREA L. TURPIN
author of *A New Moral Vision: Gender, Religion, and the Changing Purposes of American Higher Education, 1837–1917*

"In this riveting and deeply researched book, Arlin Migliazzo traces the compelling life of Henrietta Mears, one of the most important and under-appreciated leaders of modern American evangelicalism, and demonstrates how she transformed religion and Christian education in the United States."

— MATTHEW A. SUTTON
Washington State University

LIBRARY OF RELIGIOUS BIOGRAPHY

Mark A. Noll, Kathryn Gin Lum, and Heath W. Carter, series editors

Long overlooked by historians, religion has emerged in recent years as a key factor in understanding the past. From politics to popular culture, from social struggles to the rhythms of family life, religion shapes every story. Religious biographies open a window to the sometimes surprising influence of religion on the lives of influential people and the worlds they inhabited.

The Library of Religious Biography is a series that brings to life important figures in United States history and beyond. Grounded in careful research, these volumes link the lives of their subjects to the broader cultural contexts and religious issues that surrounded them. The authors are respected historians and recognized authorities in the historical period in which their subject lived and worked.

Marked by careful scholarship yet free of academic jargon, the books in this series are well-written narratives meant to be read and enjoyed as well as studied.

Titles include:

A Short Life of ***Jonathan Edwards***
by George M. Marsden

One Soul at a Time: The Story of ***Billy Graham***
by Grant Wacker

Harriet Beecher Stowe*: A Spiritual Life*
by Nancy Koester

For a complete list of published volumes, see the back of this volume.

Mother of Modern Evangelicalism

The Life and Legacy of Henrietta Mears

Arlin C. Migliazzo

William B. Eerdmans Publishing Company
Grand Rapids, Michigan

Wm. B. Eerdmans Publishing Co.
4035 Park East Court SE, Grand Rapids, Michigan 49546
www.eerdmans.com

Published 2020
Printed in the United States of America

26 25 24 23 22 21 20 1 2 3 4 5 6 7

ISBN 978-0-8028-7792-5

Library of Congress Cataloging-in-Publication Data

Names: Migliazzo, Arlin C., 1951– author.
Title: Mother of modern evangelism : the life and legacy of Henrietta Mears / Arlin C. Migliazzo.
Description: Grand Rapids, Michigan : William B. Eerdmans Publishing Company, 2020. | Series: Library of religious biography | Includes bibliographical references and index. | Summary: "The full life story of Henrietta Mears and an overview of her impact on modern American evangelicalism"—Provided by publisher.
Identifiers: LCCN 2020022484 | ISBN 9780802877925
Subjects: LCSH: Mears, Henrietta C. (Henrietta Cornelia), 1890–1963. | Presbyterians—United States—Biography. | Sunday-school teachers—Biography. | Evangelists—United States—Biography.
Classification: LCC BX9225.M397 M53 2020 | DDC 268.092 [B]—dc23
LC record available at https://lccn.loc.gov/2020022484

. . . for all the saints
who from their labors rest. . . .

Contents

Foreword

Quite simply, Henrietta Mears belongs at the center of any history of twentieth-century American evangelicalism.

Although never the public face of the movement, Mears was one of the most powerful behind-the-scenes operators during the critical midcentury decades when evangelicalism emerged as a formative religious and cultural movement. If evangelicalism is a network, Mears was the hub. As Arlin Migliazzo demonstrates in this meticulously researched account, it was Mears who helped define the contours of the movement, even as she embodied many of the tensions that afflict American evangelicalism to this day.

A product of William Bell Riley's Minneapolis First Baptist Church, Mears adhered to a fundamentalist theology. But she parted ways with fundamentalists when it came to their reactionary anti-intellectualism and their separatist instincts. Confident that the truth of the Christian gospel could transform even the most resistant outposts, Mears embraced modern culture as her mission field. Less judgmental than many of her peers, Mears modeled a fearless, often gracious evangelistic enterprise that expanded the evangelical footprint and enhanced its cultural relevance.

In many ways, Mears was a pioneering figure. As early as the 1920s, Mears was advancing a transdenominational, outward-facing conservative Protestantism. When fundamentalists came together in the 1940s to rebrand their movement, Mears had already perfected the brand. Even before the establishment of the National Association of Evangelicals in 1942, Mears had established herself as a key figure in constructing the scaffolding that would support the national movement. Moreover, Mears had relocated to southern

California decades before the region became the crucible of postwar American evangelicalism. It was there, in the shadow of Hollywood, that Mears would facilitate the rise of Billy Graham's career, and with it, help establish the trajectory of twentieth-century American Protestantism. Other "Mears boys" included Bill Bright, founder of Campus Crusade for Christ, and Jim Rayburn, founder of Young Life, along with countless lesser-known figures who would play critical roles in expanding the evangelical movement across the nation and around the world.

Mears accomplished all this as a Sunday school teacher.

By teaching, rather than preaching, Mears deftly maneuvered around the constraints conservative Protestant theology placed upon women. She would not occupy a pulpit on a Sunday morning, but she might well expound from behind the same pulpit on a Sunday evening. She trained thousands of students in biblical knowledge and evangelism, founded her own publishing house, and mentored hundreds of ministry leaders, but she did so without fundamentally challenging the gendered power structures of midcentury evangelicalism. Even so, in her role as teacher and administrator she was neither quiet nor submissive; outspoken and forceful, she could be unrelenting in her exacting leadership. Mears, then, walked the fine line that subsequent generations of evangelical women would come to know well. Staying within prescribed boundaries, she was able to exert enormous influence throughout the evangelical world.

Her position as Director of Christian Education at First Presbyterian Church of Hollywood placed her in close proximity to members of the film industry. Unlike many fundamentalists, she refused to condemn the Hollywood set as beyond redemption. Through her Hollywood Christian Group she ministered to the stars, bringing people like Dale Evans, Stuart Hamblen, Jane Russell, Roy Rogers, and many others into the evangelical fold. Her outreach appeared to be motivated by the evangelistic impulse to save souls, and she preferred to remain in the background, yet through her Hollywood ministry she nevertheless helped give rise to the celebrity culture that would indelibly shape modern American evangelicalism.

Unlike the religious movement she helped nurture, Mears's faith was not overtly political. Far more than many of her contemporaries, she saw politics as a distraction from her primary calling—to teach Christ crucified and resurrected. Bible teaching and evangelism remained at the center of all her efforts.

In this way, evangelicals today might see in Mears a refreshing counterpoint to an evangelicalism that has become enmeshed in combative partisan politics. Even here, however, the story Migliazzo tells is more complicated. Mears's reticence on political matters did not mean that the faith she promulgated had no political implications. This is particularly true around the issue of race. As Migliazzo makes clear, Mears's views on African Americans were tinged with racial stereotypes. As the national conversation on civil rights evolved, Mears had little to say on issues of racial justice. Race was rarely the focus of Mears's attention, but the evangelicalism that Mears both prefigured and pioneered was at its heart a white religious movement.

In this richly textured account, Migliazzo presents a compelling portrait of a complex, even at times enigmatic figure. Mears's evangelicalism, with all its contradictions, is one that many white evangelicals will recognize today. It is a faith that both empowers and constrains women. A faith that privileges whiteness even as it denies any racial identity. A faith that embraces celebrity culture and is in turn transformed by it. A faith that proclaims Christ over all yet applies the good news of the gospel in culturally specific ways.

Over the course of her life and ministry, Mears "negotiated the narrow ridge between judgment and grace." Mears's story is essential reading for those seeking to understand the challenges confronting white evangelicals today as they continue to struggle to navigate the shoals of judgment and grace.

Kristin Kobes Du Mez

Acknowledgments

I have accrued many debts over the more than ten years I have spent pursuing Henrietta Mears. For those many years she was known around our home as the "other woman," for I would often steal away to spend a few more minutes with her before attending to other pressing matters. So for the quarter of our forty-two-year married life during which she let me keep company with this amazing lady, my foremost appreciation goes to my wife, Judi.

The research phase of this project would not have been possible without the support of a host of generous souls. Thanks to a series of happy circumstances, it was my privilege to interview upward of sixty individuals touched personally in one way or another by Henrietta Mears. Though they are not all cited here, I remain deeply grateful for their willingness to spend time with someone most of them had never met. Among those I had the pleasure of getting to know over the course of this study, Barbara Hudson Powers, Ralph Hamburger, Jeanne Smith, Marjorie Sutton, Max Malmquist, Esther Brinkley, Barbara Becerra, Earl Palmer, Marilyn Mears Hobbs, Colleen Townsend Evans, Andrea Van Boven (Madden), and Amber Thomas Reynolds trusted me with items from their personal libraries that added particular depth to my research. Andrea augmented my set of interviews by allowing me to copy those she did in the mid-1990s for her master's thesis on Mears. I am especially indebted to former president of Gospel Light William T. Greig III and his wife, Rhonni, for their generosity and unlimited entrée to the organization's entire archive. His executive assistant, Anita Griggs, helped me navigate the records and always addressed my queries and requests with grace and more than a little patience. The late Layton Brueske Jr.—who knew the records and history of the First Baptist Church of Minneapolis like the back of his hand—was similarly helpful, and Stan White, former president of Forest Home Ministries, accorded me the same freedom there. Anna Kerr at the First Presbyterian Church of Hollywood not only facilitated my research in the church's archive, she also secured housing for me on my research trips to Southern California and organized a very significant group interview with many friends of Mears. The hospitality of Marilyn Mears Hobbs, Dennis and Carolin Migliazzo, Mary Bechtel, and Mark and Marylin Rhoads made research almost delightful. Special kudos go to Mark, who spent an entire day with me in Minneapolis to ensure that I was able to review all the salient records at First Baptist. In the same vein, thanks must go to Max Malmquist who rendered comparable service at the North Branch Methodist Church. The Whitworth University Faculty Research and Development Committee and the university's Weyerhaeuser Center for Christian Faith and Learning furnished much appreciated financial support.

I am surely not the only historian who wonders why there is no hall of fame for librarians and archivists; without their expertise our work would be next to impossible. My personal hall would include Gail Fielding and Nancy Bunker at Whitworth University; Layton Brueske Jr. at First Baptist, Minneapolis; Lorynne Budd at First Presbyterian, Hollywood; Sally Rupprecht at Forest Home; Keith Call, Wayne Weber, Paul Ericksen, and Bob Shuster at Wheaton College; Nancy Gower at Fuller Theological Seminary; Ruby Bosanko and Earle Crissman at the Marcus P. Beebe Memorial Library, Ipswich, South Dakota; Sharon Silengo at the State Historical Society of North Dakota; Barbara Krieger at Dartmouth University; Max Malmquist and Douglas Swanson at the North Chisago (Minnesota) Historical Society; Beth Kaplan at the University of Minnesota; John Hallberg at the Institute for Regional Studies at North Dakota State University; and Annie Mott at the Poultney (Vermont) Historical Society. In addition, my gratitude goes to staff members at the Chicago Historical Society, Minnesota History Center, and Los Angeles County Hall of Records for their assistance.

Once I began to shape the research into something approaching a prose narrative, I called on the knowledge and skills of many who have been instrumental in bringing this venture to a successful conclusion. Joel Carpenter, Margaret Lamberts Bendroth, Dale Soden, Barry Hankins, and Kristen Du Mez took time out from their own worthy pursuits to read and comment on all or parts of earlier versions of this tome. It is stronger for their instructive comments, but they bear no responsibility for any remaining deficits, which are mine alone. Ken Pecka gave liberally of his time and wisdom to ensure that the text, photographs, and tables would be formatted appropriately. David Jarvis was particularly helpful in digitally piecing together some of the larger historical photographs. Charity Purvis, Chloe Dye, Sarah Gambell, Chelsea Chamberlain, and Jerrica Kjorsvik contributed their abilities as student assistants in the Department of History at Whitworth University to various aspects of the research and preparation of the text—all of them under the astute guidance of our former departmental program assistant, the late Barbara Brodrick. The support of Dean Noelle Wiersma was also much appreciated.

As my work progressed, three journals accepted portions of the research for publication. I am grateful for the permission to cite in somewhat altered form substantial excerpts of those articles: "Progress of a Young Pilgrim: Henrietta Mears on the Northern Plains, 1890–1913," *The Journal of Presbyterian History* 94, no. 1 (spring/summer 2016): 16–28; "The Education of Henrietta Mears: A Fundamentalist in Transition," *Baptist History and Heritage* 46, no. 2 (summer 2011): 65–76; and "'She Must Be a Proper Exception:' Females, Fuller Seminary, and the Limits of Gender Equity among Southern California Evangelicals, 1947–1952," *Fides et Historia* 45, no. 2 (summer/fall 2013): 1–19.

Finally, I must express my heartfelt thanks to the editorial staff at Eerdmans, particularly to Heath Carter and David Bratt, for believing that the story of this remarkable woman deserved to be included in the Library of Religious Biography series. After reading what follows, I hope you will concur.

Abbreviations for Archival Collections

BGCA	Billy Graham Center Archives, Wheaton College, Wheaton, Illinois
BMC	Archives of the Beardsley Methodist Church
CHS	Archives of the Chicago Historical Society, Chicago, Illinois
FBCF	Archives of the First Baptist Church of Fargo, Fargo, North Dakota
FBCM	Archives of the First Baptist Church of Minneapolis, Minneapolis, Minnesota
FH	Forest Home Christian Conference Center Archives, Forest Falls, California
FPCH	Archives of the First Presbyterian Church of Hollywood, Hollywood, California
FTS	Archives of Fuller Theological Seminary, Pasadena, California
GAM	Minutes of the General Assembly of the Presbyterian Church in the United States of America
GL	Gospel Light Archives, Ventura, California
IRS	Institute for Regional Studies and University Archives, North Dakota State University, Fargo, North Dakota
LACHR	Los Angeles County Hall of Records, Los Angeles and Norwalk, California
MHC	Minnesota Historical Society Archives, Minnesota History Center, Saint Paul, Minnesota
NBUMC	Collections of the North Branch United Methodist Church

PCAHC	Presbyterian Church in America Historical Center, St. Louis, Missouri
PHS	Collections of the Poultney Historical Society, East Poultney, Vermont
SHSND	Archives of the State Historical Society of North Dakota, Bismarck, North Dakota
UMA	University of Minnesota Archives, Elmer L. Andersen Library, Minneapolis, Minnesota
WCA	Wheaton College Archives, Wheaton, Illinois
YPSCE	Young People's Society of Christian Endeavor

Introduction

A Gracious Orthodoxy

To the thousands who regularly travel US 101 from the San Fernando Valley southeast toward Los Angeles, the route of the Hollywood Freeway is as familiar as the masthead of the *Los Angeles Times* and probably just as much taken for granted. Even the panoramic view of the city widening out before them on a clear day over the crest of Cahuenga Pass is probably less exhilarating than the possibility of missing the traffic bottleneck that inevitably develops just past the Santa Monica Boulevard exit. A newcomer to Southern California, however, negotiating the complexity that is the LA freeway system for the first time, might have a completely different point of view. She might, for example, wonder why the freeway makes a seemingly pointless arc to the left away from the city's central district at the Gower Street off-ramp only to lean back rightward as the Hollywood Boulevard overpass comes into view. Had she traveled the route at night she might have deduced a possible reason, for she could not have missed the floodlit gothic-style bell tower of the First Presbyterian Church of Hollywood. To this day, many believe that the only reason urban planners back in the 1950s did not straighten the route was due to the outsized influence of a diminutive and physically impaired, university-trained schoolteacher named Henrietta Cornelia Mears, who became the prophetic voice of a re-forming American Protestant ethos as early as the second decade of the twentieth century.

When she arrived in Hollywood from Minneapolis in 1928, the massive sanctuary had just recently been completed, the communicant membership hovered just above 2,100, and, on any given Sunday, attendance at the church's Sunday school averaged 450. When the church hosted her memorial service thirty-five years later, the Sunday school under her care was purported to be the largest in the Presbyterian Church and one of the ten largest Protestant Sunday schools in the entire nation. In the half century between 1913 and 1963, Mears either originated, actively participated in, or significantly inspired a formidable array of organizations that would transform Christianity in the United States. Earlier than any other twentieth-century American Protestant, she shaped the contours of what would become known as the modern evangelical movement.

Mears founded a successful publishing company that grew into one of the country's largest independent religious publishing houses, whose products serviced a global clientele. She negotiated the purchase of a Southern California resort, which under her guidance became a major interdenominational conference center that today hosts upward of sixty thousand participants annually at multiple sites. She authored Sunday-school curricula used by thousands of churches around the world and helped launch the first formal organized ministry to the entertainment industry. She administered deputation service programs that were created initially for Christian youth to help underserved populations in Southern California but eventually expanded to encompass other areas of need, including war-ravaged Europe and Asia. She was an early leader of the National Association of Evangelicals—serving as a charter member of the association's Commission on International Relations—and a seminal force behind the formation of the National Sunday School Association. She created a nonprofit foundation to strengthen Christian education programs worldwide and train indigenous leaders using their own languages. A sought-after speaker, Mears regularly addressed audiences around the country and overseas on topics ranging from Christian youth work and leadership to church growth and evangelism. She carved only enough time out of her hectic schedule to author short articles, but her collected lesson materials and related notes have been in print since their release in book form. More than four million copies of her most popular volume, *What the Bible Is All About*, circulate today in at least four different editions.

Mears developed close relationships with celebrities such as film stars Roy Rogers, Dale Evans, Jane Russell, and Colleen Townsend and recording artists Tim Spencer, Redd Harper, and Connie Haines. She directly or indirectly influenced prominent Protestant icons such as Stuart Hamblen, James Oliver Buswell Jr., Harold John Ockenga, Harold Lindsell, Dawson Trotman, and

Roberta Hestenes; and she collaborated with Cameron Townsend, founder of Wycliffe Bible Translators, and Bob Pierce, architect of World Vision and Samaritan's Purse.[1] She counted West Coast governors Arthur Langlie (Washington), Mark Hatfield (Oregon), and Goodwin Knight (California) among her supporters. Excluding his mother and wife, evangelist Billy Graham called her the greatest female influence on his life and one of the greatest Christians he ever knew. Bill Bright, founder of the international ministry of Campus Crusade for Christ, patterned his lifework on principles he gleaned from her. Jim Rayburn, the visionary behind the Young Life Campaign, fashioned his ministry among high school students around what he learned from Mears. Dr. Wilbur Smith, who cofounded Fuller Theological Seminary and taught English Bible there and at Trinity Evangelical Divinity School, called her "the most inspiring woman leader in Christian causes that I have ever known."[2]

Nearly four hundred students from her renowned Hollywood Presbyterian College Department went into full-time Christian ministry, and hundreds more emerged as important civic and business leaders who served local churches as active laypersons. She motivated young women from her Fidelis Sunday school class in Minneapolis to live out their faith fearlessly in the world. They and hundreds of others trained by her or by her protégés became an integral part of the renewal of a brand of theological conservatism that developed in the wake of the fundamentalist-modernist controversy of the 1910s and 1920s, grew to prominence in the 1940s and 1950s, and continues to affect American culture in the twenty-first century. Her predominant role in the revitalization of evangelical Christianity helped transform the lives of thousands and opened a new direction for Christian orthodoxy that remains viable today, six decades after her death. And she did all this with a generosity of spirit worthy of imitation.

That generosity of spirit played out in a way particular to her. For Henrietta Mears remains something of an enigma—a woman who accepted the limitations of her time yet simultaneously pushed past those restrictions in ways few seemed to notice. She supposedly never allowed herself to fill a pulpit on Sunday morning or to be called a "preacher" as was her contemporary Aimee Semple McPherson. But she taught Scripture from more pulpits across the country than most ministers or priests. She technically never gave a sermon, but her subtle expositions of biblical texts were the stuff of legend wherever she taught. On only one occasion did she permit a female to serve as president of First Presbyterian's coeducational College Department, which ultimately grew to an enrollment of over eight hundred. Yet she encouraged women to exercise their talents in both secular and religious vocations and nurtured the young women of her Minneapolis Sunday school class in ways that her home church pastor, the Rev. William Bell Riley, could not. She never directly promoted a political or social agenda and even exhibited some inconsistency on matters of race, but her emphatic and relentless teaching on the absolute necessity of living the Christian life as an act of consecrated service led many of her students to advocate for the downtrodden and dispossessed—with her full support.

She persuaded young people and adults alike to put their faith in Christ. She interpreted the Bible almost as thoroughly as a seminary professor though she had no advanced degree in any subject and no formal training whatsoever in Christian education or theology. The flagship evangelical undergraduate college in the US and what became the largest independent evangelical seminary in the country offered her professorships, both of which she turned down. She never became an evangelist on the order of Phoebe Palmer, Paul Rader, Billy Sunday, or Billy Graham, but Fuller Seminary professor of homiletics Clarence Roddy called her the greatest preacher in Southern California. Historian Margaret Lamberts Bendroth contended that among fundamentalists and evangelicals of her time, Mears was the most renowned religious educator and perhaps the best known woman of them all. Bendroth's assertion that both fundamentalists and evangelicals recognized Mears's status as a champion of theologically conservative Protestantism illustrates not only her wide appeal, but also her ability to work productively beside those with whom she might have differed in one regard or another. Such cooperative productivity had become increasingly difficult to cultivate during the raging culture wars of her formative years in the Midwest and her first decade in Hollywood.[3]

American evangelicalism, reared in the rural, agricultural, and heavily anglicized context of the eighteenth and early nineteenth centuries, played a major role in the rampant activism and sweeping reforms of the antebellum era, but the quickening pace of the techno-industrial revolution after 1860, a massive shift in immigration patterns, and the resulting urban sprawl left Christians in America with more questions than answers about the future.

When caught up in the intellectual ferment left in Darwin's wake, they were hard pressed to advance consensual answers to the mounting dilemmas of modern life. A fault line broke open between those willing to accommodate their convictions to the new cultural environment and those who held fast to time-honored Christian doctrines. By the end of the second decade of the twentieth century traditionalists appropriated the appellation "fundamentalist" after *The Fundamentals: A Testimony to the Truth*, a series of publications bankrolled by Union Oil Company cofounders Lyman and Milton Stewart. The twelve-volume series, originally published between 1910 and 1915 and distributed free of charge, reiterated for a new generation the foundational beliefs of historic Christianity and drew a line in the sand between true Christian faith and heresy.

On the other side of the theological divide stood those more willing to reconsider core tenets of Christianity such as the veracity of Scripture and the divinity of Christ. Led by advocates such as Washington Gladden, Walter Rauschenbusch, and Harry Emerson Fosdick, "modernists" responded to the charges of infidelity to the faith with their own brand of Christian witness, which they believed spoke more directly to the predicaments of urban, industrial American society. At the outset, this wing of American Christianity embraced what was termed the Social Gospel, implying that Christian faith not only ensured salvation in the eternal sense, but also spurred a social activism in the present to ameliorate earthly problems. While this stance looked very much like the reformist impulse of Christians before the Civil War, its association with modernism in the decades after that conflict caused most traditionalists to reject the Social Gospel mandate.

The rift between theologically conservative fundamentalists and theologically liberal modernists broadened through the opening decades of the twentieth century. Fosdick threw down the gauntlet in a 1922 sermon entitled "Shall the Fundamentalists Win?" Presbyterian fundamentalist Clarence E. Macartney picked up the challenge immediately, preaching on "Shall Unbelief Win?" J. Gresham Machen followed this heated exchange with the 1923 publication of *Christianity and Liberalism,* which Shailer Matthews, Dean of the University of Chicago Divinity School, answered in 1924 with *The Faith of Modernism*. The pointed titles of these sermons and books illustrate just how far apart the two sides were by the early 1920s, and the chasm only widened. The principled pluralism of the modernist position as typified by the Auburn

Affirmation (1924) resulted in a wrenching struggle for the soul of Princeton Theological Seminary. Both the northern Presbyterian and northern Baptist churches suffered irreparable damage as modernists and fundamentalists within each denomination struggled for supremacy.

By the late 1930s Christianity in the United States had reached a crisis point. The debilitating fundamentalist-modernist struggles of the 1920s rippled outward during the opening years of the Great Depression, exposing increasingly problematic disagreements. The controversies of the twenties became more nuanced as the decade wore on. While many theological conservatives supported the orthodox precepts defended in *The Fundamentals*, they disagreed with their allies regarding the strategic initiatives to defend them as well as the tactical maneuvers that might prove most effective in doing so. On the East Coast, a rancorous parting of the ways between Machen and Macartney in 1936 over the former's decision to leave the Presbyterian Church in the USA preceded the founding by Carl McIntire of the radically separatist American Council of Christian Churches five years later. These were merely two examples demonstrating that the simplistic dichotomy between fundamentalists and modernists that materialized during the contentious 1910s and 1920s could no longer contain the range of theological diversity that surfaced during the 1930s and became even more patently obvious in the 1940s. A West Coast equivalent could be seen in the vitriol leveled at fellow Southern California fundamentalist Aimee Semple McPherson by Robert "Fighting Bob" Shuler, pastor of Trinity Methodist Church in downtown Los Angeles. How to distinguish between the growing number of theologically conservative groups and their modi operandi vis-à-vis mainstream American life and culture became confusing and divisive to the defenders of Christian orthodoxy. Consequently, a term familiar to the faithful and rooted in their collective past was vested with new meaning and fitted for service.

Prior to the first decade of the twentieth century the term "evangelical" was used most often to describe the religious fervor that pervaded the ministries of revivalist preachers like Charles Grandison Finney, Phoebe Palmer, D. L. Moody, and J. Wilbur Chapman. Such preaching filled the pews of mainline denominations so that, in the words of historian D. G. Hart, "at the turn of the twentieth century, to be part of mainline Protestantism was to be evangelical."[4] The modernist challenges to conventional Christian doctrines through the opening decades of the twentieth century, however, and the fracture lines that developed within denominations forced a reappropriation of the term. It began to denote a new cadre of theological conservatives who started to appear in the 1930s and, according to Hart and others, took viable form by the 1940s in groups like Youth for Christ, the National Association of Evangelicals with its affiliated organizations, and what became the Billy Graham Evangelistic Association, to name a few. Uncoupled from its earlier meaning then, "evangelical" came to be identified with a wide range of theological conservatives who wished to distance themselves from both strict fundamentalists and theological modernists.[5]

Yet in a very real sense a change in terminology did not actually set the new evangelicals (sometimes called neoevangelicals) apart from their fundamentalist counterparts to any great degree. David Bebbington's often cited fourfold characterization of evangelicals as biblicists, conversionists, activists, and crucicentrists could very well apply to the vast majority of fundamentalists, making the line between them hard to detect.[6] The same could be said of Alister McGrath's six-point enumeration.[7] More recent scholarship has also cast doubt on the wisdom of distinguishing between the two in this manner, contending that every expression of American Christianity has hitched its wagon securely, even if unwittingly, to capitalistic assumptions resulting in doctrinal and behavioral adaptations to an expansive consumerist mentality.[8]

When viewed from their own standpoints, however, a clear distinction between fundamentalists and evangelicals prevailed—at least through the middle third of the twentieth century. And what tended to separate the two groups had more to do with relationships and attitudes than it did with theology, with perspectives regarding American culture rather than doctrinal issues, although such attitudes and perspectives were themselves tied to particular ways of interpreting the Bible. Generally, "neo-evangelicals were those who wanted to retain an emphasis on the fundamentals of the faith while presenting an intellectually compelling case for a non-separatist, culturally engaged gospel."[9] In presenting that case, the new evangelicals established a wide-ranging interconnected set of personal and institutional relationships that cultivated a network of colleagues rooted in nearly every Protestant denomination. Their promotion of reasonable engagement with secular American culture and cooperation with like-minded Christians set them apart from other theological conservatives who continued to advocate a rigid separatism between true believers and nonbelievers.

It was this accent on a winsome engagement with secular culture and thoughtful bridge building across denominational lines that made Henrietta Mears a leading figure in the evangelical transformation of twentieth-century Protestantism. For while she came to maturity in the cockpit of fundamentalism as a member of Riley's Minneapolis church and a teacher in his Bible school, her family heritage, educational training, and personal experience of faith led her in a direction that veered off the paths taken by more reactionary iconoclasts toward a gentler but no less orthodox expression of Christianity.

Still focused theologically on the consequences of universal human sinfulness; the unmerited favor of God demonstrated toward humanity through the life, death, and resurrection of Christ; and the absolute authority of the Bible, Mears nonetheless emerged as a commanding presence at the forefront of a new brand of Protestantism. As she championed this ecumenically inclined evangelicalism, Mears made the transition from a fundamentalist Baptist to evangelical Presbyterian without a discernible shift in outlook by constructing her seamless ministry on the bedrock doctrines of historic Christian orthodoxy. She simultaneously engaged the churched, the unchurched, and secular culture in groundbreaking, sometimes stunning ways. Her aptitude for stepping across longstanding spiritual boundaries with skill and grace created new prospects for American Protestant Christians. In so doing, she invented modern evangelicalism and modeled it decades before the outbreak of the Second World War in September 1939. Her innovative practices provided a template readily emulated by a corps of leaders that came into its own under her tutelage by example, resulting in the pervasive influence of postwar theologically conservative, transdenominational, evangelical Protestantism.

Readers familiar with the current scholarly reassessment of the whole notion of "evangelicalism" will recognize that this present study largely sidesteps the current debates over its history, nomenclature, antecedents, and linkages to embedded extra-religious presuppositions. My tack is by design for two reasons. First, as a social historian I have learned to remain skeptical of (though thoroughly intrigued by) sweeping interpretations whose evidentiary basis tends to rely almost exclusively on male elites. Second, however much we might find unanimity among those elites, it is exceedingly difficult to pay due diligence to those in the trenches below them, to determine just how elite prescriptions filtered down to the rank-and-file. In spending time with

Henrietta Mears, I have come to believe that her life and work illustrate the continuing utility of the past generation's understanding of fundamentalism and evangelicalism even as we interrogate that understanding by asking new questions and advancing new interpretations.

That her life merits more extensive attention is obvious based solely on the accomplishments briefly stated here. But the fact that she lived her life at the confluence of so many significant cultural trends strikingly similar to those we currently face makes such attention all the more fitting. For example, although recent scholarship has refined our comprehension of twentieth-century Christian fundamentalism and evangelicalism, apart from the "great men"—such as Riley, Mark Matthews, Frank Norris, Billy Graham, J. Gresham Machen, Harold John Ockenga, Carl F. H. Henry, and Francis Schaeffer—not much is known about those at the grassroots level of the movements and still less about female leadership in them. Joel Carpenter and Matthew Sutton have argued persuasively (albeit contrapuntally) that fundamentalism did not dissipate after the traumas of the 1920s, but beyond their research we know little about the local institutions and personal connections that led to the sudden appearance of modern evangelicalism by the early 1940s.[10] The lively historiographical debate with respect to the nature and characteristics of modern evangelicalism has brought new questions to the table, but an overwhelming majority of the scholarly discussion has centered on the movers and shakers of the religio-economic order and the institutions they created, whether Bible institutes, retail stores, or oil companies. How substantively their predilections really affected those in the pews and at the podiums, or were absorbed by females at the local level, has yet to be adequately surveyed. Moreover, literature probing the fortunes of theological conservatism in the twentieth century has heavily concentrated on the Northeast, Midwest, and South. Scholars have begun to mine sources and explore topics related to the American West, but we need to know more about its western flavor prior to the Second World War, recent notable studies of Aimee Semple McPherson, Kathryn Kuhlman, Mark Matthews, and Lyman Stewart notwithstanding.[11]

The spirit of graceful engagement with which Henrietta Mears pursued her calling stands as an example to be appropriated in an increasingly divisive age, for *grace* is not a word that many Americans outside the faith would use to describe today's evangelical Christians. Regardless of the fact that the community of theologically conservative believers in any age or place has always been more mosaic than monolith, there is ample reason for rejecting the term as a valid descriptor for a sizable portion of the faithful in the opening decades of the twenty-first century. As our world desperately searches for the kindness and compassion that grace embodies, too many Christians in the United States appear unable or unwilling to act charitably toward those with whom they disagree. In light of the recent close identification of American evangelicals with political conservatism, reactionary social agendas, and intolerance on a wide variety of fronts, the way in which Henrietta Mears lived her life presents a refreshing counternarrative. She brought an uncommon grace to an earlier era much like ours in its oversimplified, but widely accepted, depiction of orthodox Christian belief in an age of crisis.

While a comprehensive account of Henrietta Mears's dominant impact on the evangelical reconfiguration of American Protestantism is a tale worth telling, the manner of doing so most effectively is not. In reflecting on Mears's life and work from the distance of nearly forty years, one of her close associates believed that attempting to do justice to her multifaceted legacy by adhering to a strict chronological ordering of events was fruitless. She argued such an approach would be like collecting mercury with a knife because Mears "lived in five directions every day, and in seven on Sundays."[12] My decade of research on her multistranded ministry led me to concur at least partially with this assessment—especially concerning the second half of her life. As a result, most of the chapters that follow will pursue a roughly chronological framework. At critical junctures in her life course, however, when those five directions look more like fifty, separate chapters will focus on particularly instructive aspects of her work, before returning to the main storyline. Hopefully, this approach will more accurately convey not only the depth of her significance to the modern evangelical movement, but also the breadth of her contributions, many of which continue to influence American Protestants to this day.

Chapter One

Bloodlines

In the quarter century that elapsed since Henrietta Mears assumed her duties as the director of Christian education at Hollywood's First Presbyterian Church in 1928, she had become something of an international celebrity among a worldwide Protestant network of parishioners, pastors, missionaries, and teachers. Intent on sharing her story with an even broader audience during the tension-filled years of the Cold War, one of Mears's younger devotees expressed an interest in writing her biography. Mears found the suggestion ludicrous: "Who wants to know the story of my life? I was born, I lived, I died! What's so special about that? No one wants to read the story of my life." A respected publisher, however, disagreed and in 1956 commissioned Barbara Hudson Powers to write the biography of her mentor. So began an ongoing series of discussions that took the young mother from her San Fernando Valley home to Henrietta Mears's palatial estate in the Bel Air neighborhood west of Beverly Hills. Rain or shine, Powers packed her cumbersome seven-inch reel-to-reel tape recorder into the car and snaked along Coldwater Canyon to 110 Stone Canyon Road just across Sunset Boulevard from the UCLA campus. Once she had wrestled the tape recorder from the backseat into Mears's home and switched it on, her subject regaled Powers with stories from her past shared previously with only a select few.

The faith and social activism of her mother and maternal grandmother figured conspicuously in her recollections, but Mears spent relatively little time reflecting on her father's spiritual life except to note that his was a practical faith. When she did speak of him, her memories tended to emphasize his humor or the admission that as a child she could get whatever she wanted from him—a fact certainly not lost on her older siblings. She did not mention or explain his extensive absences from home. While she characterized her maternal relatives as profoundly spiritual, Mears depicted her father's family as more materially oriented and socially connected; yet she also used the term "militant" (without explaining it) to describe her paternal grandmother's Christian commitment, which other family members also shared. She recounted the loss of her family's elite status in the wake of the economic downturn of the mid-1890s, but not the underlying reasons for that loss. Mears spoke freely of the role that physical ailments and death played in the strengthening of her faith, but she did not offer a similar interpretation regarding the many moves her family made during her formative years or the litigation that dogged them during those years. The stories Mears told Powers of abiding faith through good times and bad served as spiritual touchstones for her entire life. But so also did the more troubling aspects of Mears's youth that never made it onto any of Powers's tapes or into her 1957 biography. The interplay between the experiences Mears shared with Powers and those she kept to herself shaped her worldview and forged her character in ways that would have substantial consequences for the cause of theologically conservative American Protestantism.[1]

Henrietta Cornelia's birth on October 23, 1890, in Fargo, North Dakota, completed the family of Elisha Ashley and Margaret Burtis Mears.[2] The youngest of seven children and the third daughter, she grew to maturity in a loving family environment simultaneously permeated by piety and intrigue across four generations. Her father, born in Poultney, Vermont, in 1840, came from a family that sank its roots deep in the civic and religious life of the young republic. Elisha matured under three crucial influences: the Baptist faith of his parents, the commercial intricacies of the metals trade, and the care of a prosperous and privileged extended family. He had an uncanny ability to detect opportunities when they appeared and to seize them for personal gain. By his late teens Poultney could not ground his future nor fulfill his ambitions. Young Mears decided to look elsewhere.

He traveled west, settled in Chicago, and passed the Illinois state bar examination on his twenty-first birthday to become one of the youngest members of the Chicago Bar Association. Though now a lawyer, he utilized the knowledge and skills developed under his father Simeon's tutelage to good benefit, facilitating his entrance into the nascent manufacturing and metals industries of the growing city. By autumn 1863 Elisha was doing well enough in the tinware business to have earned a listing on the excise tax rolls of the city. The following year he advertised himself as a stove manufacturer as well. He reportedly made a small fortune in metals trading during the Civil War, clearing $25,000 in one scrap iron transaction. By the final year of the war he had added copper, sheet iron, and holloware plus stamped and japanned ware to his inventory and established a foundry.[3] While attending Chicago's prestigious First Baptist Church, Elisha met Margaret Burtis Everts, daughter of the dynamic senior pastor of the church and his second wife—the two women who were to exert the greatest acknowledged influence on the life and ministry of Henrietta Mears.

Her maternal grandmother, Margaret Keen Burtis, grew up a faithful Philadelphia Baptist, but at fourteen had an intense religious conversion experience while participating in a series of meetings at a Presbyterian church close to her home.[4] From that point forward Margaret committed herself to live out her Christian faith with a single-mindedness that transformed all aspects of her life. She shunned dancing and any clothing or ornamentation that might inhibit her ability to approach those with fewer material possessions. Money she saved went to assist others. On numerous occasions Margaret refused to accept gifts of clothing she deemed inappropriate. She began a journal, in the words of her biographer, because of a need for "vigilance and frequent self-examination."[5]

Margaret became consumed with the desire to mature spiritually and to give evidence of her faith in practical ways. She often wrote of her unworthiness and God's grace toward her. Among her earliest resolutions were those committing herself to attend all prayer meetings when possible, to spend constructive time with other Christians, and to work for the conversion of non-Christians, including members of her own family. Subsequent journal entries demonstrate the importance she placed on giving of her money and time to the needy and the absolute necessity of progressing in her Christian walk. On a monthlong visit to relatives in New Jersey one summer, she organized a Sunday school for local children. She also planned and taught an evening class for young women employed in her father's factory.

Tragically, Margaret's mother passed away soon after the sixteen-year-old entered the Collegiate Institution for Young Ladies. Bowing to her father's wishes, she traded her educational aspirations for the responsibility of running the household. In 1836 she met young William Wallace Everts, a Baptist theology student from Hamilton, New York. The two married in 1843. Over the next sixteen years the Reverend Everts pastored churches in New York State and then in Louisville, Kentucky, with Margaret providing valuable professional assistance while raising their blended family, which ultimately included five children, two of whom had been born to Everts and his deceased first wife. In 1859, with sectional antagonism building ahead of the Civil War, he accepted an invitation to lead the First Baptist Church of Chicago where he blossomed into a popular and forceful religious leader over the ensuing twenty years.

In many aspects of his work Margaret joined him as a key contributor. She wrote her own musical compositions, taught Sunday school, provided music for church functions, and visited church members and friends on her husband's behalf. She spoke and wrote on the importance of giving to church causes, appealing to the congregation for greater generosity on one final occasion the Sunday before her death in 1866. For the last fifteen years of her life, Margaret carried on nearly all Everts's correspondence and transcribed thousands of pages destined for publication. During one of his absences, she "responded to a call for Christian direction from a gentleman of position and influence, and there for hours she met his speculations, inquiries, and agonized doubts, with prayer and the Bible," acting essentially as a pastoral counselor. She worked alongside Everts in his support of the original University of Chicago, focusing on the needs of students. She ultimately became president of the Ladies Baptist Educational Society, which mobilized Baptist women throughout the state for this purpose.[6]

Never comfortable with the material trappings that came with a successful urban pastorate,[7] Margaret continued to express a deep concern as well for the underserved outside Baptist circles. Soon after settling in Chicago she became a manager of the city's Orphan Asylum and then of the Home for the Friendless. But she reserved her most passionate advocacy for women. She was a driving force behind the establishment of the first home for destitute females in the city. When the facility proved insufficient, Margaret and her small band of reformers found a larger location, which also filled quickly. Two years later, with the backing of some distinguished citizens, they secured an even bigger home and property, but need continued to exceed capacity. During the final summer of her life, Margaret joined others in soliciting funds from many sources, including the Chicago Common Council, for a seventy-five-bed expansion that included a hospital.

An evangelical ecumenism pervaded both Margaret's and Rev. Everts's sense of Christian service. While continuing their duties as committed Baptists, neither confined their interests or their efforts to Baptist circles or only those inside the greater Christian community. The need for justice and mercy meant justice for all and mercy to all. One church historian wrote of Margaret that she "devised, organized, and led in the execution of numerous systems of charity and benevolence, not only of this church, but in the wider circles of society, where all the various churches and creeds of the city were represented."[8] It was this expansive sense of Christian duty that their daughter Margaret Burtis Everts brought to her marriage with Elisha Mears and passed on to her children.

Exactly how and when Elisha and the younger Margaret met is unclear, although it is possible that their initial encounters occurred when she was barely into her teens. Soon after Elisha's arrival in Chicago his parents and sisters relocated to the city. All attended the First Baptist Church together and Simeon joined Elisha in the hardware trade. Sometime between Elisha's first visit to the church and his marriage to Margaret toward the end of the decade, he and Everts partnered in a speculative real estate development on the North Shore that would have significant consequences for the Mears family. The lure of quick success pulled his interests progressively away from manufacturing toward the financial services industry.[9]

Against the backdrop of complex transactions worth thousands of dollars and partnered with one of the most powerful men in Chicago, as well as one of the most influential Baptists in the country, Elisha courted Margaret. Little is known about the length of their relationship before their marriage and not much more about its nature, but it must have been quite complicated. After Margaret's mother died, she spent much of the next two years studying music and the arts in Germany while Elisha remained in Chicago tending his hardware company and speculating in North Shore properties.[10]

By the fall of 1868 their intentions toward each other were clear. As the wedding approached, Margaret's father, perhaps aware of either the expense or the impossibility of including all those dear to them, refused to have invitations sent, instead issuing an open invitation to the December 31, 1868, marriage ceremony directly from the pulpit. So many well-wishers attended that a contingent of Chicago mounted policemen facilitated crowd control.

Shortly after their marriage and pregnant with her first child, Margaret returned to Europe for a time, probably to attend her father's wedding in May 1869. In mid-June Elisha sent her some presents and wrote about the latest developments in his ongoing real estate transactions north of the city. By this time he had purchased at least one lakeshore lot as a potential summer home. Toward the end of the seven-page letter Elisha reflected on the pressures of the business world, hoping that she would guard him "against dissipation of any kind and never let me under any pretense take a glass of wine."[11]

Over the course of the 1870s the Mears family grew with the addition of four more children. Members of the family not only spent time with their Everts relatives, they also regularly visited their Mears relations in Poultney, remaining firmly grounded in extended family connections that stretched from New England and Georgia to the Midwest. When Elisha suffered an unspecified misfortune in 1878, Margaret's brother William tried but failed to find him a position in Providence, Rhode Island. Whatever occurred seems to have had a major impact on the family, for shortly after Norman's birth, they left for New Jersey where a sixth sibling, Margaret, was born. While they may have moved eastward to be closer to Mears family members, the more probable cause lay in the fact that Margaret's father accepted the call to serve Bergen Baptist Church in Jersey City in January 1879. By June 1880 Elisha, Margaret, and their children, along with Elisha's sisters Elizabeth and Cornelia, all lived in Jersey City. Whether by design or default, Mears left hardware behind to pursue his interest in real estate development.[12]

Although Elisha's profession is noted as real estate in the 1880 census, nothing is known about what that designation may have entailed or whether he sought advice from relatives in the industry at this pivotal point. It is also difficult to determine whether monetary or personal reverses or a lethal combination of both led the family to leave New Jersey. What is known is that oldest daughter Florence contracted typhoid fever and died on August 21, 1882. The effects of this first "Great Sorrow" as it was called by Elisha's mother, washed over the entire extended household. Although their faith sustained them, Florence's passing initiated a period of instability that would last well into the 1890s and test the Mears family in ways they could not then have imagined.[13] Memories of a long deceased, similarly named sister intertwined with Elisha's grief over the loss of his seven-year-old daughter. Within a year he cut his losses and turned his attention westward.[14]

Perhaps stimulated by the achievements of relatives in Saint Paul, Elisha moved his family in 1883 to the frontier settlement of Ipswich, Dakota Territory, where he became a prominent real estate developer. He quickly expanded his economic interests, purchasing properties nearby in Edmunds County and testing the mortgage sales market.[15] Hoping to build upon these exploits, he moved his large family to Minot in 1887. Over the next two years he burnished both his financial position and his personal reputation, founding a number of banks and serving in a variety of civic positions. As his successes multiplied, so also did his ambition; neither Ipswich nor Minot could contain it. In October 1889, less than a month before North Dakota joined the union, Elisha relocated his family to Fargo in order to manage and diversify his rapidly growing empire from the largest city in the new state. That empire ultimately included nearly twenty businesses—unchartered territorial, state, and national banks, insurance firms, and at least one livestock company.[16]

From his initial days in Ipswich, Elisha took advantage of the economic climate of a region abundantly rich in natural resources, poor in capital, and lax in regulation. Banking protocols in the late nineteenth century encouraged "creative" practices—especially in the territories—and Elisha made the most of these conditions.[17] Through an ingenious but precariously interlocked network of companies, Elisha wedded his aspirations to the intense desire for land ownership characteristic of settlers in the rural Midwest. He provided Dakota homesteaders with capital gleaned almost exclusively from eastern investors, often through contacts he reportedly made by attending church services and participating in charitable events during his regular and sometimes lengthy trips to the East.[18]

Elisha's First National Bank of Fargo served as the crown jewel of a commercial domain that covered much of North Dakota. His Mortgage Bank and Investment Company, through which he managed all of his other institutions, was housed in the same Mears Block, as the building was known. Dubbed the "Fargo Hustler" by the *Minneapolis Tribune*, Elisha installed himself as president of most of these ventures and appointed close relatives—including his mother, wife, sister, brother-in-law, and sons William and Clarence—to key management positions. Oldest son Ashley assisted his father as president of the First National Bank of Minot until his untimely death in 1890. That this approach to investment capitalism teetered on the edge of perfidy while holding to the letter of legality on the Midwestern frontier is illustrated by the fact that at the pinnacle of his power in 1890, the Bankers Association of North Dakota expelled Mears because of his questionable practices. Two weeks later he received election as a vice president of the American Bankers Association, representing North Dakota.[19]

IT WAS INTO THIS FAMILY of considerable wealth and suspect reputation that Henrietta was born just nine months after Ashley's sudden death. The spacious family residence on 13th Street in which she spent the first few years of her life, however, would not be her home for long. Until late 1891 everything her father touched seemed to yield monetary benefit, and the family lived quite comfortably with at least one live-in maid. Elisha even let young Henrietta play with coins in the bank's till. However, a tightening economy that worsened into the severe depression of the mid-1890s exposed the fragility of Elisha's jerry-rigged business model. The defining blow came in late May 1893, when Comptroller of the Currency James H. Eckels ordered the First National Bank of Fargo and another Mears bank closed for insolvency. Less than a week later, a devastating fire incinerated most of downtown Fargo and with it the opulent Mears Block. After reviewing Elisha's suspect fiscal arrangements, Eckels met with him in Washington, DC, and vowed that he would never allow Elisha to be part of another bank anywhere in the country as long as he remained Comptroller of the Currency. Over the next four years Elisha, his wife, brother-in-law, and other associates faced upward of two dozen civil court trials, most of them as defendants, as his entire enterprise collapsed. Mears served time in jail at least once during the mid-1890s for contempt of court. Judgments against him totaled nearly $9,000—the equivalent of over $272,000 in 2019 dollars.[20]

Financial and legal reverses took their toll on family relationships. Margaret Mears's sister and brother-in-law left Fargo for Minneapolis by the spring of 1893. The same year, it appears that Henrietta's oldest surviving brother, William, accepted a clerkship in Duluth. Elisha, Margaret, and their other children followed William to northeastern Minnesota in 1895, but the Duluth city directory listed no profession for Elisha that year and the Minnesota State Census designated him a retired banker. Sons Clarence and Norman became affiliated with the city's Weir-Mears Commission Company, but William left for Boston to pursue a career in wealth management with Paine Webber & Company, a firm founded by a member of the Mears extended family. In 1896 their father resumed his law practice in Duluth, but the following year he returned to Fargo alone, probably in an effort to resolve his legal problems. Clarence's administrative responsibilities with the Weir-Mears Commission Company took him to New York City, so Margaret and her two daughters boarded with Norman until late that year when the four of them moved to Minneapolis. Elisha joined them by late 1898.[21]

Over the course of the ensuing decade, the Mears family lived in several locations south of downtown Minneapolis as Henrietta's father attempted to reestablish his credibility as a legitimate businessman. He abruptly left Minneapolis after 1905, disappearing from the record until 1910. During these years, he seems to have opened banks in various small towns in Washington State, and was reputed to have had financial dealings in Idaho and Arkansas. Elisha also apparently spent six weeks incarcerated in Kittitas County, Washington, charged with writing a check on a closed bank. Authorities released him when no clear case could be presented. Although he returned to Minneapolis for good in 1910, living with daughters Margaret and Henrietta until his death in 1912, city directories list no occupation for the final three years of his life. At least one newspaper reported that he died nearly insolvent.[22]

Clearly Henrietta's childhood and adolescence were greatly conditioned by the stresses of her family's economic situation and the uncertainties caused by their constant moving—at least six times, across two states, before she completed the third grade. By the age of twelve, she had experienced the privileges of the self-made Midwestern plutocracy, followed closely by monetary crises that reverberated through her extended family. The elevated social status that came with her father's successes quickly disappeared, replaced by allegations of criminal activity that culminated in a series of lawsuits, the legacies of which would linger well into her teenage years.

While Henrietta could not have understood the origins or the implications of her father's business dealings as a young child, a lack of awareness does not imply that she remained unaffected by their consequences. According to a witness called in one of the civil cases brought against Elisha, four-and-a-half-year-old Henrietta exhibited substantial knowledge regarding her father's departure for Duluth in early 1895.[23] In a letter written to William when she was twelve, Henrietta matter-of-factly informed him that their father was in Chicago, while an earlier letter mentioned that "Papa went away Friday night at nine o'clock. He has gone to North Dakota."[24] She may not always have been mindful of the reasons for her father's frequent absences from the family, but she was fully aware of the fact that he was not at home. Whether these details indicate a pattern of emotional distancing from a father who was often gone, or simply a child's acceptance of her family's realities is indefinite, but it is certain that she and other family members were shaped directly by her father's struggles.

A deeper impact of Elisha's frequent trips on family life can be observed in a letter William wrote to Henrietta before she began school in Duluth. In light verse he wrote about their mother and father, communicating a relative regard for each parent to his sister. An entire page describes Margaret, recording how she cared for them when they were sick, instructed them, read to them, cooked, and made sure they did not overindulge in sweets. He said she "makes your dresses and 'pantlets' small, paints the doors and papers the wall. Hoes the garden and waters the lawn and is up in the morning at early dawn." William also reminded Henrietta of their mother's charity toward the less fortunate and her service to the church. He wrote his sister that "I know she's the best (mother) to be had, that's why we should both be glad." The section concludes with "You love your mama I know you do, and so does your brother Willie *too*." The final page contains but a few lines about Elisha and conveys a starkly different message:

> Now it would not do for me to stop without writing a Rhyme
> about your pap(a).
> But he is such a funny man I don't see exactly how I can.
> Still I'll try my level best to get off just one little jest.
> He is getting old and gray on toward sixty years they say.
> He was once a bright and lively youth now he has but
> one little tooth.[25]

It is impossible to miss the strong positive identification with Margaret and a nearly dismissive indifference toward Elisha communicated to Henrietta in his poem. Given her father's acknowledged absences from home, one cannot help but wonder about the implications for her formative years.

As a young girl, Henrietta sustained an exceptionally strong bond with William. By her own admission, he acted as her surrogate father. His departures for Duluth and then Boston appear to have been especially difficult for her. Although he initially left home when she was only a toddler, "Willie," as he referred to himself in his letters to Henrietta, cherished his "darling little sister." His surviving letters to her are full of rhymes and pictures that express his affection. That she returned his sentiments is obvious, opening one of her letters with "My dearest Will" and concluding it "with many kisses, your loving little sister."[26] Her fondness for him, however, could switch to frustration at his absence. In a letter probably written when she was between eight and ten years old, she turned spiteful as only a child might at his failure to visit.[27] It is not clear how often he was able to make the trip to Minneapolis, but he did host her a number of times.[28] Exactly why William ended his affiliation with his father and opted to settle in Boston is open to speculation, but whatever the reason, Henrietta interpreted his absence in an acutely personal way. He may have served as the only adult male figure she could both openly adore and soundly criticize, giving vent to the emotions of love and loss that she could not express toward her father.

While it is difficult to assess the collective impact of Elisha's personal and professional circumstances on family relationships, there certainly were other consequences for Henrietta and her siblings. Perhaps the most traumatic event they endured occurred in late March 1895. Two months earlier, in the midst of his legal and financial problems, Henrietta's father had moved to Duluth to explore business opportunities. Henrietta, then four and a half, remained in Fargo with her mother, brothers Clarence and Norman (then aged twenty-two and sixteen), and fifteen-year old Margaret, awaiting word from Elisha to sell the family home and most of the furniture. Cass County Deputy Sheriff Henry Hanson went to the Mears residence to serve a warrant, but Henrietta's sister refused to admit him. According to testimony from their mother, Hanson then tried to open the locked door forcibly. Failing this, he went to the back door and tried again, but it too had been secured, so he resorted to pounding on the doors of the home, soundly terrifying its occupants. The anxiety this encounter engendered in the family's youngest child would not have been softened by her ignorance of the reasons for the deputy's actions. Although other incidents precipitated by her father's machinations were probably not as jarring as Hanson's actions were, they did little to impart a sense of security as Henrietta matured. Irrespective of how much she actually understood with regard to the severity of her family's problems when she was a preadolescent, she undoubtedly learned to live with a significant level of instability, uncertainty, and sometimes fear.[29]

In addition to the many moves made by her family during her formative years, as a senior she had to transfer from Central High School, the largest secondary school in Minneapolis, to newly constructed West High closer to her home. By the time she began her studies at the University of Minnesota in September 1909, she had known the death of two siblings (Ashley and Florence), the temporary loss of her Aunt Henrietta and Uncle John when they left Fargo and brothers William, Clarence, and Norman as they struck out on their own, and numerous periods—two of them extended—without her father's presence. During her university years she tended her mother, who died of kidney disease in late December 1910. Her father succumbed to pneumonia in early May 1912, a month before the end of her junior year.[30]

Even before Henrietta reached puberty, tragedy and health problems had wreaked havoc on the Mears family and marked each surviving member. Both her parents began their married life grounded intimately in their Christian faith, but also well-acquainted with the fleeting nature of life and the ubiquity of death. Though Henrietta never knew her oldest brother and sister, their passing deeply affected other family members and she was raised in the shadow their deaths cast. Florence's decease at seven seems to have fallen most heavily on Margaret, while Ashley's sudden death during a visit to his maternal grandfather in Chicago rent not only familial bonds, but also professional ones since he had already begun to exercise leadership in his father's financial empire after graduating from the University of Chicago at sixteen.[31]

These deaths shrouded Henrietta's formative years. But her own direct encounters with debilitating health conditions predated her mother's illness by more than a decade and added another dimension of personal angst to her life as she passed from youth into young womanhood. Her brother William lost his hearing after an ill-advised swimming adventure led to the onset of spinal meningitis, so from an early age Henrietta had firsthand experience with physical impairment.[32] Her own health challenges materialized quite early in life and began with optic afflictions that appear to have had some genetic base as she was not the only family member to endure serious eye problems.[33] She suffered a general weakness of the eyes, and they were often irritated and painful. Severely myopic, Henrietta wore glasses from her first day of grade school in Duluth. A few years later in 1903, following her visit to relatives in Boston and Poultney, she contracted an acute case of muscular rheumatism, which incapacitated and nearly killed her. Several cases were reported in Minnesota that year and many succumbed, including Henrietta's best friend. Henrietta suffered excruciating pain and had to be carried everywhere through the winter, spring, and summer. An aunt who witnessed her struggle with the disease remarked that "Henrietta was so very patient during her siege, although I saw tears in her eyes often." At nearly the same time, Henrietta also began to experience frequent nosebleeds. She inadvertently contributed to her own medical problems when at sixteen she accidentally drove a hat pin into the pupil of one of her already damaged eyes. Doctors warned her that she would be blind in that eye, and probably in both within fifteen years.[34]

Given this formidable array of potentially destructive influences present in young Henrietta's life, it is not difficult to understand her need for stability, comfort, and certitude. She discovered in Christianity the source by which all three of these needs could be met. In later life, she spoke openly of the spiritual heritage to which she was heir, and related story after story illustrating the legacy of Christian faith she traced through the generations to her own parents.

After their marriage, Elisha and Margaret made regular church attendance, membership, and service a priority. Shortly after their arrival in Ipswich they were among a group of nine Baptists who met on January 20, 1884, and voted to organize a church. Within a week the small band had written and adopted a constitution and elected officers including Elisha as one of the three church trustees. Margaret worked to mitigate the suffering of the less fortunate members of the growing community.[35] Her volunteer work and Elisha's money also helped organize and build the First Baptist Church of Minot. They were two of the six founders of the congregation, which organized in April 1888. Elisha assumed primary responsibility for the construction of the sanctuary, which neared completion in November. He served as one of the first trustees while Margaret became the initial superintendent of the Sunday school. According to the *Minot Journal,* Margaret was "always in the front rank of Christian workers, and always on some errand of mercy." Just before the Mears family moved to Fargo in October 1889 the local newspaper declared that "she is one of God's noblest women and Fargo has reasons to rejoice that her lot is to be cast with them."[36] Margaret became one of the early leaders of the First Baptist Church of that city. The entire family attended regularly, and all but Henrietta, who was too young at the time, were received into full membership. Margaret taught a large Bible class for young people and led music for the

Sunday school. She also advocated for neglected women—just as her mother had in Chicago—serving on the Board of Managers of the Fargo Florence Crittenton Home for unmarried mothers, including at least one term as president.[37] The move to Duluth found the family worshipping at the First Baptist Church and though only associated with the congregation for three years, Elisha, Margaret, and Henrietta's older siblings joined as full members.[38]

The full range of Margaret's leadership and service became evident with the family's move to Minneapolis. Almost immediately on their arrival in the city, Margaret, son Norman, and daughter Margaret became members at the First Baptist Church.[39] Less than five months later Margaret began her involvement with the Women's Baptist Home Mission Society.[40] Over the next few years she led in prayer and presented Bible lessons to the members gathered for regular monthly meetings of the society. Her sister Henrietta Everts Buckbee often joined her in sharing with or singing for society members. At the April 20, 1898, meeting the nineteen women present "enjoyed the beautiful and earnest manner in which Mrs. Mears commented on the different passages."[41] She taught from various books of the Bible including the Gospel of John, Romans, and First Corinthians.

The topics of her lessons ranged from the practice of Christian witness and the call to care for "fallen women" to the need for diligence in all areas of activity. At the December 20, 1899, meeting, for example, Margaret read Dostoyevsky's short story "The Priest and the Devil" to drive home the danger of taking on too many obligations. That tendency, she warned, could lead to a failure "to do the little things well . . . the little things that count for so much." On more than one occasion she assumed leadership of the meeting at the last minute when formal program plans went awry. Such was the case for the meeting on July 20, 1898, when the women expected to hear about the work of the Minneapolis Rescue Home. When the speaker failed to appear, Margaret stepped forward to share about her mother's work in establishing the home for women in Chicago and also related her experiences working with the poor in Fargo. She spent many hours visiting the girls and women at the local Florence Crittenton Home and shared the importance of that work with her fellow society members. Given such an active interest in Baptist Home Missions, it is not surprising that the sixty-five women attending the annual meeting on October 19, 1898, elected her a vice president of the First Baptist branch of the society. Margaret was reelected to at least five more consecutive terms as vice president, serving in that capacity until late 1905. She was made a life member in December 1900.[42]

On top of her work for the Women's Baptist Home Mission Society, Henrietta's mother worked with other committees and groups associated with the church.[43] All deacons in the Baptist church at this time were male, but in her charitable work Margaret represented the deacon board after petitioning it in February 1903 for funds to assist a local indigent family.[44] She often took food baskets to needy families at Christmas and invited guests for holiday dinners at her home. Her concern for the deprived led her to turn in first-class train tickets and take a less comfortable seat so that she could use the money saved to buy coal for those who struggled. Other members of the Mears family and its extended relations in Minneapolis served the First Baptist Church in a variety of capacities, but after Elisha successfully transferred his membership from the First Baptist Church of Duluth in February 1902, there is no clear record of his involvement in any leadership role in the church, although he may have taught Sunday school classes for young men and briefly served on a church committee.[45]

From a very young age Henrietta was drawn to the family's fervent Christian expression. The sorrow of losing Florence brought Margaret to a spiritual crisis that affected the rest of her life. As remembered years later by Henrietta, her mother experienced a time of guilt, fearing that her intense love for her firstborn daughter had been too obsessive, too consuming. When Florence died, Margaret "felt that the whole world drained out through a small hole and left nothing." Her only surety became her Christian faith and she passed that confident spirituality and its disciplined expression on to her children. She appears to have been the parent who instituted devotional practices and initiated most conversations about faith in the home. Elisha often deferred to her judgment and spiritual insight when it came to Henrietta and her siblings, but he did lead in family prayers.[46]

The Mears family regularly read the Bible, prayed, and sang together directly after breakfast and often entertained Christian leaders in the home. On Sunday afternoons they would place ribbon bookmarks in copies of the New Testament and then stack them on a table in the receiving room ready to hand to callers during the week. Margaret often engaged salesmen and other visitors in conversations about their relationship with God, and each received a testament as a gift whether they professed faith in Christ or not. She maintained a small box into which family members placed coins so that Margaret could allow her laundress to take a day off with pay. She had other boxes to collect money for distribution to disadvantaged friends and acquaintances. There was always a bedroom available for a guest in need.[47]

As the children grew and their schedules diverged, Margaret met each one for prayer before saying goodbye at the front door. When the siblings had friends spend the evening they could count on Margaret's knock on their door near bedtime; no matter what age, offspring and guest knelt beside her as she laid her hand on their heads for prayer. Keenly aware of the passing of time, her mother made sure that Henrietta, her sister, and her brothers made the most of it. During the school year she insisted that the children do all their homework on Friday afternoons. Margaret refused to allow them to sleep late on holidays or summer breaks.[48] In the summer months, chores and other purposeful pursuits such as poetry memorization and music study, which for Henrietta meant voice or piano practice, took up the morning hours.

Margaret held the children to a high standard and remained unafraid to bring them to heel when they did not meet her expectations for them. She once tracked Clarence down in a pool hall and on another occasion took a streetcar across Minneapolis late at night to retrieve seven-year-old Henrietta, who had decided to stay with friends that evening against her mother's express instruction. When one of the children misbehaved and expressed sorrow at the transgression, Margaret forgave the offender immediately. But to demonstrate that there were always consequences to illicit behavior, she informed the transgressor that *she* would do penance for the deed; this often involved denying herself butter at mealtime. When she decided that the lesson had been duly absorbed she asked the wayward sibling to pass the butter because only then would she allow herself half a pat. With this practice she hoped to impress upon her children the reason for the sacrificial death of Christ.

Margaret also instilled in her sons and daughters a strong sense of accountability in a variety of ways. Henrietta recalled that her mother would often walk up to her as she was reading, close the book, and ask her to explain the content. If Henrietta came home from a church meeting or a party at a friend's home disappointed with the event, Margaret would challenge her to think about what she could have done to make it more worthwhile. In addition, she taught her children to see any activity or assignment through to its conclusion.

There was no room in Margaret's world for self-pity or half-completed tasks. Neither would there be in Henrietta's.

Since Henrietta was so much younger than her brothers and sister, Margaret was able to spend even more time on religious matters with her, which became apparent quite early in Henrietta's life. Just as Margaret desired to introduce her children to the best Christian practices, so also did she hope to introduce them to the most winsome examples of Christian faith in action. She took a very young Henrietta to the last meeting that D. L. Moody held in Minneapolis so that she could introduce her daughter to the noted evangelist she had known in Chicago. Henrietta never forgot shaking his hand.[49] The first recorded evidence of her interest in Christianity occurred when she was still a preschooler in Fargo. It was Margaret's practice to spend up to an hour each day on her knees in prayer alone in her room. Everyone left her undisturbed except Henrietta, for whom a closed door meant nothing. When interrupted, her mother stopped to pray for Henrietta, who then would get up and leave only to repeat the process the following day. She decided she too would spend an hour praying, and though she fell far short of her goal as a youngster, her ongoing desire to emulate her mother's example would drive much of her later success.

Henrietta's precocious nature surfaced in various ways during her early years. Music played an important role in her life as both her mother and her aunt studied and performed. Her parents hired opera coach Edward Skedden to give their daughter voice lessons, which led to numerous solo performances in Minneapolis. She also shared her mother's affinity for the piano under the tutelage of Grace Feltus, performing a ragtime-tinged piece by Karl Bechter in her first recital at the age of ten.[50] Henrietta demonstrated a keen interest in learning that could on occasion approach arrogance. She could tell when her mother simplified the wording of Bible passages while reading to her, and she reacted viscerally, interrupting Margaret repeatedly to assure her that she understood the text as written. Henrietta eagerly anticipated beginning her formal education in the Duluth school system. Kindergarten, however, failed to impress her. Upon returning home after her first day, she relayed to Margaret in no uncertain terms her frustration with the absence of any real instruction.[51] Soon after her disenchantment with kindergarten, Henrietta informed her mother that it was time for her to become a Christian and join the church. Because her daughter was so young, Margaret demurred. But exhibiting the single-minded conviction that would serve her well as an adult, Henrietta apparently convinced her that she understood the implications of her desire. Margaret promised to speak to their minister.[52]

Margaret's example of service to all regardless of their religious affiliation left a deep impression on her young daughter. Just after her eighth birthday Henrietta began to participate in a children's group called the Willing Helpers at First Baptist, Minneapolis. In July 1899, the Willing Helpers staged a program for the Women's Baptist Home Mission Society in which Henrietta played a major role. She also accompanied her mother to the local Florence Crittenton Home and helped shop for food items that her mother arranged in baskets for indigent families at Christmas. She went so far as to take naps after school so she could attend evening church meetings.[53]

After Sunday service on May 6, 1900, Henrietta Mears appeared before the pastor and deacon board of the First Baptist Church. She confessed her faith in Christ and requested baptism and church membership. Even though the issue of formal church membership had been deferred until now, Mrs. Mears feared that formal interrogation by church leaders might be somewhat overwhelming for her daughter. She also harbored some concern that the deacons might believe that she or Elisha had pushed the youngster to seek church membership. But the leadership saw no impediment to her desire to join the church and, duly satisfied with her answers to their questions, gave their consent for her to be recommended to the church for baptism and membership. With the public profession of her faith preceding baptism on May 17, she became a full member of the church. Henrietta was not yet ten years old.[54]

The church to which young Mears pledged her allegiance had only recently called a new minister, and she would draw significant lessons from his leadership. The Rev. William Bell Riley accepted the First Baptist pastorate in 1897 and from the beginning of his ministry placed his theologically conservative stamp on the church. He spearheaded a reorganization of the church's leadership bureaucracy into an advisory board under his authority that made most key decisions about church policy. Riley also saw First Baptist as a center of theological orthodoxy that would prevail in the ongoing battle with modernism. To this end, in 1902 he championed the creation of a Bible school, christened the Northwestern Bible and Missionary Training School, which utilized the church's physical plant for many years. Riley served as its chancellor and made sure that all the professors hewed to his theological line. A major figure in the fundamentalist-modernist controversy for nearly fifty years, Riley filled the First Baptist pulpit with like-minded guest preachers and assistants.[55] It was in this confrontational religious context that Henrietta Mears matured and found solace and stability in the midst of the personal trials she faced during her formative years.

OVER THE THIRTEEN TURBULENT YEARS following her baptism, the church anchored a maturing Henrietta Mears. She taught her first Sunday school class at eleven when her brother Norman requested assistance with the Beginners class of the Berean mission Sunday school, which he helped lead for First Baptist. Shortly thereafter, when battling the physical afflictions of her early teens, Henrietta turned to her faith for comfort and relief. After a family friend offered prayers of healing from her persistent nosebleeds, the hemorrhaging stopped—and never returned. As her struggle with rheumatism progressed and her discomfort increased, Henrietta asked her mother whether he could return and pray for her healing from the disease. Directly after his prayer Mears reported a complete cessation of pain. Within three months her strength returned and no sign that she had ever battled the disease remained. She had full use of her body and her heart suffered no ill effects—a singular occurrence among those who knew the young survivor.[56] Two years later, when she was sixteen, Henrietta asked the same friend to pray for the healing of her eyes, but this time she could detect no change. She lived the rest of her life free of nosebleeds and rheumatic complaints but bound to thick eyeglasses, which became one of her most distinctive features.

A further deepening of her spiritual life came during her senior year at West High School when Henrietta attended a series of meetings at First Baptist with her friend Evalyn Camp. Both young women committed themselves to Christian service as missionaries to Asia after one of the sessions taught by Riley. Over the next few years Evalyn became convinced of her calling to Japan, while Henrietta became less sure of hers. Evalyn arose as a major young leader at First Baptist while preparing to go to Japan. She also seems to have been quite active during the years that she and Henrietta spent at the University of Minnesota. Henrietta, on the other hand, retreated from much engagement both at church and university from 1909 through much of 1911. This nearly three-year span was undoubtedly triggered by ongoing reservations about her future and by her mother's illness and death. Taken together, these circumstances comprised her first and most intense crisis of faith.

In the interviews Barbara Hudson Powers conducted with Mears about these years, Mears candidly shared her frustration at sensing no clear direction after her commitment to mission service. She believed that God wanted her to go to China because "China was the only place that the Lord did call anyone in full-time missionary work." She, however, had no desire to go. Her anxiety regarding the future, especially when she had committed that future to God, who had given her life meaning and stability, became a turning point for Mears. At nearly the same time, her mother's health problems during her first year at the University of Minnesota caused Mears further emotional duress. Not only did the young woman confront the reality of her mother's mortality, but in attending to her growing list of needs, Mears's studies suffered. Margaret had survived typhoid fever and pneumonia, but her kidney function steadily deteriorated over the last year of her life. After her passing, Mears entered a period of introspection much like her mother had when the family lost Florence nearly thirty years earlier. She trimmed her academic coursework at the university and appears to have cut herself off from most social interactions, causing her sister and father to worry about her withdrawal from nearly everyone. Powers explained this as a time when "her entire life were [*sic*] narrowed down until it became a relationship that existed exclusively between herself and the Lord, as though the doorway was so small that only she and the Lord could go through." It only made matters worse for Mears when, at her mother's funeral service, Riley put an arm around her shoulder and said, "I hope the spiritual mantle of your mother will fall upon you."[57]

She slowly emerged from her dark night of the soul, renewed by a more incisive grasp of the Christian doctrine of grace thanks to Paul Rader, pastor of Moody Memorial Church in Chicago, who held a series of meetings in Minneapolis. For Henrietta, this new awareness of faith unbound by expectations or conditions freed her from the fear of disappointing others:

> I [had] felt absolutely powerless from the thought that I could possibly live up to what my mother had been and had done, and I prayed that if God had anything for me to do that He would supply the power. I read my Bible for every reference to the Holy Spirit and His power. The greatest

> realization came to me when I saw that there was nothing I had to do to receive His power but submit to Christ, to allow Him to control me. I had been trying to do everything myself; now I let Christ take me completely. I said to Christ that if He wanted anything from me that He would have to do it Himself. My life was changed from that moment on.[58]

This revelation to young Mears was a manifestation of the Keswick Convention's perspective on Christian living. Otherwise known as Higher Life or Victorious Life teaching, it emphasized complete surrender of the will to God's direction. It would be her theological North Star from this point forward.[59]

In light of this powerful revelation, Mears's involvement at the First Baptist Church greatly expanded after 1911. In 1912 she served as a member of the Social Committee of the church, superintendent of the Junior Department of the Bible (Sunday) School, corresponding secretary of the Young Women's Missionary Circle, and president of the Girl's Club. She continued her service in all four positions during her senior year at the university and added responsibilities as Intermediate and Junior Committee chair and member of the Executive Committee of the Young People's Society of Christian Endeavor chapter at First Baptist, which also selected her in late March 1913 to co-chair the Lookout Committee. It was during her administrative leadership of the Sunday school's Junior Department that Mears first realized her call to serve the Christian cause would not be fulfilled as a missionary in foreign lands, but as an educator and trainer of young people.[60]

Her years at the University of Minnesota also played an important role in the renewal of her faith and the resolution of her doubts about the future. The first evidence of her engagement with her student colleagues beyond the classroom came less than two months after her mother's death. Shevlin Hall served as the center of women's activities at the university, and in February 1911 she was named to its third-floor house committee for the month.[61] In October 1911, during the fall semester of her junior year, Mears was one of four students to lead Bible classes at the university. Most of the classes were taught by professors, pastors, or missionaries. Her class, "Getting Acquainted with the Bible," attracted only a few students at first, but by the time the eight-session course had ended more than sixty women attended.[62] She also became involved with the campus YWCA, Women's League, and Tam o' Shanter, which was the junior women's social organization.[63]

By the time Mears graduated from the university in June 1913, she had persevered through troubling times both before and during her university days. She also possessed a confidence in her abilities that had grown with the difficulties of her youth and been sharpened by a fervent faith heritage that gave her life direction. Her early years on the Midwestern frontier had taken Henrietta Mears through periods of ambiguity and heartbreak, but they had developed in her the personal strength of character and professional expertise that would carry her through an exemplary teaching career in North Branch, Beardsley, and Minneapolis public schools. Those years also prepared her to assume the responsibility for teaching a Sunday school class of a few recalcitrant girls in 1917 and shape it into an energetic group of young women so large that the First Baptist Church of Minneapolis built an entire auditorium to house the five hundred who were attending the class by the mid-1920s.

Chapter Two

Teacher

On a warm June evening in 1956 Henrietta Mears sat across from the microphone and spent more than a half hour reading from a prepared script as Barbara Hudson Powers's hefty tape player recorded her words. In a distinctive staccato delivery known to theologically conservative Protestants around the world by this time, she shared details about her family life and the vision for training young people that had led to her singular accomplishments. After rattling off the names of a number of Protestants who had influenced her early Christian walk, Mears seemed a bit lost as the tape rolled on, recording nothing but silence for nearly ten seconds. Finally, Powers asked Mears if she would like to say something about "the young man in Minnesota." The abrupt shift in mood is profound. At first the older woman hesitated to say anything—she rarely had in the more than forty years since she first met him. She admitted that her closest family members knew next to nothing about their relationship, and she told Powers, "We let that drop. They would have just died if they'd even thought I was serious." She seemed unsure about going any further. After some urging by Powers and another long pause, she fell back momentarily on the trope she so often used over the years when asked why she never married—Saint Paul was not available. But she suddenly stopped, hesitated, and after a third lengthy period of silence, set aside any scripted text or glib answers, and over the next eight minutes revealed the impact on her life and ministry made by the only man she ever loved. As she told their story, it became apparent that, at twenty-three, she still had much to learn, not only about life but also about the call to Christian service.[1] The three years following her graduation from the University of Minnesota were the only months that she lived on her own without other family members in the home until the early 1950s. They proved to be a thousand days that completed her education and reinforced the values that she brought with her into young adulthood. A ripening of her inquisitive spirit, care for the downtrodden, unfettered love of knowledge, and practice of extending grace to those with whom she differed marked these years, all grounded in a vibrant faith that she discovered could meet any challenge.

HENRIETTA MEARS ENTERED the University of Minnesota in the fall of 1909, just as Progressives began to wonder whether President William Howard Taft could faithfully bear the reformist standard passed to him by Theodore Roosevelt. Mears had a strong background in both the humanities and mathematics and language preparation in French and Latin. Her interest in languages continued at the university as she studied German, Latin, and Greek, but she also pursued coursework in mathematics, physics, English, rhetoric, animal biology, and sociology. The College of Science, Literature, and the Arts allowed Mears significant latitude in choosing courses that would permit her to emphasize a classical, scientific, or literary program, and she appears to have picked all three to some extent. The freedom to explore many interests, when coupled with her intellectual curiosity and indecision about the direction of her post-collegiate life, explains the potpourri of courses she selected during the first two years of her matriculation. Her quandary over a career direction, however, progressively dissipated as she proceeded through her university studies, particularly in her junior and senior years. As early as her first semester Mears began coursework in chemistry that would eventually become her major—quite a rare choice for a woman at the time. She also satisfied the requirements for a secondary teaching certificate by taking the appropriate philosophy and education courses. These classes introduced Mears to the latest thinking with regard to educational psychology. She also received instruction in the most up-to-date teaching strategies.[2]

Her choice of a major in the College of Science, Literature, and the Arts meant that she purposely chose a more challenging course of study than the more direct route of affiliating with the College of Education. Had she done the latter, her training would have been oriented more toward professional preparation and somewhat less toward the liberal arts. Because of her decision to major in chemistry, she had to meet alternative and more stringent requirements to achieve her Minnesota state teaching certificate. Over and above fifteen credits in approved education, philosophy, and psychology courses, she also had to receive the recommendation of the chemistry faculty for teacher certification and provide evidence of "a good average of scholarship" at the university. The teaching certificate she received, like those granted to all other students, lasted two years. The provisional credential could then be made permanent with evidence of successful teaching experience, attestations from the superintendent of education and the president of the university, and payment of a five dollar fee.[3]

Even as Mears juggled her academic work, Bible teaching, and cocurricular involvement, she faced a second crisis of faith that would not only provide answers to her personal concerns about the relationship between Christian faith and the world's wisdom, but would also animate her lifelong conviction that religious beliefs and the pursuit of knowledge should complement each other. Upon entering the university, she resolved to approach her classes with an open mind. In order to do so she engaged in a "sincere and earnest study" of evolutionary theory spurred by the animal biology course she took during the first semester of her senior year. Discrepancies between the biblical account of creation and the implications of Darwinian natural selection led to a time of protracted intellectual and spiritual ferment. Clarity came when "God met her in a real and victorious way—one that cleared away all doubts." Mears never elaborated on exactly what transpired, but although she encountered daunting personal and professional experiences throughout the rest of her life, nothing would shake her confidence in Christian orthodoxy or the inherent worth of rigorous intellectual inquiry again.[4]

When she received her undergraduate degree in June 1913, Mears could look back on fruitful academic preparation in a major field largely dominated by males, and she could look forward to a career in public education, where females rarely rose to midlevel supervisory roles. In both circumstances she not only succeeded but excelled. She prospered in the academic culture of her time, probably just missing election to the university's Phi Beta Kappa chapter because of the strain of losing both her parents within two years of each other prior to her graduation. Her superb academic skills apparently allowed her to graduate without having to take final examinations.[5]

Though more than amply prepared to embark on a high school teaching career, Mears still had not secured a post by the late summer of 1913. She sent her credentials to the board of the recently created North Branch Independent School District but failed to receive a contract. The rural district, which just a few years earlier had revamped its curriculum and built a new three-story school to accommodate all students, appeared quite ready to begin the academic year without her services. Passage of compulsory school attendance laws by the Minnesota state legislature, the introduction of interscholastic high school sports in the fall, and the addition of vocational courses in domestic science (for girls) and agricultural science (for boys) in September 1911 stimulated high school enrollments in the years just prior to Mears's entrance into the job market. In an effort to further cajole students to enroll beyond the eighth grade, the North Branch school board mandated four years of practical training in both domestic science and agricultural science for graduation by the fall of 1913.[6]

In spite of these educational improvements, teaching and administrative staff changes occurred annually. In 1913, hiring and reshuffling of personnel in the small district fifty miles north of the Twin Cities began in the spring and concluded with the abrupt resignation of its recently hired principal in late August. As the board faced the prospect of beginning the school year in less than four weeks without one, frantic members directed newly appointed school superintendent J. O. James to "attempt to find a gentleman to take Miss Cheney's place at $70.00 a month. If no suitable gentleman can be found Miss Henrietta Mears 4337 Colfax Avenue South, Minneapolis [should] be employed." In such an inauspicious manner, Mears began a teaching and administrative career that would last for five decades.[7]

Her days were undoubtedly full, for she not only administered the North Branch school but also taught. Her expertise in chemistry deepened the school's science curriculum since the subject had not even been offered during the previous academic year. Because students could not register for chemistry courses until their third year of high school, Mears's primary teaching contact must have been with junior and senior students, although as principal she also worked administratively with all the other grades.

Relatively little can be discerned regarding her specific directives as principal or the scope and sequence of her pedagogy, but she clearly adopted some of the ideas of the progressive education movement most closely identified with philosopher John Dewey. The Progressive Education Association would not be founded until 1919, but the redirection of educational practice toward child-centered learning had made significant inroads both in teacher training and professional curricula—the founding of the Park School in Baltimore in 1912 being but one example. Throughout her career, Mears advocated a pedagogy that shunned a dry recitation of factual material and allowed students to ask questions and explore areas of interest as active participants. She always believed that character development played a central role in the education of every student and that it could be cultivated through an array of opportunities inside and outside the classroom. The teacher's role in the educational process centered on encouraging young people to find their own voices and assisting them in understanding how to speak confidently with those voices: "I am convinced that learning is more than the ability to repeat the sayings and ideas of another; rather it is a dynamic development of the conduct and character of the pupil."[8]

She began her work with a flourish, securing money for textbooks and laboratory supplies through Superintendent James within the first week of the fall term. An oil stove for the domestic science students and remodeled facilities for the agricultural science students were also on her mid-September "must have" list.[9] Mears taught all the chemistry courses in addition to performing her administrative duties, but because her record books have not survived, it is not possible to determine either how many students or how many courses she taught.

Arguably the most valuable scholastic activity over which she exercised leadership was a mid-December series of eagerly anticipated meetings that included an academic course for farmers and community members and ran concurrently with a Chisago County teachers' institute.[10] She bore direct responsibility for a midweek evening reception at the school, complete with a program and refreshments, for all community members interested in the course. Mears invited three ministers from different churches in the area to participate. Superintendent James wrote about the evening for the *North Branch Review* and waxed rhapsodic about the communal and spiritual impact of the event: "Such a big get together meeting as this means a lot to any community. After touching elbows like this we become less prejudiced and have more true Christian spirit of love and friendship for our fellow men." This academically themed event planned by a northern Baptist and featuring ministers from three churches different from her own—along with the sentiment it provoked—foreshadowed both the ecumenical approach to

Christianity Mears took for the rest of her life and the response to it by those so engaged.[11]

She also played an essential role in organizing an innovative spring event in mid-May that combined a public exhibition of academic work produced by the North Branch students with the first track meet ever held in the town. While it cannot be determined whether the day was exclusively her idea or whether in her role as principal and chemistry teacher she merely facilitated the ingenuity of another colleague, it is clear that the affair displayed important aspects of Mears's philosophy of education. Her superintendent and the greater community supported it enthusiastically. At the conclusion of the athletic competition, attendees viewed the academic exhibits showcasing student work.[12]

Graduation came just two weeks after the track meet and student exhibition with a baccalaureate service on Sunday and the graduation ceremony on Monday, June 1, 1914. Without corroborating evidence it is not possible to ascertain with any degree of certainty which aspects of the proceedings fell to Mears and which were the plans of others. But in looking at the programs—particularly for the baccalaureate service—the same inclusive Protestant spirit evident in the fall reappeared at the end of the academic year. It is also worth noting that on graduation Monday, the seven seniors, their parents, and the junior class enjoyed an afternoon banquet after which an estimated five hundred people crowded into the new auditorium for the graduation ceremony featuring A. O. Eberhart, governor of Minnesota, as commencement speaker.[13]

As an administrator Mears had to concentrate on the general welfare of the entire student body and the execution of policies already in place or decided upon by her superiors during the course of her service to the district. But as a chemistry teacher she had the chance to develop her own pedagogical style and determine the nature and quality of her relationships with her pupils. The evolution of her association with high school chemistry student Everett Alvin perhaps best illustrates her approach to her students as persons as well as the impact of her treatment of them.[14]

Alvin came from a large well-to-do clan whose patriarch, John Elof Alvin, had emigrated from Sweden with his family.[15] By the time the young Alvin entered Mears's chemistry classroom as a junior, he had acquired quite a notorious reputation as a chief mischief maker. Other teachers warned her about him, but Mears chose not to act preemptively, instead treating the boy as if she knew nothing about his previous escapades. In this way she called him into an expectant comradeship with her. But such a strategy went only so far. One afternoon, Mears looked up from her desk to catch Alvin preparing to launch a spitwad at another student. When their eyes met, instead of giving him a disapproving scowl, Mears smiled graciously as if to affirm her faith in his ability to make the right decision. Her unexpected response disarmed him. A nonchalant scratch of his ear transformed his former course of action and also signaled the end of his belligerence.

The next day young Alvin handed her a written invitation from his family to join them for dinner at their elegant home on the west side of town, which Mears passed every day on her walk to school. When word of the engagement circulated among the teachers, Mears became an instant celebrity as none of them had ever been invited to the Alvin home for dinner. That evening turned out to be the first of many shared with the Alvins. They grew closer through the school year, so close in fact that Mears served the family as a spiritual advisor and trusted friend. Nearly forty years later, when the eldest Alvin daughter visited her in Southern California, she reminded Mears what her friendship meant to the entire family and what her leadership meant to the community: "You revolutionized North Branch. Our whole family was changed because of your influence on our lives."[16]

While charged with responsibility for the physical and educational welfare of more than two hundred students combined with all the pedagogical burdens of a first-year chemistry teacher, Mears did have a life outside the physical confines of the school. As her relationship with the Alvin family demonstrates, however, the impetus behind much of her social activity in the small community proceeded from her professional role as principal and teacher. She and her colleagues were invited to dinners and parties, often with students also in attendance. On one such occasion nearly forty students enjoyed watching their teachers compete in a series of lighthearted contests including hat design and sculpture. Mears won the "best memory" competition and later joined a few others in presenting unspecified "selections of various types." A group picnic to nearby Fish Lake in late May brought the high school teachers and students together to celebrate the end of the school year.[17]

Of all the choices Mears made during her first year as a professional, none caused her more distress nor illustrated the centrality of her Christian faith more clearly than her romantic relationship with a young financier associated with the town's Merchants National Bank. He had supposedly graduated from Dartmouth and traveled extensively. Mears never revealed his name nor how they met, but due to the nature of small town life they ran into each other constantly. She described him as "outstanding and splendid and fine in every way—intellectually challenging and socially a delight." The attraction seems to have been almost immediate and reciprocal. They began walking out together, but Mears harbored some concerns that intensified as their relationship progressed—for her young banker was Roman Catholic. They continued to see each other and broached the subject of marriage. At this point the misgivings Mears tried to ignore took new form. She doubted the sincerity of his affections and perhaps her own value when measured against his character and achievements.[18]

As real as these doubts may have been, in light of the yawning divide between Protestants and Roman Catholics in the early twentieth century her suitor's faith remained the principal issue. For although Mears had been raised to respect religious perspectives other than her own, she had decidedly strong feelings that she should marry only someone who shared her most earnest religious beliefs and practices. There is no indication that she doubted his faith, but it seemed increasingly apparent to her that some of their spiritual differences were insurmountable. As they tried to work through their difficulties, he assured her of his admiration for her religious views. He promised Mears that "he'd want me to go on and just believe as I believed and do as I felt that I should do." He even offered to move from North Branch so they could start over together in another town if that was what she preferred. He obviously loved her, but she could not escape the conclusion that should she marry him, she would be putting him in front of her desire to be fully available to God. Mears may have reflected on her mother's anguish in trying to make sense of Florence's death in her own turmoil over where her primary commitment lay. She kept returning to the thought that marriage to him would be like

> establishing a home and deciding that my husband would eat in the dining room and I would eat in the den every night. We would both have a good meal, and I knew that I just could not sit around the table unless I could sit around the table and have fellowship together and eat at the same table. It would be impossible.[19]

Mears ultimately concluded that she had to end the relationship, but she hoped to find a way out of her romantic dilemma "in such a way that the issue need never be faced squarely." While her meaning here is open to interpretation, her actions in the spring appear less so. Perhaps in an attempt to prod him to break up with her, Mears stepped out with a local dentist, George Rowell, when her banker left town on a business trip knowing that he would hear of her relationship with Rowell. He soon returned, but her social engagements in his absence did not cool his ardor. This only made the situation intolerable for Mears. She seems not to have ended her association with either of them via direct conversation, instead resolving to resign her post at the North Branch school. It is also unclear whether she told either young man of her decision to leave at the end of the school year in June 1914 before boarding the train. She may have merely said goodbye and never returned. Regardless of the questionable means by which she extricated herself from these relationships, this was a deeply significant move on her part. Her resolve, however imperfectly implemented, led Mears "to a place of knowing what God really wanted me to do." She believed that through this surrender of her desire for marriage and family to her faith commitment, God showed her

> that He had something peculiar for me to do, and something special. . . . I didn't know just when, but I could just see doors were closed here and there until finally, this was it. And after I once went through that final door where it was just the Lord and myself . . . I found out that life can become very creative in every way.

The decision to reject the only man she ever loved marked another turning point in her maturing Christian faith and provided a decisive personal lesson she would draw upon countless times over the next five decades.[20]

Most likely in an attempt to put as much distance as possible between herself and her thwarted suitors, Mears accepted a position in Beardsley, Minnesota—a short distance from the South Dakota border and more than two hundred miles west of North Branch. A somewhat more ethnically diverse community than North Branch though overwhelmingly Caucasian, the small town of under a thousand in the Minnesota corn and wheat belt prospered with the coming of the railroad. As with her North Branch appointment Mears taught chemistry and served as principal of the high school, which was similarly housed in a modern three-story building containing all grades. But unlike her previous position, she also assumed responsibilities as the speech and drama coach and athletic director. Enrollment in the high school fluctuated between thirty-five and forty-five, with a total student population between 130 and 180 during her two-year tenure in Beardsley. She and two others appear to have taught the entire secondary curriculum. Grades one through eight were covered by four other teachers. The entire staff stayed together for two full years—quite unusual for rural school districts at this time. Mears was one of the very few of her colleagues in all the county's schools who had earned a university teaching certificate, which meant that she did not have to take competency examinations as did most of her contemporaries. She joined an even more select group among her Big Stone County peers when she secured a grade one lifetime teaching certificate by September 1915 at the beginning of her second year in the district.[21]

Although the school district was not an independent one like North Branch, Mears operated under the same bureaucratic constraints; her role as principal remained a leadership position secondary to the local male superintendent. Superintendent Schopmeyer and the school board, however, were under the jurisdiction of Big Stone County superintendent Anna Swenson, who visited quite often. It fell to the new principal to ensure that the Beardsley school served the surrounding community as an "educational center, with the special function of training boys and girls to be more capable and useful citizens."[22]

If North Branch introduced her to the academic profession, it was at Beardsley where she seems to have blossomed, both as a multitalented administrator-educator and as a respected Bible teacher. Yet she began her position there with a somewhat pessimistic view of rural life in western Minnesota. Upon arriving in Beardsley shortly before the school term began in early September 1914, Mears perceived a decided lack of initiative and moral direction among the older students, particularly the boys, which caused her to lament that "God made the country, man the city, and the devil the small town." She was also less than ecstatic about the pool halls and other forms of suspect entertainment that existed for the young people of Beardsley. Mears decided to tackle the problem with "enthusiasm, stamina, and a progressive program" to supply more appropriate diversions for them.[23]

From the first days in her classroom, students realized she meant business. She utilized the tools at her command to reinforce order and build an academic culture conducive to learning. With perhaps upward of forty students in any given class session, Mears maintained decorum by relocating talkative students—and she did so repeatedly during the opening months of 1914. Consistent with progressive educational theory, she appears to have let her pupils choose their own seats initially; one student noted that on the first day of school everyone arrived early to stake out the back seats. It did not take long, however, for Mears to make her first strategic changes by moving the freshmen and sophomores to different seats while leaving the juniors and seniors alone except for one student who was probably very disruptive. But during the last week of October, the seniors fell from grace as she moved all five of them. This left only members of the junior class in their preferred seats by the beginning of November. For a short time no seating changes were needed, but by the end of November some of the senior boys needed relocating again. Mears's chess-like positioning of students achieved the desired results soon after the new year as she only moved some of the freshmen prior to January 14. As if to demonstrate the positive effects of her seating strategy, an upper class student correspondent for the *Beardsley News* wrote with a whimsical touch, "Ask Dean how he likes the front row. Poor Ralph, at last he can no longer hold those nice little conversations with Ruth." After this midwinter seating adjustment, there is no further mention of Mears shifting seats during the remainder of the year. During the ensuing year the only seating change seems to have occurred as a reward for *good* behavior as "Annie Miller was given the back seat for the first time during her checkered career."[24] A more stable seating arrangement did not, of course, mean that her students made no mischief at all.

One of the most amusing pranks with which Mears had to contend happened in the autumn of her first year in Beardsley. The seniors had placed a class pennant bearing their motto in the school assembly room. Sensing a chance to humble their elders, some boys in the lower high school classes surreptitiously removed it. When Mears discovered that the senior pennant had been pilfered, she cross-examined a number of potential perpetrators until she deduced their identities. They then faced the ignominy of having to restore the pennant to its rightful place of honor. Sometimes embarrassment went the other way, however, as when Mears confronted a high school girl about eating in class. But she was not eating. As a student wrote later, "Poor Estella can't have a toothache in peace! Miss Mears must think toothaches are sweet things—she told Estella to take her candy out of her mouth." For decidedly differing reasons, both teacher and student probably wished the event had not happened.[25]

Consistent, even-handed discipline was only one approach Mears employed to inspire a sense of pride and accomplishment among her Beardsley students. She also offered a myriad of opportunities for them to excel, making them wide-ranging enough to appeal to nearly every student. She directed two senior theatrical comedies that were performed for the community at a packed Beardsley Opera House. Proceeds from both plays were used to meet graduation expenses. She also most likely directed the high school students' presentation of *Santa's Santaplane*, a fifteen-song Christmas cantata performed at the opera house in December 1915 with a full cast of characters including Santa, Christmas Eve (Santa's love interest), Fusty Boots, Cinderella, the Snow Queen, Mars, and Earth Children. Even the grade-school students appeared as Pinkies and Winkies (Good and Bad Fairies). The *Beardsley News* ran a full-page advertisement that noted that the production's admission price benefited the Beardsley High School Athletic Association.[26]

The athletic association itself may have been Mears's idea. She championed the competitive spirit that animated interscholastic sports and sought to institutionalize that spirit in the small town in much the same way as she had with the track meet in North Branch. When she arrived in the summer of 1914, Beardsley had no high school football team although the very first team (1910–1911) had gone undefeated, allowing no ties and holding opponents scoreless.[27] Recognizing the positive role sports could play in the lives of young people, she set about organizing a team by persuading a member of a prominent Beardsley dry-goods merchant family to take on the challenge of resurrecting the program. Coach Prevey exuded confidence in his players as the team approached its first game in early October 1914 against the alumni—the score was not recorded. The team lost three of its remaining four games, but Mears showed up at every contest, whether home or away, to cheer on her boys. Beardsley fielded boys' and girls' basketball teams during her time there, the boys team doing especially well both in 1914–1915 and 1915–1916. Mears may have also had a hand in helping organize the high school baseball team in 1915.[28]

Along with the avenues for student success that Mears provided in academics, theater, and athletics, she also spearheaded the formation of a new student organization that proceeded from her expertise in rhetoric and from her desire to recognize excellence in thought and deed. The formation of the Athenian Literary Society most readily demonstrates her commitment to the intellectual and moral development of her students. The society was first organized in late October 1914 to "promote the literary and social welfare of the school." Those enthusiastic about its creation believed that it was "impossible to have a good high school unless there is formed some good literary organizations," and the Athenian Literary Society fit the bill. A constitution was written, bylaws drawn up, and a motto coined ("Let your speech be better than silence or be silent"). Proceeds from the society's events went toward the purchase of equipment needed by the Beardsley school. Students took charge of the programs, but under Mears's guidance as advisor and coach. She insisted, for example, on a direct linkage between literary endeavors and other aspects of student life by choosing "Athletics as conducted in the Beardsley High School are a benefit to the school as a whole" for the debate topic of winter 1916 as the boys' basketball team headed toward a championship season.[29] To her, students were never "bowls to be filled, but torches to be lit"[30] and multifaceted individuals to be nurtured—but not without assistance.

Mears also fully supported the rural mission of the Beardsley school, signaling to students that an education could be of practical benefit. Less than a month after she assumed her responsibilities, the high school students spent a day at the Big Stone County Fair to show their work and participate in fair competitions. The next year, Beardsley students won fifty awards at the same fair in multiple categories including sewing, cooking, canning, drawing, and farm crops. The high school girls did particularly well with their home gardening and canning entries, and Adelaide Lumphrey took second prize in the reading contest. In November, county school superintendent Swenson made a special trip to Beardsley to present forty dollars in prize money to Mears's students. A week after the county fair, Mears dismissed students to show Beardsley's loyalty to another agricultural exposition at which the Beardsley boys won all the prizes and fifty dollars in cash in the corn-per-acre growing contest. Such success bred more interest, for by April of 1916 the Beardsley school had cataloged twenty-two entries from students in agricultural competitions such as corn growing and pig raising. By virtue of their earlier triumphs, Mears's students Ross Clymer and Victor Eastman looked forward to their free weeklong trip to the Minnesota State Fair in the fall.[31]

Under her leadership the domestic science program at the Beardsley school delivered important services to students and community members alike. In mid-January 1915, the older students began offering hot lunches at the domestic science laboratory with Mears's home economics instructor supervising production of the meals. This practical application of school-based skills to meet a material need appears to have initiated a pattern of hospitality. The following month the high school domestic science department served lunch to about one hundred in the village hall after the regular meeting of the Beardsley Farmer's Club. In May a domestic science class prepared a four-course meal for the members of the school board and their wives. The following year the junior domestic science class served breakfast to the faculty of the Beardsley school, and less than two weeks later their senior counterparts began serving luncheons that continued at least into mid-May 1916. The advanced domestic science students treated the school board members and their wives to an elegant dinner that same month. When the school held its open house for parents and community members later in May, the domestic science students provided a lunch for all visitors. The preparation and presentation of meals not only gave the students occasions to hone the culinary and hospitality skills learned in their classes, but also met practical and substantive community needs. As in the case of a similar North Branch program, it is unclear whether Mears created it, encouraged it, or merely followed through on directives from higher up, but it is intriguing to note that neither school had such an initiative before she arrived. Whatever her role, her advocacy for the students in her school and the community at large is unmistakable. The Beardsley school's dedication to rural issues during Mears's tenure is further demonstrated by the fact that in February 1916 the high school received copies of the 1915 *Minnesota Farmers Institute Annual* for distribution to community members.[32]

Her involvement in projects related to the educational mission of the Beardsley school offers another example of her promotion of its rural mission. At a November 1914 teachers meeting, Superintendent Schopmeyer floated the idea of forming a village and rural teachers' association. Mears accepted appointment to a committee charged with choosing an appropriate name and developing an agenda for the body's first meeting. She and two colleagues worked quickly to pull together an instructive program before the end of the week. After this initial gathering, it was assumed that the group would take up issues related to schoolwork during the course of the year. In addition to her role in the creation of this teachers' organization, Mears also participated in the Beardsley Farmer's Club, giving a dramatic reading to the gathering of close to one hundred in February 1915 as part of a program that drew heavily on the talents of the sons and daughters of the members.[33]

Even as Mears set about to provide multiple pathways for student success and to support the rural community in which she lived, her dual responsibility as administrator and teacher meant that matters both major and mundane required her regular attention. Barely a week into her first month in Beardsley, the school received a new disc phonograph to be used as a pedagogical tool for the younger students. Unfortunately, the teachers and pupils had to pay for it. Mears concocted an ingenious method of payment by suggesting that proceeds from the programs of the Athenian Literary Society be earmarked for that purpose. She also procured funds to purchase records. The resourceful principal found money to pay for everything from a pencil sharpener for her high school room to burners for the chemistry lab so that she could proceed with chemical bonding and distillation lessons, which had to be postponed until their arrival. The school's library converted to the Dewey decimal system during the fall of 1914, and Mears apparently assisted in this task, which necessitated rearranging the library's entire catalog. The resolution of problems ranging from poor student achievement and protracted staff illness to a temperamental boiler fell under her purview. Mears periodically welcomed Superintendent Swenson to her campus, and on at least one occasion, had a visit from Minnesota state inspector R. B. MacLean. Other dignitaries and members of the local visiting committee also made stops at the school.[34]

The many academic hats she wore carried extracurricular implications as well, and provided her with opportunities to socialize and serve in ways not spelled out by her contract—from dinners with community members, Christmas festivities, and theatrical cast parties with her students, to school open houses and exhibition days, fundraising events, and year-end celebrations. Mears had no trouble filling her calendar or showcasing her talents and celebrated sense of humor.[35]

Other duties allowed Mears to invite an array of guests to campus for special presentations on an assortment of pertinent topics. In her first year of service the school had at least seven different lecturers including the local Roman Catholic priest, the Rev. P. J. Shanahan; the Rev. Shannon of the Society for the Friendless; prohibition advocate Rozette Hendrix; and the Rev.

Rice, Methodist minister from nearby Clinton.[36] It is striking that within the first six months of her arrival in Beardsley, Mears selected guests to address her students who exemplified not only her inclusive sensibilities but also her concern for the welfare of the less fortunate and her desire for her students to be engaged with the world in which they were maturing.

Mears quickly won the students over with her administrative acumen, pedagogical expertise, and care for them beyond the classroom—and they were not shy in expressing their appreciation. Perhaps it was her fair-minded discipline coupled with an obvious regard for the welfare of her students that resulted in a surprise party for her less than two months after her arrival. Adelaide Lumphrey enlisted some partners and planned an elaborate celebration for Mears's twenty-fourth birthday. They furtively sent invitations, planned refreshments, decorated the room, and devised a program. Lumphrey and her collaborators even enlisted the local superintendent as a coconspirator. Early on the evening of Friday, October 23, Schopmeyer asked Mears to assist him in reshelving library books after their conversion to the Dewey decimal system. When she arrived, he led her to the domestic science room where the entire high school hid, waiting to shout "Surprise!" to the flummoxed principal. At that point, "she began to open up her eyes and think of something else besides working in the library." The festivities included "playing games, singing, and listening to Miss Mears portray some of her powers in 'elocuting'"—no doubt in a jovial spirit fitting for the event. The assembled well-wishers presented their young principal with a clock selected by Lumphrey and her committee. The party lasted until 11:00 p.m. and clearly demonstrated the affection her students and colleagues had for her even at this early point in her service to the community.[37]

WHILE HER READINESS TO "ELOCUTE" for the guests at her surprise birthday party illustrates her playful spontaneity, Mears took quite seriously her efforts to educate Beardsley students in the Christian faith. She limited her church involvement to worship services at the Beardsley Methodist Episcopal Church for the first few months as she shouldered her professional responsibilities in the new district during the fall of 1914. Upon her return from the Christmas holiday, however, the superintendent of the Sunday school appointed Mears teacher number two on January 8, 1915. She began teaching the Doers class (ages unknown) on January 17 and taught through the rest of the academic year. After summer recess she returned to the class for the entire 1915–1916 school year. Neither her class nor the Sunday school was very large. Average attendance did not reach sixty-five students during her two years in Beardsley and the highest recorded attendance for class number two was a mere seventeen students. However, two observations merit attention regarding her class because they foreshadow patterns that became even more characteristic of her ministry in the future.

First, her students comprised a significant percentage of the total student population of the Sunday school. The first two weeks of January 1915, before she began teaching, show attendance figures of seven and eleven. In the two succeeding weeks, after she accepted the position, the numbers increased to twelve then sixteen, the latter being the largest enrollment in any of the classes that quarter. Attendance fluctuated as it did in the other seven classes, but tended to be in the mid-teens. With an average attendance for the entire Sunday school at fifty-three, Mears's class had the highest totals of all eight classes for every week in the quarter but one. The average attendance jumped to sixty for the quarter ending in June, with her class having the highest attendance for eight of the thirteen weeks even though she was gone for six of those weeks. Overall average attendance dropped to fifty in her summer absence as did the totals for class number two. Fall average attendance in the Sunday school stabilized at fifty. Mears's class attendance, though up somewhat from the summer, remained fairly low through the quarter ending in December, but her weekly class figures were still often the highest in the school.

Second, throughout 1915, with relatively few exceptions, her class gave more money to the church than any other class—sometimes double, triple, even quadruple the amount donated by the next most generous class. Similar patterns can be seen for the first quarter of 1916, but Mears's class was not quite as dominant as it had been in 1915. The attendance and giving trajectories of her class, even in this small western Minnesota farm town, signaled two major emphases of her educational practice that would be reproduced again and again through the years. It should also be noted that, in keeping with her belief that spiritual teaching had to be integrated with other aspects of life, she treated her students to "secular" events, such as a progressive dinner and an outing to Bonanza Springs. On top of her role as a Christian educator, Mears also found time to contribute her vocal talents to the church as second alto in the ladies' quartet.[38]

During her second year in Beardsley, Mears also taught a Monday evening Bible class of up to twenty girls at the L. J. Oren home where she boarded.[39] The exact nature and composition of this group, however, is difficult to ascertain. Not only are the ages of the students in her Sunday school class unknown, so is their sex. Articles in the *Beardsley News* reported that members of the Monday evening Bible study were female and presumably of high school age, but the newspaper also identified them as members of her Sunday school class. So it is unclear whether Mears taught the girls during the Sunday school hour (noon) and then conducted a Bible study with them on Monday evenings or whether these were two different, though most likely overlapping, groups.

Powers's conversations with Mears in 1956 add another layer of complexity. She reported that Mears taught a young people's class that included most of the football team. As if Mears did not have enough on her plate already, Powers wrote that two high school football players approached her after class to ask her to start an evening Bible study for them. She consented and began the study that very evening—also at the Oren home. Mears told Powers that the study became so popular that the parlor windows had to be opened in the spring so interested students could hear her teaching. If all these accounts reflect the actual state of affairs, Mears never slept and the Orens never had an evening to themselves![40] Whatever the exact nature and extent of her ministry to students, it is evident that Mears's formidable influence on the young people of Beardsley went well beyond her role as public school administrator and teacher. Her spiritual leadership both at the church and in the Bible studies she led played well in an environment that also saw a woman fill the evening pulpit of the Methodist Episcopal Church at least once during Mears's sojourn in the town.[41]

If aspects of her Christian service remain somewhat ambiguous, the importance of Mears's relationship with Father Shanahan is not. The Roman Catholic Church of St. Mary had been a mainstay in the community since its founding in 1884, predating by three years the first Methodist church building. Shanahan came to the parish from Minneapolis and assumed his office in early September 1914 within a few days of Mears's arrival in town. It is unclear whether the priest or the principal initiated their first contact, but the two developed a close relationship that appears to have lasted the duration of her stay in Beardsley. Soon after the fall term began, Mears invited him to speak at the high school. He accepted her invitation and gave a well-received presentation on the benefits of an education. Either as he was planning his remarks or just after he had addressed the high school, the rectory caught fire and burned to the ground in spite of community members' attempts to save the building. The priest lost most of his furniture, clothing, and other personal effects, though he was able to save his library. Until suitable lodging for him could be secured, he moved into the sacristy of St. Mary's, making his home among the clerical vestments and sacramental objects of the worship preparation room. Even in the wake of his personal loss, however, Shanahan assured Mears of his support for her work. He visited her numerous times at the high school, offering to assist her in any way he could. Over the two years of their association in Beardsley they had many conversations on a range of issues and extended discussions on spiritual matters. Their ongoing relationship meant that Shanahan stayed current with respect to Mears's attempts to nurture the minds, bodies, and spirits of Beardsley's young people from the very beginning of her appointment. Before she left town in June 1916, he expressed his personal admiration for all she had accomplished, and the entire town's gratitude for her achievements.[42] Mears never forgot his kindness and support.

Her years in Beardsley held one other relationship that illustrated her willingness to bend toward compliance for the sake of a greater good. During one of the community's harvest parties, Mears became acquainted with the son of the local hotel owner. Apparently a Harvard student, this also nameless young man took an immediate interest in the educator. They became constant companions over the next few weeks, for Mears found him polite, intelligent, and gracious, "very charming in every way" as she recalled decades later. Their relationship seemed destined to deepen if not for a visit from J. L. Fitzgerald, president of the local school board. He warned Mears of her suitor's scandalous reputation and told her in no uncertain terms to terminate contact with him. She agreed and, unlike her North Branch experience, broke the news to him personally. He confessed his past misdeeds to her and his desire to make a fresh start. He also thanked Mears for her role in motivating him to turn his life around and shortly thereafter left town. His mother subsequently called to express her appreciation to Mears: "I just want to thank you for making him change and for inspiring him to want to be different."[43] Mears fondly remembered the banker and dentist she left in North Branch and the hotelier's son in Beardsley, but she would never again pursue a romantic relationship, believing that she would find all her needs met through the exercise of her Christian faith.

THE YEARS HENRIETTA MEARS SPENT in North Branch and Beardsley provided her abundant opportunities to showcase her many talents and gifts. Students and colleagues respected her integrity, enjoyed her sense of humor, and prized her contributions to the community. Her consistent witness to a vibrant and ecumenical Christian faith had been noticed by those within and outside the Methodist Episcopal Church. Her years in the rural Midwest augmented her pedagogical insight, validated her interpersonal skills, challenged her personally, and sharpened her focus on living and teaching a holistic Christian life. Yet North Branch and Beardsley were very small towns and quite far from her sister, brother, and extended family in the Twin Cities. By the spring of 1916 Mears began to search for another position.

At her request, Fitzgerald wrote a letter of recommendation that accurately summarized the professional and personal attributes of his twenty-five-year-old principal as well as his regard for all she offered to students and community members. Fitzgerald began by praising her "as a teacher and a citizen" and certifying her worth by noting that she "has been re-elected for next year and can practically name her salary if she will stay." He then became more specific about all she had brought to her position:

> Miss Mears has made herself so popular with students, faculty, parents, and the rest of the community that it is difficult to try to write an itemized account of her qualifications. She is well prepared in education and natural talent, is full of ambition, industrious and tireless. She accepts suggestions from proper sources in proper spirit, - still has a "mind of her own." She maintains control of her pupils without finding it necessary to be eternally cracking the whip.

Fitzgerald noted especially that Mears "interests herself in her pupils out of school hours, in church and society."[44] So convinced were school board members of her value to Beardsley, they implored her to remain even after receiving her resignation letter in June. In a last-ditch effort to retain her services for the 1916–1917 school year, a delegation from the board followed her to the train station, offering her a bonus if she would stay for the coming year.[45] But she would not be dissuaded; Mears had set her course for Minneapolis even though she had no position in hand when she boarded the train.

In a real sense, North Branch and Beardsley served as a kind of social, intellectual, and spiritual laboratory where Henrietta Mears advanced practical, real world applications for the educational theories she studied at the university and the theological beliefs of her family heritage. The proven viability of those applications would carry her forward from this point on, and she would clarify and expand upon them in ever more significant ways in the decades to come.

Chapter Three

Passages

With the United States avowing neutrality even as it became more closely identified with the Entente powers fighting the Great War overseas, 1916 turned out to be a difficult year to find work as a public school educator in the Twin Cities—particularly for young female chemistry teachers. Though the population of Minneapolis had ballooned from 203,000 in 1900 to over 300,000 in 1910 and would add another estimated 70,000 by 1917, Mears had no luck finding a teaching position in any of the city's six high schools, even armed with Fitzgerald's glowing recommendation. Her three years of experience as a principal, science teacher, rhetorician, dramatics coach, and athletic director counted less for her than age and gender counted against her. However, 1916 was also the year when Minneapolis public schools introduced a junior high department enrolling seventh-, eighth-, and ninth-grade students partially to remove population pressures on the district's high schools. Fortunately, Mears's skills as a mathematician coupled with the necessarily rapid implementation of the junior high curriculum in September secured her an appointment teaching that subject. She refused to accept a permanent posting, however, and taught the entire year as a substitute because she set her sights on returning to the high school classroom as soon as possible. She moved in with her sister Margaret and began her temporary position.[1]

At year's end Mears received a contract to continue in the junior high department, but she declined, opting to reapply for a high school chemistry teaching post against the advice of district officials. Disheartened at the dismal prospects for teaching in her chosen field, Mears accepted a late-summer offer to teach mathematics at the high school she had attended as a student between

1905 and 1908. It was her old school in name only, however, as the dramatic population growth of Minneapolis led the city to construct a new Central High School physical plant in 1914 to accommodate up to 1,800 students.[2]

Fortuitously for Mears, just as the fall 1917 term began, one of Central's chemistry teachers resigned to report for duty with the American Expeditionary Force, which was then preparing to deploy to the battlefields in France. Desperate to find a suitable replacement at this late date, the principal appealed to his faculty for the names of possible candidates. One of Mears's former teachers at Central put forward her name based on a superlative endorsement submitted by University of Minnesota chemistry professor Lillian Cohen, who insisted that Mears "had the most brilliant mind of any student she had taught." Her commendation won over the principal, but he expressed some concern about Mears's ability to maintain the chemistry rooms filled with hazardous materials. When asked if she felt up to the challenge Mears responded demurely, "May I try it, and see?" With that coy rejoinder the twenty-six-year-old began a decade of service at CHS. During those years Mears would apply the latest pedagogical methods and demonstrate through her own example that preparation for life happened both inside and outside of the classroom.[3]

High schools of the era, even large ones like Central, spun their academic purpose into a broader web of intersecting functions addressing the intellectual, social, and physical welfare of maturing adolescents. Since African Americans comprised less than one percent of the Minneapolis population, with other persons of color a fraction of that, Mears and her colleagues directed their attention to the perceived developmental needs of white students. Faculty members served not only as disciplinary experts, but also as models of respectable adulthood. From the moment she walked into her room, Mears demonstrated her commitment to this holistic educational philosophy. Chemistry classes were apparently open only to upper level students, as they had been in North Branch and Beardsley, so she probably had the greatest impact on juniors and seniors. Mears served as one of the advisors and party chaperons for the junior-senior Girls Club (1921–1922) and advisor to successive senior classes from 1921 through 1927.[4]

The discipline of chemistry lent itself quite well to the experiential learning most valued by progressive educators. Central's science teachers not only utilized popular scientific journals and the new medium of film,[5] they also often made use of special demonstrations and speakers to link classroom activities to issues of wider import. Mears, for example, had students bring a piece of soft coal to school. Each student then heated the specimen and observed the various stages of its transformation. She concluded the lesson by listing all the products that came from bituminous coal. She also took her students on field trips to the Minneapolis Gas Light Company so they could see how the city used coal on an industrial scale for illumination. A few years later Mears and a chemistry colleague hosted a University of Minnesota graduate student who demonstrated the preparation of chlorine gas. Employed by a New Jersey company that manufactured inhalators used in the experimental treatment of lung disorders, he offered the high school students a clear connection between chemical processes they studied and amelioration of the human condition.[6]

Mears worked diligently to clarify for students just how central her discipline was to the future. In an article published in the student newspaper she expounded on the merits of chemical knowledge and its application to nearly every industry as well as the impressive job prospects not only in chemical engineering but also in a number of related fields.[7] She was not above a bit of good-natured chicanery to popularize the wonders of chemistry, which she demonstrated by creating a colorful underwater garden of chemical salts for her students. Interviewed by an intrigued student reporter, Mears took the opportunity to link chemistry and popular culture by commenting that gardens similar to the one she created were used by the film industry.[8] She also emboldened her students to show off the marvels of their discipline. They often performed experiments for high school open house sessions. On one such instance, after visitors passed a banner announcing the "Mysteries of Chemistry," her pupils treated them to "magical" displays of chemical processes. Mears's devotion to her chosen field of study and to her students quickly caught the attention of her peers, who invited her to address the fifty-seventh meeting of the Minnesota Education Association in November 1920.[9]

Her pedagogical creativity, however, could not avoid the occasional mishap. In October 1919, paradoxically during Central High's "No Accident Week," Mears's students gathered around her desk as she conducted an experiment with chlorine gas. Suddenly flames arced toward the chemist and her startled audience. Two quick-thinking students knew that chlorine gas did not burn and, reasoning that the laboratory desk's gas line had somehow ignited, turned the flow off at the spigot. A somewhat amused Mears calmly explained the cause of the flame and assured her students that all would be well. A few years later when an eager pupil splattered sulphuric acid over her clothes and legs, Mears took no chances with either safety or propriety and sent her home to recover.[10]

Attending to the academic and physical welfare of her students comprised a significant portion of Mears's attention, but from the opening years of her service at Central High, she often melded these most important matters with the psychosocial needs and desires of her charges. As a senior class advisor, whether for the A, B, or C student advisory group, she met with her portion of the class every day and never shied away from challenging her scholars to do their very best. One autumn when teachers received midterm failure notices from the advisors to distribute to their hapless charges, Mears reminded her students that the "marks on these notes will depend largely on your showing during the next few days," thereby issuing both a warning of dire consequences *and* a hope for redemption to those on the brink of academic disaster.[11] But she tempered her challenging words with a care for students that endeared her to them. Over the years she chaperoned dances, participated in plays and pantomimes, created and performed comedy sketches, hosted students in her home, and perhaps exercised her skills in dramatics and rhetoric to advise informally a rather renowned and highly selective boys' literary arts club called The Wranglers.[12]

Mears's fondness for comic humor must have been most entertaining to her students and colleagues alike, and it presented itself at the least provocation. In early 1921 she helped plan the program for a social after the January 14 faculty meeting. Place cards with appellations such as "peanut," "prune," "sardine," and "shrimp" awaited the teachers in the school lunchroom, and they were instructed to sit by the card they believed described them best. After supper Mears and her comrades recruited male teachers to sing parodies of the latest songs about women. Female faculty members responded in kind. They also created riddles with answers that included the names of their colleagues, awarding a prize to the one who had the most correct guesses. However dated such amusements appear to the contemporary reader, the playfulness of the evening must have brought welcome relief after a long Minneapolis winter's week.[13] As the student population of Central High approached 3,500 in 1923, seniors decided to throw a party for all the class to get better acquainted.

After-dinner entertainment included a pantomime entitled *Molly's at Home* by Mears and the other senior advisors.[14] At a later soirée, Mears joined her colleagues in serenading the students with "Oh! Mister Mitchell!"—Mr. Mitchell being a fellow senior class advisor.

In a more serious vein (and one that would reappear in her Sunday school work), Mears managed the formal bureaucratic organization of her seniors, complete with officers, committees, and requisite duties. Mears also supervised her share of senior proms. When the A Senior Class Council decided to publish its own newspaper, Mears became one of the paper's directors and kept the submission box for story ideas in her room. At a special celebration hosted by the seniors of 1927 for the graduated seniors of 1926, Mears and her fellow senior advisors performed for the guests of honor.[15]

She also added her support to extracurricular campus-wide initiatives and events. To raise money for a fence to enclose the athletic field, Central's faculty staged the play *Is French Spoken Here?* in the spring of 1925. Mears played Anna Marie, otherwise known as the maid-of-all-work. For the 1926 Faculty Day assembly, teachers structured their presentation as a radio broadcast from station CHS. Mears contributed a reading to the program enjoyed by the entire student body. She also found the time to host in her home not only the officers of her own senior advisory group, but also the editor in chief of the *Centralian* yearbook and the president of the senior council.[16]

The informal *nom de plume* of Mears's character in the above play communicated a truth about her life at Central High School that neither pupils nor peers missed. If work needed doing, she could be counted on to contribute. She challenged her students academically and her colleagues professionally, when necessary, and made mischief alongside them whenever possible. She endeared herself to them with her ability to communicate a love of learning during class sessions, to counsel students about their deepest concerns after school, and to lighten the mood with her witty sense of humor when needed. Perhaps with some level of hyperbole but nonetheless with earnest sincerity, Margaret White, a chemistry student and senior advisee during Mears's final year of teaching at Central, remembered how highly students regarded her: "Everybody liked Miss Mears as an advisor and as a chemistry teacher. . . . everybody who knew her loved her. . . . she was everybody's friend." Mears's engaging personality drew young people to her classroom at the end of the school day. Students, particularly male students, sought out her advice and counsel or just dropped by for challenging conversation.[17]

Central High students demonstrated their esteem for "Miss Mears" in manners both serious and whimsical, reciprocating the ways in which she expressed her care for them. They worked to make sure she felt accepted at Central because she had graduated from archrival West High. Students reasoned that since she spent her first three years at the old Central High School, they could legitimately claim her as one of their own. The yearbooks included jokes that poked fun both at Mears and the discipline she so ably taught. One year the *Centralian* noted that she dismissed her seventh-period class ten minutes early with the request to "go out quietly so as not to wake the other classes." The 1924 edition contained a recitation between Mears and a chemistry student: Mears says, "State the property of H_2O." L. Catton responds, "It always freezes with the slippery side down." In the section entitled "Would you suspect?" the same yearbook shared that "Miss Mears took a dare to wear a green and orange hat, on which protruded balls fastened to the hat by long wires, to her Latin class at the university." At a year-end senior party in May 1925 the students took turns impersonating Mears and her faculty colleagues. She had just begun her sixth year at Central High when students voted her the second best female "all around teacher." She was so popular that when it was discovered her niece, Peggy Greig, had begun writing poetry, the student newspaper covered the story, which included comments from a critic and a reprint of one of her poems though Mears's niece was only eight years old.[18]

As Mears concluded ten years of service, the *Centralian* editor expressed rather effusively what she had meant to the June 1927 seniors: "Miss Mears, with her everlasting generosity together with a wonderful gift of understanding, has been instrumental in making our last year at Central one of the happiest of our lives." It had been common knowledge since mid-March that the chemistry teacher would be spending the summer traveling in Europe. By early May the students learned that she would also take a year's leave of absence to winter in California. They did not know that she had taught her last chemistry class. Neither did Mears. All she knew was that she decided to take the advice of her pastor and step back from her responsibilities at Central High and First Baptist for a year to consider the future. The timing of the Rev. William Bell Riley's suggestion proved to be impeccable.[19]

WHEN HENRIETTA MEARS RETURNED to a much larger Minneapolis in the early summer of 1916, she also returned to a much different First Baptist Church. During her three-year absence, Riley had built First Baptist into one of the largest churches in the Twin Cities. His reputation, influence, and ambition had also grown proportionally. By 1914 he was universally acknowledged as one of the foremost leaders of the fundamentalist movement, speaking at conferences across the country and also bringing an international cast of like-minded pastors and Bible teachers to First Baptist. Riley entertained the notion that First Baptist and his Northwestern Bible and Missionary Training School could serve as bastions of fundamentalist Christianity to rival Moody Bible Institute of Chicago and the Bible Institute of Los Angeles.[20] The First World War severely curtailed his aspirations in the short term, but the global conflagration did not diminish Riley's goal of defending theologically conservative Protestantism against its perceived enemies nor of building a greatly enlarged campus for First Baptist ministries to do so most effectively. His role in founding the World's Christian Fundamentalist Association in 1919 coupled with the success of a somewhat downscaled building campaign cemented his central role in the postwar struggle for the soul of American Protestantism.[21] With Riley at the helm of First Baptist and Northwestern, Henrietta Mears, like all those associated with either institution, was assured of a front row seat in the showdown that had been building for decades between orthodox Christian believers and their critics.

She dove back into active participation at First Baptist immediately upon her return to Minneapolis. By September of 1916 she resumed a minor leadership role in the Young People's Society of Christian Endeavor group at First Baptist—now the largest chapter in the entire state.[22] Even though her teaching duties increased once she moved to Central High in the fall of 1917, Mears augmented her service to First Baptist and to the Northern Baptist Convention. In October 1920 she began a term on the church's tithing committee. Two years later when the city feted Riley to mark his twenty-fifth year as pastor at First Baptist, Mears read a congratulatory letter from Mrs. Riley, who could not be present for the celebration. She also accepted an invitation to join the faculty at Northwestern, initiating "a long period of the most effective assistance the School had ever had and so greatly needed" according to one close to the Bible institute. So significant was her influence that the church leadership chose Mears as a delegate to the 1925 Northern

Baptist Convention meeting in Seattle. By the time of the national gathering Mears had also assumed directorship of the church's large Tuesday evening Girl's Club.[23] As impressive as this list of service commitments might be, it does not include the most significant of her ministry efforts. For it was her creation, leadership, teaching, and administration of the Fidelis Sunday school class that not only proved to be beneficial to the Christian education of young women in Minneapolis but also became the springboard for Mears's greater impact on the Protestant cause.

Henrietta's sister Margaret worked variously as a stenographer and secretary and maintained an active church life during her sister's absence. She taught one of three classes in the Sunday school for late adolescent young women. Over the years she became increasingly exasperated with their behavior (they called themselves the "Droolers" after all) and with her inability to hold their attention.[24] Whenever Henrietta visited Minneapolis, Margaret asked her younger sister to teach in her stead. Her move back to the Twin Cities found Margaret still soldiering on with the Droolers. By the following year, however, believing that Henrietta's youth and professional training would equip her more ably to connect with the girls personally and communicate Bible lessons more effectively, Margaret persuaded her to assume primary responsibility for the class.

When she took the reins in autumn 1917 membership at First Baptist hit two thousand, but the Sunday school enrolled only three hundred. Church leadership recognized the necessity of improving its educational ministry if the church hoped to prosper. Perhaps as a preliminary strategic move, it appears that three classes of Droolers collapsed into one under Henrietta's leadership. Guided by Mears's sense of Christian service, class members soon jettisoned their previous nickname to become the "Great Eighteen," signifying the number of charter members in the class. They remained together for only a few weeks, however, because the superintendent decided to reorganize the entire Sunday school. He shifted the education hour to precede rather than follow the morning worship service, introduced a grading system to track attendance, and doubled the teaching corps. Nearly all of the Great Eighteen joined the teaching staff, leaving Mears on the first Sunday in December 1917 with only two or three in her class, one of whom had only paid a solitary visit. Mears believed in the importance of a personal connection, so she and the remaining membership called on every home in the immediate vicinity of the church with an 18–25-year-old single young woman to recruit new members. The following Sunday forty-four attended the second meeting of the Fidelis class.[25]

Mears's biblical teaching, combined with her focus on meeting the social and emotional needs of students, generated phenomenal support for the new class. The official attendance figures from early March 1918 pegged the enrollment at fifty-three with an average attendance of thirty-one. Two years later the statistics had increased to 135 and 111 respectively. By November 1920 the class passed two hundred. Barely five months later, enrollment hit 257 with an average attendance of 144. The Fidelis women added nearly another hundred members by late March 1924. The number swelled to 375 by March of 1926 and expanded to 449 a year later. Within the first three years of its founding, the Fidelis class became not only the fastest growing class in a rapidly expanding Sunday school, but also the largest and the most generous with its monetary contributions.

It grew so quickly over the course of its first five years of existence that the class had to relocate into successively larger rooms. The first move came in mid-July 1918, when First Baptist's education newsletter announced, "The Fidelis moved to a larger room downstairs today. Their next objective is the Barnabas room but what is really worrying is what the rest of us will do when they fill the auditorium." When attendance hit 200 an observer wrote "The Fidelis class a few Sundays ago, passed the high water mark of 200 in attendance having 202 present. This is a great crowd of young women and now they take possession of the Social Room by right of conquest. We predict for them 300 by January 1st."[26] Mears used the occasion to write to her "Fideltians," urging them to take up the challenge.[27]

As attendance mushroomed, Mears noticed that members failed to welcome visitors adequately. She could not let this tendency pass. In early January 1921 she wrote again but with a quite different tone. She began by acknowledging the opportunity the new year provided "to have one of the *greatest* classes in the country." She commended her Fideltians as a "splendid class" with a "splendid room which can easily hold 300." Then she addressed the core problem of such rapid growth: "It makes me heartsick to see forty or fifty girls come to visit our class on Sunday and not see our own girls invite them to join or ask them to come again. Girls, it is thoughtlessness on our part and I believe we must pray that the Lord will make us more courteous and unselfish." She linked her admonition to the future welfare of the class by reminding her students: "We must fill the room or we cannot expect to keep it. Let's do it!! Bring some girl with you Sunday." Mears concluded with an appeal to action based on Saint Paul's charge to the Corinthians (1 Cor. 15:58): "Be ye steadfast, unmoveable, always abounding in the work of the Lord, inasmuch as ye know that your labor is not in vain in the Lord."[28]

Mears's reprimand yielded astonishing results as the class grew larger still, far surpassing all the other Sunday school classes. It took over the area formerly occupied by the entire junior department, and by April of 1921 the Fideltians commandeered the largest room in the building apart from the sanctuary itself. Using as a benchmark the year of highest Fidelis enrollment (1927), the young women's class contained more than twenty percent of the total Sunday school registrants excluding infants and the housebound. Riley used the Fidelis class in his written comments to members and friends of First Baptist as a model to inspire similar growth in other Sunday school departments at the church.[29]

Since Mears's class had outgrown every meeting room in the church, she attended an April 1920 meeting of the leadership that adopted a motion to move forward with a feasibility study for remodeling and enlarging the church. The need for additional space became so acute by the end of the year that contingency plans had to be implemented for temporary housing of some Sunday school classes off-site and the initiation of a church service for junior-age children during the 11:00 a.m. worship service to free up seating in the sanctuary for more adults. Riley advocated a simultaneous expansion of the sanctuary *and* creation of a new education building. Though the board's decision was not unanimous, his plan received approval. Jackson Hall opened in April 1923 and included spacious classrooms to serve both the Sunday school and the Northwestern Bible and Missionary Training School.

Two months before the grand opening Mears wrote a personal letter that probably went only to Fidelis leaders. In it she expressed her hopes for the class, whose members were "as anxious as I am to see it prosper and grow." Reaffirming the "many spiritual blessings" that had come to it, Mears then turned to her dream for the future: "I do want so to see *five hundred* active members on our roll and I want to see *three hundred* present on Sunday morning, to hear the message of our Lord and Saviour Jesus Christ. I believe this is our challenge!" She wrote that "big things are easy for us when 'each has a mind to work,' but these things are hard when only a few try to accomplish them." She then pulled the recipient in as a partner in her vision: "I am writing to you because I remember that the dear Lord says, 'one can chase a thousand, and two can put ten thousand to flight,' so you see I need to add your forces to mine so that my strength may be multiplied by ten in adding yours to it." Mears wanted "to see FIVE HUNDRED girls on fire for Jesus Christ, telling of His love and winning others to Him."[30] Her invitation to join her in achieving a common goal demonstrated both her desire for continued growth of the class and her skill in challenging and encouraging her students at the same time.

The extent of her successful strategy became evident when Jackson Hall opened. The largest room in the new building, the chapel, was designed specifically to seat the better than three hundred young Fidelis women now on the membership roll—with an overflow room on the south wall. Fortunately, this gave Fideltians room to grow because they did, reaching their highest recorded daily attendance of 532 on October 11, 1925. Since the chapel only held four hundred, even the overflow room overflowed.[31]

While it is a relatively simple matter to track the explosive growth of the Fidelis class under Mears's leadership, it is somewhat more difficult to determine the exact content of her Sunday school lessons as none of her teaching notes from this period seem to have survived. Since she tended to repeat her lessons every few years during her time in Southern California, she most likely did the same for her classes at First Baptist, expositing selected books of the Bible as well as preparing topical studies informed by Scripture. She also employed acrostics to fix the main points of her teaching in the minds of her students.[32]

Mears's Fideltians attested to the power of her teaching. They spoke of sitting "spell bound as she opened to us the word." Harriet C. Blank appreciated her "intelligent presentation of scripture truths." Mears's erudite exposition of the Bible so affected Adabelle Christensen that she "never wanted to miss any service." Others believed that her "passion for the Word of God" motivated Mears to teach the Bible "in such a way that it took on a new dimension. The Word was for every day living." Gene Fornell spoke of the "rich privilege" it was to sit under Mears's teaching:

> Her Bible lessons were not about someone whom she had only read, but she seemed personally acquainted with the Bible characters and especially

her Lord and Saviour Jesus Christ. She had such enthusiasm for carrying on the work of her beloved Father in Heaven that it was contagious and we all searched for ways in which we, too, might . . . "preach the gospel of peace and bring glad tidings of good things."[33]

If the precise content of her teaching remains somewhat uncertain, there is no doubt about the objectives to which she taught, for they remained constant. Mears often spoke of them and reiterated them regularly at conferences and teacher-training meetings for over forty years with minor wording changes for coeducational applications. Christian educator Antoinette Abernathy Lamoreaux investigated what Mears was accomplishing at First Baptist and wrote a short piece for *The Sunday School Worker* that first put into print what at this early stage of her ministry Mears called the "I Wills."

- With God's help I will win the personal allegiance of every one of my girls to the Master.
- I will not think my work is over when a girl has made her decision for Christ.
- I will see that every girl finds a definite place of service in the kingdom.
- I will try to bring religion out of the unreal and intangible and interpret it in terms of daily life.
- I will try to help each girl discover her powers, because the world and the Master need every talent hidden away in the heart of every girl today.
- I will instill a divine discontent into the mind of every girl who can do more than she is doing.
- I will make it easy for every girl to come to me with the deepest experiences of her inner life, not by urging her confidence, but by such consistent sympathy and understanding that she will naturally turn to me in an hour of need. I will reverence her personality as the Master reverences it, and with the Master's eyes see its glorious possibilities. No girl shall ever feel that I am disappointed in her, nor however tense the cords of love may be stretched, that I have given her up.
- I will put the cross back in the Christian life where Christ placed it, and challenge my girls to carry it.

- I will pray as I have never prayed in all my teaching life for wisdom and for power.
- I will spend and be spent in this battle between good and evil.[34]

As her ten principles make clear, Mears devoted her life to further the cause of theologically conservative Protestantism by committing herself completely to her faith and to those for whom she took responsibility. Fideltian Fornell recalled that "Her faith was so positive that when she prayed we felt she was having a conversation with her Heavenly Father with whom she was in constant contact."[35] She held herself and her students to lofty standards of personal devotion to and deliberative action for Christ, with both lived out through the application of scriptural injunctions for daily life. It is no accident that the former Latin student chose a name for her class that evoked this sense of faithfulness and loyalty. She believed that even biblical knowledge, without practical outlets for examination and expression, deformed the human personality. Biblical teaching remained at the heart of everything she did, but it is clear from her ten I Wills that such instruction had to be applied to the welfare of students in ways that would lead them to further explore the implications for their entire lives of a faith commitment to Christ. She strove to ensure that biblical knowledge led to practical service.[36] As one of her Fidelis class members said, "She radiated joy and assurance and gave to us the knowledge and experience of Christian living and service." Another remembered that Mears "led me to see that a young woman who walked close to her Savior would live a loving, fruitful life."[37]

Mears believed that a structured but purposeful environment facilitated intellectual learning and also deepened relationships both socially and spiritually, so she guided her Fideltians with this holistic goal in mind. The Fidelis Constitution and By-Laws introduced the framework Mears believed would most likely stimulate optimal Christian development.[38] The class verse (Dan. 12:3) linked the appropriate pursuit of knowledge and personal evangelism. The class actually appears to have had three mottos—all of them connecting the ethos of the class to classic elements of the Christian life. "Once a Fideliser, Always a Fideliser" spoke to the importance of looking inward and fostering personal relationships even as the class grew larger with each passing season. "Organized for Service" advanced the absolute necessity of looking outward to those in need. "The Class Where One is a Stranger Only Once" in a sense served as the bridge, inspiring those within to embrace those from without. Henrietta and Margaret would always be on hand to welcome students on Sunday morning, but the young women assumed responsibility for contacting visitors and new members, thereby pulling them more closely into the group. From the first meetings of the Fidelis class Mears placed great emphasis on making personal contact with prospective members and saw herself as a spiritual mother to those under her care. Her ability to initiate and nurture connections between class members and visitors resulted in lifelong friendships and Fidelis class reunions that continued for more than sixty years.[39]

The creation and maintenance of such strong relationships proceeded from the model of hospitality and acceptance Mears provided. It could begin with something as simple as a handshake and special greeting for every young woman regardless of the class size and continue with a loving Christmas greeting. The personal interest Mears took in students convinced them of her care for them as Christian sisters. She could persuade even the reserved young woman that with God's help she could do anything.[40] Her relationship with Nell Petersen changed the young Fideltian's life, for "she was a real true friend and was never too busy to give help, counseling and encouragement. She had a vital interest and concern for people and her enthusiasm was unequalled.... She was unique and without a doubt one of the greatest women of the century."[41]

Article II of the Fidelis Constitution clarified that the multilayered class objective focused on Bible study, Christian growth, evangelism, and service. The class granted official membership to young women nineteen or older who had visited for three Sundays upon the recommendation of the membership committee. Members were assessed monthly, noncompulsory dues of twenty-five cents to pay for "flowers for the sick, temporary help for needy Fidelis girls, and for social purposes." Mears involved as many members in leadership positions as possible because she believed that responsibility made leaders out of visitors, who then became more vested in the welfare and ongoing mission of the class. Those young women "who have served the class in some efficient manner, thereby proving themselves entitled to nomination for office," could stand for election. Election of the slate of officers by majority vote of the class membership occurred annually in the early spring unless circumstances necessitated a special election to fill an open office. The constitution restricted voting in such elections to the officers of the class, with a two-thirds affirmative vote necessary to fill vacant offices. Even the teacher had to be elected each year. In April 1921 the Fideltian officer corps numbered just under twenty and rose to twenty-seven by the end of the decade. The officers met for supper and cabinet meetings on the Monday after the first Sunday of each month.[42] It is probable that the sitting officers in cabinet sessions approved ballots with only one candidate per office so the majority vote required for election merely rubber stamped the choices of the leadership, no doubt guided by Mears.

The Fidelis class met weekly at the Sunday school hour. Supplementary meetings included Thursday evening prayer meetings, which also involved Bible memorization. Prayer meeting attendance more than quadrupled from April 1920 to April 1921 to between thirty and thirty-five even as the duration of meetings increased from thirty minutes to an hour. Fideltians were also involved in the Tuesday evening Girl's Club. Mears's aunt, Henrietta Everts Buckbee, formed and directed a Fidelis Glee Club. Midway through 1921 seventy-five women comprised its membership. The class also had its own orchestra that performed at venues across the city.[43] Special programs for the class appear to have been determined by the officers' cabinet, with the input of both Mears sisters, and then regularly printed in small booklets. Class members edited and published an informative magazine and developed their own songbook with Fidelis-themed lyrics set to popular tunes of the day. By 1921 Fideltians had been able to hire a half-time assistant and looked forward to expanding the position within a few months. The class even had its own stationery.[44]

The service orientation of Fidelis young women swung in two directions. The above examples illustrate an inward focus as members shouldered responsibilities to ensure the vitality of their class. But as demonstrated by the Great Eighteen, many left to teach in the Sunday school at First Baptist. Over the years others followed similar courses by volunteering in Sunday schools across the US and Canada. Fideltians also visited those struggling with infirmities. For example, Mary Anderson, a resident at Parkview Sanatorium "always looked forward to the Fidelis girls spending Sunday afternoon with her."[45] Some Fidelis members prepared for full-time Christian ministry by attending the Northwestern Bible and Missionary Training School. While an accounting of all those from the class who entered Christian service positions as missionaries, nurses, or administrators is not possible, at least thirteen who did can be identified. The class supported its own array of missions causes and also contributed to the missions fund of another group within the church. Mears formed former

Fideltians into a young married women's auxiliary group that met monthly to sew needed items for missionaries. This Dorcas Society, named after the New Testament figure, also contributed monetary support to missions causes.[46]

Bible study, prayer, and service constituted central aspects of the holistic ministry Henrietta Mears advocated, but she never minimized the absolute importance of social activity to facilitate relationships and build community. Ann Kludt, an early president of the Fidelis class who went on to serve as a missionary to Japan, recalled that "she brought clean wholesome fun into our lives."[47] Class picnics, teas, wiener roasts, banquets, and special parties occurred regularly throughout the year. These events provided opportunities for service in organizing events and planning programs, as well as occasions for social engagement via games, skits, and general levity. Jokes, riddles, and profiles in the pages of the class magazine furnished another outlet for humor and ingenuity, as did the class songbook. And Fideltians could always count on their teacher to add her special comic flair when called upon. They especially remembered her trademark corsaged outfits and hats—particularly the "rusty frock coat and a smashed silk hat" she donned when "preaching the famous sermon on 'Old Mother Hubbard.'" Fideltians howled with laughter when Mears sang "Oh, in the moonlight I want to hold somebody's hand."[48]

Her phenomenal success at First Baptist in proclaiming the historic Christian faith with depth and grace to her Fideltians proceeded from her ability to value individuals authentically and to make biblical teaching both relevant and appealing to those for whom she cared. One of the young women Mears encountered during a Fidelis house-to-house visitation campaign explained how that meeting affected the rest of her life:

> My mother and her people were Roman Catholics, but the personal evangelism and subsequent interest and prayers of Miss Mears, and the impact of the Word of God, brought conviction and conversion to me and to the members of my home. . . . She is the one who reminded us that Sunday school is the time of impression but Christian Endeavor (coeducational evening youth meeting) is the time for expression. Though the emphasis was ever on the spiritual, she never did neglect the mind and body. Laughter and fun, wholesome play and entertainment, sightseeing, and conversation were ever in high gear. I adored her, copied her, shadowed her and quoted her.[49]

Many other Fidelis class members over the years expressed similar sentiments.

One of Mears's most enduring qualities was her gift for making anyone who approached her feel not only welcomed but singularly important. Late one evening after counseling one of her Fideltians, she wrote a letter that epitomized this trait. She first thanked the unnamed young woman "for the generous way you have expressed what you call appreciation." Then she turned the tables:

> I can assure you that all the appreciation of our being brought together has not been one sided. The Lord has brought a blessing upon my life too in letting me know you in just this experience you have gone through. I have been so glad if I could have been used to help you just a little bit. I hope and yes, pray that your being with me (no matter what the occasion) may always be attended by a real blessing to both of us. Always know dear child that our home welcomes you and the latch string is ever out, pull it whenever you want to.[50]

As a teacher in the First Baptist Sunday school and as a professor at the Northwestern Bible and Missionary Training School, Mears adhered to Riley's requirement that she annually affirm the Christian Fundamentals Association Confession of Faith.[51] She could do so because of her theological conservatism. Since Mears grew to maturity under Riley's ministry at First Baptist, it is no surprise that his fundamentalist theological perspectives played a significant role in her spiritual development. It would be difficult to imagine that he would have allowed her to occupy such a conspicuous place in his Sunday school and Bible institute had she not absorbed his views. Yet while hewing to his fundamentalist theology—which included a dispensational hermeneutic and an adamantly anti-Darwinian predisposition—Mears refused to adopt many of the sociocultural implications of Riley's diatribes against modern American life. Her affinity for historic Protestant teachings did not equate to a philosophical kinship with many of the positions taken by Riley or other fundamentalists of the day. During the decade when the culture war between modernists and fundamentalists moved inexorably toward its destructive denouement, Henrietta Mears began to forge a new direction for theological conservatives while serving at the epicenter of American fundamentalism.

MEARS'S GENUINE CARE FOR STUDENTS and her call to practical, graceful service combined with incisive scriptural exposition that joined mind and heart in a manner both challenging and appealing. This attractive amalgam led to results that caught the attention of other theologically conservative Protestants. By the early twentieth century a network of orthodox Protestant pastors, teachers, missionaries, church administrators, and lay leaders transcended denominational lines and stretched from coast to coast. It was only natural that as they fought to hold the line against their modernist adversaries they would call on each other for moral and practical support.

Nearly two thousand miles from First Baptist in Minneapolis, the Rev. Stewart P. MacLennan at the First Presbyterian Church of Hollywood, California, built upon the theologically conservative foundations of his predecessors, teaching the supremacy of biblical authority and welcoming to his pulpit others who shared this outlook. Because of Riley's uncompromising stand against modernism, MacLennan invited the Minnesota Baptist to preach during the 1923 Easter season at First Presbyterian.[52] Riley accepted and returned the favor, offering his pulpit to MacLennan in the early spring of 1925.

After morning worship the Mears sisters asked the distinguished West Coast minister to dine with them. Aware that he would be preaching again during the evening service, Henrietta promised to drive him to his hotel directly after their meal so that he would have most of the afternoon to relax. MacLennan, however, preferred to spend the time conversing with his hosts and seeking their responses to a new series of sermons he had begun to develop. As the hours slipped by, MacLennan must have been intrigued by what he learned about Mears's extraordinary educational work, and perhaps he imagined what she might be able to do for his own Sunday school in Hollywood. It is doubtful that he offered her a position in his church at this time, but he probably made overtures along that line for her to consider because he suggested that the Mears sisters visit Hollywood to see the work at First Presbyterian for themselves. As enticing as his offer sounded, their many commitments seemed to preclude any trip to Southern California.[53]

Yet because Henrietta's academic schedule lightened in the summer, she traveled to California in July 1925, just a few months after MacLennan's visit. She spent time with friends and relatives in San Francisco and Fresno, but it is unknown whether she ventured any further south before returning to the

Twin Cities.[54] As fall approached, Mears resumed her many duties at First Baptist and began the 1925–1926 school year at Central High. Her educational work in both places flourished, and she and Margaret settled into the new home they had recently purchased. So although she had seen at least part of California for herself, there were plenty of reasons for her to remain ensconced in her Minnesota life surrounded by successes and close to extended family members throughout the greater Twin Cities metropolitan area.

But other issues forced their way into Mears's thinking about the future. Between 1925 and 1927, fallout from the infamous Scopes trial, the mysterious disappearance of Aimee Semple McPherson, and the sensational murder trial of J. Frank Norris combined to sully the collective national reputation of theological conservatives.[55] Closer to home, Riley's prime role in the fundamentalist struggle trained a spotlight on First Baptist whose beam only intensified scrutiny of the church through the early and mid-1920s. His displeasure with secular American culture led him to confront officials at the University of Minnesota in 1926. A personal conflict between Mears and fellow Northwestern professor Marie Acomb simmered as well.[56] How much these events provoked Mears is anyone's guess, but her own personal stake in the contested contours of Christian orthodoxy remained steadfast. She may have become increasingly disillusioned by Riley's anti-Semitism and confrontational style. The undisclosed rift with Acomb—who would eventually become Riley's wife—may have also played a role. But perhaps more than anything else, her discussion with MacLennan on that March afternoon gave her pause.

During the 1926–1927 academic year Mears faced a personal crossroads as well. She reasoned that after fourteen years as a teacher she should enroll in a graduate program to prepare for an administrative post, but she still struggled with the ramifications of her decision from two decades earlier to dedicate her life to full-time Christian service. At nearly thirty-seven Mears remained unsure about what that commitment looked like because she did not sense God's call to the foreign mission field as she expected, yet she longed to find her specific place in the kingdom.[57] Somehow Riley discovered her discontent, which led to a critical discussion probably sometime in early 1926. During their conversation, Riley proposed that she consider taking a sabbatical from her responsibilities in Minneapolis. He thought the experience of visiting other places might be just what she needed to discern where and how she was to serve. With his prompting, Henrietta and Margaret decided to spend the summer in Europe and fulfill their promise to visit Southern California in the fall and winter of 1927–1928.[58]

The Mears sisters could not afford to spend the summer of 1927 traveling in Europe on their salaries, but other members of their family were quite wealthy. Norman and cousin Charles E. Buckbee founded the Buckbee-Mears Company in Saint Paul, and uncle John Colgate Buckbee headed the Bureau of Engraving in Minneapolis until his death in 1921. Both companies were major stakeholders in the commercial life of the Twin Cities. Clarence served as president of the Itasca (Grain) Elevator Company and was a member of the Duluth Board of Trade and a director of the Minnesota National Bank at his death in 1926. William worked for the Paine Webber wealth management company in Boston.[59] These relatives probably helped the Mears sisters in one way or another to afford their nearly three-month European holiday as well as many of their later adventures abroad.

They left the day school ended for Henrietta. Over the next three months the sisters and their entourage traveled across Europe and Canada.[60] Henrietta filled her travel diary with particulars that ranged from shopping and dining excursions to visits to religious sites. She often merely chronicled the days' events, but occasionally her words reflect more about their author than where she went or what she bought. Mears valued the many conversations she had with members of her party, some of them lasting hours. She remained as approachable and empathetic as she had in Minneapolis and would engage fellow travelers on religious topics, though she was not sure her words had any lasting impact.[61] She wrote a letter to her Fidelis class soliciting their prayers for her trip and praising their Christian devotion, which differed markedly from the rampant unbelief among people she met.[62]

Germany was of particular interest. She saw Paul von Hindenburg and visited the site of the German war declaration of 1914. Mears also made a pilgrimage to the Baptist church where her mother worshipped during her stay in Berlin. She called her visit to Oberammergau, location of the renowned Passion Play, "a benediction."[63] Her reactions to aspects of Roman Catholicism encountered over the course of the trip seem to indicate a level of appreciation that many theologically conservative Protestants of the era would not have shared. She confessed a fascination with Copenhagen's Church of Our Lady, with its "gorgeous statuary of the apostles—so wonderful in its simplicity."[64] A highlight of her visit to Rome was meeting Pope Pius XI, though for some inexplicable reason she could not reach far enough to kiss his proffered hand.[65]

Throughout the journey Mears exhibited an openness to experiences that would have been suspect to many of her fundamentalist contemporaries. She had no compunction at all about shopping for fashionable attire or dining in chic restaurants. In both Nice and Monte Carlo, she visited the casinos and did the same in Monaco. Although she refused to gamble, Mears found such exquisite beauty in the garden outside the Monaco casino she almost forgot that "just inside the casino men were playing themselves to hell!" She also appears to have explored nightlife in Paris to a limited extent, visiting the macabre Cabaret du Néant in the bohemian Montmartre section of Paris.[66]

The travelers returned to Minneapolis on September 12, but Henrietta still had no clear direction about the future. She and Margaret remained in the Twin Cities for the next month preparing for the trip to California. Before leaving, the sisters participated in the tenth-anniversary celebration of the Fidelis class attended by hundreds of young women.[67] The ensuing drive to Southern California proved uneventful, and they quickly adjusted to their temporary home, paying the first of many visits to the First Presbyterian Church of Hollywood shortly after their arrival. They found MacLennan's church to be welcoming and vibrant. Henrietta often spoke at the church and also accepted invitations from other churches. In a late winter letter to her Fidelis class Mears wrote that "the Lord has used me to His honor and glory since I have been here. I have spoken numberless times in various churches. . . . Everyone has been so interested in the simple message of God's love and have urged me to come back again and again." So many transplanted Fidelis women came to hear her speak that she felt right at home.[68]

It appears that as early as February 1928 she had been encouraged to take up what she called "definite work" in Southern California, for she received numerous offers for her services, although apparently not from a large church of her own denomination in downtown Los Angeles.[69] Mears, however, determined just to rest during her sabbatical.[70] Her resolve did not last. Sometime in the late winter or early spring MacLennan invited her to become the director of educational programs at First Presbyterian Church. She could not give him an answer before she and Margaret departed, but he left the offer on the table for her to ponder on the long drive back to Minneapolis.[71]

And he did not let the matter rest. Over the next few weeks, MacLennan inundated Mears with letters, telegrams, and telephone calls touting the opportunities First Presbyterian could provide her for expanded service in a rapidly growing part of the country.[72] He also attempted to address her many concerns. She would not move without Margaret, and much of her extended family lived in and around the Twin Cities. Their home would have to be sold in a less-than-promising housing market. Her life had pivoted around Central High School since 1917 and First Baptist since girlhood. Both institutions had benefited from her considerable influence, and she had strong ties to them that would last into the foreseeable future. Mears also had to confront her own anxiety about whether her successes at First Baptist could be reproduced in Southern California. As she wrestled with these issues and communicated with MacLennan, it became clear that she needed to return to Hollywood.

Most likely traveling alone this time, Mears probably arrived sometime in the mid- to late spring to confer with MacLennan and assess her own suitability for the position. In a very real sense she put her own theological assumptions to the test. She believed that God called individuals to specific labors, but she had always thought that her call was to foreign missions. That call, however, had never been evident to her and, as her work in North Branch, Beardsley, and Minneapolis had demonstrated, she had a real aptitude for facilitating the education of young people. Mears prayed for clarity of vision, and received it in a most unlikely way.

MacLennan asked her to join him for lunch at a popular restaurant on Hollywood Boulevard. As they walked toward the front entrance, the door opened automatically, allowing them to enter without any exertion on their part. Mears had never before encountered what was then called electric eye technology, and its operation brought everything into focus for her. To enter the restaurant all she had to do was to step forward. In the same manner, she now saw MacLennan's offer as God opening a door for her. All she had to do was step forward. While this revelation set her on the path toward Hollywood, she wanted to be absolutely sure before making such a life-changing decision.

Persuading Margaret and resigning from her position at Central High School proved to be the most straightforward and least complicated matters—the sale of their home was among the most difficult. Mears needed one more indication that she correctly perceived God's direction, and so she intentionally pegged the selling price of the home two thousand dollars *above* her asking price. Although the population of Minneapolis grew substantially throughout the 1920s, spring in the upper Midwest was not the most propitious time to sell a home. The first person to view it rushed through so quickly Mears supposed that he had absolutely no interest. Shortly thereafter when he tendered an offer exactly two thousand dollars above the asking price, she discovered that his haste proceeded from a desire to secure the home before anyone else could submit a competing bid. The cords binding Mears to Minneapolis were gently being cut one by one. She could see that a new life waited for her in California, but the tremendous difficulty of leaving her Fidelis young women caused her to waver momentarily before accepting MacLennan's offer.

The Mears sisters moved in June 1928. They lived initially in an apartment house with six other people ranging in age from sixteen to fifty. Henrietta called it a "hectic but happy existence" but admitted that such an arrangement, even though temporary, made it difficult "to 'be still and know that I am God' in the midst of such a crowd." Although September 15 was Mears's first official day in her new position, she actually taught on Tuesdays and Sundays at the church for much of the summer and found great satisfaction in her work. Writing to one of her Fidelis friends she explained that "the atmosphere of the church is like our own. They all love God's Word and there is such a wonderful consecration among the young people." Still, Mears seemed to be grappling with the implications of her decision, confessing, "I have been trying to wait on the Lord to know His will." She may have only meant his will for the future because she remained convinced that she made the right choice: "I know that I am there because I believe the Lord has led me there." Yet she could not shake a lingering ambivalence: "I only want to be in His will! I know not what a day may bring forth."

As Mears concluded her letter, she assumed a mothering role to her friend as she often did with others, supportive of her decision for Christian service and praying "that the dear Lord will lead you in a very plain path to do His good will." But the final page reads like a farewell love letter to her Fidelis women from their mentor and teacher:

> It does not seem possible that I am to be there no longer to help pull and lift. But God has a plan which He will work out in a glorious way if we but wait upon Him. Give my dearest love to my own girls! They will always

> belong to me, as far as I am concerned my heart will always be with you all! I do not believe that my other group will ever take your place in any way. There is a peculiar and a particular spot there for you and you alone. But I am going to try to serve the Lord in His own way here in this new place.[73]

With this poignant goodbye Henrietta Mears closed the door on the foundational chapter of her life and gingerly opened the door to the next, unsure of what lay ahead but undaunted in her belief that God would make that clear as she stepped forward.

Chapter Four

The Remarkable Miss Mears

By the time the Mears sisters first visited Southern California, the region had entered a rambunctious adolescence, though one tempered by the quest for order, stability, and propriety. The village of Hollywood, barely a quarter century old, had been platted in 1886 but not formally incorporated until 1903 with an adult population of 166. Tethered to Los Angeles by the interurban railway system, the small town existed on the furthest periphery of its much larger neighbor to the southeast and to the distant beach city of Santa Monica to the west. Its mostly dirt, tree-lined streets cradled more orchards than homes, but on December 20, 1903, in a small upstairs room in the unfinished Masonic building on Highland Avenue, twenty-five adults gathered to organize the First Presbyterian Church of Hollywood.[1] Membership hit 174 by the end of the first decade of the new century and led to the purchase of property on Gower Street in 1908 for the construction of a sanctuary the following year.[2]

The crush of in-migration to the Southland from other parts of the country increased the population and allure of Hollywood as well as the number of occupations, simultaneously offering new fields of work to the members of First Presbyterian and new challenges for theologically conservative Protestant Christians. While the population of Los Angeles and its metropolitan area rose from 50,000 in 1890 to 319,000 in 1909 and 2,208,000 in 1929, Hollywood grew from 4,000 in 1911 to 36,000 in 1920 and 235,000 by 1930. The Southern California film industry generated a $20 million payroll in 1915 and by the end of the 1920s included more than fifty studios; they employed 15,000 workers, who received $72.1 million in compensation and produced films worth $129.3 million.[3]

The church kept up with the region's exponential growth and selectively adapted to the emerging electronic technologies. It surpassed 650 communicants and 350 Sunday school members in 1920. Five years later the church had more than doubled its communicant membership and nearly tripled the Sunday school enrollment. By the early summer of 1928, First Presbyterian reported 2,104 members and a Sunday school of 1,624. Soon after the completion of a new sanctuary in 1924 with seating for 1,800, local studios began a longstanding practice of requesting permission to photograph the striking gothic structure and film on church property. The leadership quickly demonstrated its willingness to utilize mass media for its own purposes by accepting the donation of a "fine apparatus for presenting motion pictures," stipulating, however, that its use was "to be made only upon weekdays, and not upon Sundays." By the mid-1920s Warner Brothers's Los Angeles radio station broadcast the worship services at First Presbyterian while the church screened films like Cecil B. DeMille's *King of Kings* (1927).[4]

The educational program and organizational structure of the church expanded considerably during the 1920s to meet the needs of a growing congregation and Sunday school.[5] Viewed in this context, the appointment of Henrietta Mears was actually the culmination of more than five years of concerted strategizing on the part of the church leaders. First Presbyterian had a Sunday school from its founding year, but until the arrival of Stewart MacLennan as senior pastor in 1921 no committee of session, the church's governing body, appears to have been charged with oversight of the educational ministry. This all changed in 1923 when church leadership appointed a committee on Christian education.[6] A short time later, the Hollywood church hired its first director of religious (later, Christian) education. Over the next three years church leaders heard concerns, implemented policies, advocated organizational reform, and hired personnel that they hoped would meet the needs of the hundreds of young people attending the Sunday school.[7]

In August 1926, perhaps in response to the raw emotions brought to the surface by the Scopes trial in Tennessee, the session passed a "Department of Education Declaration of Faith" to be affirmed by all teachers and workers in the education program. Very similar to the document Mears signed at Riley's First Baptist Church, the theologically conservative statement placed First Presbyterian squarely in the fundamentalist camp with its emphasis on the authority of Scripture. Unfortunately, although new staff positions were subsequently added, further organizational and personnel changes led to institutional instability even though Sunday school numbers continued to rise.[8] A particular need for more-effective and better-trained Sunday school teachers preoccupied the leadership. At the annual meeting of the congregation on April 11, 1928, recent progress made by the Sunday school was duly noted and the Christian education report for fiscal 1927–1928 highlighted alterations yet to come—including a Vacation Bible School, teacher training classes, and curricular adjustments, "which will put the Sunday School on the dignified basis of knowledge acquired—gaining promotions that will be comparable to the public schools."[9] New opportunities appeared on the horizon, but institutional equilibrium and stable leadership had been in short supply—a situation that no doubt somewhat blunted the good efforts of church staff members and lay leaders. Henrietta Mears would change all that.

Shortly after beginning her official duties in September 1928, barely a year before the stock market crash, she recorded her vision for the work. It encompassed the entire educational program of the church. The extensive list included: (1) separate departments for all age groups from infancy to old age and individual classes for each year of age in the departments, with teaching centered on the spiritual and psychosocial needs of each age group; (2) an inviting atmosphere in all departments that encouraged adults and young married couples to continue their Christian education thereby nurturing a strong faith-based home life; (3) an enthusiastic leadership and teaching corps and specialized training for its members that equaled the quality of teaching and training in the public school system; (4) a curriculum for all classes that challenged students to Christian maturity; (5) interest-focused clubs for all ages, including gender-specific ones for adolescents from middle school through high school; (6) a summer camp and conference program to teach and train young people socially and spiritually; (7) an evangelistic outlook and missionary program for each age level; (8) a financial strategy in the young people's groups that provided personal involvement in the greater work of the church; (9) the cultivation of an ethos of camaraderie to stimulate the creation and maintenance of deep friendships within the church that could sustain and strengthen Christian witness in the world; (10) Sunday school graduates who dedicated themselves to some form of full-time Christian service; and (11) appropriate brick-and-mortar building projects to facilitate the educational mission of the church.[10]

Mears deemed the church's educational mission central to its overall vitality and so set high standards and clearly articulated objectives for its pedagogical programs and curricula. A few years after her arrival in Hollywood, she shared her expansive conception of Christian education with members of the church:

> We are trying to put the *school* in Sunday school and have it mean all that the word signifies. We want our Sunday school to be an educational institution with standards of credit so high that a graduation from it will mean a preparation for any walk of the Christian life. We not only have a training school for preachers and missionaries, but we are preparing men and women to live and to serve in any capacity that God calls them, for we believe that all Christian life is a full-time service whether it be in a bank, in a store, in a school room, or as a professional man.[11]

At the heart of Mears's comprehensive educational responsibilities lay Sunday school, which, as the primary conduit for Christian education, had been in serious decline nationally since the end of the previous century.[12] But not so at First Presbyterian. In fact, MacLennan had wooed her to Hollywood in order to shape the direction of an already robust entity. Recognizing the collective effect of rising enrollments, organizational instability, and frequent personnel changes on the morale of the staff she inherited, Mears approached the first monthly meeting of her Sunday school workers with the skill of a behavioral psychologist. When called to the podium Mears paused, peered over the top of her glasses, and smiled at her jaded if not skeptical audience. Then she began: "I believe I know just what you're thinking. You're thinking, 'Oh, now here's somebody else to tell us what to do! If I have to reorganize my class once more, or try out some fancy new theory, I'll just die. What does she know about Hollywood, anyway?'" Her self-deprecating tack completely disarmed them. Many caught themselves laughing at her histrionics. Mears went on,

> You don't like changes and neither do I. You've been getting along without me up to now and it would certainly be a great burden on me to have the responsibility of rushing in here and having to try to reorganize everything overnight. So here is my plan. We'll all relax for six months and use the time for observation and then we'll sit down and evaluate the situation and decide together what we want to do. You'll undoubtedly have some ideas and I might just possibly have one or two myself.[13]

In just a few moments Mears demonstrated her preeminent concern for relationships over program as well as her ability to lead with empathy. Once her staff members knew that she saw them as valued contributors to the educational direction of First Presbyterian, she had their loyalty and their enthusiasm.[14]

With revived vigor, her Sunday school teachers and officers gave Mears the green light to proceed as expeditiously as possible. She apparently waited only four months before meeting regularly with the staff to consider new initiatives. In subsequent monthly strategy and planning sessions, she discussed with them the importance of what they did as church school teachers; she also discussed the goals they shared together as Christian educators. She often spoke of Christian education as "big business" because it was God's business. She stressed the necessity of having a well-formulated educational strategy because "business" would be conducted according to the plan. But she argued no business model could be successful unless there were goals in sight. Since she believed that clear articulation of the goals of her "big business" was of paramount import, she presented them publicly to the congregation in April 1930—the beginning of the church's first fiscal year after the Great Crash of October 1929:

1. To bring each life into vital relationship with the transforming word of God—from the youngest to the oldest. This is our major concern.
2. To lead each one to an acceptance of Jesus Christ as a personal Savior.
3. The formation of Christian ideals of Character and Conduct.
4. The expression of Christian life in Missionary and Service enterprises and recreational activities.
5. To bring people to recognize the Lordship of Christ.[15]

These five goals, when operationalized via her ten "I Wills" for teachers, formed the core assumptions upon which she based her entire ministry.

Within the first eighteen months of her arrival, Mears made significant progress toward her objectives and laid a solid foundation for her remarkable ministry. The themes she focused on during those initial monthly meetings remained her constant priorities: (1) a genuine concern for the well-being and training of her staff; (2) effective organization and implementation of the total educational program of the church; (3) a central emphasis on evangelization;

(4) the development of a biblically based curriculum that was attuned to the needs of each age group, that utilized teaching methods that engaged the whole student, and that met the wide range of student needs: spiritual, mental, emotional, and physical; (5) the necessity of cultivating spiritual maturity and a sense of service to others; and (6) programs and practices that connected the Sunday school student of any age to the work of the larger church body. [16]

From the first meeting of the administrative cabinet on January 23, 1929, Mears exhibited a great respect for her staff members and a simultaneous desire to challenge them to aspire to greater possibilities. One of her first actions was to lay out the traditional Sunday school calendar and ask the superintendents of each department what they thought should be emphasized over the course of the year. By soliciting their perspectives, Mears drew them in as colleagues in the planning process. She would do this again later in the year when she asked staff members whether anything special should be done for Mother's Day and how the Sunday school might celebrate Children's Day. She asked them their opinions about topics such as stewardship, circumstances in other departments, and the length of opening exercises.

After the Sunday school programs had been up and running under her leadership for a few months, Mears sought candid feedback from her staff on what was working well and what needed to be changed. A "Survey of our Religious Education Needs" taken in the summer or early fall of 1929 asked staff members to assess systematically all aspects of the Christian education program. Mears raised the issue of the social side of Sunday school life for both the cabinet and the teaching corps to contemplate. By October of 1929 she began asking leaders in each department to share with the rest of the staff how they were moving forward in this regard. At the January 6, 1930, teachers' and officers' meeting Mears asked her staff to reflect on what their policies should be for the coming year. Her query prompted the attendees to brainstorm on the enduring purposes of the Sunday school at the beginning of a new and, in many ways, uncertain year because of the precarious nature of the national economy. She even solicited their thoughts about whether teachers' meetings should be held during the summer months.

Mears also took to using pithy quotations to cheer and challenge her teachers. They first began to show up in the summer of 1929 when she quoted Charles Kingsley. ("I don't want to possess a faith, I want a faith to possess me.") To remind them of the profound consequence of their work, she shared that "a first rate teacher may have some third rate pupils, but no third rate teacher can long have first rate students." At opportune moments from that point on, thought-provoking quotations became an integral part of her ministry. Sometimes she would cite others to emphasize a certain precept. (Louis Entzminger's "It is impossible to grow a Sunday school without personal visitation." Or Martin Brumbaugh's "God has so planned that what we plant in a human soul may bloom perennially.") Other times she would wax eloquent on her own. ("The Sunday school which lays small plans will measure its accomplishments accordingly.")[17] She always used quotations to provide a measure of comfort in difficult circumstances or to drive home a salient point to be remembered: "'How can we gain the interest of our young people?" she asked in 1932. "Let me answer, 'Never lose it.'"[18]

While focusing on the welfare of her staff and promoting the open sharing of their viewpoints, Mears could deftly transition to matters that needed further attention, such as their duty with respect to absent or irregularly attending Sunday school students or the importance of teacher training classes to improve pedagogical skills. She introduced a reading on new teaching methods for consideration early in 1929 and announced the heady goal of 2,222 Sunday school attendees for Easter 1929, thereby pushing her colleagues to greater achievement. It also became obvious that she hoped representatives from the Sunday school departments would participate in the weekly presession prayer meetings at 9:15 a.m., ultimately proposing that each department have its own prayer time. To the cabinet members she posed the challenge of assessing the quality of supervision they provided for their department, including how (or even whether) they encouraged their teachers. At the November 27, 1929, cabinet meeting Mears bluntly inquired, "Are you really a leader?" The following month at a teachers' and officers' conference she asked, "What definite things have you done since the November meeting? Have you called on each member of your class?" After such a potentially sobering end to the December conference, Mears assumed a cheerleading stance in January, urging each of her colleagues to be "a go-getter in the Lord."

She wanted go-getters in the Lord on her staff because they understood the necessity of hard work. For while Henrietta Mears placed individuals and relationships above programs and organizations, she also knew that little could be accomplished without programs that met the needs of individuals and without organization that stimulated healthy relationships. Work was her four-letter word, and she never soft-pedaled how much of it was necessary for success. On November 4, 1929, she told her staff members that "Sunday school teaching or being an officer in any department means *work* and it has the same meaning as Webster gives it in the dictionary." By the late winter of 1929 Mears had begun the process of streamlining the Sunday school bureaucracy in order to make the respective departments more responsive to the needs of their students. The resulting increased workload fell to the entire teaching corps, including Mears. In short order she revamped the system of taking and reporting collections in the departments, instituted committees in each department for the purpose of calling on visitors and absent members, and formed another group to oversee the commemoration of special days in the Sunday school year. Calling committees were the first step toward building a strong visitation program, and Mears believed they were crucial to the health of her school, something she learned well at First Baptist. For example, in preparation for Roll Call Sunday (March 17, 1929) cards were sent to all Sunday school enrollees, and teachers were charged with contacting every student by telephone or personal visit—a total of well over 1,400 contacts. With such large numbers Mears also wanted to make sure that the church had accurate records for each pupil, including an alphabetical list containing all their contact information. This was such an important practice to her that she met with the new departmental secretaries to review the procedure. From her point of view there were only four reasons to remove a person from the roll: death, removal from the community, evidence of membership in another Sunday school, or at the student's request. She never deleted students from the roll if there were any possibility that they might return, and she warned her teachers not to do so without authorization.

Perhaps recalling her days in North Branch and Beardsley, Mears paid particular attention to attendance records because she believed that aside from one of the four exceptions, there remained no legitimate reason for students to absent themselves once they visited the Sunday school. Concerns about enrollments, absentees, and the personal contact of students appear regularly in meeting agendas. At a training session in mid-1929 she listed five reasons why students exhibited irregular attendance patterns, all of which she said could be mitigated by appropriate action on the part of teachers and officers. A few months later she spoke about the necessity of formally recognizing new members in each department. The teachers' and officers' meeting in November 1929 was wholly given over to a discussion of how to grow the Sunday school, and the first item addressed was how to persuade absentees to return. Mears's solution was quite simple: "They must be personally visited. This must be done every week." She believed it was fine for teachers "to write letters or cards or telephone but only as opening the way for *personal visitation.*" The director expanded on her strategy for making this possible:

> Sunday School should be so organized that no class up through the Intermediate Department is so large that the teacher cannot get in personal touch with those who are absent. Above the Intermediate is Junior High. The class should be organized into small groups with somebody responsible for each group. No more on [*sic*] a group than the leader can keep in touch with *every week*. No absentee committee will do the work. They may look up those who have been lost track of but some*one* must be responsible.

Her directives regarding new members and evangelism were just as labor-intensive. She argued that only personal visitation could increase membership and wanted teachers to report their contacts weekly to their respective superintendent. To ensure accountability Mears requested that a record of telephone calls, letters, and personal visits made by staff members be shared at the next Sunday school meeting. That Mears expected great things and held her educators and herself to extremely high standards of performance became quickly apparent to the members and friends of the First Presbyterian Church of Hollywood.

Mears also sought go-getters in the Lord because they shared her conviction that a personal conversion experience was absolutely essential to the work of the Sunday school and they willingly utilized every opportunity to introduce their students to the gospel message. Since the Bible was the great repository of the message, Mears suggested as early as February 1929 that the church give Bibles to all children in the Sunday school who did not own them. While it appears that the entire Bible was not supplied to students, copies of John's Gospel were. Beginning in June 1929, each year's third grade graduates of the Primary Department received complimentary copies of the Bible from the church.

Though the Bible was *the* textbook of the Sunday school under Mears, that fact did not necessarily mean students either understood what conversion meant or had a conversion experience. Consequently, Mears kept the necessity of personal evangelistic work on the part of her teachers foremost in their minds. In December 1929, the first of eight questions she asked her staff came right to the point: "How many of your pupils have you led to Christ in the past three months?" At a teachers' and officers' conference early that month she asked the key question: "Do we really know who the saved are in our classes?" She revisited the question in February 1930 by asking her teachers and officers, "What are you doing definitely to win souls for the Lord?" Mears's unrelenting focus on evangelistic work proceeded from her foundational belief that the conversion of students had to be a primary task of the church's educational program.

If evangelism remained a central objective of the Christian education program at First Presbyterian, then it fell to the curriculum of the Sunday school to facilitate conversion by presenting biblical texts and concepts clearly to students of all ages. It became quite obvious early in her tenure that Mears wanted something more for her scholars than the educational materials she inherited in 1928. Her lack of enthusiasm for the curriculum the church session had approved in December 1926 was on full display when she placed the issue of the Sunday school workbooks on the agenda for the January 1929 cabinet meeting. By the following summer curriculum committees had been formed—a general committee chaired by a church elder and departmental committees for the Beginners, Primary, Junior, Junior High, and Senior High departments. A short while later, Mears initiated a discussion of curricular concerns and invited suggestions from her teachers. The subsequent "Survey of our Religious Education Needs" marks the takeoff point of Mears's vision for the Sunday school of First Presbyterian.

In the twelve months or so between her hire and the dissemination of the survey, there had been a flurry of activity, but Mears waited to introduce consequential changes until she had ample time to observe the ministry through an entire church year. As the new fiscal cycle began, she moved ahead with a complete review of all aspects of the church's educational program. "The purpose of the coming year," she began, was "to start the practice of systematically studying the needs of our Church school program and of discovering how they may be met." The survey requested responses from the entire staff about pupils (how much outside work to expect, what memory work to assign, contacts with students at home, impact of the program upon their lives), accommodations (room and equipment needs), finances, personnel concerns (teacher problems, issues with assistants, teacher training), and their personal perceptions of the educational program. She asked teachers to evaluate its strengths and weaknesses and pushed them to be specific about possible improvements. The most detailed information requested, however, related to curricular and instructional issues. Mears wanted to know what teachers needed to help them do their jobs better. Listed specifically were texts, leaders' manuals, reference books, maps, and charts. Related questions dealt with better teaching methods for communicating the lessons, standards for teachers to meet, the role of music, and the size of classes.

A series of experiences Mears had during her initial months in Hollywood motivated, at least partially, such a comprehensive assessment of the Sunday school. A concerned mother of one of the junior age boys in the First Presbyterian Sunday school confessed to her that her young son was less than enthusiastic about his class. He had told her that "Sunday school just gets dumber and dumber and they tell the same old stories every year and when I don't have to go to Sunday school any more I'll *never* go back!" After listening to the discouraged parent, Mears must have wondered how many other children held similar opinions. She soon discovered that it was not only children who harbored such sentiments. Jack Wilson, a doctoral student at UCLA with a Phi Beta Kappa key who had been raised in the church, put a penetrating question to her and provided a sad commentary on his own Sunday school experience. Wilson asked, "What's wrong, Miss Mears? I've gone to Sunday school all my life and I have average intelligence, yet if I were to take an examination on the Bible tomorrow, I'd flunk it."[19]

Added to these demoralizing conversations was Mears's own frustration with the curriculum used in the Primary Department. As a university-trained educator with more than a decade of teaching experience as well as service on a curriculum committee for the Minneapolis school district, she found the lessons far removed from the cognitive and affective capabilities of these young students. Perhaps the title of one of the primary lessons, "Amos Denounces Self-Indulgence," best illustrates Mears's distress at the irrelevance of the curriculum to the lives of the children. Most likely stirred by these and similar troubling encounters, Mears approached MacLennan to discern his perspective on the Sunday school curriculum. "Use anything you want as long as it teaches the Bible," he replied. With his support, her quest for a more satisfactory curriculum began.[20]

At the early November 1929 teachers' and officers' meeting Mears jotted a note on her agenda to "find out just what each department is teaching." Later that month at the cabinet meeting, still attempting to discover the content of lessons being taught in her Sunday school, she directed each department superintendent to "give exact quarterlies used in each dept. or state book in the Bible being taught or state any course." By March 1930 change was in the wind, for she made a note to herself to "protest to Board on publications." Whether her protest originated from an evaluation of the types of Sunday school publications for which the board had authorized funds or from the fact that the publications expenditures line in her budget had decreased to less than $415 in the current fiscal year from more than $740 in fiscal 1928–1929, a significant shift in the Sunday school curriculum appeared imminent.

Notwithstanding her personal disaffection for the curriculum, a number of other interrelated factors made a change of direction imperative. Perhaps as early as the summer of 1929, when the curriculum committees formed, Mears and her associates began reviewing materials. By 1930 the group had studied a rather broad spectrum of Sunday school curricula for primary through junior high, including publications from Methodists, the United Church of Christ, and the Religious Education Association.[21] At roughly the same time, the publisher of the church's junior department curriculum informed Mears that the series would be discontinued. Unlike the primary materials, the junior lesson books appear to have been rather more practical. The fact that they would soon be unavailable drove Mears to desperate measures. She inquired as to the possibility of purchasing the type from the publisher so that the church could contract with a local printer to make its own copies of the material. Unfortunately it had already been consigned to the furnace, so she quickly purchased as many junior books as she could. Mears soon realized, however, that her stockpile would last only three years at best.[22]

Meanwhile, as the curriculum committees reviewed Sunday school materials, none could be found that passed muster. Problems clustered around the presentation, not solely the content. For example, while many of the reviewed lessons were graded by age to some extent, some were devoid of pictures or excluded age-appropriate teaching aids. There was also a decided lack of coherent chronology, and committee members believed that could confuse young students.[23] Mears soundly indicted this practice: "Piecemeal. The children cannot see God's Plan. The lessons should be planned with thought about what the child will study throughout his years at Sunday School and graded to meet the need of each age."[24] Finally, in the most widely used curriculum (probably the International Uniform Lessons), if the student missed the one lesson on the Genesis creation account, years would elapse before it reappeared.[25]

Perhaps the tipping point for Mears came when she placed an order for new junior lesson books after she exhausted her cache. Upon their delivery to her office, she opened one of the boxes to review the lesson content. When she discovered that the book informed the student that Saint Paul had survived the ferocious storm and destruction of the ship he was on—described in Acts 27—because "he had eaten carrots and was strong," she packed up the books and promptly returned them to the publisher. For while she remained concerned about how lessons were packaged, biblical accuracy was paramount to her. No curriculum that denied the authority of Scripture or minimized biblical miracles would have a place in her Sunday school, no matter how attractively presented.[26]

Since Mears could find no curriculum that met her expectations, only one choice remained. She decided to write her own. By late 1929 Mears had recruited Esther Ellinghusen as her co-author. Like Mears, Ellinghusen brought impressive professional credentials to the job. She was a trained educator who had worked for the Los Angeles public school district for some years and also served as superintendent of the Junior Department of the Sunday school. Both women committed themselves to produce lessons that were closely age-graded, biblically based, educationally appropriate, and Christ-centered. They began with lessons for the Primary and Junior departments in 1930. To ensure that their efforts compared favorably with the corresponding graded curricula utilized by the public school systems of Southern California, Ellinghusen consulted the head of the remedial reading department of the Los Angeles school district, studied vocabulary lists, and "compared school textbooks for size of type, vocabulary, sentence structure, and illustrative material." She wrote the junior lesson series called *Old Testament Heroes* and began a memory work course for that level in early 1931. Mears wrote the primary curriculum with assistance from Ellinghusen and started a junior high series on the life of Christ before the end of the 1930–1931 fiscal year. Biblical stories differentiated for each age comprised the primary lessons. "The pupils' books were readers with few words, short sentences and large type for first graders." The books became progressively more detailed for the second and third graders, "keeping pace with the child's everchanging [*sic*] interests, abilities and learning capacity." Because the deepening nationwide economic depression forced budget cuts at First Presbyterian, the authors collected out-of-date religious calendars and cut out the pictures to paste on the front of the lesson books, making them more visually appealing with minimal expense. The church also had to slash funding for Sunday school activity papers, so in addition to the lesson books they made up crossword puzzles, mazes, and other age-appropriate amusements to occupy the children.[27]

Writing the weekly lessons and composing the activity papers was one matter, but they also had to be typed, duplicated, and stapled together. Fortunately, Ethel May Baldwin, an early member of the College Department who had been hired to assist Mears in October 1928, proved more than capable serving as "production manager." Because of the size of the typed copy for each lesson, only four could be constructed at a time instead of the more common run of thirteen manufactured by the major publishing houses. Baldwin's mother became so concerned that her daughter's constant stapling of hundreds of lesson booklets would lead to cancer of the hand that she enlisted her husband as stapler in chief. Ethel May realized that mimeography, the duplicating process then in vogue, could actually bleed ink onto clothing if used for the booklet covers. Consequently, she pressed the church's multigraph machine into service; it used nontransferable printer's ink to make copies on its rotating cylindrical drum. This change protected Sunday clothes and provided a more professional look to the lesson booklet covers.[28]

Enough progress had been made on the new curriculum by the end of the fiscal year that Mears gave the congregation of First Presbyterian a look at the future of the Sunday school in her annual report of April 9, 1931.[29] With the coming of fiscal 1931–1932 curricular revisions of earlier lessons began and work on visual aids moved forward. Mears and Ellinghusen would continue to revamp lessons for years, keeping what proved useful and either discarding or radically modifying what had not in order to supply students with the best content and teachers with the most up-to-date methods and pedagogical tools. Mears also thought strategically about the entire Sunday school curriculum. On her teachers' and officers' meeting agenda for September 4, 1930, she listed each Sunday school department through the adult classes and then, to the right of the list she wrote down subjects for each class. Some of the subjects were quite different from those revealed just six months earlier at the April annual meeting.[30]

Her "Outline for Sunday School Course" laid out the subjects and also proposed a series of pertinent questions to be addressed. Cradle roll, beginners, and primary students would study "Stories of God's Word" and participate in a memory work program. Juniors would focus on Old and New Testament history emphasizing heroic figures. They too would have an active program of memory work. Seventh-grade pupils would have lessons on the life of Christ, what it means to be a Christian, and what church membership entails. Other materials would be added later. Eighth graders began a chapter-by-chapter study of the Gospel of John with questions related to the text. Ninth-grade students would learn about God's plan and government as well as the creation. The three-year senior high curriculum began in tenth grade with "the Scope of Scripture given and the Six Periods of the Scriptures mastered." High school juniors would participate in a book-by-book study of the Bible centered on main events. Seniors concentrated on "Christian Evidences, Great Words of Scripture," and doctrinal teaching. College Department members would study the epistles of Paul and Bible prophecy. At all levels Mears directed her teachers always to make their instruction Christocentric and evangelistic. She wanted the "great facts of God's Word" taught and, whenever possible, prophetic teaching highlighted. Mears reminded her teachers that "what we are teaching is not the curriculum, but the Bible."[31] To ensure that her teaching corps was proficient in the latest pedagogical methodologies and comfortable with their responsibilities, the church conducted a highly recommended weekly teacher training class on Wednesday evenings at 7:00 p.m.[32] As the years passed, required monthly teacher and officer training meetings led by Mears for the entire volunteer staff moved to Monday evenings.

The emphasis on evangelism and biblical literacy, a dedicated and well-trained teaching staff committed to establishing personal relationships with each student, and the introduction of the new closely graded curriculum with activities for all ages had almost instantaneous effects. First Presbyterian's Sunday school had experienced increases nearly every year since its inception in 1904, but enrollments skyrocketed as the new curriculum found its way into the classrooms. The total count (including teachers and officers) stood at 1,624 at the end of March 1928. Two years later it had ballooned to 2,440, and that figure nearly doubled to 4,131 by April 1, 1932. Classes convened in nearby homes and sundry less-than-optimal locations in the sanctuary including the kitchen, offices, and mimeographing rooms. Even the bell tower was pressed into use to accommodate children reportedly brought by their parents from as far as fifty miles away. Those parents attended adult classes, which also grew briskly. The church purchased and renovated nearby apartment houses and had a row of bungalows constructed to meet the demand for space. After the Sunday school hour, adults attended the worship service while their children attended their own junior church exercises.[33] The transformation of the American Protestant Sunday school was underway.

MEARS'S PHENOMENAL EARLY ACHIEVEMENTS in Hollywood confirmed the legitimacy of a Christian education program that owed as much to her professional training and experience as it did to her dynamic faith. Her ability to imbue the best of secular educational theory with sacred purpose modeled a progressive synergy practically unknown among theological conservatives of the early twentieth century. It served as the template for those who would become the new evangelicals by mid-century. At the same time, because she never departed from her adherence to the fundamental tenets of the Christian faith, theological modernists who might applaud aspects of her educational theory and practice recoiled at her didactic teaching methodologies and solidly evangelistic agenda.[34]

It would be inaccurate to maintain that Mears developed a definitive theology of Christian education. She probably never went beyond Proverbs 22:6 or 2 Timothy 3:16–17 in defense of her educational program. But she very clearly articulated a philosophy of Christian education that owed a great deal to child development theorists of the era. Her ten "I Wills" included injunctions committing the teacher not only to evangelize students and motivate them to Christian service but also to inspire their self-actualization, facilitate strong relational bonds, value the whole person, and accept each one unconditionally. She also believed that recreational pursuits were as integral to the Christian education program as the cultivation of Christian character, conduct, and service.[35] Such an expansive understanding of Christian formation indicated that the Sunday school hour—though permeated with significant meaning—comprised only one component of a much larger educational task that included the mind, heart, and body of each student.

Though her curricular emphasis on evangelism and biblical literacy remained paramount, she believed that full spiritual maturity could not be achieved without some external expression of an internal faith commitment. So strongly did she believe in the necessity of fostering the practice of serving others that she proposed the creation of a young people's council with "expressional directors" charged with meeting monthly to "promote the expressional part of our young people's work" and to coordinate expressional opportunities.[36] To Mears, the expression of faith included a broad range of possibilities. Underpinning any form of expression, however, was the call to serve those outside as well as inside the church proper, a call she knew firsthand thanks to her family history. It pervaded nearly all aspects of her work. She constantly communicated the necessity of service to her students, her teachers, and her colleagues, for it was in meeting the needs of others that a personal connection to the larger work of the church became most real.

Service itself could take many forms—and did so in her Sunday school.[37] Students traveled around the greater Los Angeles area to ministry sites such as the Sailor's Rest and Union Rescue Missions to conduct Christian meetings of various types. Older students visited local jails and honor detention camps. The Senior Young People had their own gospel team for such work. Some volunteered their time at the Hollywood Japanese Church to teach Sunday school, and one, Katherine Miller, organized a junior church there in early 1930. In late winter of the same year, Mrs. Goodner's Class for women (abbreviated MGC in church records) supplied furnishings for a recreation room at the Hebron Center, a missionary outreach to Jewish Southern Californians. By 1938 Sunday school students from First Presbyterian took over leadership of the local Chinese mission. A number of smaller groups representing the Sunday school, called deputation teams, traveled to churches throughout the region to share their personal experiences of faith. In June 1935 young adults (probably affiliated primarily with the College Department) organized and conducted a ten-day youth conference, which drew five thousand participants from 175 churches resulting in nearly one hundred conversions. Daily Vacation Bible Schools held during the summers for local children up through high school age also served as an outlet for the expression of faith. During the year the weekday programs of Boys' and Girls' Clubs, sponsored by the church under the auspices of the director of Christian education, gave further avenues for service.

Mears's Sunday school emphasized personal financial stewardship as another avenue of faith expression. Students were encouraged to give regularly to their departments, which provided pledge cards for those as young as junior age. She reported in February 1930 that more than 110 junior high students pledged to the Sunday school. A few months later in June the entire Sunday school committed to purchase a new Ford for the Rev. Jesse Smith, First Presbyterian's missionary in Santiago, Chile. By mid-1935 the departments of the Sunday school had sent money to at least seventeen different mission concerns, both foreign and domestic. Some missionaries supported by the Sunday school—such as Bernice Ludlow, Margaret Hartsock, Kenneth and Eleanor Wilson, Julius and Ruth Raplee, and Bill and Betty Blackstone—had been sent out from the church, most of them since Mears's arrival. Until the Blackstone family's evacuation in late 1935 because of the advance of the Japanese in China, her Sunday school met all their financial needs.

Faith expression in these early years of Mears's ministry in Hollywood, whether of time or money, heavily favored evangelistic or church-growth endeavors but not exclusively so. The Sunday school also had an active relief program during the Depression years. Just prior to Christmas 1929, a group from the Sunday school traveled to the Los Angeles County Hospital and staged a holiday party for one of the wards. Thanksgiving and Christmas baskets were distributed to the indigent, and as the economic outlook dimmed further the Sunday school's Meal Barrel program collected food. Staff in the Sunday school office became the conduit for relief requests and the apportionment of relief supplies to the needy. During fiscal 1933–1934 alone the Sunday school helped clothe and feed 112 of its own children. In addition, the departments provided similar aid to fifty congregant families and to other families who were not associated with the church but had children attending the Sunday school. Material assistance extended beyond the immediate vicinity of First Presbyterian, as illustrated by the Macsmen class's commitment beginning in the summer of 1930 to provide $50.00 monthly to the local Jail Commission. Like her mother and maternal grandmother before her, Mears recognized the preeminent need for spiritual sustenance but did not forsake the more immediate needs for material assistance.

From Mears's perspective, active service and faithful giving embodied two of the important ways an inward faith commitment to Christianity should be expressed. But faith could itself be energized by times of study, reflection, and recreation. While regular weekly meetings at the church, social functions sponsored by church groups, and informal gatherings at Mears's home presented occasions for such pursuits, participants could not spend more than two or three hours at a time on them because the rhythms of daily life intruded at every turn. Since her Minnesota days, Mears recognized the value of withdrawing from the regular workaday environment to focus on spiritual things in surroundings more conducive to such an undertaking. It is no surprise then to discover that she launched a retreat program for her students less than a year after her arrival. What began in the summer of 1929 as a single conference for older youths within a decade became the foundation for a comprehensive camping and conference ministry that spanned denominations, generations, and continents.

While thoroughly committed to such a program for her students, Mears struggled to find an appropriate location from which to launch it. It was not for lack of trying. Beginning with her first summer in Southern California and over the course of the next nine years, she took her students to seven different conference grounds and investigated the viability of at least two others. Most of the facilities were functional to one extent or another, but none of them offered the combination of alpine surroundings, a satisfactory physical plant and facilities, ready access from Hollywood, and amenities suitable for all age groups she so ardently desired. Still driven to find such a retreat center but perturbed because of her protracted search for one, Mears received an unexpected telephone call from the father of some of her Sunday school students in the summer of 1937. William Irwin told her about a resort along Mill Creek in the San Bernardino Mountains that might soon be available.[38]

The original owners had been Thomas and Catherine Akers, who purchased a quarter section of land in Mill Creek Canyon from the Southern Pacific Railway for $800 in 1897. In July they filed for and received homestead rights to the surrounding acreage, which included an orchard, garden, and natural springs. The Akers added tent cabins with stoves and other outbuildings to entice guests and made a series of infrastructure improvements including an irrigation system and several bridges. They also cut trails through the forest. The campground soon became a destination resort with as many as five hundred gathered there on summer weekends. After a series of ownership changes and further upgrades, the Forest Home Outing Company became "the summer headquarters of the 'sporting set,'" hosting more than three thousand visitors in 1914. A swimming pool, dance pavilion, and miniature golf course designed by Hollywood architect J. Bryant Severance were soon added.[39]

From the 1910s well into the 1920s the outing company and its neighboring vacation getaways along the canyon played host to middle-class professionals and wealthy celebrities alike, but in the years just prior to the stock market crash of October 1929, the appeal of Forest Home began to fade. Title passed to new owners and finally to Pasadena manufacturer Edward Durant. With his son, Harlan, Durant struggled to revitalize it, but by then the stock market crash had given way to the Great Depression and the resort business dried up and dissipated like soil on the Great Plains. By 1936 the elder Durant's enthusiasm for the property flagged and his health deteriorated. Knowing that in the event of his death, his heirs would be saddled with an exorbitant inheritance tax burden, he contemplated selling the outing company.

It was the following summer when Irwin informed Mears about the camp. He reported that the Forest Home Outing Company comprised "320 acres of land, fifty-two cabins, swimming pool, stables, an eighteen hole miniature golf course, cement tennis court, outdoor barbeque pit, badminton court, soda fountain, coffee shop, general store, post office, and filling station, all nestled down between two sheer mountains . . . away from LA."[40] A short time later while at a high school conference at nearby Camp Radford, Mears suggested that she and some of her associates visit the site during an afternoon break. Chauffeured by Cyrus Nelson, dean of the camp, Mears set out to find Durant's property. When they arrived she took one look at the impressive grounds and told Nelson to drive on: "I know we can't afford all of this. . . . This is just ridiculous! The buildings alone are far too elaborate for our pocketbooks, and certainly we can't begin to pay for the land."[41]

At the conclusion of the Radford conference, Mears returned to her responsibilities at First Presbyterian. When Irwin called to ask what she thought of Forest Home she reiterated her dismay at the prohibitive expense to purchase and maintain such a facility: "What could we ever do to run such a big place even if we could afford to buy it, and we can't afford it!" Irwin, however, had some new details regarding the property. The elder Durant now faced an imminent operation and in his weakened state could not be assured that he would survive the surgery. The bank had assessed the property at close to

$350,000, which meant that the inheritance tax could financially ruin his sons. Given these circumstances, Irwin believed that a good-faith offer of $50,000 might be acceptable, so Mears took an option on the property for $50,000. She later recalled, "Everyone at the church thought I was crazy! It was such a terrible time!"[42] She also said, "But this is the moment for action and not speculation. The option will close before I know it. I have to get people up to see Forest Home."[43]

To do so Mears called a "church day" at the resort. She hoped that as members of First Presbyterian visited it they would recognize the value of owning the property. Capital would be raised from those who made down payments on cabins purchased for their personal use. Those dollars would then be bundled to make a down payment on the entire site. Her enthusiasm for the venture proved contagious, and a number of congregants and friends took advantage of the prospect and selected cabins. At the end of the day, however, Mears began to doubt the wisdom of the arrangement she had presented to the attendees, for if she sold the cabins, her students would have no place to stay and she would have no real center in which to hold conferences.[44] She let the option lapse and considered the matter closed.

Summer turned to autumn and autumn to winter—a winter that saw snow accumulate up to thirty feet in the upper reaches of Mill Creek Canyon according to one resident. Then in late February and early March 1938, three days of warm rain followed directly on the heels of three days of snowfall, saturating the snowpack up and down the canyon. The unusually heavy snow and warming temperatures proved a catastrophic combination. By some accounts a twenty-foot wall of water roared down the canyon, sweeping with it boulders the size of automobiles. In a matter of minutes Mill Creek boiled over its banks and flooded the entire valley floor, uprooting massive trees and rushing them downriver before they had the chance to fall. Those that did topple over blocked the flow, trapped debris, and forced the deadly current in other directions until the dam broke causing even more detritus to tumble through the canyon, destroying whatever lay in its path. For three days the water rose precipitously; for a week after Mill Creek finally crested, residents found themselves isolated and pinned to the sides of the canyon. As the waters receded, the full impact of the flood's fury became apparent. The torrent had swept away a total of fifty-four dwellings along with personal property and belongings. Bridges, walking paths, and roads disappeared, as did much of the flora. "All that was left of the once green forest at Forest Home was a barren landscape of boulders and logs and a large steep bank."[45] The physical topography of the Forest Home Outing Company property had been radically altered by the disaster, but only five of its fifty-two cabins had been washed away and no other building was damaged.

The built environment of the resort had been largely spared the desolation elsewhere visited on the canyon, but the severity of the storm deeply affected Durant. He recognized that the effects of the flood had diminished the value of the campground and decided to lower his asking price to $30,000. Irwin quickly contacted Mears, who was preparing to embark on a lengthy excursion with some of her closest associates and former College Department members. They called off the trip and a number of them, including David Cowie and Robert Munger, traveled with Mears to Forest Home the next day. They thoroughly examined the grounds and facilities. Mears recalled, "I remember how flabbergasted we were! Everything was there. . . . It was just perfect!"[46] Cowie and Munger pledged their financial support and urged her to buy the property, but she hesitated, unsure of the direction she should take. She spent the next few days in contemplative prayer and Bible study. When she read in Scripture of God's promise to deliver the land to Joshua (Josh. 1:2b–3) she took it as divine confirmation. It became even more evident that she made the right decision when Durant spurned a much more lucrative offer and agreed to sell the entire property to her.

All Mears had to do was scrape together $7,000 for the down payment, but the nearly decade-old Depression made that somewhat challenging. Investment capital had evaporated long ago, and the church carried a $350,000 mortgage on its physical plant that needed regular servicing. The money therefore had to come entirely from Mears and her friends. She suggested that since their trip had been cancelled, they donate the money they would have spent to the down payment fund. Their gifts motivated others to give to the project, enabling First Presbyterian to purchase the Forest Home Outing Company. On July 3, 1938, Mears, Irwin, MacLennan, John G. Hormel of the meatpacking family, and David Cowie formed Forest Home Inc., a nonprofit, nondenominational corporation to "conduct conferences for all ages where Christ will be upheld and magnified. We desire that each person attending will be introduced to Christ as Savior and will commit his life to Him as Lord. We are a nonprofit corporation held in trust, operated by a Board of Directors, set up to handle the Lord's money as He gives it to us."[47] After searching for nearly ten years, Mears had her retreat and conference center.

As the first camps at Forest Home drew to a close late that summer, it was apparent that Henrietta Mears had found her true calling. The vague uncertainty with which she began her work in the Southland melted away, for the ministry model she crafted in Minneapolis transferred remarkably well to Hollywood. As she completed her tenth year of service, Mears could look back on significant progress toward her ambitious goals for First Presbyterian's Christian education program. She won over the Sunday school teacher and officer corps by demonstrating her care for them as individuals and her willingness to lead by example—especially with regard to the necessity of hard work and long hours. She wove regular training workshops directly into the fabric of every department under her jurisdiction. Her holistic educational program balancing biblical knowledge with occasions for social growth and active service sparked an astonishing spike in Sunday school attendance. Her desire to conduct an internal curriculum review would soon have ramifications far beyond her initial objective of providing First Presbyterian students with age-appropriate and biblically based Sunday school lessons. In her quest to establish a camping and conference program for all ages as an extension of the educational ministry of the church she acquired a major resort in the San Bernardino Mountains more than suitable for such purposes and open to participants well beyond her own congregation. She had already sent a substantial number of her students off to seminary or to the mission fields of the world, initiated service opportunities for young people that took them to places of need throughout Southern California, and inspired laypersons to live lives dedicated to Christian ministry no matter what their vocation. With so much accomplished during her first decade in Hollywood, close observers of Mears's work might well have wondered what the next ten years might hold.

Chapter Five

A Faith of Her Own

Undergirding every one of Henrietta Mears's formidable achievements lay a rock solid certainty in the theological fundamentals of the Christian faith. Yet a shift in her application of those fundamentals, introduced with her Fidelis class in Minneapolis, became even more apparent by the late 1930s. Mears and her students had faced the course and consequences of the Great War, the excesses of the Jazz Age, worldwide economic devastation, and the rise of totalitarian regimes. But while she navigated those troubled waters with much of the rest of world, she also negotiated a distinctly personal faith journey. Suspended between the stridently confrontational fundamentalism of her home church pastor and a personal family history of graceful compassion toward the wider human community, Mears appropriated a model of Christian faithfulness that blended aspects of both with the overarching reality of human sinfulness and the need for personal absolution through Christ.

Her move to Southern California placed Mears at the center of the region's own culture wars, which pitted older generations of transplanted white middle-class Protestant midwesterners against a rising tide of working class, ethnically and religiously diverse immigrants from the urban North and rural South. Political, economic, social, and religious conflict broke out on all sides, stimulating her thoughtful reflection on how best to communicate the gospel in such a fractious time. Mears worked tirelessly from the media-blitzed entrepôt of Hollywood to promote appropriate linkages between faith and modernity resulting in what seemed to her a winsome and relevant orthodoxy. In forging her own way through these tensions, she served as an archetype for theologically conservative Protestants who aspired to model a vigorous and culturally engaged Christianity in the 1940s. The ways she managed the transition from the 1910s into the 1930s would play a significant role in reorienting fundamentalism and transforming the ways evangelical Protestants perceived human culture throughout the rest of the twentieth century and well into the twenty-first.

The extent of the Rev. William Bell Riley's influence on Henrietta Mears and her family cannot be overestimated. They continued to support Riley and First Baptist after many of its other well-heeled families bolted to form Trinity Baptist Church in opposition to the pastor's desire to increase the appeal of the church to working class families.[1] Yet while sharing his fundamentalist theology, Mears refused to adopt Riley's strident judgments about modern American life. Differences between Riley and his protégé emerged quite early and centered on her reluctance to politicize the faith, the breadth of her ecumenism, and her preference for more nuanced perspectives vis-à-vis American culture.[2]

Early in her career Mears reached across ecclesiastical differences to work collaboratively with Roman Catholic and other Protestant denominational groups. Riley responded in kind only when such alliances served his own purposes, as demonstrated by his unqualified support of Father Charles Coughlin, one of President Franklin Roosevelt's most vocal critics, only after the Detroit priest's descent into rabid anti-Semitism. Riley also publicly and regularly criticized the Roosevelt administration and the Democratic Party. Mears, on the other hand, kept her political leanings to herself.[3]

As early as 1921 Jews surfaced as a threat in Riley's public pronouncements and writings. He stated flatly that his "most annoying hecklers were young atheist Jews," though one wonders how he could have known the ethnic or religious composition of his audiences.[4] His sermons, conference speeches, and writings assumed a more pointedly anti-Jewish stance as the Great Crash stretched into the Great Depression, convinced as he was that an international Jewish-communist conspiracy had co-opted the New Deal. His open admiration for Hitler's anti-Semitic policies continued until the coming of the war.[5] Riley's alienation from the mainstream of both American culture and American Protestantism by the late 1920s probably sparked his anti-Semitism, although his premillennial dispensationalist way of understanding the Bible could also have been a contributing factor. This interpretive framework bent toward an embedded ambivalence about the Jews, since it considered them God's chosen but disobedient people. That inconsistency could lead to full-blown conspiratorial anti-Semitism under the right conditions. Riley and a few other well-placed contemporaries made that leap.[6]

Mears, however, was not one of them. While a lingering equivocation toward Jewish people is somewhat noticeable in her writings, so also are many elements of what David A. Rausch calls philo-Semitism and pro-Zionism.[7] She most clearly revealed her views in the 1937 booklet *Highlights of Scripture—Part 2: God's Great Covenants*. As a good dispensationalist, Mears made it clear that God's care for the Jews depended "not on Israel's faith, but on God's covenant," yet "God will punish them for their disobedience." Nonetheless, "His plan is to preserve them."[8] Temporary loss of their political kingdom was one consequence of their disobedience, and although "the jealousy of other nations has made it possible for the Turk to hold it [the land God promised to the Jews] as long as he has," God will make good on the promise to return them to it (24–25, author's brackets). Mears believed the Jews will turn back to God and will "be gathered from the four corners of the earth," cementing the spiritual connection between Jews and Christians. From her observation of world events she believed that "the great gathering already has been commenced" (24–25).

Given these perceptions, Mears's enthusiasm for Zionism should come as no surprise. She also tipped her hat to the effect of the Balfour Declaration (1917) and to a lesser extent the Sykes-Picot Agreement (1916) on the restoration of the Jews to their ancient homeland. Her Zionist proclivities were so unqualified in the 1930s that she made no mention of the conflicts, evident since the 1920s, between native-born Palestinians and the swelling number of returning Jews. She did, however, concede that the increased immigration of Jews to Palestine (which she applauded) surged despite the efforts of the League of Nations to manage it (40).

While her positive opinion toward the Jews was the main focus of the booklet, Mears also exhibited a tendency toward stereotypical thinking about them, illustrating the premillennial prevarication toward Jews noted by William Trollinger and others. For example, she partially attributed their ability to survive so many centuries without a land of their own to a Jewish physiognomy (23). A more egregious instance involved her discussion of the wealth and influence of Jews (23). Aside from these rare but telling exceptions, Mears exhibited a wholehearted support for the Jews. Not only did she maintain a solid commitment to the Jewish people, she also looked forward to their return to full nationhood, as any good premillennial dispensationalist would. Whether her acquiescence to demeaning stereotypes was due to her theological predilections or to American chauvinism, it is clear that Riley's vitriolic anti-Semitism, which had reached fever pitch by the time Mears published her booklet, had no place in her theological or social consciousness. But as was the case with regard to other racial issues of the era, her restrained, sometimes indeterminable response left the exact nature of Mears's position open to question.

Such, however, was not the case with her appraisal of higher education. She rejected out of hand her mentor's antagonistic outlook as much by her actions as her words. Although Mears had dedicated herself to mission service as a teenager, she seems never to have considered attending Riley's Northwestern Bible and Missionary Training School, opting instead for an education that Riley viewed as riddled with anti-Christian biases. If merely attending a public university was not perilous enough, Mears studied some of its most dangerous disciplines. She graduated with her orthodox beliefs tested but still intact. As might be deduced from her choice to major in chemistry at the University of Minnesota, Mears had little dread of being tainted by the intellectual atmosphere of the modern university. Nor did she fear for her students attending state institutions of higher learning or private ones whose Christian moorings had disappeared or were held suspect by other conservatives. She regularly encouraged them to get the best education they possibly could to prepare for a life of greatest service to God. Recognizing that Moses, David, and even Christ spent years in preparation for their work, she admonished her students to do the same.[9]

While some of her Fidelis young women attended Riley's Northwestern Bible and Missionary Training School, others went to New York to study at Columbia University and art school.[10] She relished the fact that her college young people in Hollywood matriculated at schools like the University of Southern California, Stanford, Oberlin, UCLA, the Chouinard School of Art, Penn State, Cal Tech, Harvard, and the Otis Art Institute. Others studied overseas at Oxford and Edinburgh. Many also attended Christian institutions such as Occidental College, Wheaton College, Moody Bible Institute, and the Bible Institute of Los Angeles. Perhaps most surprising in light of the 1929 founding of Westminster Seminary in Philadelphia as the fundamentalist rival to Princeton Seminary was Mears's continued advocacy of the latter as the preferred seminary for those seeking a vocation in the church. And though more of her graduate students during this era enrolled at Princeton, others went to Westminster, Dallas Theological Seminary, the Biblical Seminary, and San Francisco Theological Seminary.[11]

Since her worldview asserted that God authored all truth no matter who discovered it, Mears held to the inherent virtue of knowledge irrespective of its source. She peppered her formal addresses and more intimate talks with citations from eminent Christian leaders while focusing on the centrality of Scripture or timeless biblical principles. But she also referred to the latest psychological research on human development theory. In her 1931–1932 annual report, for example, directly after quoting evangelist Henry Drummond, Mears cited research regarding the perceptual capabilities of six-year-olds and the mental acuity of ten-year-olds. After reaffirming that in the educational work of First Presbyterian, "The Bible is our only text book, the Cross is our only power, Christ Supreme is our only motto," Mears elaborated on the "principal mental characteristics of the adolescent period." A few years later, she began her wildly successful interdenominational Sunday school teacher training classes, which utilized "new methods of modern psychology" applicable "to the fundamental teachings of God's Word" so that participants might learn "a new and scientific way of mastering the Greatest Book in the world."[12] While she always held the Bible in highest regard, unlike other theological conservatives of her day Mears had no misgivings whatsoever regarding the value of advanced education. One of her greatest concerns was not that students would lose their faith as they pursued higher education; it was that they would not pursue *enough* education to prepare them adequately for their vocations as believers in a secularizing world.

But if that pursuit led to an education devoid of Christian assumptions, how would young people develop a rationally informed and thoughtful faith? To Mears, the answer was obvious—through a more intellectually satisfying and pedagogically superior Christian education program. She argued categorically that "we're the ones who are sending our children away from the Sunday schools and the church. The public school, I do not believe, is nearly as responsible as we are, as much as we've been told so. . . . We're not careful in our presentation. We're not careful in our approach. We're not careful in our methods."[13] She assumed that Christian youths would be challenged by secular learning as a matter of course. But instead of urging students to retreat from the halls of intellectual power, she charged the educational program of the church—"Christ's college," she called it—with the responsibility of equipping its students with a biblically and intellectually robust faith with which to meet those challenges. If the church took its educational mission seriously, Mears held, students would "have an answer for every question that is asked them" and be able to stand firm against any cultural opposition with a mature and confident faith.[14]

Another trait Mears clearly did not share with Riley and a host of other fundamentalists was the propensity to vent their pervasive detestation for modern culture in vindictive and very public ways. Historian George Marsden may have had his tongue firmly planted in his cheek when he opined that "a fundamentalist is an evangelical who is angry about something," but facetious or not, there is at least a significant kernel of truth in the observation.[15] One just does not think of the fundamentalist firebrands of the era with smiles on their faces or a lighthearted spring in their step.

In rather stark contrast, Mears exuded a public optimism and personal playfulness that belied the seriousness with which she approached life in general and her duties in particular. Her quick-witted sense of humor could be wry, ironic, and sometimes self-deprecating but was always hilarious to those around her. She never shied away from laughing with others or at herself because she believed in the spiritual benefit of wholesome amusements. The jokes and skits comprising those long ago amusements would seem silly or maudlin to a contemporary audience, but even those sentiments highlight the personal distance between her and so many of her dour brethren of the fundamentalist fold. Aside from personality differences between herself and fellow theological conservatives, Mears's upbeat persona may have proceeded in part from her family heritage as well as from the fact that her critique of American culture remained more selective and subtle than Riley's. She therefore focused on issues she believed were absolutely crucial to gospel concerns. It would be wrong to suggest that Mears never muttered an angry word, carried on a heated exchange, or harbored a malicious thought. But it is also apparent that such episodes, if and when they existed, were conducted in an appropriately private venue and were exceeded in number and degree by her proclivity to address even the most important topics with more than a little whimsy.

Mears gave her students permission to laugh too—and laughter, particularly among theological conservatives in the 1920s and 1930s, was in admittedly short supply. The young women in Mears's Fidelis class felt free enough to satirize even theological issues in the pages of their class publication *The Fid'ler*, poking good-natured fun at modernists *and* fundamentalists.[16] A story entitled "A Young Kentucky Uprising" played humorously on the spreading fear of communism. The story's protagonist, who ironically (or purposely?) was a schoolteacher, mistakes a lovestruck swain and his friends for a backwoods Bolshevik cell. While true motivations eventually get sorted out, the lighthearted treatment of such a serious phenomenon could have been perceived as both unpatriotic and unchristian since by this time the country had already passed through its first red scare and communism was seen by many, including Riley, as a dire threat to the American way of life.[17]

Mears also allowed herself to be included in the merriment and more often than not entered into it with gusto. On numerous occasions she poked fun at her singleness, noting that "she never married because she did not live in the same dispensation as the Apostle Paul and she had never found anyone to match him in this age." When she taught the story of Christ meeting the Samaritan woman at the well who had multiple husbands, she invariably interjected that "she must have been a real glamour girl. She could get five husbands, and I couldn't get one!"[18] Chief among Mears's antics was her rendition of Old Mother Hubbard. She would dress up in an outlandish costume, pick up a telephone book (the "Book of Numbers"), open it randomly, pull her thick glasses forward to the tip of her nose, bend low over the book with a finger on the page, and proceed to explicate the nursery rhyme by interpreting the "deeper meanings" of the "text":

> "Old Mother Hubbard went to the cupboard"—I want to read this passage clear through, so you can get the full meaning, and then I will come back and we shall look at it statement by statement. . . . "Old Mother Hubbard went to the cupboard." Can't you see the pathos of this o-l-d, o-l-d woman going to the cupboard? "To get her poor dog." No! She didn't go to get her poor dog, but that's the way some of you read Scripture. You stop right in the middle of a thought. What did she go to get? What is the object of her "wenting?" You've all seen an old woman "wenting" haven't you? She's all bent over low, with furrowed brow.

By all accounts, every time she performed the skit her audience laughed so hard tears streamed down their faces. Another variation on her "Book of Numbers" send-up found Mears opening the telephone book and reading with revivalist fervor and dramatic, exaggerated inflections the names on the page to the same effect.[19]

Mears's Fideltians also exhibited a flair for the fashionable, unlike so many of their fundamentalist counterparts. Bobbed hair as a sign of the "modern" young woman was everywhere to be seen in the class. One issue of *The Fid'ler* took note that Margaret Bergman's melancholy after receiving her first bob proceeded not from religious considerations but rather from her fear that it was not attractive. While Margaret faced the future with anxiety, Ruth Nelson relished her new look. The daring hairstyle was so evident among Fidelis members that one of the writers quipped that someday, when *The Fid'ler* would publish a list of all those with long hair, it would take up a scant quarter of a column. The same issue even carried an advertisement from a local beauty shop specializing in the cut. Mears herself sported a modified bob throughout the 1920s.[20]

That Mears could embrace aspects of the surrounding culture did not mean she jettisoned her theological fundamentalism—only that she willingly engaged and challenged her students to engage the secularizing environment in which they lived as long as it did not contradict their core beliefs and could further the Christian mission of evangelization and dedicated service to others. Her willingness to bring the fundamental tenets of Christianity into conversation with modern American culture represented a more gracious theological conservatism that would contribute significantly to the emergence of interdenominational evangelicalism in the early 1940s.

A CLOSER LOOK AT HER EARLY YEARS OF MINISTRY in the College Department at the First Presbyterian Church of Hollywood provides the clearest window through which to observe Mears's graceful blend of conservative Protestantism and American culture. While she administered all aspects of the educational program at First Presbyterian, she took special interest in the eighteen-to-twenty-five-year-old young people—just as she had at First Baptist—but this time in a coeducational context. A relentless advocate for the college- and career-age contingent at First Presbyterian for nearly thirty-five years and the group's primary Bible teacher for thirty, Mears brought the personal philosophy and methodological strategies that had served her so well in Minneapolis to even greater effect in the Southland. She not only replicated the success she had with her Fideltians, she also exceeded her expectations thanks to the lasting results of her labor evident in succeeding generations of Christian young people.

The preeminent emphasis Mears placed on personal relationships and evangelism led to alterations in attendance patterns at First Presbyterian within the first year of her service. She pushed her college-age students to invite others to Sunday school class, Christian Endeavor programs, social gatherings, and midweek prayer meetings. Her care for them and her enthusiasm for growth proved contagious. Soon after she began teaching the "young people's class," as it was known in 1928, Mears set before members the objective of achieving a total enrollment in the college Sunday school class of 222. Reaching that number by December, she raised the bar again to 333 by December of 1929, and again to 444 by October 1930. Her collegians met every goal. Local media reported the attainment of the latter figure on Sunday, October 5, 1930, and observed that 500 was the goal for the following week.[21]

By the early 1930s Mears's emphasis on evangelism in the Sunday school transformed the church. From the first year of record-keeping (1904), both communicant membership and Sunday school enrollment at First Presbyterian had trended upward regularly and quite dramatically. That dynamic continued after her arrival. What changed, however, was the *type* of new member admitted to the church. Those admitted by transfer from another church had always outpaced those admitted by confession of their faith in Christ—until 1931. For every year thereafter through 1938, admission of new members professing their faith exceeded those joining by church transfer. Through Mears's first decade at Hollywood, large numbers of her students, from juniors through college and career age who made a confession of faith, joined the church and helped increase the membership from 2,104 in 1928 to 2,627 by 1938. Total Sunday school registrations grew even more dramatically, from 1,624 to 3,477, countering the observed decline in church activity nationally during the 1930s. *(See table 1 on page 279.)*

If evangelism remained among Mears's highest priorities for her Sunday school, developing the intellectual life of her students was not far behind.[22] While Mears remained a staunch anti-evolutionist, she simultaneously championed the absolute congruence of proper biblical interpretation and the findings of experimental science—a standpoint that found its roots in the natural theology of the Scottish Common Sense Realists of the eighteenth century. Trust in the verities of both science and Scripture led to quite a difference of opinion among theologians and scientists for three generations following the Civil War,[23] but Mears maintained a dual allegiance throughout her life and offered her students ample opportunities to experience the harmony of faith and learning. She often invited Christian apologist Harry Rimmer to speak to her collegians on topics revealing their agreement. Bud Moon, who later as Dr. Irwin A. Moon directed the Moody Institute of Science, entertained them at camps with science experiments that illustrated biblical themes.[24]

Mears's own educational background propelled much of her teaching on science and faith. In a lesson entitled "The Bible Confirmed by Science" she explained her outlook on the difference between scientific inquiry and evolutionary theory. She contended that

> The universe teems with life, but we know that there is never any life without antecedent life of that particular kind. Many and exhaustive experiments have proved that fact. If life only comes from life from whence did the first life come? To this question science can only reply, "We do not know." In science we do not deal with origins. Science gathers the known and proved facts on any subject and makes a record of it. Science is knowledge gained and verified. . . . When things originated who was there to observe? What experiments verify these observations? The question of origin is therefore either in the field of philosophy or revelation. Evolution is the reply of philosophy to man's questions, "How and where did man originate?"[25]

This clear distinction between the proper domain of science (direct, observable evidence) and philosophy (theoretical reasoning based on assumptions that cannot be authenticated by direct observation) drove both Mears's uncompromising stand against evolutionary theory as it was understood in her day and her lifelong love affair with empirical science. She taught her students not to fear science but to recognize when it strayed from its experimental tether. Her reticence to endorse the findings of the historical sciences such as geological and evolutionary theory proceeded from her belief that true scientific conclusions had to be based solidly on empirical evidence—an assessment that was also reflected in the church's root conflict with Galileo over the heliocentric theory of the solar system. Like Princeton luminary Charles Hodge, Mears always held the Bible in highest regard, but unlike other theological conservatives of her era, she had no reservations whatsoever regarding the value of scientific inquiry.[26]

She frankly acknowledged that college students would most likely experience a period of cognitive dissonance between what they learned in church and what they learned in the public university, much as she had. She knew that the authority of Christian education teachers could very well be called into question by a university professor whom students looked up to "as a real intellectual with a winning personality" but who also might denigrate the Bible in some way, steering students toward the assumption that "only morons believe the facts of the Book." At that point it was perfectly understandable, she argued, that students seeking true knowledge would find themselves "in a position of conflicting loyalties to church, pastor and . . . parents and the teachings of this new voice." Considering the prominent anti-intellectual bent of many theologically conservative Christians, one might expect Mears at this point to denounce the secular academy. But in a bold strategy born of her supreme confidence in the power of Scripture to anchor sincere believers and in the ability of consecrated Sunday school teachers to make it vital and enthralling, Mears merely charged those teaching college-age young people in the church to study constantly the intellectual and cultural contexts of their lives in order to speak Christian truth to secular suppositions in ways that students would respect and honor.[27] One of Rimmer's well-attended visits during the early fall of 1929 illustrates the angle on science and faith cultivated in her College Department.[28] According to a writer for the department's monthly newsletter, Rimmer's presentations made clear that either ignorance or wrong thinking was responsible for the belief that discrepancies between Scripture and science existed.[29]

In addition to her views on science and Scripture, Mears's millenarian tastes also surfaced regularly in the ongoing educational program of First Presbyterian. Neither she nor other leaders in the church shied away from a strong prophetic voice, particularly in the early years of her ministry. The Pike Bible class for adults continued for years after Mears arrived and focused exclusively on the examination and interpretation of prophetically understood scriptural texts. MacLennan himself taught prophecy in his Macsmen Sunday school class for adult males. Ella Pohle, former secretary to C. I. Scofield, taught the Scofield Bible Class on Thursday evenings in the 1930s. One of the first books Mears taught to her Hollywood collegians was the book of Daniel—a central text to premillennial dispensationalists. She also enjoyed expositing the apocalyptic book of Revelation. The May 1933 issue of the College Department's publication (*The Quest*) spent an entire page listing the wars, dictatorships, and disasters worldwide with separate paragraphs dedicated to events in the Soviet Union and Palestine all leading up to "Miss Mears' Message," which served as an introduction to prophetic themes in the book of Revelation. Her extended series, "The Seven Dispensations," which included a full-color schematic, appears to have stretched across a considerable portion of the year. Thanks to donations from her and others, the College Department library contained a number of books on prophecy and related topics. Her Sunday school curriculum, in its early iterations, included a healthy dose of prophetic study. Mears's dispensational inclinations lingered throughout her long career; they did become more subdued over time but remained apparent to her close associates.[30]

Along with her lifelong support of dispensational theology, Mears also continued to uphold historic Christian teachings, which she clearly communicated through her teaching, administrative leadership, and invited speakers. The session-approved "Department of Education Declaration of Faith" had to be signed by all teachers and officers, and she made sure that happened. Special speakers like Rimmer reinforced doctrinal orthodoxy, sometimes in no uncertain terms.[31] The statement of faith upon which Mears would soon found her publishing company contained an even more explicit and detailed enumeration of key doctrines, including sections on universal human sinfulness, the Trinitarian nature of God, the work of the Holy Spirit, the character of the church, the coming kingdom age, and the future judgment of humanity. The camping program at Forest Home produced a similarly orthodox proclamation of faith to be honored by all who worked at the facility, although it was not quite so detailed.[32]

All of these formal pronouncements bolstered a theological conservatism that Mears humanized through her recognition that doctrinal priorities had to be accompanied by a concurrent commitment to meet the emotional, physical, and social needs of students. She believed that the "church must reach the *entire* life of a college person or you cannot hold them at all. . . . If you do not incorporate the whole life of that college person in the church you don't have them at all."[33] Her faith in God and love for her students stimulated a natural complementarity between the divine call and the human condition—in all its manifestations. Mears's genius proceeded from her uncanny ability to blend a serious commitment to theological orthodoxy and a Christian way of living in the world with a wink or a tear.

Her passion for a holistic ministry began with proper organization and leadership. Much as had happened in the Fidelis class, at the top of the list for the College Department was work on the constitution, which the church session approved in late September 1928.[34] Mears perceived that the quality of the leadership determined the vitality of the department, so she did not leave the selection of officers to chance. Addressing the Presbyterian Fellowship from Fuller Seminary more than a quarter century after arriving in Hollywood, Mears candidly lined out the philosophy of leadership that had characterized her success:

> You have to build a college department by training the leaders all the time. And there's nothing democratic about leadership in a college department. And I'm perfectly willing to tell you that. I've been called everything—all kinds of names—that I just don't take a crowd and work in—no, I don't, because I learned all my psychology-leadership from the Scriptures, so I never did it. (5)

"Elections" occurred much as they had for her Fideltians. Because the elections resulted in a slate of officers handpicked by Mears and the current leadership, she sought to quell potential dissent with an explanation of the process in the department publication. Once they were installed, Mears regularly called these leaders—now the members of the College Department executive—together for planning and prayer. She constantly reminded them of the significant role they played in training the leaders that would follow them.[35] Weekly early Saturday morning prayer meetings at her home saw all members plus their teacher on their knees seeking guidance and blessing for the department.

Mears shared with the seminarians her hope for the College Department and her rather blunt evaluation of the leadership potential of its members when she first arrived:

> I wanted to start a college department at the First Presbyterian Church of Hollywood, and I wanted it to have a little atmosphere—a little prestige. I knew that the shadow of a leader made all the difference in the world how far that department was going to go. I looked around at the crowd and nobody looked as if he could be the president of the department. I didn't exactly like their looks. Now, no reflection—they were just young, and innocent. So I thought, well, now listen, what will we do? (4)

What she did was to ask her students who served as the student body president at the University of Southern California, located just a few miles from the church. Upon discovering that the president, Rand Richey, was not a Christian, Mears sought an introduction. In short order she converted Richey to Christ and he then became the first president of the College Department. She told her Fuller audience that Richey's leadership established a prestige that attracted others to the class. This strategy worked not only to draw new members but also to attract more potential leaders. When Ford Palmer, captain of the USC football team, began attending shortly after Richey, "he used to bring all the football fellows, the whole line would come and sit right across the class—every Sunday" (5). Summing up her philosophy of leadership, Mears contended that "if you don't start with that crowd, who do you get? A list of names doesn't mean a thing to me . . . you have to find the leaders. You have to build a college department by training the leaders all the time" (4–5). She firmly believed in recruiting and training leaders with star power, for that was the way to attract others to the church and its programs. Given the relational dynamics of the era, she focused especially on recruiting and training males—for as she often said, if the men come, the women will follow. Though many women held positions of leadership in the College Department over the years, only one woman ever served as president of a department organization.

Even attractive leaders could not sustain a thriving College Department ministry if its programs did not meet the needs of college students. So Mears followed the formula for success that had served her so well at First Baptist. She worked hard from the beginning to ensure that all the programs of the department met at least one of what she called the "great urges in a college student's heart and mind" for security, recognition, adventure and experience, social interaction, and service and cooperation (11, quotation from 13).

The centerpiece of the College Department ministry was the morning Sunday school hour, with other Sunday meetings filling out the rest of the day. The morning session would usually commence at 9:30 a.m. with singing, announcements, and special presentations orchestrated by the departmental officers; the session was always preceded by a time of prayer with Mears and her collegians on their knees. Unless there was a special missionary or guest speaker Mears would step forward to teach the lesson, following a straight lecture format and most often doing systematic exegesis through a book of the Bible or offering a topical study based on Scripture over a number of weeks. Members of the department would then make their way into the sanctuary for morning worship. Late Sunday afternoon the collegians convened for a purely social hour. Female members prepared refreshments while male members took care of the dirty dishes. The Christian Endeavor meeting followed with a student leader (male or female) or guest speaker (often a missionary) providing a message. The meeting then moved to a time of personal reflection during which any member who felt inclined could share with the group. The session concluded with about twenty minutes of group prayer.[36] Following the evening worship service, collegians would gather again for an informal time of singing and games at a leader's (often Mears's) home or go to a favorite restaurant for an evening snack.

If one attended only the regular Sunday activities for collegians, most of Mears's five "urges" as well as her overall educational goals would have been met on that one day. But Sunday was only the beginning. Wednesday evening dinners and prayer meetings probably looked much the same at First Presbyterian as they did at other churches and provided another chance for faith expression like the Sunday afternoon and evening meetings. But the resumption of regular College Department dinners and prayer meetings after students had returned from summer break in September of 1929 carried a special appeal to males with the reminder that "it's great to get down on bended knees with several real *men*." To promote a "muscular Christianity" that would appeal to young males, *The Quest* turned up the virility factor associated with prayer editorializing that "This praying is no weakling's play, but a real HE MAN'S privilege. Not one of you can get along without it."[37] In later years, as attendance increased, Mears or one of her associates gave short messages and then the large group would be broken into a number of smaller ones, with a leader for each to facilitate greater individual participation.

By the end of 1929 specialized groups had been formed for college-age young people in order to incorporate more smoothly new members and visitors to the College Department. Perhaps most valuable to this effort was the work of a relatively small group who set aside Tuesday evenings to call personally on recent visitors and those members of the class who had been absent for some time. If the group could not make personal contact with a student that evening, there were follow-up telephone calls made and letters sent. This "Calling Squadron" was first organized in January 1929 and became a significant relational bridge that assisted in turning casual visitors and lapsed attenders into active members of the College Department.[38] After the calls had been made, the evening often concluded with a social activity, such as a potluck supper, taffy pull, or party. As the class grew, the entire membership was divided into sex-segregated subgroups according to home address, each with its own leader to facilitate easier contact. By early 1930 the Tuesday evening calling group was augmented by a "Telephone Squadron" headed by the vice president of the College Department. After checking the department roll following Sunday morning services, members of the group called the absentees to let them know they were missed and invited them to the Christian Endeavor meeting that would start in a few hours. Other telephone-calling "specialists" kept department members abreast of important news and pushed the total number of calls made in February 1930 to 856. Department members hosted semimonthly teas for college- and career-age females, many at Mears's home, to introduce newer members and visitors to some of the old hands in the department. Regular reminders in the department newsletter urged members and class officers to seek out new faces and make the visitors feel welcome, sometimes gently chastising them for not doing so.

Students also banded together around shared skills and interests. The College Department Orchestra first organized in February 1929, followed a year later by the formation of a College Department Choir. Tennis enthusiasts met at 6:00 a.m. on Saturdays through much of the year beginning in late April 1929. Female golfers could pursue their passion with other members of the department at 2:00 p.m., while the riding club brought together the equestrians at 4:00 p.m. The all-male basketball team boasted an undefeated season into January 1930. Those interested in studying theology could attend a Thursday evening class, and a men's Bible study limited to fifteen members began meeting on Sunday afternoons at 4:30 in May 1929. If more than fifteen expressed an interest, another small group would be formed so all could be accommodated.

A Young Men's Club joined the above organizations in late 1930. Its target membership was men in their twenties for it provided career advice in a spiritual setting. The Thursday evening programs were analogous to the meetings of popular civic organizations with complementary components including a spiritual message. In November 1930 the group began a series of meetings on vocational guidance to assist in the selection of and preparation for an occupation. Two recent meetings had been led by the vice president of public relations for Southern California Edison, a major power company, and a human resource administrator for the Southern California Telephone Company. Besides furnishing occasions to hear from Christian business leaders, the club also selected two men each week to present extemporaneously a three-minute speech on a designated topic. The week following their presentations each participant received a written critique intended to sharpen his public speaking abilities. With the shadow of the economic depression still lengthening, this club afforded openings to network with Christian business and professional leaders and to receive mentoring in matters both personal and professional.[39] The Rouzee Club served business and professional women on Tuesday evenings, but it appears to have had a somewhat more spiritual emphasis as Mears usually gave the message.

Christian service played such a central role in Mears's educational philosophy that it remained a high priority for her collegians. The pages of their newsletter included information on service projects and often contained news from foreign and domestic missionaries supported by the department. Mears challenged her students to service by her behavior as well as her words. In the early spring of 1929 she "packed her powerful Packard full of pretty packers, preaching the gospel of the perfect Prince" in the vernacular of a *Quest* writer. A second carful followed her to the rescue mission in downtown Los Angeles where her students conducted a gospel meeting. From this evening forward for many years, they led the program at LA's Main Street Union Rescue Mission on the fourth Thursday of every month. During the summer of 1929 local radio station KTBI broadcast an hour-long program in support of the mission that included nearly forty department singers and musicians.[40] That same summer, a small group of six traveled to the Sailor's Rest Mission in San Pedro to begin what became a regular evangelistic outreach that committed department members to provide services on the third Tuesday of each month. By September of 1930, members of the College Department had also begun to serve at the LA Chinese mission. As with the other mission activities, evangelization was the ultimate goal, but unlike the two previously mentioned endeavors, which were primarily concerned with Christian conversions, volunteers at the Chinese mission assisted students with English language acquisition skills—meeting a practical need with the hope of a spiritual benefit. This mission, too, engaged College Department members over a span of years.

These three groups were among the first organized into what would later be called deputation teams. Such teams would be formed for some specific purpose, often evangelistic in nature, and would be sent out as representatives from the College Department, "deputized" as it were by the department and the church. Membership could fluctuate—especially if the particular activity was ongoing—but the teams always acted on behalf of the entire department. Individual department members also served in a variety of capacities. The September 1929 issue of the newsletter reported on collegians "scattered very widely doing the Lord's work." Although probably somewhat overstated, the article nonetheless highlighted the breadth of service obligations undertaken by Mears's students just a year after she arrived in Hollywood.[41]

Early issues of *The Quest* not only profiled members of deputation groups and individual missionaries sent out or supported by the College Department, but they also carried updates on the work of some of these individuals. Barbara Parish, for example, accepted a teaching position in Miami, Arizona, and volunteered at the Community Church as the Sunday school missionary supervisor and a junior high Sunday school teacher soon after her arrival. To supplement her weekly Sunday school class, she presented a monthly twenty-five-minute program on missions. She also took it upon herself to begin a Wednesday prayer meeting.[42] In late August of 1929 at Lake Arrowhead in the San Bernardino Mountains, Bob Burns presented gospel messages to campers.[43] By the fall of 1930, many College Department veterans had begun to enter full-time Christian service, including Bernice Ludlow with Native Americans in Oklahoma, Ruth Russell (Raplee) in South America, and Eleanor and Kenneth Wilson in China. The activities of these and others showed up in College Department publications.

Ludlow, Russell, and the Wilsons were early members of the DEBTORS, a group comprised of those committed to a vocation of full-time Christian service that had predated Mears's arrival. The fellowship greatly expanded during the 1930s as more of Mears's collegians chose to pursue Christian professions.[44] Renamed the Life Work Recruits, the group met regularly to listen to missionaries and other Christian workers and signed a pledge giving themselves "wholly to the service of Christ and the Church." Missionaries, directors of Christian education, pastors, and evangelists came from this group in growing numbers over the course of the decade.[45] In April 1930 there were forty-one members; by the late 1940s membership increased further and the group affiliated with the Celtic Cross, the national Presbyterian organization for those seeking full-time Christian service. Their fellowship eventually grew into the hundreds.[46]

In all likelihood, after her graduation from the University of Minnesota Henrietta Mears had no overarching strategy to propagate a more gracious Christian faith other than what had been modeled for her. She merely moved forward, embodying the beliefs she held and living as authentically a Christian witness as she possibly could before her students. But Mears's progressive approach to Christian education during the cultural crises of the 1910s through the 1930s put her on the leading edge of fundamentalist Protestants reconfiguring the relationship of theological conservatism to American culture. Committed more to conversation than confrontation, Mears rebuilt linkages between the sacred and the secular that had been snapping for most of her adult life. By the end of the 1930s her comprehensive and holistic educational program at the First Presbyterian Church of Hollywood not only conveyed a worthwhile model to the coming generation of new evangelicals, but placed her at the forefront of those most able to shoulder leadership for it.

Chapter Six

Unexpected Opportunities

Many of Henrietta Mears's most enduring contributions to the reformation of Protestant America flourished well beyond the walls of the First Presbyterian Church of Hollywood. But all the initiatives and achievements associated with her ministry radiated outward from the church campus at the corner of Gower and Carlos. As confirmed by the multilayered programs associated with her College Department, a complete Christian education program operated at many levels for many reasons in order to meet the challenges of contemporary life. Not surprisingly, however, as Mears diligently applied herself to the task at hand in Hollywood, unanticipated avenues of opportunity opened, presenting new pathways for her to revitalize Christian orthodoxy.

Her extraordinary accomplishments since the move to Southern California brought Mears to the attention of major players on the theologically conservative national stage, including her old friend J. Oliver Buswell Jr. They attended the University of Minnesota together and had been fellow parishioners at the First Baptist Church of Minneapolis, where Buswell's father served for a time on Riley's staff. In 1926 Buswell assumed the presidency of Wheaton College in Illinois, probably the most widely recognized fundamentalist Christian college in the country. They stayed in touch over the years, and Buswell even paid Mears a visit soon after her move to Hollywood, participating in a meeting of the teachers and officers in early June 1930. As a direct consequence, he had firsthand knowledge of what she had attained both at First Baptist and First Presbyterian.

That knowledge led Buswell to write two letters to her during the winter of 1936. The first elaborated on a conversation they had earlier regarding his conviction that she could greatly increase her influence if she would join the Wheaton College faculty as its first professor of Christian education. He invited her to spend some time on campus, deliver a few lectures, and confer with members of the faculty during her stay. Buswell wanted her to visit soon because he hoped to hire staff for the following academic year as early as possible. He let her know that visiting campus would not obligate her in any way and that while he did not know what salary she might require, he believed that Wheaton could make her a viable offer. Buswell concluded the letter by assuring her that the "trip need not take you long. Come by air or rail as you prefer at our expense."

His second letter was more personal and somewhat more pointed than the first. He began with another plea for her to consider Wheaton and then addressed an unspecified concern with regard to the Genesis creation narrative in her Sunday school curriculum. Buswell observed that there were respected Bible teachers who held the same interpretation, but he also made it clear that he was not one of them. He quickly informed her, however, that at Wheaton nobody "criticizes anybody else for holding either the one view or the other" and assured her that as Wheaton's president he never allowed his personal opinion on "non-fundamental" subjects to intrude on a faculty member's academic freedom.[1]

Nearly two months passed with no word from Mears. Buswell wired on March 10 to ask one question: "When may we expect your visit?" Mears sent a brief telegram two days later letting him know that she could not come.[2] Puzzled by her terse reply and quite concerned that she might decline his offer, Buswell wrote the next day. He spoke directly and on behalf of his colleagues at Wheaton: "We are quite united in wanting you to join our staff next September." He offered a specific salary of "twenty-five hundred dollars, less the ten percent reduction which temporarily applies to all college salaries." His concluding sentences reveal his fear that the second letter of January had been problematic for her:

> If your wire means that you might come for a visit sometime later this spring, and would give consideration to an invitation for next September, please wire again. In any case, please use the enclosed stamped envelope and let me have some assurance that my long critical dissertation of last January did not cause any offense.[3]

Mears replied by letter on March 25. The salutation "Dear Oliver" matched the intimacy of his last two letters to her. She wrote that she had taken no offense at his previous letter. She expressed an interest in hearing the ideas of others and even prompted Buswell to "send some more dissertations. I like 'em." She referred somewhat lightheartedly to the flurry of correspondence from his end meant to entice her to Wheaton but left no doubt this time that she would not be traveling to Illinois: "I say again that I do sincerely appreciate your invitations and your flattering importunity, but ------I feel that my work here has not been completed."[4] Although Mears closed the door on this prospect it would not be the last time that an institution of higher learning would recognize her distinctive accomplishments in the Christian education of youth and do its best to recruit her into its faculty ranks.

FIRM IN HER COMMITMENT to the students at First Presbyterian, Mears riveted her attention on an educational enterprise increasingly unable to accommodate an exploding enrollment. As word spread across Southern California of the unprecedented growth of First Presbyterian's Sunday school, visitors flocked to the church, intent on observing for themselves what animated such phenomenal numbers. Mears also accepted invitations to speak at churches in the region. Many who heard her or visited her Sunday school inquired about the curriculum she utilized because it seemed to fuel the expansion. When asked about the origin or content of the materials, Mears replied frankly, "Oh, just some mimeographed material some of us are writing and putting together here." Doubtless hoping to replicate the same results in their own churches, pastors, teachers, and Sunday school superintendents tried to purchase copies of the lessons. But already more than fully occupied with the process of creating an entirely new curriculum with Ellinghusen and informed by experienced printers that the cost would be prohibitive, Mears countered, "Such a thing would be out of the question, as we are hardly able to produce it fast enough for our own use. . . . I'm just producing it for my Sunday School and have no way to do more."

One church leader, however, would not take no for an answer.[5] Marion Falconer worked as a pharmacist in Orange County, California. A dedicated layperson, he served as Sunday School superintendent at Anaheim's First Presbyterian Church. When he learned of the success Mears generated in Hollywood, he invited her to speak to his teachers, probably sometime in late 1931 or early 1932. From this point on Falconer and Mears became rather well-acquainted as they attended some of the same regional Sunday school conferences and shared a profound commitment to Christian education. He soon recognized that the curriculum being written by Mears and Ellinghusen had exactly the focus and emphasis he wanted for his Sunday school and began a campaign to secure copies for his teachers. Repeatedly rebuffed by Mears, Falconer decided to make a personal visit to Hollywood in 1933. After services he cornered her and proceeded to argue his case with decided passion. Mears tried to defuse his resolve, but Falconer became even more insistent, vowing not to leave the church until she relented. His zeal won her over, and she promised to investigate the matter further.[6]

Mears subsequently conferred with longtime friend Harry Rimmer regarding the key issues related to printing her Sunday school lessons. He sent her to his printer in nearby Glendale. Whether out of the goodness of his heart or because the Depression had severely curtailed his contracts, Cary Griffin of Griffin-Patterson Printers agreed to extend a generous line of credit, promising to defer billing except for absolute necessities, such as the engraving plates, until the books sold. He also assisted with design concerns. The authors decided to order two hundred teachers' books and one thousand student books for the fourth-grade edition. When Esther Ellinghusen used her salary to pay for the engraving plates, her mother fretted, "That's $84.74 down a rat hole." During the summer of 1933 the books were printed and delivered, though storage space was at a premium at the church. Thrilled when she saw the finished product, Mears went to work immediately on the junior high book so it could be printed by mid-September and ready for the fall quarter.[7]

At this juncture, Stanley Engle, one of Mears's Junior Department teachers, began asking questions of the authors regarding storage of unsold books, shipping procedures, and other details. Engle naturally saw the practical side of the operation since he worked as an accountant for the Union Oil Company. Realizing that Mears, Ellinghusen, and Baldwin had not given much thought to these important issues, Engle offered to store the books in his garage and to keep the records in his spare time. He soon became the fourth partner in what all agreed to call The Gospel Light Press. The new partnership received its initial copyright on August 23, 1933. Fittingly, the first order to be invoiced went to Falconer for eighty-four junior student books, four junior teachers' books, and forty-six junior high student books.[8]

The Gospel Light Press curriculum met a deep need among theological conservatives. Even though it had begun with no capital, and from 1933 to 1936 had no full-time employees and no rented facility, production could hardly keep up with demand. Paralleling but far exceeding the growth rate of Mears's Hollywood Sunday school, the biblically based Sunday school materials proved an instant sensation. By the end of 1933, twelve different books were available and 13,366 copies had been sold to 131 Sunday schools in twenty-five states. So successful were the curricula that in early April 1934 the church's Board of Trustees requested clarification regarding the relationship of The Gospel Light Press to First Presbyterian Church, seeking "to discover what interest, if any, the church has in this corporation."[9]

The partners prepared a promotional brochure and dispatched personal invitations to a preview of the current curriculum to be held at the church on May 12. These tactics, coupled with radio and newspaper advertisements disseminated throughout the Southland, resulted in a "Demonstration Day" crowd that exceeded their wildest expectations. Griffin-Patterson printed teachers' books for seventh-grade classes, eighth-grade student books for the Gospel of John, and junior teachers' books. Visual aids (flannelgraph patterns called Scripturegraphs) were also fashioned for juniors. Sales of the twenty-five existing books more than tripled to 44,837. A garage could no longer hold the inventory, and soon the Engle home had books stacked under tables and in every vacant corner. Mrs. Engle took orders over the telephone and by mail while her beleaguered husband kept the books and packaged and shipped orders to more and more churches around the country. The Engle dining room became the shipping and (order) receiving office for the fifty-seven books in print by the end of 1935. Ellinghusen took a year's leave of absence from her teaching position to finish work on the primary and junior teachers' books while Mears wrapped up the course on the book of Acts for eighth-graders and began the ninth-grade book. Sales for the year nearly tripled again as 125,737 books were sold to 723 churches representing twenty-seven different denominations.[10]

By 1936 work commenced on the kindergarten curriculum and Mears started the tenth-grade course, *Highlights of Scripture*. Ellinghusen completed the primary and junior teachers' manuals ahead of schedule and spent the final portion of her leave in the Pacific Northwest visiting churches, demonstrating the materials, and holding workshops that further accelerated their popularity. It became obvious that the sheer volume of items printed required a larger facility than Engle's residence. In November 1936 he discovered a vacant storefront space at 1443 North Vine Street, just two blocks from its storied intersection with Hollywood Boulevard. With financial details ironed out and stock moved, the four partners held a service on Thanksgiving Day to express their gratitude for the new headquarters of The Gospel Light Press.

Because Mears, Ellinghusen, and Baldwin were preoccupied with the production of new lesson books, the partners hired staff in 1937 to see to other aspects of the growing business. Engle found his responsibilities enlarged at the new site. The accusation that he walked to work through the alleys of Hollywood to locate the best used packing cartons began as a gentle jibe at his thriftiness, but soon clerks, assistants, and shipping employees all joined in the search for Campbell's Soup boxes, deemed the best containers for the ever-expanding line of Gospel Light Sunday school materials. Halfway through the year, Engle resigned from Union Oil to devote his full attention to Gospel Light. The Vine Street location functioned not only as the headquarters of the company but also as a Christian bookstore. Margaret Mears provided funds to purchase assorted Bibles and books, and the partners hired James Forshaw to run the operation. Meanwhile, work continued on the kindergarten lessons, and the *Highlights of Scripture* curriculum appeared as did a new Christian education magazine called *Light*, edited by Cyrus Nelson. Nelson had been among the early graduates of Mears's College Department at First Presbyterian who committed his life to full-time Christian service, and after graduating from Princeton Seminary he returned to become youth minister at First Presbyterian under her.

By the end of the year, the number of lesson books sold surpassed a quarter of a million (257,997). In addition to the publication of the first books in the kindergarten series, 1938 also saw substantial revisions of the primary, junior, and junior high curricula in order to keep them editorially and pedagogically current. By year's end 1,544 churches representing forty-two different denominations from forty-three states had purchased 365,286 lesson books.[11]

The meteoric rise of Gospel Light unfortunately led to a protracted personal conflict for Mears. It issued not only from the exceptional demand for Gospel Light goods but also from the interconnections she helped establish within the company between her family members, the original owners, and her associates at First Presbyterian. Such rapid expansion of a project that began merely as a curriculum for a single Presbyterian church in Southern California placed a tremendous burden on Mears and the partners to make wise and often difficult decisions not only about production and facilities but also about personnel and organizational concerns. As might be expected, a company that started as a kind of quasi-extended family operation struggled to maintain the intimacy of such an environment while simultaneously facing the consequences of success that none of the principals could have foreseen in 1933.

It should be recalled that Baldwin, Ellinghusen, Engle, and Nelson were close associates at First Presbyterian and worked in the educational ministry of the church under Mears's leadership for some time before the founding of The Gospel Light Press. By mid-1937 the scale of Gospel Light's expansion made more formal organization necessary. Mears assumed the position of founder and editor in chief, Ellinghusen associate editor, Baldwin assistant to the editor, and Engle general manager. Upon incorporation, all four of the partners became directors of The Gospel Light Press and divided the company stock between them. They also acquired new titles: Mears as president, Ellinghusen as vice president, Baldwin as secretary, and Engle as treasurer and assistant secretary.[12] Two other important figures joined the four partners and Nelson before the end of the year.

The two really were members of Mears's extended family. William T. Greig Sr. had married Mears's cousin Margaret Buckbee at the First Baptist Church of Minneapolis in April 1917.[13] He worked for his father-in-law, John Colgate Buckbee, at the Bureau of Engraving in Minneapolis and eventually rose to the vice presidency. Mears approached Greig regarding his potential interest in assisting with some of the early production work for The Gospel Light Press. He also became the business editor of *Light,* while Engle served as its manager as well as general manager of The Gospel Light Press. To complicate the situation further, Greig's daughter, Peggy, had visited Mears in Southern California for an extended period, during which time she and Nelson began a romantic relationship culminating in their marriage. These complicated and overlapping business and personal relationships among Mears, First Presbyterian, and Gospel Light led to a tense test of the company's leadership and organizational structure that originated in December 1937 and lasted nearly a year.[14]

Even while wending her way through these troubles, Mears continued writing for The Gospel Light Press and added another duty as president of its board of directors.[15] The skyrocketing sales of Gospel Light wares across denominational lines indicated that Mears and her partners filled a massive need for an all-ages, biblically orthodox curriculum in a time of global uncertainty. They raced constantly to keep pace with the relentless market demand their materials engendered. Throughout the 1940s and 1950s Gospel Light introduced new products, added staff members, upgraded facilities, and streamlined operations in a concerted effort to ensure that its unapologetically evangelical curriculum would be accessible to all who desired to utilize it.

Mears and her staff updated existing programs of study and regularly created new teaching aids to meet the ever-increasing demand. As early as 1945 many of the Sunday school materials were translated into Spanish and then into Chinese, signaling the international appeal the curriculum would gain over the coming decades. Two years later The Gospel Light Press began its imprinting program for other denominations, allowing them to insert their own theological distinctives directly into Gospel Light products. Aimee Semple McPherson's International Church of the Foursquare Gospel and the Colorado Baptist Convention were among those that took advantage of this generous provision.[16] In 1948 the authors finished *Sailing with Christ*, a three-week course for Vacation Bible School, but delayed its publication to make sure that a needed reworking of the kindergarten series could be completed in 1949. Substantive and stylistic improvements in the primary course proceeded concurrently as did new adult studies on the epistles of Romans, Galatians, and Ephesians. In the latter year Gospel Light added activity sheets to complement the workbooks, and these immediately found a receptive audience with a circulation of 100,000 within five years of their introduction. Under Mears's supervision a twelfth grade course was developed in 1951, the same year that the first publications for two- and three-year-old children rolled off the presses. A series of four books for worship in small churches rounded out the new offerings. With other projects accomplished, Gospel Light finally released *Sailing with Christ* in 1952, close on the heels of a new adult course under the guidance of Nelson. A second Vacation Bible School course called *Crusading with Christ* appeared in 1953 and a third, *Pioneering with Christ*, the following year. New editions of these three vacation curricula appeared in 1955, 1956, and 1957, respectively, and were well-received. The mid-1950s also saw the broadening of Gospel Light's product line to include audiovisual materials beyond traditional print media. The company created its first filmstrip in 1953, with the first sound recordings (songs for two- and three-year-olds) added in 1954. A map kit was introduced in 1957 as were a new series of worship books. In 1958, when the first cradle roll course appeared and a new twelfth-grade course was published, the company could boast a curriculum for all ages, including a line of supplementary Sunday school papers that had just been added.

As writer and editor in chief, Henrietta Mears presided over a significant expansion of the company as the popularity of its products exceeded all expectations. By the end of 1940 The Gospel Light Press shipped its materials to more than 2,100 churches—359 Baptist, 307 Presbyterian, 224 Methodist, 140 Foursquare, and 463 community and independent, among others. Serviced directly by Gospel Light, these churches were heavily concentrated in the West but included churches in all but one of the states. Seven hundred thirty-six of the churches were in California, 338 in Washington state, 195 in Illinois, 157 in Oregon, and 125 in Minnesota. The other 600 churches were scattered among forty-two states. The press sold more than 1.7 million curriculum books that year—120 times the sales volume of 1933. Requests for Gospel Light items came from denominational publishing houses, Christian bookstores, and from churches in every state but Alabama. Fifty-three bookshops offered Gospel Light publications by 1940. In 1943—only ten years after its founding—The Gospel Light Press was recognized as one of the four largest independent publishers of Sunday school supplies in the United States. Thousands of Sunday schools in Australia and Canada, as well as the US territories of Alaska and Hawaii, also utilized Gospel Light curricula. The five full-time and two part-time employees of 1941 increased to twelve full-time staff members by 1945 and forty by 1956, including more than a dozen in the editorial and production departments.

Gospel Light's Christian Education Service Bureau debuted in 1944, functioning as a resource for Christian educators who desired assistance in sharpening their teaching and administrative skills. Mears and others participated directly in this branch of the work, contributing practical workshops for interested parties regarding Sunday school work and tips on integrating Gospel Light curriculum into their churches' broader educational program.

The company received a constant stream of requests from churches and conference organizers for speakers. An education services department, established in 1958, arranged speakers for 337 different requests in twenty-four states and Canada. The department engaged a field consultant in the Pacific Northwest and selected personnel to speak at fifty-three conventions throughout the United States. And still the demand increased.

In February of 1945 Gospel Light organized a religious art department and in June a merchandising department. *Trade Winds*, a monthly newsletter sent to dealers to inform them of the growing range of company products, began publication by the end of that year. The first three full-time editorial staff members joined in 1950. The following year Gospel Light was able to begin a direct business relationship with the Times-Mirror Company, publisher of the *Los Angeles Times*. The company continued to develop specialized departments and hire personnel as the popularity of its literature called for further expansion. A small production department emerged in 1953. A director of biblical research was hired in 1955, when a total of thirteen persons were employed in just the editorial and production departments. Hires in 1957 augmented the company's expertise in the latest media technologies.

After the fledgling enterprise outgrew the Engle home in late 1936, 1443 North Vine Street not only served as the headquarters of The Gospel Light Press but also its only directly managed retail facility. In May 1939 the company leased an adjacent space to provide more room for retail sales and stock storage. Two years later a third space next door temporarily met the need for expanded facilities. The company itself retained only the retail bookstore in Hollywood until 1946, when it opened two other Southern California sites in Long Beach and San Diego.[17]

The complexity of managing both the retail and publication aspects of the business, however, led to a reassessment of the company's priorities in 1949. The board decided to concentrate on the publication of curricular materials and sold all three bookstores to their respective managers. The Gospel Light Press headquarters moved to progressively larger buildings in nearby Glendale over the next decade. Earlier in its history, the company had used depositories around the country to expedite the delivery of orders nationwide. But the persistent increase in the number of purchasers and the ballooning growth of product volume made this business model untenable. As a result, a branch company office and warehouse opened in Mound, Minnesota, in 1950 to assist midwestern and eastern dealers and to facilitate more efficiently the shipping of orders. So effective was this business strategy that barely three years later the Mound staff relocated to more spacious quarters.

A series of major organizational changes altered the structure and debt service of Gospel Light in 1949 and 1950 but strengthened the personal connection Mears had with the highest level of company leadership. The shift actually began in 1948 when the directors attempted to recruit Cyrus Nelson as the company's executive director nearly a decade after he had left Gospel Light to assume leadership of the Mount Hermon Christian Conference Center south of San Francisco.[18] In May 1949 the board moved to divest the company of the retail end of the business and conveyed title of the Vine Street store to Engle.[19] He then withdrew as director, assistant secretary, and treasurer of The Gospel Light Press, thereby severing his formal relation with the company.

Engle's departure meant the top leadership even more reflected Mears through her family members.[20] Sometime between mid-May 1949 and early June 1950 Nelson assumed the office of treasurer and joined the board of directors with Mears, Ellinghusen, and Baldwin. A special meeting of this board on June 6, 1950, in turn led to a wholesale shuffle of the leadership team. Mears, who had been reconsidering her role in the company for some time, submitted her resignation as president and director. The remaining directors immediately chose Nelson as her replacement, and he presided for the duration of the meeting. Ellinghusen then resigned as director and vice president to be replaced by Mears's second cousin William T. Greig Jr., manager of the company's Mound, Minnesota, operation. Following Greig's election, Nelson relinquished his role as treasurer to be replaced by Greig. Then Baldwin, the last of the original founders of The Gospel Light Press, tendered her resignation as director and secretary. The final leadership shift came with the election of Margaret Greig Nelson—Cyrus's wife, Greig's sister, and Mears's second cousin—to the board of directors. Whereas the initial leadership team included three of Mears's church family, this new board included three lineal family members, one of whom had been mentored by her in the College Department.[21] Although Mears, Ellinghusen, and Baldwin left their formal leadership roles, as writers and editors of the Gospel Light curriculum their influence remained practically undiminished and they continued to receive royalties on a sliding scale in proportion to their authorial and editorial contributions.

The Gospel Light Press celebrated its silver anniversary in 1958. To signify clarity of purpose and continuity of mission, the company changed its name to Gospel Light Publications to reflect more accurately its primary objective of publishing, rather than simply printing, theologically conservative Christian educational literature and related materials. Nearly a decade earlier Mears had turned over the day-to-day operation of the company to her family members and trusted colleagues, but her stamp remained imprinted on everything the firm developed as she retained her post as editor in chief and her status as founder. When the staff gathered at the end of 1958 for the annual Christmas banquet, more than one hundred attended—a five hundred percent increase from the twenty who were present at the first event just ten years earlier. Encouraged by the marvelous acceptance of Gospel Light products, Mears imagined greater possibilities for theological conservatives even as her impact on a transforming American Protestantism broadened and deepened. And as always, her ongoing work as First Presbyterian's director of Christian education served as the catalyst for those bigger dreams.

In her annual report for fiscal 1940–1941 Mears reiterated her priorities as the director of Christian education:

> It is incumbent upon us to mold ideas and ideals, to change the thinking of our youth, to create standards of character and conduct, to prepare young people for this life, — yes, more, — for the life to come. . . . We must not only help him to know a Savior but instruct him in the way of righteousness and build him in the things of the Word of God. . . . We must teach him how to live with others, how to consecrate and use his talents for the glory of God, how to find the path of service that Christ has for him, to help him in his career and teach him the art of playing in a wholesome way and let him find an outlet for his particular genius.[22]

In crucial ways Mears's thinking presaged current educational theory by emphasizing the learning process over the act of teaching. Yet she tied both together in an ingenious way, contending that teaching had not occurred unless the student learned. Learning for her did not mean the mastery of ideas; it entailed "the integration of ideas into the personality." To her, "Real teaching should help the student to demonstrate an increased ability to meet the problems of life and to act on his own initiative. As he comes in contact with the experiences of others, his own experiences are enriched. This is learning one's lesson."[23] Hence Mears placed tremendous responsibility squarely on the teacher's shoulders, famously remarking that "the most powerful part of a Sunday school lesson is the teacher behind it."[24] While she did not believe that teachers were born to teach, she did acknowledge that they must have a desire to be taught, must be curious about the grand questions of life, and must work hard. Successful training would result in teachers who knew the subject, carefully observed students, and were able to do something about both.[25] Her resolute commitment to personal conversion, spiritual growth, ongoing vocational discernment, leadership training, and meaningful service spawned an increasingly diversified and truly compelling educational program stretching from the cradle to adulthood, centered squarely upon meeting the spiritual, intellectual, emotional, and physical needs of her pupils.

Mears's creation of differentiated groups to meet those student needs at identifiable developmental stages did not end with young people, as the launch of the Rouzee Club for business and professional women early in the 1930s indicated. She divided educational activities by age, gender, and even life station, tailoring classes and activities to meet particular needs of specific groups at specific times. Through the first ten years of her tenure at First Presbyterian, the eleven departments of the Sunday school sufficed, but with the growth of the College Department (and the related uptick in marriages) that configuration began to change in the late 1930s. Not surprisingly, the first new department added was the Homebuilders class for young marrieds, first meeting in March 1939.[26] Members of this group had previously been included in the College or Senior Young People's departments, but Mears decided they should have their own class to maximize cohesion around a similar life station and age (roughly twenty to thirty-five). The Homebuilders joined the SYP (Senior Young People—married couples with nontoddler children) class, the MGC (women only) class, the prophecy (coeducational) class, and the MBC (Macsmen Bible Class—men only) as the adult departments of the Sunday school.[27]

MacLennan left the church in 1940 to begin work as vice president of Cathedral Films and was succeeded by Louis Evans Sr. in 1941. This change in pastoral leadership coincided with significant educational adjustments. By March 1941 the prophecy class had been discontinued. Soon thereafter Mears supported the formation of a class for single business and professional men and women aged twenty-two to thirty-five whose needs were not being adequately met by either the College or the SYP departments. It first met on December 14, 1941, but lack of available space during the morning hours meant this group had to gather initially on Sunday evenings at 6:30. In short order young women in the membership formed the World Fellowship Guild to promote mission service. Adult classes changed names but not direction in the early and mid-1940s. The MGC class was renamed the Women's Bible Class to reflect more accurately its clientele, and the business and professional class was christened the Christian Forum Club. The former Macsmen class became Evans's class of adult married couples appropriately called the Adult Bible Class. Many groups adopted specific age and life station designations during these years. Christian Forum Club members were singles aged twenty-five to forty; Homebuilders, married couples aged twenty-five to thirty-five; SYP, married couples aged thirty-five to forty-five; and the Adult Bible Class (renamed the Westminster Class by 1946), mature married couples.[28]

Mears's belief in the vital importance of relationships nurtured in the church meant that Sunday school classes, once founded, should carry cohort members through the different stages in their life course together. By the later 1940s this meant that no specific class existed for middle-aged couples or for young couples under twenty-five married after the war. Mears's recognition of this fact led to further reorganization with the formation of two new classes: the Harvesters during the 1946–1947 fiscal year and the Mariners in 1949. By 1951 the adult classes reached a new level of age and station specificity: the College Department (eighteen-to-twenty-five-year-old men and women), the Ambassadors (formerly the Christian Forum Club, now meeting on Sunday mornings, twenty-five to thirty-five), Mariners (married couples with a combined age of sixty or younger as of 1948), Homebuilders (married and over thirty years of age, roughly thirty-five to forty-five), Harvesters (forty years of age and older, generally forty-five to fifty-five), and Westminster (men and women fifty-five and older). The Women's Bible Class had no age designation at this time. The Mariners Class appears to have split into two groups in 1958 to meet more adequately the needs of the younger adult cohort. One group maintained the Mariners designation and was comprised of the youngest married contingent—those aged twenty to twenty-eight. The new group, the Voyagers, focused on young marrieds ages twenty-eight to thirty-five.[29]

Aside from the age and station stipulations for the adult Sunday school classes, Mears left it to the membership and officers to plan their curriculum, establish giving priorities, decide on mission and service assignments, and devise social engagements to meet their needs. The Gospel Light Press developed adult curricula, but it is unclear whether all the adult classes used them. While she was often called upon to speak to adult groups at their functions, her direct intervention tended to be minimal, though her oversight was significant. For those below college age, however, she took a much more decisive role. Her Gospel Light curriculum provided the core of biblical teaching to prepare her younger students for committed service to the world. (It is intriguing to note that the only group for which no curriculum was written by Mears or her associates at The Gospel Light Press during these decades was the department for which she served as teacher—the College Department.)

By the late 1930s most children's departments of the Sunday school used her Gospel Light curriculum. As soon as Mears and her partners wrote new materials they were adopted by the requisite department down to the two- and three-year-old nursery children (1951) and the one-year-old toddlers (1958); she did, however, utilize the Presbyterian Faith and Life curriculum for her kindergarteners in the late 1950s.[30] Primary and junior students had workbooks that stimulated their study of Scripture and participated in gender-segregated smaller classes for each week's lesson after meeting all together for opening exercises. As pupils advanced, workbooks became more detailed and included acrostic puzzles and fill-in-the-blank sections taken directly out of the King James Version of the Bible. Bible memorization played a large role in these departments. Staff members took time during the Sunday morning session to listen to students recite their verses. The Gospel Light Press produced colorful badges that the young scholars received after successful recitations. They would be affixed to a red ribbon with the student's name at the top and hung in the departmental room for all to see. Competition for the most decorated ribbon resulted in some that hung eight to ten feet long festooned with emblems announcing that the student had completed assignments that included memorization of the books of the Bible, the Ten Commandments, the Beatitudes, John 3:16, and other important passages.

Rooted solidly in knowledge of the Old and New Testaments through the Gospel Light curriculum and a regular program of recitations calibrated to their developmental abilities, pupils then graduated successively into the

Junior High, Senior High, and College departments. Graduation ceremonies from department to department became quite elaborate affairs staged every spring on Children's Day to coincide with the termination of public school instruction. As they moved through these departments, maturing students took a progressively greater role in morning Sunday school activities giving them practical training. By the time they reached the College Department, members had been exposed to leadership and service as cabinet officers and departmental assistants. The curriculum cultivated intimate knowledge of Scripture and also instruction on vital matters such as vocational choices, relationships, science and faith, and world missions. Mears always emphasized the importance of personal connections between the Sunday school teachers and their pupils and prompted her instructors to foster relationships with their students that transcended the Sunday morning education hour. Fishing trips, miniature golfing expeditions, parties, and hiking adventures bonded teachers to students beyond the classroom experience in her holistic training strategy.

As mentioned previously, under Mears's guidance each Sunday school department encouraged students to give regularly so that in pledging their money to the Sunday school, they might learn responsible stewardship of their resources for the rest of their lives. Donating their own money (or dimes and quarters passed to them by their parents to drop in the collection plate) out of a grateful heart not only aided the Sunday school program, but also sustained domestic and foreign mission causes. Mears saw her role in the process as educating "our youth as well as our adults in systematic giving 'on the first day of the week.'" Pledge drives occurred annually and resulted in substantial revenue. Even members of the Cradle Roll Department (though probably not part of the pledge drives) gave to support the Sunday school.[31] In fiscal 1937–1938 more than five hundred students pledged $7,800. From April 1939 to March 1940 pupils raised $8,221.34 for the Sunday school and mission causes. The following year $6,750.90 was contributed for the work of the Sunday school and an additional $1,839.63 for missions. During fiscal 1941–1942 the $10,813.68 raised by the Sunday school meant that it only needed $176.00 from the church's general fund to meet the school's expenses for the entire year. The later war years saw a pronounced increase in giving by the classes, and that remained fairly constant from the late 1940s well into the 1950s, often topping more than $20,000 annually.[32]

Mears also maintained that her students' giving should be split between local church needs and national and international missions. Each department from the Beginners (roughly four- to five-year-olds) upward selected its own mission causes, which meant that the Sunday school supported a sizable number and wide variety of missionaries and agencies—many of whom held membership at First Presbyterian and some who came from Mears's own College Department. In 1948 the Sunday school supported twenty-nine different foreign and domestic mission organizations and individuals. The following year, Mears's students supported local mission projects and other causes in Alaska, Arizona, Africa, China, Japan, South America, and Thailand. Many of the departments gave to multiple mission endeavors. So strong was the mission emphasis in Mears's Sunday school that a Mission Education Department was organized in 1947 with a specific missionary program for each department in the Sunday school.[33] Her students did not just give to missions, they participated in mission. From the High School Department through the adult classes, her students contributed their time and energy to local, regional, national, and international concerns. Many of these ventures had a definite social-service emphasis, although the ultimate goal remained the conversion of those served.[34]

To Mears, Christian training entailed more than just an hour on Sunday morning, so she instituted other educational opportunities for the children and young people of First Presbyterian. During the fiscal 1941–1942 year separate nursery and primary church programs joined the junior church program established in the early 1930s to create a worship experience for children through the sixth grade at the 11:15 a.m. hour. Older children seated their colleagues and collected the offering. Not only did the three programs inculcate the habit of worship in the attendees, they also freed parents to attend regularly the sanctuary worship service. Junior high, senior high, and college-age students met on Sunday evenings for Christian education meetings that gave them openings to express their faith before others. Monthly Youth Night services, which began in the early war years, allowed young people to take part in Sunday evening worship services. Weekday programs ranged from Bible and activity clubs for junior through high school boys and girls to sporting and artistic events and "hot rod" aficionado meetings. These engaged young people and drew them into the network of relationships that Mears hoped would lead to Christian faith development. The desire to draw youth on the periphery into church life led the leadership to build a roller skating rink on church grounds in 1955 and to purchase skates so that young people could join in one of the most popular leisure activities of the day without charge.[35] A three-week Vacation Bible School was held annually in the summer and provided Bible training and activities for ages four through eighteen to twenty depending on the year.[36] It served as a five-day-a-week day amplification of the Sunday school and as an outreach to the community surrounding the church campus. Mears also offered a full camp, conference, and retreat program for all ages.[37]

Innovative programming and a progressive educational ministry continued to be the hallmark of Mears's work as she challenged her young people to live out their faith and fully utilize their gifts and talents. She was delighted when Lucy Hirt arrived in 1941 to initiate a full slate of youth choirs for juniors through college age. The Crossley doll collection allowed sixth-grade Bible lessons to take material form through the use of the figurines in period costume with appropriate background scenery. Mears and her assistant Ethel May Baldwin were the driving forces behind the church library, which first opened during fiscal 1946–1947. The Missionary Education Department began the same year. Mears's desire to ensure that students were taught with the most up-to-date methods led to the formation of an audiovisual department in 1949. Her commitment to an inclusive camp and conference program found her students not only at Forest Home but also at a variety of other local sites. Many departments sponsored newsletters authored by their own members. Discipleship groups for collegians and older people joined the multidimensional ministry in 1959.[38] When addressing matters of dating and marriage in her Sunday school, Mears brought experts in the field to the church and rented sex education films from the public school film library because she wanted Christian young people "to learn about these things in the context of the church and not to be ashamed to ask their ministers anything that is on their minds."[39]

Statistics tell only a part of the story, but they are also indicative of the fact that her steadfast philosophical assumptions, work ethic, and educational strategies struck a responsive chord among theological conservatives. An exhaustive list of all the programs, organizations, and meetings under Mears's administrative purview would be nearly impossible to compile had it not been her practice to keep meticulous records of her activities. She estimated that in fiscal 1937–1938 she was "responsible ultimately for the leadership of between 6,000 and 7,000 meetings and over 2,000 private interviews and speaking at the meetings mentioned above and attending the innumerable committee meetings, executive meetings, vacation institutes, women's councils, which are incumbent upon one in this capacity."[40] As time passed, Mears's tasks grew even more varied and extensive as the more than four-page single-spaced compendium taken verbatim from her 1951 annual report indicates.[41]

The tremendous membership gains in her Sunday school made Mears's ubiquitous administrative duties worthwhile and spoke to the necessary connection in her mind between careful planning, successful execution, and desired result. The Sunday school grew from 1,624 in 1928 to 4,167 in 1933—an amazing increase in just five years during the worst years of the Great Depression. The next half decade saw some fluctuation from a high of 4,107 in 1935 to a low of 3,315 two years later. (By way of a rough comparison, between 1926 and 1936 Sunday school numbers in the northern Presbyterian Church fell by eighteen percent.)[42] Between 1938 and 1958, however, only six years posted a decrease in the number of students over the previous year (1939, 1941, 1943, 1948, 1951, and 1957). The 2,673 reported in 1941 as war clouds gathered was the lowest enrollment since 1931, when a polio outbreak severely curtailed attendance during the summer. While there were years of decreased attendance, the general trajectory of membership surged upward. The 3,477 of 1938 rose to 3,783 in 1947, to 5,929 by 1958, and to 6,102 in 1960—making Mears's Sunday school the largest Presbyterian Sunday school in the country.

Perhaps just as remarkable was the proliferation of classes, departments, and staff members. In 1939 Mears administered twelve departments with 209 teachers and officers. Two years later 219 teachers and officers conducted seventy-five different classes in the twelve departments. By 1948, 309 teachers and officers were responsible for ninety-four classes in fourteen departments. After a major reorganization of the Sunday school in 1951, Mears had 359 teachers and officers in eighteen different departments including four classes of two-year-olds, six classes of three-year-olds, seven classes each of four- and five-year-olds, eight classes for first-graders, nine for second-graders, and eight for third-graders. There were 314 in the Junior Department (fourth through sixth grades), 248 in junior high (seventh through ninth grades) with thirteen teachers, 311 in high school (tenth through twelfth grades) with twelve teachers, and 449 in college. The church also included more than 1,600 adults in its Sunday school program. Five years later 501 teachers and officers (aided by eighty others) served in the eighteen departments conducting 119 Sunday school classes. If the home and extension departments are included in the calculation, educational enrollment for 1956 was 6,821. By the end of the decade her fabled College Department alone boasted 807 members.[43] *(See table 2 on page 281.)*

With such large numbers, Mears faced a constant search for viable teaching stations, which often included holding classes in houses purchased by First Presbyterian or in nearby public buildings such as schools. After many years of making do with less-than-ideal class space, the church opened its first education building in 1950. Just six years later it constructed a second to house classes for infants through third grade, with a third soon added.[44] Growth in the Sunday school also meant growth in church membership as Mears's emphasis on evangelism permeated the classes. Rally Days and Decision Days were particular evangelistic foci. She stressed to her teachers and officers that most conversions occurred during childhood, and so the push was on. She was not disappointed—and neither was the church.[45] Because of the terrific geographic mobility of Southern Californians, the statistical increase in students and volunteers is all the more astounding.[46]

Early in her ministry Mears became acutely aware that significant population shifts not only affected Sunday school numbers, but could also severely hamper the work of adequately training Christian young people because of the associated turnover in her teaching corps, nearly all of whom were volunteers. Consequently, the identification and development of capable and committed leaders remained a constant theme throughout her years in Hollywood. The emphasis Mears placed on training leaders not just for her growing Sunday school but for the benefit of the church's worldwide mission remained a core priority for her. She called it "our greatest concern."[47] Like many other theological conservatives of the time, Mears believed that youth had to be trained for world leadership to assist the church in the current age of crisis. She firmly believed that her Sunday school could provide Christian leaders for a world in desperate need, but that its purpose was laden with consequences far beyond the immediate needs of a world in turmoil. The motto of her Sunday school, "only the best is good enough," applied to the obligation before her—to train young people whose leadership carried both temporal and eternal implications.[48] In her 1950 Christian Education Department Annual Report, Mears reflected on the importance of the new educational building's completion for her students. She summoned all to sacrificial service and leadership—especially the young:

> The years ahead are dark and ominous, and already youth today realizes it is going to be called upon to make heroic sacrifices. Never before has the world been so lacking in leadership in which everyone can trust and believe. In these increased facilities we now have the opportunity to build with greater care and accuracy, youth that shall be leaders who have a firm foundation and who know where they are going and why![49]

Teaching in her Sunday school provided one crucial platform for leadership. But the need for thorough and comprehensive teacher training intensified as the student population exploded. Many of those teachers came from her Sunday school classes and needed instruction in the most effective teaching strategies. As the renown of her Sunday school spread, a steady stream of visitors from other churches (and countries) sat in on classes and quizzed Mears and her staff, hoping to duplicate her achievements in their own congregations.[50] The needs of her own "student" teachers, the requests pouring in from visitors, and the widespread adoption of her Gospel Light curriculum opened the door for Mears to introduce regular teacher training institutes.

Offering a "fresh approach to the world's greatest literature," the workshops aimed to train an interdenominational teacher corps who could in turn train the next generation of Christian leaders. Mears began the first training course on Tuesday evening, January 18, 1938. She recruited notable experts who "had worked out in the laboratory of a great Bible School new methods of modern psychology in their application to the fundamental teachings of God's Word, and are now ready to present their findings and completed lesson material." An early evening start time accommodated those who worked. Clifford Clinton, a member of First Presbyterian, offered to host the meetings on the second floor of his large restaurant in downtown Los Angeles. A registration fee of $1.50 entitled participants to attend the entire sequence of sessions stretching over the next six months. Because of the popularity of the sessions and limited seating, unregistered guests had to pay fifty cents per session. Mears and her colleagues optimistically reserved places for two hundred at that first session, but the capacity crowd forced many to eat dinner standing up. Over the next eight years Sunday school teachers from all over the Southland came together at Clifton's Cafeteria to learn how to improve their craft. The unmitigated popularity of the institutes, however, caused a shift in location and form; when the regular attendance approached five hundred in the mid-1940s, the restaurant could no longer accommodate the crush of participants. The training institutes moved to Forest Home and became multiple-day conferences.[51]

As initiative after successful initiative pooled outward from her home base at First Presbyterian, a cadre of professional and lay church leaders committed to theologically conservative Protestantism took notice. Much like Mears had been modeling for two decades, these young reformers believed that engagement with—not separation from—the secular world remained the most effective way for Christians to live as salt and light in desperate times. And they committed themselves to a thorough recasting of the stereotypical image of Christian fundamentalism fixed in the minds of Americans since the 1920s. In late October 1941 an interdenominational group of college professors, ministers, missionaries, and Bible institute and lay leaders met in Chicago at the Moody Memorial Church to discuss issues, voice concerns, and develop strategies. Before adjourning on the afternoon of October 28, the group agreed in theory to create a national front to serve American theological conservatives. The nascent organization eschewed sectarian doctrinal statements and avoided any belligerent attitude toward other individuals and groups. Those present also resolved not to use the lightning-rod terms "fundamentalist," "modernist," or "council," substituting instead "conservative." This Committee for United Action among Evangelicals appointed two other committees to ensure adequate representation in the fledgling enterprise and to determine who should be invited to a future three-day convocation to discuss problems facing evangelicals. In early February 1942 organizers drafted a letter signed by nearly 150 "executives and leaders of many denominations, mission boards, religious journals, gospel broadcasters, Christian colleges, seminaries, Bible Institutes and interdenominational organizations" inviting interested parties to an April conference in St. Louis. Expressly devoted to "the purpose of exploring the possibility of closer cooperation and coordination in the work of the gospel," it was hoped that the meeting would result in "measures for creating a clearing house in matters of common interest and concern based upon the groundwork of a common faith." With these actions American theological conservatives launched the National Association of Evangelicals.[52]

One of those matters of common interest pertained to the current state of Christian education. In a business session at the second national convention of the NAE on April 17, 1944, Chairman Harold John Ockenga led a spirited discussion regarding the Sunday school movement. Statistics that graphically portrayed the decline in attendance—particularly in the Presbyterian, Episcopalian, and Congregational denominations—heightened the urgency among evangelicals to strengthen Sunday school curricula and programs at the national level. Delegates called for a consultative assembly of Sunday school workers to investigate the feasibility of establishing a permanent national organization affiliated with the NAE for that purpose. The meeting was to be held in conjunction with the next national convention of the NAE, and "as much time as is consistent with the program" was to be set aside for this national discussion.[53]

The NAE Commission on Church Schools began planning in earnest for the conference, which was initially scheduled to take place in Chicago from April 30 to May 1 of the following year. Key leaders from across the nation who, like Mears, were known to have an "interest in evangelical standards in the work of the Sunday school" received a letter inviting their "counsel and co-operation in making this preliminary meeting a success." The letter admonished "all those interested, regardless of their attitude toward the NAE," to participate and asserted that the convocation would be "thoroughly constructive in character and without prejudice to existing organizations." Members of the commission "expected that a permanent organization will be created by those in attendance."[54]

They put together a program, secured appropriate personnel, and publicized the event in one hundred state and national journals, but because of the wartime interposition of federal authority over the allocation of domestic resources, the Office of Defense Transportation cancelled all national and state conventions. The widespread positive response of Sunday school leaders and lay workers, however, led the commission, in consultation with the Boston office of the NAE, to gather a much smaller body together for the same purpose. Letters again went out, but this time to a highly select group. Nearly one hundred came to the two-day meeting and discussed a number of issues including the general state of the Sunday school, the causes of its decline, curricula, and future options. Specifically chosen because of her multifaceted educational accomplishments, Mears contributed her practical insights to the deliberations and spoke confidently about what the Sunday school movement would need if it was to succeed.[55]

The only female chosen to address the conferees, she took the podium on the afternoon of April 30, focusing on the need for trained leadership to provide evangelical Sunday school education for all ages. Mears challenged her audience by arguing that the "church is dying for lack of leadership. . . . The Sunday school has had its artery cut and it is bleeding to death." Unlike her contemporaries she did not believe that many students lost their faith in college. Rather, she contended that those who fell away from the church during the university years did not have any faith to lose because the church did "not make the Bible attractive." Mears spoke to the desperate need for trained Sunday school leaders to ensure that the students who attended Sunday school classes (seventy percent of whom at First Presbyterian came from unchurched families) would be "established in the things of God." She believed that students could benefit from attending youth rallies and special programs, but she said such activities did not certify that they received adequate instruction in biblical literacy or leadership training. The church, she argued, has not "captivated the big men and women who could draw them in." Mears took the NAE itself to task and concluded by prodding her listeners to comprehend the gravity of the need:

> Today the young person needs glamour, thrills, and challenge because the world is offering so much. It is our business what we are going to do with these people after we get them. . . . We must put the Word of God in the hands of men and women who know God, and then God will give the increase. Our responsibility, under God, is to produce leadership. We need to be salesmen of the Gospel of the Lord Jesus Christ. We ought to be on our toes filled with the Holy Ghost.[56]

Others joined Mears's powerful call to recharge the American Sunday school, which on the following day resulted in the formation of the National

Sunday School Association as an NAE affiliate. Planning began immediately for a nationwide Sunday school convention to be held in Chicago in 1946. The conference membership met on May 1, 1945, to accept the nonsectarian doctrinal statement of the NAE as binding on members of the new organization and to forge a formal bond between the Church School Commission of the NAE and the NSSA. Members also issued an invitation to all evangelicals to "participate in the NSSA and the convention without regard to their relationship to other interdenominational organizations." Among the few women present at its creation, Mears accepted a call to serve as a member of the NSSA Advisory Board and 1946 convention planning group. Thus began fifteen years of service in what was to become an international organization dedicated to the revitalization of Sunday schools throughout the United States and Canada.[57]

Between 1946 and 1959, Mears remained a fixture at annual national conventions of the NSSA and many regional and local Sunday school conventions. She taught workshops, offered institutes, authored articles, and often headlined NSSA conferences as a featured speaker. According to participant Howard Hendricks, Mears spoke to nearly five hundred at the first annual NSSA conference at Chicago's Moody Memorial Church in early October 1946. At the second annual convention in Cincinnati in 1947, Mears not only gave one of the main messages but also led the Youth Department groups. She so impressed the leadership during this formative stage of the association's development that her name was put forward to chair the NSSA's Commission on Youth, one of a very small group of evangelical women deemed capable of leading subdivisions of the organization. At the regional level Mears's ongoing involvement in the renewal of the Southern California Sunday school movement via the Greater Los Angeles Sunday School association cannot be overestimated.[58]

In 1948 she keynoted both the Greater Chicago Sunday School Convention in mid-September and the NSSA national conference the next month in Denver. From the fourth national convention in Oakland (1949) through the dual tenth annual conventions in Spokane, Washington, and Providence, Rhode Island (1955), Mears delivered major plenary addresses to audiences as large as six or seven thousand and led specialized workshops for smaller groups. In the later 1950s she pulled back somewhat from her commitments to the NSSA and its allied Sunday school organizations but still spoke at regional gatherings and taught at national conference workshops. In 1959, however, when there were actually three national conventions, Mears at the age of sixty-nine not only assumed responsibility for directing an institute regarding the work of the young people's department (eighteen- to twenty-five-year-olds), but also agreed to participate as a principal speaker alongside Clate Risley, Charles Blair, Arvid Carlson, and Bob Pierce, sharing with her national audience why "Youth Needs God."

Over the years Mears was asked to address topics related to organizational and administrative issues affecting Sunday school classes, superintendents, and directors of Christian education as well as the spiritual, psychological, and intellectual needs and capabilities of students at different stages of their development. At the sixth annual convention in Detroit (1951) Mears joined a panel of prominent church leaders, including the pastor of Aimee Semple McPherson's Angelus Temple, to discuss "Elements in Building a Successful Sunday School." At the Providence convention four years later, she gave an impassioned apologetic for the necessity of a Christian education curriculum that would provide students with religious teaching not occurring in the public schools:

> We in the Church face a tremendous task but not a hopeless one. All we have to do is teach the Word of God. It is sufficient; you don't have to add anything to it. We're feeding the children nothing but husks—superficialities instead of realities. We must put God into our education to make it good.

She also led discussions for lay Sunday school workers, pastors, and other church professionals.[59]

In addition to her ongoing commitment to the National Sunday School Association, Mears served the international cause of evangelical Christianity through her eight-year association with the NAE's Commission on International Relations from 1950 to mid-1958. Her election in the spring of 1950 was most likely precipitated by the recognition of her longstanding interest in world missions, but another factor was her role in facilitating relief work in western Europe and Asia soon after the end of World War II. Other members of her elected class included Billy Graham, Charles Fuller, Bob Jones Jr., Paul Rees, Oswald Smith, Louis Talbot, and C. Davis Weyerhaeuser. Aside from the secretary to the commission Mears remained the only other female member for her entire eight-year term. Harold John Ockenga chaired the commission, which sought to mobilize evangelical Christians and Christian organizations worldwide in much the same way that the NAE hoped to do in North America. A critical imperative of the commission was to create an international association coordinating global evangelistic initiatives. International conferences and consultations held throughout the 1950s fostered a connection between the World Evangelical Fellowship and the Commission on International Relations resulting in the formation of the Commission for World Evangelical Fellowship of the NAE. Toward the end of her service with NAE's world evangelical concerns, Mears agreed to an appointment to the advisory board of this commission, which had evolved out of the World Evangelical Fellowship American Office. She had also served on the advisory board for America of the latter organization since at least 1956.[60]

THAT HENRIETTA MEARS EXCELLED in educating and training the next generation of Christian leaders would have been obvious enough if only her plans for First Presbyterian had borne fruit. But because her work yielded such an abundant harvest year after year, Hollywood could not contain it and unanticipated opportunities to extend her ministry multiplied. The curriculum she developed as a way to provide for her own students at First Presbyterian quickly evolved into a publishing juggernaut with an international, interdenominational clientele by the 1940s. The teacher preparation classes she administered for her own Sunday school teachers broadened into training institutes that drew hundreds of participants, ensuring that her educational strategies would be adapted for congregations far removed from the church at the corner of Gower and Carlos. And her substantial impact as a prophet and pragmatic educational entrepreneur intent on reshaping Protestant Christian orthodoxy well before the Second World War guaranteed that her presence would be required as others worked to organize an international network of new evangelicals that she had a large part in creating in the first place.

Chapter Seven

For Such a Time as This

The 1930s proved to be the death rattle of a world system that had been deeply shaken by the trench-mired horrors of the First World War. Sobering peace settlements attempted to buttress and extend the hegemony of desperate victors at the expense of the vanquished. They only succeeded in creating new contexts to aggravate international rivalries and provoke domestic revolutions that wracked the world during what turned out to be not the peace sufficient to end all wars, but merely a volatile twenty-year truce before a culminating holocaust. The Second World War in turn generated seismic alterations in world power relationships that are still playing out generations after the defeat of Tojo, Hitler, and Mussolini. The rise to global prominence of the United States and the Soviet Union in the postwar nuclear age coupled with the dissolution of old colonial empires tinged everyday life with a collective sense of insecurity and uncertainty. Ironically, Americans, who enjoyed greater international influence, political stability, and economic prosperity than at any other time in history, also exhibited perhaps the greatest angst about their future. For all its power and affluence, postwar America faced tomorrow with more than a little trepidation.

Henrietta Mears believed passionately that she had the answers America and the world needed during these decades of massive change, and those answers found their source in an evangelical expression of the Christian faith. The tangible results of her labors during the 1930s clearly demonstrated the appeal of her tempered fundamentalism, for her accomplishments at First Baptist in Minneapolis were far surpassed during her initial ten years in Hollywood. Wheaton College's offer of a professorship in Christian education recognized the significance of her work with youth even though she had no formal training in theology or Christian education and no advanced degree in any subject. The quarter century following Buswell's offer proved to be the most perilous of times, but also the most fruitful years for the prolific ministry of "Teacher," as Mears was now affectionately known. For it was in the midst of those unstable decades that a 1946–1947 sabbatical abroad radically refined her vision for a culturally engaged, theologically conservative Christian faith and resulted in the extension of her influence to encompass the world.

MEARS RELISHED ADVENTURE IN ALL ITS MANY GUISES, and international travel proved to be one of its most frequent manifestations. The 1927 trip to Europe only whetted an appetite she continued to feed into her seventieth year. That initial excursion took her to exotic locations primarily for sightseeing, but by her 1935 world tour Mears's periodic trips served the additional purpose of connecting with and speaking to missionaries (many of them sent out from her College Department) and others supported by the expanding interdenominational network of evangelicals. But of her dozen journeys outside the United States, none matched the impact or the effect of the trip she took with her sister Margaret that began in February 1946.[1]

From Mexico the sisters made their way through Central and South America, arriving in Rio de Janeiro on the Fourth of July. Much as she had done in diaries of her earlier travels, Mears exhibited a keen if somewhat biased awareness of the history and culture of the places she visited. But unlike other journeys, underscoring her narrative was a palpable sense of danger that became apparent after their arrival in Buenos Aires in late May 1946, just as Juan Perón took office. From that point on, Mears craved the latest news and editorialized repeatedly about the impact of international developments on the faith.[2] Often interspersed with observations on the relative vigor of Christianity in the locations she visited were observations about her fellow travelers. She and Margaret had been able to book passage from Buenos Aires to Rio on the French passenger liner *Formosa* on its way to France for the first time since the cessation of hostilities. They met refugees, some of whom had lost everything and yet eagerly anticipated their return home. After witnessing violent Brazilian student demonstrations in late August, Mears wrote, "I can now imagine how folks in Europe felt when they saw their businesses devastated."[3]

She hoped to visit South Africa or Europe after leaving Rio, but neither transportation to nor permission for either destination in 1946 was assured because their passports had only been issued for travel in the Western Hemisphere.[4] By September any chance of going to South Africa faded. But in reading the latest news from Europe Mears discovered that some American civilians (she mentioned syndicated columnist Drew Pearson and former First Lady Eleanor Roosevelt in particular) had been cleared to visit European destinations. After some persistent wrangling with US diplomats, the Mears sisters also received clearance to travel to France. They hurried to the French Line shipping office and discovered that two cancellations left room for them on the *Desiradi* leaving October 26. Now confident that they were going to Europe Mears acknowledged, "I had prayed so definitely that the door would be closed if it was not the Lord's will. Now it seemed that everything was opening up. . . . We feel very thankful for this open door. What an experience it will be to visit Europe." Ultimately the determined Mears sisters were granted permission to travel throughout the continent.[5]

During their voyage across the Atlantic they again met many displaced persons returning home after the war. One young French Jewish woman who lost her entire family in the Holocaust took meals with the Mears sisters. On November 13 Mears wrote, "all the tragedy of her life became real again" because her murdered parents had married on that date. Though an opponent of gambling in any form, Mears confessed she was "almost glad when she made 1,200 francs on the horse race" as it might temporarily relieve some of her grief.

On November 17, 1946, Henrietta and Margaret Mears arrived in Le Havre, among the first American civilians to be allowed access to Europe after Germany's surrender and six weeks before President Truman officially proclaimed the end of the war on December 31. They spent the next three months traveling from one city to another, Henrietta often writing in her travel journal of the physical and emotional desolation she observed. Le Havre, Paris, Brussels, Antwerp, Amsterdam, The Hague, Rotterdam, Marseilles, Rome, Naples, Brindisi, Athens, Florence, Milan, London—at each place she recounted the misery war visited upon the city and her sorrow at the tragedy replayed over and over again at nearly every stop along the way. As the trip continued, they met more European Jews who had lost their entire families, accentuating the anguish the sisters internalized during their solemn pilgrimage.

They booked passage on the *Queen Elizabeth*, arriving back in the United States on February 17, 1947—a year to the day they left Los Angeles. Even had they not been able to visit Europe, Henrietta would still have returned to Hollywood profoundly affected by what she had seen. After all, she had called on former Mexican President Lázaro Cárdenas and his wife, witnessed the inauguration of Juan Perón, read with apprehension about the atomic bomb test on Bikini Atoll, heard General Eisenhower speak, watched proceedings of the Nuremberg trials, experienced the violent Fifty Percent Club riots in Rio, written a personal note to fellow hotel guest former President Herbert Hoover, challenged the acting US ambassador to Brazil, observed the agitation over former Vice President Henry Wallace's foreign policy speech regarding the USSR, and expressed relief at the resolution of the US seamen's strike. But the final three months spent in war-ravaged Europe powerfully moved her and transformed the remainder of her ministry into the most productive years of her life. The sense of divine purpose that had motivated her work to this point became even more pronounced. The prophetic words of Mordecai to Esther (Esther 4:14) took on added meaning for Mears. She wrote, "I was overcome with a sense of destiny, of crisis, of God speaking to me. All of my ministry was now in a different light. 'If I perish, I perish!' But as I returned from Europe, I knew that God had called me into the kingdom for the hour."[6]

She resumed her life in Hollywood with a renewed sense of urgency but no clear direction about the future beyond her continuing responsibilities at First Presbyterian. Mears spoke often and ardently about what she had seen in Europe and the necessity for Christians to make a difference in a world choked with despair. But during the first few months after her return she lived "on the tiptoe of expectancy" without knowing exactly what to expect.[7] As spring gave way to summer, mounting international tensions drove Mears and her comrades to their knees in prayer seeking clearer direction about the role they should play on the world stage.

And it was the world that consumed Mears. Although the war years laid bare underlying sources of unrest in Southern California, her preoccupation with overseas affairs drew her attention away from matters of consequence much closer to home. The quest for wartime factory employment had fueled a massive migration of African Americans to the region much as the Bracero program did for Mexican agricultural workers. When combined with the incarceration of Japanese immigrants and Japanese Americans all along the West

Coast and the restrictions placed on those of Italian ancestry in Los Angeles and other California coastal cities, prevailing white social conventions sparked escalating racial animosity. But the LA riots that erupted in the wake of the legally flawed Sleepy Lagoon murder trial of seventeen Mexican American young men failed to elicit the same response from Mears as did her interactions with the distraught European Jews she met or her fascination with the proceedings of the Nuremberg trials of Nazi racists. She may have exhibited a compartmentalized social consciousness in 1947, but she did have one. And it would be substantially expanded by a series of events that began with a conference at her retreat center high in the San Bernardino Mountains.

In late June, Gospel Light held a teacher training conference at Forest Home with Mears as featured speaker. On Tuesday evening, June 24, she gave an impassioned presentation recounting her European experiences and linking the tragedies of World War II to a much longer historical trajectory that had severely eroded robust allegiance to the Christian faith. "Atheism and moral expedience had been at work for centuries before Hitler's rise to power," she said, and the same debilitating forces could be found in America itself. She warned that "there must be a Christian answer to the growing menace of communism." The answer, she declared, was evangelism and discipleship: "We are to take the gospel to the ends of the earth. . . . And we must present the full doctrine of Christian truth. God is looking for men and women of total commitment." She spoke frankly about the consequences of such total commitment by reminding the audience of those wartime volunteers known as expendables who gave their lives in service to a greater cause. Mears drove home the unmistakable parallel: "We must be expendables for Christ." Then she issued a solemn warning: "If we fail God's call to us, we will be held responsible."[8]

At the conclusion of her call to arms, a number of participants—women as well as men—asked Mears if they could meet with her for a time of prayer in the Biltmore, her personal cabin on the conference grounds.[9] Among those who gathered were recent convert Bill Bright; Mears's assistant Jack Franck; College Department President Louis Evans Jr.; and Richard Halverson, assistant minister at First Presbyterian. Several others including Bill Dunlap joined the prayer circle as the evening wore on. As Halverson later commented, "Although we were not soliciting any special work of the Spirit that evening, He seemed to meet us in special power, and the meeting turned into an unusual period of blessing and spontaneous planning."[10] Bright remembered that "we were overwhelmed by the presence of God. It was one of those things I had never experienced and I didn't know what to do. I just got on my knees and began to praise the Lord."[11] Evans asked the critical question, "What could happen if we, the [members of the] College Department, really gave our lives to Christ?"[12]

The response to Mears's call for radical discipleship soon began to manifest itself in concrete ways. For years, college-age students had been attending a Labor Day weekend retreat at Forest Home. In light of Mears's charge to young people that evening, however, it was decided that, in order to equip them to live a completely surrendered life and to raise up leaders commissioned to evangelize the world, the conference should be extended to eight days and a much broader potential constituency contacted. Renamed the College Briefing Conference to reflect the militant faith and uncompromising commitment Mears advocated, deputation teams of young people from the College Department fanned out across the region after the teacher training conference, speaking at churches to get the word out about the late summer gathering by bearing witness to the movement of the Spirit at Forest Home on June 24. Hundreds of telephone calls were made and thousands of fliers produced. Mears sent innumerable letters encouraging attendance.

Her mid-August letter to "Don," with an enclosed brochure about the meeting to come, underscored the aura of bold anticipation surrounding the first College Briefing Conference. After beginning her letter emphatically ("I need you and God needs you!") she unpacked the crisis motif triggered by her trip, concluding the first paragraph with a vote of confidence in his future: "I believe, Don, that you are a young man of destiny, for who knows but that 'you have come into the kingdom for just such a time as this.' I believe God has made no mistakes and that He has a plan for you in this hour." She called him to join her as an expendable for Christ because "there is a tremendous work to be done among college men and women today and how can I do it alone?" Mears then listed some of her protégés who exemplified what could be done by a committed person, declaring, "We need men who will put God first!" She continued her personal appeal to him by reiterating how important he was to the greater Christian cause. After her exhortation for his help with the work at First Presbyterian, Mears invited his participation in the College Briefing Conference, assuring him that there would be a "galaxy of stars for leaders" and reminding him how much she was counting on him.[13]

The spirit of urgency cascading from the June conference at Forest Home contributed to a revival among young people on the West Coast in tandem with what was occurring in places like New York with radio evangelist Jack Wyrtzen's Madison Square Garden youth meetings and in Chicago with Torrey Johnson's Youth for Christ rallies. A week after the prayer meeting in Mears's cabin, for example, she and five others traveled north to Mount Hermon as a deputation team to share with the leaders of a high school conference about what had occurred at Forest Home. Many of those in the audience who had been deeply influenced by Mears and were serving as parish ministers—people such as Bob Ferguson, Homer Goddard, Robert Munger, and Bill Dunlap—persuaded the group to speak to the entire gathering. Conference center director Cyrus Nelson agreed. That evening, after Mears and her colleagues had spoken to nearly a thousand students, hundreds of them came forward offering themselves as expendables.[14]

When the first College Briefing Conference began in late August 1947, six hundred students from eighty-seven colleges and universities from nearly every part of the country converged on Forest Home for a week of inspiration and training to impact the world for Christ. Publicity for the conference had pulled no punches about the theme of the week emphasizing the crises facing the world and also the crucial role of young people in confronting those crises:

> The tragedy of our times is that we live in a militantly pagan world. Social, economic, political, and spiritual chaos has overwhelmed world leaders, and the urgency of the hour has brought God's people to their knees in one last plea. God, in His tender mercy and loving kindness, has granted a revival to stave off what many of our leading statesmen have termed "the complete annihilation of civilization."[15]

Several of those in attendance had banded together soon after the June prayer meeting in Mears's cabin to pursue a common objective. With the College Briefing Conference already in the planning stage,[16] Mears, Richard Halverson, Bill Bright, Jack Franck, and Louis Evans Jr. crafted specific guidelines expressing their desire to live as expendables and to work toward the mobilization of college and university students for the cause of Christ. This Fellowship of the Burning Heart took as its emblem Protestant reformer John Calvin's depiction of a hand offering a flaming heart as a sign of consecrated service to God. The inscription surrounding the image, "My heart I give thee, Lord, eagerly and sincerely," embodied the pledge the members made to each other and to God. College-age young people "who had offered up their hearts as a sacrifice to the Lord Jesus Christ in behalf of a needy world" could be counted as members of the fellowship. Those who wished to be identified with the fellowship committed themselves to four basic principles of surrendered Christian living: (1) since such discipleship is "sustained solely by God alone through the Holy Spirit," members promised "through prayer, Bible study, and devotional reading to give God no less than one continuous hour per day" to develop a disciplined devotional life; (2) because discipleship begins with Christian character, participants also committed to holy living through self-denial and self-discipline; (3) since discipleship "exercises itself principally in the winning of the lost to Christ," fellowship adherents pledged to take every chance to share the gospel with others seeking to win at least one person to Christ every year; and (4) because discipleship demands "absolute consecration to Christ," members vowed to offer their lives as "living sacrifices" so that they might be "expendable for Christ."[17]

The founding document of the fellowship makes clear that its ecumenical purpose was not to siphon young people from local churches but to "provide a new motivation for Christian youth which would make them more effective in their own churches." Members bound themselves "to other Christian youth who want to live and witness and work for the evangelizing of the whole world." The fellowship developed a structure that ensured continuity, accountability, and decentralized leadership. Founding fellowship members believed that "as God leads other young people into this experience of complete discipleship, the Fellowship will move on. As it moves it will flame for Christ until the world is set on fire by a new work of the Spirit of God." Just as the original signatories surmised, others soon joined the five as deputation teams dispersed to share what had happened at Forest Home in June and what subsequently occurred at the 1947 College Briefing Conference.[18]

As the College Briefing Conference began, Mears and other leaders—such as Louis Evans Sr., David Cowie, and Robert Munger, among others—wanted to leave the program open to the wisdom of the group with regard to who would speak and when. Mears headed the subcommittee that would make that decision on an hour-to-hour basis. From the introductory four-hour meeting at Victory Circle, atheists, agnostics, lapsed Christians, and the already committed conversed in an open environment that affirmed honesty and introspection. To stimulate students to consider the entire planet their sphere of ministry, Mears placed a large world map in the main meeting hall and pressed conferees to place their names where they felt called to serve. The map remained up during the entire conference. On the last evening she challenged students one final time, "Young men, young women, there is no magic in small dreams. Go to the map and place a large "X" where you propose to invest your life for Jesus Christ."[19] Listening to Mears in the assembly hall were two men who would transform her vision of a world renewed by committed evangelical Christians into a reality she had no way of imagining on that warm summer evening.

ORIGINALLY FROM THE MIDWEST, Walter James specialized in working with disadvantaged youth. He moved to Hollywood and headed the YMCA's community work with area gangs from 1940 to 1946. Less than three weeks before Mears left on the trip that would eventually take her to Europe, First Presbyterian hired James as assistant minister of weekday activities. He "was there to put people to work for God, to help them find and be Christ's answers to pain and alienation."[20] One of the leaders of this first College Briefing Conference, James worked with Louis Evans Jr. and heard Mears and others develop the theme of expendables for Christ throughout the conference. He watched on the final evening as students rose in response to Mears's challenge to locate their place of intended service on the map. James noticed a young man sitting quietly in the back listening closely to each person who spoke. He resolved to greet the stranger, but when the opportunity arose, the man had disappeared into the night.

That young man, Ralph Hamburger, was a war refugee from the Netherlands and a member of the Dutch Reformed Church. Of partial Jewish heritage, Hamburger had been involved in the Dutch underground during the war and helped Jews and others survive and ultimately escape Nazi-occupied Holland. Haunted by his experiences with the underground and the Nazi atrocities that drove the resistance, Hamburger could not exorcise the ghosts nor rid himself of his hatred for the Germans, who had nearly killed his father and murdered his friends and fellow citizens. The end of the war brought no relief for him. Hamburger bounced from one job to another, never finding his place in a shattered Europe. Dissatisfied with his prospects, he explored the possibility of emigrating to the United States. Ultimately an uncle in Beverly Hills agreed to sponsor him—a necessity for refugees seeking asylum. He arrived in Southern California in February 1947, a week to the day after Mears returned to Hollywood.[21] Coming from a Reformed background and having a strong interest in music, Hamburger gravitated to the First Presbyterian Church of Hollywood because of its similarity to his Dutch Reformed heritage and its comprehensive music program. There he

> saw all these fantastic young people. They were attractive. They were full of joy. I came out of trauma and destruction. And these young people, they were sure who God was and they talked with Him. . . . To me this was a new experience . . . but I saw the genuineness of them. And so I said, "this is the way to go." . . . So I went to everything that went on at Hollywood Presbyterian Church. And I went to the College Department, of course, also.[22]

Preparations for the first College Briefing Conference were well underway by late June 1947. As the conference drew near, Mears let her College Department know that the gravity of the world situation meant "only people who wanted to do business with the Lord" were invited. Scrupulous by nature and somewhat skeptical by experience, Hamburger wrote a letter informing Mears that he would very much like to attend the conference but he was not at all sure that he could meet that criterion. She honored his sincerity and interest, and so still unsure about his own spiritual moorings Hamburger joined the collegians at Forest Home. At the evening dedication services Hamburger listened to students testify about their faith, but he struggled with what he perceived to be a lack of sincerity on the part of some. He had known Richard Halverson from the Hollywood church and approached him afterward with his observation. When Halverson affirmed that Hamburger's perception matched his own, his candor touched the young refugee.[23] He became Hamburger's spiritual mentor as he struggled to find peace and purpose. Following the College Briefing Conference, Hamburger continued to attend College Department functions. In a letter he wrote to Mears shortly after the conference, Hamburger vacillated between tremendous gratitude for his developing

Christian faith and recognition of his own propensity to fall short of his expectations, concluding, "I thought I had to tell this to you, who planted the seeds in my heart."[24] For nearly two years, under Mears's teaching and Halverson's counsel, Hamburger wrestled with his demons. In due course during the summer of 1949 God met him in a powerful way, easing his hatred of Germans and providing him an overwhelming sense of purpose. Finally at peace, Hamburger now had the foundation upon which he could rebuild his life:[25] "Christ is teaching me that he can deal with my hate. He is draining it out, healing the wounds, showing me the meaning of unconditional love."[26]

By the time Hamburger had this cleansing encounter, both Halverson and James had been Mears's associates at the Hollywood church for some time and had watched the deputation programs flourish. Prior to his 1949 spiritual awakening Hamburger had not participated in any of them, at least partially because he remained something of a spiritual searcher during that period. After that liberating event, however, he found his true vocation:

> I saw all these young people [at First Presbyterian] who had an experience of Christ and I knew that my friends and fellows back in Holland . . . they were depressed, the economy was down, they had nothing to do. And I said "We've got to get this message over there." And so then we began with a very small group of young people to pray, Miss Mears church prayer [group].[27]

Guided by James, five[28] summer prayer partners from Mears's College Department grew to two dozen by the fall of 1949, and Hamburger's focus sharpened; he wanted to "export" Christian young people from the College Department to Europe. As Halverson wrote later, "Ralph became a conscience for many of us [at First Presbyterian]."[29] Hamburger furnished the vision, Mears's collegians supplied the volunteers, and James provided formal leadership to what would be called First Presbyterian's World Deputation Program. The objective was to introduce Christ to those who suffered, but merely conducting evangelistic meetings without any vested interest beyond saving souls would not be welcomed in a Europe still prostrate from the war. Corrie Ten Boom, who had lived through the barbaric brutality of Nazi concentration camps, spoke to the group and emphasized the importance of solidarity with those they hoped to evangelize. She said: "To make a vital witness to the power of your faith, you must identify with the pain and suffering of the people, work alongside them, eat what they eat, sleep where they sleep. And if you do it well enough and long enough, they may hear what you have to say. You must earn the right to be heard."[30]

The first team of collegians trained for nearly a year. They met every Tuesday evening for three-hour sessions consisting of Bible study, linguistic and cultural study, and special lectures. On Sundays they arrived at church before 7:00 a.m. for what was termed a "starvation breakfast" to acquaint themselves with the nutritional privation faced daily by those they hoped to serve. Then they spent two hours of prayer on their knees before the College Department Sunday school session. They also formed domestic deputation teams that fanned out among marginalized groups in the greater Los Angeles community. In the Watts neighborhood of South Central LA, Cleland House in the East LA barrio, and Hicks Camp, a shantytown along the Rio Hondo Wash, deputees tutored students, developed recreation programs, and taught Bible classes. In befriending dispossessed Americans they put into practice what they were learning so that they could be most effectively prepared to serve destitute Europeans.[31]

In the summer of 1950 James and ten College Department members who raised their own support comprised the first World Deputation team sent out from the Hollywood church. Six served in German work camps, five in French work camps.[32] During the first six years of the summer program, sixty-two young people pursued eighty-one different assignments. By 1956 the work had expanded to include Austria, France, Germany, Greece, Italy, the Netherlands, French Cameroun, Japan, and Korea. Mears's long-running domestic deputation program also broadened under James's influence to send volunteers to Alaska, Pacific Coast migrant workers' camps, and to the marginalized immigrant populations of New York and Los Angeles. The World Deputation program at the First Presbyterian Church of Hollywood gained such notoriety that the director of the Presbyterian Board of Foreign Missions told Hamburger that involving young people in short-term overseas mission work is "of inestimable value. Please continue this."[33] English Bible scholar, author, translator, and clergyman J. B. Phillips's 1954 visit to the United States was prompted by his interactions with members of the work camp and rehabilitation center deputation team members.[34] Some believed that the ongoing ministry with those in East Germany through the 1980s saved the German Democratic Republic from a bloody revolution as the Soviet bloc dissolved.[35]

Although Mears was never directly involved in the World Deputation program, her imprint on it is unmistakable. From the emphasis on Bible study, prayer, and service to the training sessions, from the challenge to live as expendables for Christ to the very students who went, one only needs an awareness of the precedents Mears established in her ministry long before 1950 to recognize her pervasive influence. Even the ecumenical nature of the deputies' placements demonstrated continuity with Mears's longtime advocacy for interdenominational cooperation. She made a special point to call on Berlin pastor Alfred Schröder of the Protestant Evangelical Church, a major figure in the ongoing deputation work, during her European trip in 1956. Schröder had been associated with the well-known anti-Nazi Martin Niemöller of the Confessing German Church before the war and had since spearheaded a multipronged ministry to youth in both East and West Berlin. The following year she promoted his three-week visit to First Presbyterian sponsored by the College Department. He was the featured speaker at the spring college conference at Forest Home and Mears relinquished the podium to him back at the church so her students could hear more from him.[36] As Hamburger, who became the administrative secretary of First Presbyterian's World Deputation program, remarked at one point, "Henrietta Mears was really never involved centrally in this [the World Deputation program], which does not mean at all that her influence did not reach into that."[37] The same could be said about how her influence reached into his own life and through his, to hundreds of others around the world.

If the formidable contributions Mears made to the NAE and its associated organizations elevated her national reputation, the global consequences of her June 24, 1947, discourse at Forest Home amplified her significance even further, for she came fully into her own as one of the most revered figures among theological conservatives by the late 1940s. The fact that she taught the Bible as the authoritative Word of God endeared her to the rising neoevangelical movement and took her across the country on speaking engagements at churches and conferences representing many different denominations. Notwithstanding her immense popularity, however, Mears still operated under the constraints of a rigidly constructed social framework that reinforced limitations on female leadership among the new conservatives. But the landmark successes she brought to the evangelical cause even before the end of the war exposed weaknesses in that framework. It illustrated the fact that not all evangelical believers were cut from the same cloth regarding the role of females. Her part in complicating evangelical perspectives on women in ministry most clearly surfaced in Fuller Theological Seminary's search for a professor of Christian education.[38]

In 1946 well-known radio preacher Charles Fuller approached Harold John Ockenga, pastor of Boston's Park Street Church, about the possibility of his involvement in the creation of an evangelical, interdenominational graduate theological academy in Southern California named in his father's honor. Intrigued by Fuller's vision for the seminary, Ockenga agreed to assume the title of president in absentia. Other leading evangelicals including Wilbur Smith of Moody Bible Institute, Carl F. H. Henry and Harold Lindsell of Northern Baptist Seminary, and Everett Harrison of Dallas Theological Seminary joined him in the venture. Fuller Theological Seminary, which had aspirations of becoming a Princeton on the West Coast, opened for its first classes in the fall of 1947.[39]

Gendered assumptions of the era took hold by default as faculty and administrators alike presumed that women would assist their student-husbands and care for their children rather than seek admission to the seminary. Yet within two years of its founding, Fuller moved from not allowing women access to classes to permitting academically qualified wives of matriculating students to take courses for credit, then extending the offer to enable other women to enroll. Under sustained pressure from Helen Dunsmoor Clark to grant females access to bona fide graduate programs, the faculty approved the creation of the Bachelor of Sacred Theology degree for women in September 1950.[40] They believed that the program would be of practical value to those who might find positions as professors or directors of Christian education while holding the line against the ordination of women, which was largely opposed by American Protestants at the time. The creation of the BST degree resolved one problem but created another. How could the young seminary, already growing faster than anyone could have foreseen, prepare itself adequately for the anticipated increased participation of female students?[41]

In an early December letter to seminary dean Harold Lindsell, President Ockenga surveyed the strengths and weaknesses of the faculty, concluding that "the greatest need which we have in the curriculum of Fuller Theological Seminary is in the practical theological department. We must reinforce this by adding a professor in Christian education." Ockenga urged the faculty to endorse his perception of the seminary's preeminent need and then turned to a discussion of the person who would best fit the bill. He made his assumptions about the faculty and his own choice for the position quite clear:

> Now I presume that the faculty will want nothing but men teaching on its staff. However, I am perfectly sure that the greatest Christian education leader in America today is Miss Henrietta Mears, and I believe we could persuade her to come to our staff if the faculty desire to have her. To me it would be a stroke of genius to get her on that faculty. She has achieved in the Sunday School realm, she has achieved in Christian education, she is the outstanding leader of college young people in a church program, she is the publisher of Sunday School literature, she is in demand all over the country as a speaker on both Sunday School and young people's topics.[42]

The faculty agreed on the need for a faculty position in Christian education to meet the needs of the new BST students. They also agreed that the position "by way of exception" could be held by a woman since female students would need a faculty advisor. When the prospect of calling Henrietta Mears to the professorship came up, faculty members responded in a generally favorable manner, although Lindsell was charged with looking into her academic pedigree before the faculty could make any definite recommendation. The only other name advanced by the faculty was Rebecca Price—the same person Buswell hired when Mears declined his offer of the first faculty position in Christian education at Wheaton College in 1936. In a letter to Ockenga apprising him of their deliberations on this issue, Lindsell mentioned that both he and Henry knew Price and that "should nothing develop in the direction of Dr. Mears we are convinced that perhaps Dr. Price may be the woman we would want."[43] At this point Lindsell, Ockenga, and perhaps Henry favored Mears over Price with the only possible impediment being her academic credentials. The fact that the Fuller leadership settled on two women as the top candidates for the new full-time position in Christian education highlights the negotiable boundaries between males and females among West Coast evangelicals at Fuller—a scant three years after opening its doors and only two years since deciding to admit females.

Once the faculty discovered that Mears had earned only a bachelor's degree and received an honorary doctorate in humane letters from fundamentalist Bob Jones University in 1949, the discussion of her candidacy turned to other issues. Members raised questions vis-à-vis her ability to function in a graduate academic environment as well as her partiality for dispensationalism. Given these concerns, faculty members recommended that Ockenga check on Price's academic qualifications and theological perspectives before further considering a Mears appointment.[44]

The crux of the matter, however, emerged when several faculty members expressed a desire to separate her beliefs from "whether or not her personality . . . would make it possible for her to fit into our situation without difficulty." While, to a person, the all-male seminary faculty applauded Mears's outstanding contributions to Christian education and recognized the "incalculable benefit to us among her wide field of acquaintances," they remained skeptical enough of her candidacy that they continued looking carefully at Price. Those who knew the latter candidate "felt that in terms of faculty relationships her personality is such that she would be quiet and submissive and would fit into the picture beautifully." Such was not the case with the outspoken and forceful Mears. In acquainting Ockenga with the matter Lindsell added his own assessment writing that "it was my reaction that the faculty was enthusiastic about the work of Doctor Mears, although, for reasons more intangible than tangible, the men hesitated to give a positive verdict in favor of her until we had checked over the case of Doctor Price."[45] For his part, Ockenga continued to support the Mears candidacy, writing to her in late December, "I still have a cherished plan in my heart that you might some day be actively identified with Fuller Theological Seminary."[46]

Early in January 1951 Ockenga made arrangements to meet Price in New York to follow up on the faculty's recommendation. When the faculty met on January 10 it had been discovered that Mears would be traveling in Europe for the next two or three months, making her candidacy somewhat problematic because of the time constraints within which the faculty operated. Her absence and Price's superior academic credentials impelled the faculty to move that the seminary offer Price the position.[47] In a letter to the president relating the sentiments of the faculty, Lindsell went off the record to give Ockenga his personal take on the debate over Mears vs. Price. While not discounting the latter's teaching experience or academic qualifications, Lindsell believed that there was more to the recommendation for Price over Mears than classroom expertise and advanced degrees. He wrote:

> It is my reaction that in general the faculty members exhibited a lively fear that an invitation extended to Dr. Mears might result in the subjugation of the faculty to her own personality and persuasion. I gather that they felt the maleness of our faculty would be protected far more by the addition of Dr. Price.[48]

With no extenuating circumstance prohibiting the invitation, Fuller tendered the position to Price—which she turned down in late winter. After receiving the news of her decision at their meeting of March 2, the faculty voted unanimously to extend the offer to Mears, with the caveat that she be informed Fuller did not carry a strong commitment to dispensationalism. It must have been sometime after faculty approval of her appointment on March 2 that Ockenga spoke about the position directly with Mears, who of course was completely unaware that Price had declined it. Shortly after their conversation on March 5, Ockenga wrote to her in Paris confirming that the "project of which we talked when I was in Boston, namely, your acceptance of the chair of Christian Education at Fuller Theological Seminary, has now come to the point of decision." He proposed an annual salary of $8,500—more than $83,000 in 2019 dollars. March passed into April without word from Mears, who continued her sojourn overseas.[49]

She finally replied to Ockenga on April 4 to verify her interest in the position but also to seek clarification on important issues that Ockenga hoped to discuss with Cyrus Nelson at the annual convention of the National Association of Evangelicals to be held in Chicago later that month. Mears expressed particular concern about the timing of her appointment, the nature of her future connection to Forest Home and Gospel Light, the status of her future relationship with the First Presbyterian Church of Hollywood, and the growth potential of the Christian Education Department.[50]

Before corresponding with Mears, Ockenga conferred with Lindsell on the issues he had discussed with Nelson in Chicago. One of her concerns turned on the growth of the Christian Education Department and the potential for its massive expansion if she accepted the offer. He asked Lindsell:

> Do you think our men would be disposed to letting this Christian Education Department under Miss Mears really grow to some proportions so that we would not limit our student body necessarily to two hundred? One thing that concerns her is that the crowds usually follow her and from experience I know that is true. Moreover there is no really vital Christian Education Department anywhere providing the merit necessary in our evangelical position. I think Miss Mears might have such a tremendous following that it may be necessary to provide additional facilities and if necessary even give her certain assistants if the department warranted it.

Ockenga encouraged Lindsell to check with the faculty on the topic and then report back to him so that he would have "some idea of what to do." The potential financial windfall Mears could bring with her was also not lost on the president. He noted that "if we had Miss Mears, we would also have a great number of financial leaders in the West who would be interested in the school and perhaps in her department." Ockenga reaffirmed his trust in Mears's leadership, academic ability, and motivation: "I have no fears of her running away with the school, so if anybody brings up such an idea, please dismiss it. She is willing now if God calls her to devote herself a great deal to writing and publication and to teaching."[51]

By mid-April Lindsell had solicited faculty input. He agreed substantially with the view that Mears's coming to Fuller might very well result in significant growth of the student population, which in turn could necessitate additional help. Faculty members supported this eventuality. Once he secured faculty buy-in, Lindsell telephoned Mears and invited her to campus so that he could share prospective building plans "and acquaint her with the fact that additional space can be obtained at any time, should enrollment require it." The dean also wanted to make it clear that "she would not be hindered in the development of a Christian Education program" at Fuller. After her visit on April 18, 1951, Lindsell believed that, given her enthusiasm for the possibilities open to her at Fuller, she would accept the position. He even invited her to speak to a class in May, which she accepted. Before the day ended Lindsell wrote to Ockenga providing his positive assessment of Mears's visit. After receiving Lindsell's letter, Ockenga echoed his dean's optimism.[52]

Once fully cognizant of all aspects of the Mears candidacy, Ockenga composed a three-page letter on April 20 to provide the details she needed to make an informed decision and to induce her to join the Fuller faculty. Ockenga first expressed his delight at her interest in the position and confirmed that her desire to begin teaching at Fuller in September squared perfectly with Fuller's need and his wishes. He then communicated his conviction that perhaps God was guiding her to join his faculty; he wrote that "everyone at Fuller from Dr. Fuller himself to all the members of the faculty" wanted her to join them at the seminary. In retrospect, however, his use of a qualifying phrase indicating that all were "fairly sold on your coming to Fuller if God leads you that way" might have been somewhat off-putting to a woman used to being praised by all manner of devotees. Ockenga then assured Mears that her involvement with Forest Home, her work at Gospel Light, and her speaking schedule could proceed without interruption. He made a special point of letting her know that the seminary had recently rescinded its policy of requisitioning the honoraria of its professors from outside speaking engagements. Because of Presbyterian policy, however, she would have to sever her connection to First Presbyterian, which he acknowledged would be "a great wrench" for her.

He tempered his enthusiasm for further growth of the student population under her influence by noting that the present faculty could only accommodate two hundred students—a threshold the seminary rapidly approached. A larger enrollment would necessitate the hiring of new faculty members that budgetary priorities would not immediately allow as the short-term objective had to be on bricks and mortar. Nonetheless, he assured Mears that "a priori we have no objections whatsoever to numbers in the Department of Christian Education. The only difficulty would arise in reference to our financial ability to handle such a program. God sending the finances, we certainly would be willing to have it expand."

The final topic Ockenga addressed related to how well Mears's own philosophy of teaching would comport with the objectives of the seminary. Given her numerous successes over nearly three decades in an assortment of contexts with all age groups, he believed that she could serve students most effectively by emphasizing the practical application of Christian education precepts while leaving the theoretical niceties to others. Ockenga's affirmation of her perspective on the "doing" of Christian education must have given her a strong sense of satisfaction. He concluded his letter with a prayer for God's guidance in her decision-making process and offered to answer any questions she might still entertain about the position.[53]

It must have been quite a shock to a faculty that believed its members had made many a concession on principle (and prejudice) to entice Mears from Hollywood to Pasadena, when she decided against joining them at Fuller. Her response to Ockenga's offer bore a striking parallel to the one she gave President Buswell in early 1936 when she turned down the Wheaton position. Although she would have had a major role in the training of hundreds of committed believers at Wheaton or at Fuller, Mears's vocational center remained the training of lay and professional church leaders and the cultivation of biblical literacy in parish ministry. As she told one of her closest associates a few years later, "the privilege and honor of teaching the Word of God to college men and women more than equaled being a professor at Harvard or UCLA or anyplace else."[54] Just past her sixty-first birthday in the spring of 1951, Mears sensed that work remained for her to do at First Presbyterian. Events over the next twelve years proved her right. The 1950s saw not only the continued expansion of her ministry at First Presbyterian, by the dawn of a new decade her global influence epitomized for evangelicals the grand possibilities for a time such as this.

Chapter Eight

Teacher and "the Industry"

By the time the Mears sisters moved to Southern California, Hollywood had already established itself as the center of the booming entertainment industry. Although the accouterments of celebrity culture were already affecting the population, manners and mores grounded in a deep strain of Protestant theological conservatism flourished alongside the seductive allure of all things Hollywood. Aimee Semple McPherson's theatrical style certainly played at spectacle, but other, more traditional institutions parsed the Christian message in a rather less sensational manner. Undoubtedly some members of First Presbyterian shared the sentiments of landlords whose signs indicating "No Dogs or Actors Allowed" cluttered the area and looked with jaundiced eye at the metamorphosis of the sleepy village into the unabashed capital of glitz and glitter. After all, the intersection of Gower Street and Sunset Boulevard just four blocks south of the church featured three different studio complexes by 1927. "Gower Gulch" attained further distinction as the spot where would-be cowboy actors congregated, anxiously awaiting casting calls.[1]

The strides toward respectability taken by the film industry during World War I quickly dissipated in the early 1920s. The Roscoe "Fatty" Arbuckle-Virginia Rappe case was only the most lurid scandal of the era. Less than acceptable behavior off-camera coupled with Hollywood's output of post-war films that flouted social norms regarding sexuality, divorce, smoking, and drinking (during Prohibition) "provoked outrage from women's clubs, educators, clergymen, literary societies, newspapers, magazines and other sources."[2] In an attempt to repair the damage, the Motion Picture Producers and Distributors of America hired Presbyterian elder Will Hays to surveil the film industry from the inside. Hays pledged to promote decent entertainment and persuaded the studios to include morality clauses in contracts that allowed them to dismiss those not in compliance. But the jury would remain out as to whether he succeeded in sanitizing an industry that was both loved and reviled.

As film, radio, records, and later television, exerted a progressively broader impact, Mears carried a deep concern for those in the industry. From her earliest days in the Southland she hoped to craft a sustainable Christian witness to the Hollywood set. Because she viewed the entire world as needing salvation, she thought no part of it unredeemable.[3] While more than a few of her coreligionists looked with disgust at Hollywood and all it stood for by the late 1920s, Mears wrote that "my heart ached for this place so far removed from any influence of righteousness or God." She did not shrink from the hope that Christianity could pervade mass media culture and wanted to be of service to those in the industry who sought to live out their Christian convictions as well as to those who held no religious faith. As one of her associates said, "She was a friend of show business people. Anyone who had a speck of responsiveness to the Lord, she was in their corner cheering. . . . She did not have a whit of judgmentalism in her."[4]

Mears could not help but notice that although plenty of churches dotted the film capital, "none of them seemed to reach the gifted and successful actors that acted upon its screens and played such a part in effecting [*sic*] the thinking of the world." No less a figure than Billy Sunday, who held a series of meetings at the First Presbyterian Church, confided that Hollywood "was the hardest city in the world to reach and lift broken hearts." Rather than discourage her, the apparent difficulty of bearing an effective Christian witness to those in the industry challenged Mears to work intentionally toward that end. From her perspective, celebrities seemed to have everything, "money, fame, the adulation and the praise of the world and yet they had nothing." This fact was driven home to her shortly after she arrived in Hollywood. Following one of her early speaking engagements, a young woman rushed up to Mears and wrapped her in a warm embrace. "You have what we all want. You are wonderful!!" Before Mears could respond the attractive blond melted back into the crowd. She did not see Thelma Todd again before her apparent suicide in 1935. To Mears, Todd's success in the industry belied a spiritual void that she had been unable to fill. But as the years spooled by without a perceptible entrée to the celebrity culture surrounding her, Mears had to admit that the effort to penetrate the celluloid curtain with a faithful Christian witness proved more daunting than she had anticipated.

Though nearly twenty years elapsed before Mears cofounded the first organized Christian ministry to Hollywood celebrities, the entertainment industry was no stranger to her College Department. By the 1930s some members, like Leonard Eilers and Harold "Slim" Nyby, had gone into the business and renditions of pop music, including blues recordings, could be heard at department socials. College Department member Ethel Edwards sang with the Goose Creek Broadcasters prior to 1937. Paul Wendt worked in the processing department of Technicolor Laboratories. Jim Ferguson spent the summer of 1937 at Warner Brothers Studios, and fellow First Presbyterian collegian Eleanor Wilson appeared as a guest artist with the Glendale Symphony. Young radio personality Ernie "Skeeter" Hubbard brought his guitar to department singing events and participated in a trio with fellow department members Joel Allen and Johnny Johnson. Allen enjoyed minor success as a character actor, and Hubbard went on to work with cowboy star Stuart Hamblen on his radio program.[5]

In the mid- and late 1930s Mears's students organized a Creative Arts Club and a Drama Club. In addition to establishing an affirming environment to showcase the vocal, literary, and artistic talents of its membership, the Creative Arts Club also hosted local artists, including the head of the animation department at Disney Studios in March 1937. Club member Mary Rogers had an original radio play produced that was only the latest in a rather long list of radio accomplishments. Ernest George, a humor writer for the monthly College Department publication, also wrote for radio. He not only had his own program by November 1938 but was also interviewed for another—the redoubtable "Man on the Street" series. The Drama Club performed both religious and secular repertoire, and members honed their skills in set-building and costuming, producing at least six plays by early 1939. Two members of the club, Mark and Frances Smith, decided on a whim to audition for a radio play. Both won parts in the production, with Frances finding further opportunities in the medium. The College Department Glee Club performed regularly on the radio by 1938. Mears's niece Marguerite in 1937 held the comedic title role in one of the Drama Club's productions, which was restaged the following year and taken on the road because of its popularity. Over the ensuing decade

Mears's students and her Christian education program continued to embrace the entertainment community.[6]

Many of those already in the industry gravitated to First Presbyterian. Child star Jane Withers, a contemporary of Shirley Temple, enrolled in Mears's Sunday school and brought many of her friends. She promised to sign autographs—but only after the Bible lesson. Noted stage and screen character actor Porter Hall served First Presbyterian Church for years as a board member. By the 1940s Dennis Morgan and his family became communicant members of the church as did Donald Crisp, Virginia Mayo, Michael O'Shea, and Rhonda Fleming, among others. Robert Hunter, head of personnel at Paramount, served as an officer in the church, and Don and Jean Harvey were active members by the mid-1950s.[7]

Nineteen forty-nine proved to be pivotal for Christians in the industry. Early in the year evangelist J. Edwin Orr accepted an invitation from the Christ for Greater Los Angeles Committee to spend March teaching and preaching in Southern California to prepare the region for the upcoming Billy Graham Campaign slated to begin on September 25. On one occasion Orr spoke to Mears's College Department and came away favorably impressed with her several hundred collegians. His evangelical fervor so impressed Mears that she invited him to speak at the Forest Home College Briefing Conference. He and his family spent much of the summer of 1949 at Forest Home, where he met a small group of Christian entertainers. They included popular radio star Connie Haines, a former vocal partner to Frank Sinatra and member of both Harry James's and Tommy Dorsey's bands. Orr also got to know recent convert Tim Spencer, a founding member of the popular western recording group the Sons of the Pioneers.[8]

Mears continued to be impressed with Orr's forthright and sensible approach to Christian orthodoxy and thought he might partner with her to reach the entertainment world. As Ethel May Baldwin observed: "Miss Mears knew that no tricks or gimmicks could be used on a crowd who made the mastery of gimmicks their livelihood. The secret of reaching the stars was Christ crucified and resurrected, the source of abundant life; and Miss Mears believed that Dr. Orr represented this approach."[9]

Haines, who had become a guest in Mears's home, took part in the Young People's Interdenominational Conference at Forest Home in early July. She desired a deeper Christian experience for herself and those in her industry and had talked and prayed with Mears about these concerns. During the conference Haines sought out Orr for counsel regarding her future. Somewhat chary of show business, he advised her to go to Bible school and use her vocal talents there, even suggesting one such institution with its own radio station for that purpose. It became clear to Haines that she could willingly give up her career for a full-time Christian service vocation. Yet she felt constrained by a desire to bring a faithful witness to her friends and colleagues in the entertainment world.[10]

She also spoke with Mears during the week, discussing with her, Tim Spencer, and perhaps a few others the impediments to an ongoing, visible Christian presence in Hollywood. They came to the conclusion that convening a group comprised solely of those in the industry could provide the supportive context for such a witness. At this critical point a member of the group thought a decision to organize a meeting should be deferred until the fall, but Mears voiced her disapproval in no uncertain terms: "Then forget all about it! If it is worth doing in the fall, it's worth doing now, but if you wait until fall all the sparkle and enthusiasm will be gone. What is the first night you can get started?"[11] That was enough for Haines. She told Orr that until she sensed a definite call to serve elsewhere, she would continue her work so that she could "make the most of the opportunity of telling the stars of radio and screen what Christ had done for her."[12]

Haines and Spencer returned to Hollywood invigorated by the possibility of an organized Christian fellowship and outreach program. They telephoned Colleen Townsend, member of Mears's College Department and a relatively new Christian under contract to 20th Century Fox, along with Porter Hall and a number of others. Haines called Orr to ask if he would be willing to speak to a gathering of media celebrities. The following Wednesday evening, July 13, 1949, just over two dozen industry insiders met at Mears's home a few blocks east of the UCLA campus. Orr brought a gospel message based on Matthew 6:24 regarding the impossibility of serving two masters.[13] The group present that evening included several leading personalities, with perhaps as many as ten having already starred in various films. Western star Dale Evans remembered the first meeting, "when a small group of the Hollywood entertainment industry knelt in the living room of Miss Mears' Westwood home and unconditionally surrendered our lives to be used of the Lord Jesus Christ in reaching others for the Kingdom of our Lord through the industry."[14] They strategized until well after midnight and resolved to meet again "to pray and then invite their friends." This inaugural meeting of the Hollywood Christian Group represented a new direction for the support of Christians in the entertainment world and the evangelization of their friends and colleagues. It also marked the culmination of years of prayer and discussion by Mears and her allies regarding how best to be of service to members of the industry.

Over the next year, the group met weekly on Monday evenings, alternating relatively small, intimate Bible study and prayer meetings for committed believers (usually held in Mears's home for the first year) with larger meetings, designed to draw the attention of the spiritually curious, held at the homes of Jane Russell, Roy Rogers and Dale Evans, George Eastman, and others. By mid-1950 the membership roster of the HCG included more than forty people of varying reputation in the industry—some of them top tier stars. At the end of the summer of 1951 one hundred plus celebrities from all branches of the entertainment industry (stage, film, radio, and television) had been reached by the fellowship's programs, which were conducted by the members themselves. Many in the industry—including Stuart Hamblen, Louise James, Redd Harper, Lee Childs, Cindy Walker, Georgia Lee, Ralph Hoopes, and Buddy and Abigail Dooley—had been converted by that time, and Christians in the field had been substantially encouraged. By January 1955 the HCG counted over 135 regular Screen Actors Guild and associated union members (excluding visitors) from nearly every studio. Between July 1949 and 1955 in excess of twenty media celebrities converted to Christianity and at least fifteen members entered specialized Christian service vocations. Orr served as chaplain of the group for two years. Richard Halverson, assistant minister at the First Presbyterian Church of Hollywood and later chaplain of the US Senate, succeeded him. Jack Franck and Bill Bright, two former members of Mears's College Department, also became involved in the evangelistic outreach to celebrities, spending hours with her and Orr in prayer for the work of the group. By the time Orr left for a South American ministry in the summer of 1951, the HCG had become a self-sustaining entity with Mears still serving as its advisor. The decision to incorporate came from the leadership in the early 1950s. Throughout the decade, a wide variety of speakers supplemented the sharing of personal conversion stories by members at group meetings.[15]

From its inception, a central purpose of the HCG was the evangelization of those in the entertainment industry. Yet even with such a clear—some might argue triumphalist—goal, those of Jewish, Eastern Orthodox, Roman Catholic, Christian Science and other nonevangelical persuasions participated, as did people without any faith affiliation. William A. Moses, religion editor for the *Los Angeles Times* who attended a number of meetings, explained how the group could be committed to the evangelization of their religiously diverse colleagues while still providing a welcoming atmosphere for them:

> They call and think of themselves as theological conservatives with the evangelical's desire to spread the Gospel among those who happen to live in a gaudy, tinseled world of make-believe. . . . The first question they will ask you is, "Have you accepted Christ?" The pleasant manner of inquiry holds no offence except to the most sensitive.[16]

As one of the early leaders of the group later recalled, "Our effort was to get our friends involved . . . [who were] open to the Gospel, in a way that wouldn't turn them off and where we wouldn't be inviting them to a specific church."[17] Orr affirmed that "no attempt was made to proselytize anyone. . . . The Hollywood Christian Group tells its story only to those who are eager to hear. There is no urging, no pleading, no coaxing, no pressuring."[18] Big-band entertainer and radio personality Redd Harper attended his first meeting in February 1950; he remembered that during the social hour after the message, "no one asked *me* any questions about what or how I believed, or even what I'd thought of the 'sermon.'"[19]

Besides promoting a winsome evangelistic ethos,[20] the HCG worked "to provide Christian Fellowship for artists of the entertainment world and to unite them in witness to those of their profession who lack a vital relationship with the Lord Jesus Christ." The foundational principle noted in the group's "Resolutions" was "acceptance of Jesus Christ as only Saviour and acknowledgment of the supremacy of Holy Scripture in matters of faith and practice." The body restricted membership to "all artists of radio, television, stage and screen and allied professionals, also their husbands, wives, parents or adult children, and all so invited are welcome to participate in group discussions, irrespective of standing or experience in matters religious."

For those who had a religious faith, the HCG maintained a nonsectarian, interdenominational character so that all would feel equally comfortable, but also reiterated that it desired to reach "people with any faith or no faith with the gospel."

While all were welcome to attend meetings, only "regular attenders who profess an experience of the New Birth [i.e., Christian conversion] shall be entitled to share in the direction of affairs." An annual meeting held in July appointed a six-person steering committee, "preferably three men and three women of mature Christian experience," to lead the group. Three members would be replaced each year. The steering committee had the authority to appoint subcommittees as deemed prudent and agreed "to adopt a scriptural attitude toward intoxication, profanity or immorality." Connie Haines, John Holland, Jane Russell, Tim Spencer, Colleen Townsend, and Porter Hall comprised the initial steering committee.[21] A key provision concerned privacy issues and stipulated that

> all participation in Group discussions and exercises shall be regarded as strictly private. Guests and members will be asked not to release publicity not previously released by the Group. Names of visitors or participants shall not be used without the consent of the person and the committee. Publicity calculated to advance the professional interests of any individual is unwelcome. The purpose of all publicity shall be to further the work of the Group only.[22]

The opening paragraph of the document and the concluding section highlighted Mears's seminal role in the genesis of the HCG. The final paragraph recognized that "Miss Henrietta Mears, honorary matron, Dr. Edwin Orr, Honorary Chaplain, together with Connie Haines, Colleen Townsend, Jane Russell, Porter Hall and Tim Spencer, founded the group." Dr. Jack MacArthur of the Fountain Avenue Baptist Church (Hollywood), Leonard Eilers, and Richard Halverson were named as cosponsors and members of the Advisory Board charged with ensuring adherence to the resolutions.

Mears's impact went far beyond merely facilitating the formation of the HCG. Her engaging evangelical witness and counsel, coupled with her mentoring of leaders, played a crucial role in its growth and development. Second chaplain Richard Halverson is one example. A former child vaudeville performer, he relocated to Hollywood at nineteen to break into films. Less than a year later, shortly after he began attending the Vermont Avenue Presbyterian Church under the leadership of David Cowie, Halverson had a conversion experience and jettisoned his cinematic aspirations for a full-time Christian service vocation. After attending Wheaton College and Princeton Theological Seminary, Halverson returned to Hollywood as assistant minister at First Presbyterian in 1947. Not only was he converted under the ministry of one of the early graduates of Mears's College Department (Cowie), but Halverson's faith was further affected through the Fellowship of the Burning Heart, the organization that developed under Mears's influence at Forest Home in 1947.[23]

The effect she had on Leonard and Frances Eilers, main figures in the evangelical ministry to Hollywood celebrities, is impossible to quantify, for they became colleagues as well as friends. Leonard grew up in North Dakota under trying circumstances and had been converted at seventeen through the ministry of Billy Sunday. After spending five years as a cowhand in Wyoming, he moved to Hollywood in 1923 and became a cameraman for Cecil B. DeMille at Paramount Studios. Shortly after his arrival, he joined the First Presbyterian Church of Hollywood where he met Frances, a secretary at the church. They married in 1926. The Eilerses had probably been associated with the Young People's Department at First Presbyterian prior to Mears's arrival, but under her teaching Leonard's spiritual life deepened considerably. He eventually left Paramount to attend the Bible Institute of Los Angeles. He also assumed a leading role in a number of the programs coordinated and supervised by Mears beginning in 1929. He traveled with members of the College and Senior Young People's departments, respectively, to provide gospel messages at the Los Angeles Union Gospel Mission downtown and at the Sailor's Rest Mission in San Pedro. Leonard also joined the Life Work Recruit group sponsored and hosted by Mears, signifying his commitment to full-time Christian service. In the fall of 1930 he became the pastor for Junior Church and Junior Christian Endeavor, two children's ministries at First Presbyterian. By the mid-1930s he was an ordained Baptist minister and recognized evangelist. Leonard often gave devotional messages at young people's meetings while mounted on horseback and performing rope tricks, but he was best known for his ministry to the western stars of Hollywood. It was said that Leonard and Frances befriended nearly all the top western celebrities of the era. According to one historian, the Eilerses "became the advance guard of the movement which was to wield such an influence in the field of western entertainment." Their friendship and Christian witness touched many of the most notable western celebrities, one of whom said that Leonard "was the real 'prayer warrior' behind all the cowboys who have been converted to Christ in Hollywood." Orr held that behind "the conversion of Tim Spencer, Stuart Hamblen and Roy Rogers was a quiet cowboy evangelist. . . . Leonard Eilers." And behind Leonard and Frances Eilers was Henrietta Mears. They remained close friends and ministry associates throughout their lives. Their daughter, Joy, who also went into the entertainment business, was raised with Mears in their home for times of prayer and conversation so often that she thought of her initially only as a close family friend and not a "great woman of God," as she put it.[24]

Mears's influence on Tim and Velma Spencer, significant leaders of the HCG, was ubiquitous—directly through personal encounters and indirectly through others she mentored and ministries she nurtured. In 1933 Tim Spencer teamed with Bob Nolan and Leonard Slye, soon to be known as Roy Rogers, to form the western singing group the Sons of the Pioneers. Earlier that year while barnstorming through the Midwest, Spencer had met seventeen-year-old Velma Blanton. They married in 1934. The rapid success of the Sons of the Pioneers, the endless round of Hollywood parties, and Spencer's penchant for using liquor as a muse to unlock his songwriting talents sent the family into crisis by the latter part of the decade. During these difficult years when Spencer spiraled into extended alcoholic stupors, it was often Leonard Eilers who would search the bars and other haunts until he could be located. Eilers then made sure he got home and put to bed. Their high life sent Velma back to the church. In 1938 she joined the First Presbyterian Church of Hollywood and enrolled their children in the Cradle Roll Department of Mears's Sunday school. By her own admission she "went to church on Sunday, but during the week I lived just like any unbeliever." Their children, however, each found Christian faith in the Sunday school.[25]

Nine years later, with the support and counsel of Mears's friends, Leonard and Frances Eilers, Velma experienced a renewal of her faith. She then became a spiritual advocate for her husband. And there were other advocates; Leonard had been praying for Tim Spencer's Christian conversion for fifteen years. Mears and Frances would join Velma and Suzy Hamblen at the Eilers's ranch "on their knees in the living room. . . . just crying before God for the salvation of their husbands."[26] Then, during the summer of 1948 while touring with the Sons of the Pioneers, Tim Spencer had a powerful conversion experience that transformed his family and his career. In December 1948 he confessed his faith before a thousand congregants at First Presbyterian. He could not, however, break free from indebtedness, which soon forced the sale of the family home. In spite of their financial predicament, Spencer resigned as a member of the Sons of the Pioneers so he could spend more time with matters related to his new faith. He remained the group's manager but seemed unable to write music for months following his conversion. After having penned two hundred songs of varying quality over the years (usually "under the influence") and enduring a severe case of writer's block, Spencer resolved to commit his songwriting abilities to God, vowing to quit the profession completely if he could not write without the aid of alcohol. On that same day he sat down and composed a simple love song. While attending the July 1949 conference at Forest Home, Spencer sang it for Orr and asked him to pray for God's blessing on the song. Shortly after its subsequent publication, "Room Full of Roses" shot to the top of the pop charts for three weeks and remained in the Hit Parade top ten for fourteen weeks, ending the family's financial difficulties. As she reflected on her family's faith journey in the mid-1950s, Velma specifically singled out two First Presbyterian leaders, Clair Gahagen and Henrietta Mears, "for the comfort they gave me when the going was rough. I just pray that the lives of each member of the Spencer family will be a tribute to their faithfulness."[27] When she received advance copies of her small book *How to Have a Happy Christian Home* in late 1956, Velma gave one to Mears inscribed, "To Miss Mears, In grateful appreciation for all you have done for us!" Tim Spencer and Leonard Eilers continued to cultivate their friendship and became close associates in the HCG.[28]

Mears's gracious hospitality and bold Christian witness, experienced both firsthand and obliquely through her other endeavors, often worked to inspire members of the HCG to service and evangelism, thereby multiplying Mears's own personal influence. For example, although Mears was not intimately connected to the conversion of either Roy Rogers or his wife, Dale Evans, Rogers gave the first public testimony to his faith at Forest Home. Both stars became integral members of the HCG. By the later 1950s Mears had made room on the Forest Home schedule for an annual conference specifically for the association. It was largely the initiative of Mears's invited houseguest Connie Haines and Henrietta's connection to the Spencer family that resulted in the first meetings of the HCG in Mears's own home.

Rising 20th Century Fox film star Colleen Townsend came to Christian faith because of her experience with Mears and others in the College Department at First Presbyterian. Townsend's roommate, Mary Standley, feared that "Coke," as her friends called her, had been overly influenced by religious fanatics—until Standley attended the College Briefing Conference at Forest Home, resulting in her own conversion experience. An invitation from Townsend to attend a meeting of the HCG brought Georgia Lee of Warner Brothers face to face with Christianity. Lee and her husband, fellow entertainer Ralph Hoopes, shortly thereafter became Christian converts. Townsend's Christian witness played a major role in scriptwriter Robert Cherry's decision to make a Christian commitment. She also was instrumental in encouraging studio artist Walter Jolley and his wife Louise to attend their first group meeting, which led to their ongoing active participation. Perennial film heavy George Slocum knew both Townsend and Lee and attended Mears's College Department, drawn by the apparent satisfaction with life exhibited by his friends in the class. Slocum became a tithing member of the HCG in 1954. After their respective conversion experiences Tim and Velma Spencer often invited nonbelievers to open meetings of the group. Together they were at least partially responsible for the conversion of Redd Harper, western singer/songwriter Cindy Walker, performers Buddy and Abigail Dooley, and at least one noted producer and his wife. Tim Spencer became such an active evangelist among his colleagues that he earned the nickname "the Lord's Sherlock Holmes." In addition to inviting their colleagues to meetings of the HCG, many members of the group spoke at hospitals, colleges, jails, missions, and churches regarding their Christian faith experiences.[29]

As the HCG grew in numbers and its members became more vocal about their faith, the organization gained credibility among those in the entertainment world. Less than a year after its formation, word had already spread within the industry, as one member discovered when the producer he was inviting to the next meeting interrupted him saying "I know about your meetings and what you are doing. It is the talk of Hollywood."[30] Generally, the mainstream national media and international observers viewed the group with a mixture of admiration and incredulity. Townsend graced the cover of the August 30, 1948, issue of *Life* magazine. A few months later a feature story on the First Presbyterian Church of Hollywood in the same publication (January 10, 1949) included a section on those in the entertainment industry. When Townsend decided to walk away from her film career for full-time Christian service, newspapers across the country picked up the story. Hollywood columnist Louella Parsons expressed her surprise in an essay released to the International News Service on January 15, 1950:

> In all my years of reporting, this story is the most unusual one I have ever written. Colleen Townsend, beautiful 20-year-old actress, is not re-signing with Twentieth-Century-Fox when her contract expires in February. The promising young player is giving up a lucrative movie career to answer the call of God and to dedicate her life to religion.[31]

South African publisher Fred Crous included a favorable report on the HCG in a memoir of his visit to the United States in 1950, and William F. McDermott's essay "I Found God in Hollywood" in the February 1952 issue of *Pageant* magazine did the same.[32]

Favorable press came with a price, however. The importance of the faith commitments of HCG members sometimes clashed with the norms of life in the industry. Lee and Hoopes had been a dance team and appeared in films before their conversion during a group meeting at which Mears and Orr explained the way of salvation to them. By mid-1951 Lee had her own television program, and while her husband decided to leave show business to enter seminary, Lee believed that she could model the best Christian witness by remaining in the entertainment world. Her musical variety program, *The Georgia Lee Show,* reached a large television audience, and her success garnered the admiration of her peers. The series began as a sustaining program, meaning that it went on the air without a sponsor. The ABC network tried for weeks to secure one for the show in order to maximize revenue. Finally a beer company agreed to sponsor it, but this left Lee with a dilemma. Though only a few weeks removed from her conversion, she struggled with the possible contradiction between her new faith and the necessity of having to promote the company's product. She brought her concern to Tim and Velma Spencer, who counseled her to seek God's guidance in the matter. Convinced that she had to maintain a consistent witness, Lee told her producers that she could not support the new sponsor and that another would have to be found. As she shared at a HCG meeting a week after her decision, "So I got fired. *Praise the Lord!* He has a better job for me, I know!"[33]

Stuart Hamblen, a star of longer and more illustrious reputation than Lee, had a similar experience in radio. After a frank discussion on the air about his conversion, Hamblen pledged that he would not "preach" at his audience. "All I'm going to do is try to live a good Christian life," he promised.[34] Very soon, however, he began to have reservations about a cigarette company's sponsorship of his program. He tried to thread the needle by reading the commercial script and then launching into a thinly veiled soliloquy that was anything but an endorsement ending with, "if you're going to smoke anyway, you might as well smoke my sponsor's cigarettes, the best of a bad lot."[35] On other occasions Hamblen warned his fans about the connection between smoking and cancer, but the cigarettes continued to sell. As might be surmised, his sponsors were not very supportive of his novel approach to marketing.[36]

Hamblen, however, drew the line at alcohol. He refused to endorse his sponsor's beer telling the executives of his radio station that "I'm not going to be a party to helping my listeners become boozers. I got kids in my audience; you don't think I'm going to make barflies out of them, do you?" Even his immense popularity could not induce the sponsor or the station executives to concede, and Hamblen left radio after twenty-one years on the air. Thousands wrote asking him to reconsider, but Hamblen held his ground, convinced that he had made the right decision. On the day of his final broadcast, loyal fans waited in long lines in the rain for a chance to enter the studio to watch him perform one last time. "I can't afford to dilute my testimony," he argued, even turning down an offer of a nationwide broadcast platform. He later confided to his wife, "I don't know that I want to be back in radio. I'm thinking maybe that radio and I have had it. I won't sell beer and I don't want to sell cigarettes. And there's a lot more junk that I just can't sell. I can't lie any more, I guess, and I'm not sorry."[37]

Other members of the HCG may not have been fired for taking a stand they believed was congruent with their Christian commitment, but they often found themselves swimming upstream from the accepted way of doing business in Hollywood. Joy Eilers carved out a successful career in the entertainment industry even though those she worked with sometimes expressed skepticism regarding her stand on moral and ethical issues.[38] A year or so after his conversion, Roy Rogers felt compelled to make films with a higher moral tone than was possible under his current contract in order to foster an unambiguous Christian witness. He broke with Republic Pictures over his decision.[39]

Ironically, the HCG in the early years found its relationship with other Christians far more troublesome than with those outside the faith. There were some examples of Christian reportage sympathetic to the organization, such as British evangelist Tom B. Rees's commentary in a London newspaper that was otherwise rather critical of American evangelism. Mears associates Bill Bright and Richard Halverson as well as Phil Kerr also wrote favorably, but when Bright's essay appeared in the conservative *Christian Life* magazine the dam broke. Because of Bright's connection to Mears, he had opportunities to attend meetings of the HCG at the homes of Jane Russell and Roy Rogers and Dale Evans. He also accepted invitations from group members to visit movie sets. He therefore wrote from an insider's perspective. But although Bright included a list of trusted Christian leaders who echoed his assessment of the genuine spiritual renewal underway in Hollywood—including Billy Graham, Carl F. H. Henry, and the editor of the very magazine that published his article—the fundamentalist readership recoiled at the thought that Hollywood could actually harbor committed Christians. Bright quoted one woman who eerily foreshadowed the often mindless reactions to his assertion that there were actually Christians working in the industry. In chastising a Christian leader for working with celebrities, the irate churchgoer fumed, "I wish you and your friends would stop getting these stars converted. It makes it hard for my pastor to prove to the young people that everyone in Hollywood is either a drunk or a prostitute."[40]

The nationwide expression of outrage even found its way into the pages of *Time* magazine. Scathing references by one livid believer to a "Prostitutes Christian Association" and a "Bartender's Christian Fellowship" demonstrated the cynicism some felt toward the possibility of a Christian presence in Hollywood. Another writer in a religious periodical lambasted "Movie Religion." The author of this article focused on the alleged misconduct of one star who attended the meetings—completely ignoring the fact that plenty of members were living lives of consistent witness in accordance with biblical injunctions (and HCG affirmations). Orr dashed off letters to both malcontents, but while the former appeared contrite, the latter declined to be confused by the facts. Orr even chided the esteemed conservative Bible scholar, author, teacher, and pastor A. W. Tozer for his sweeping indictment of celebrity culture and its deleterious effect on American evangelicalism. He feared that Tozer's overwrought condemnations could lead Christians mistakenly to blame members of the HCG for this development. For his efforts, Orr found himself vilified, accused of selling out to the film studios, whose bosses supposedly had built him a Beverly Hills mansion as payment for "services rendered." Both Orr and members of the HCG remained confounded by the graceless treatment they received from believers such as these. [41] As time passed the attitude moderated, but even a member of Mears's own College Department dashed off a scathing letter to her, soundly condemning the role Hollywood celebrities played at a 1950s Christmas party for the department.[42]

One of the biggest hurdles Christians in the industry had to overcome was the widespread belief that conversion led a believer naturally out of Hollywood and into a more respectable line of work. Mears stood steadfastly against this notion, believing that all lines of employment could result in honorable service to God. There is no indication that Mears ever advised anyone associated with the HCG to leave the field, although she was very selective about whom she encouraged to enter the industry from her College Department and Sunday school. Orr, on the other hand, had a more difficult time with converts from the group remaining in the entertainment world.[43]

The articles written by Bright, Kerr, and Halverson that reported sympathetically on the work of the HCG reiterated Mears's belief in the possibility of a faithful witness to Hollywood celebrities. Bright's essay "The Truth About Hollywood" demonstrated that Christians in show business, like believers elsewhere, sought God's direction for their lives. He observed that Colleen Townsend, who by that time had decided to leave her secular film career to act in Christian films and prepare for full-time Christian service, nonetheless believed that "God may have called others of the group, at least for the present, to be a witness in the industry." Bright concluded that because of the influence of Christians within Hollywood culture, "God may see fit to take over this and related channels of communication in order to reach the world for Christ in the shortest possible time." Four years later Kerr's article in the same periodical raised similar issues.[44] Likewise, Halverson's contribution, "Any Good—from Hollywood," published by *Christianity Today* in December 1957 answered with a resounding "NO!" the prevailing notion that Christians should abandon the industry because of its less than savory aspects. Halverson spoke for those believer-celebrities when he wrote that, "aware of its [Hollywood's] overwhelming potential influence for good, they see it as their mission field. At the risk of censure by those without [the industry], they labor and pray for a spiritual awakening that will capture its talents, in part at least, to evangelize the world."[45] At one of the HCG meetings Halverson heard a recently converted actor declare that "Jesus Christ must want me in this business because I couldn't do it otherwise. Every time I go before a camera I pray my life will be a witness to the others working on the picture." Halverson believed that "it would be unrealistic to pretend that there are not those who, lured by prospects of popularity and riches, remain in pictures at the expense of their witness, but it is unjust to assume that all in the business are thus motivated." The former chaplain of the HCG insisted that "no group in the writer's experience is more insistent for the Gospel or less willing to compromise. Believing no one can reach people in Hollywood like people in Hollywood, they accept as a divine mandate the responsibility to begin where they are to make disciples." Halverson compared the entertainment industry to any other venture, maintaining that no human undertaking would ever be completely or even mostly Christian. He concluded that "there abides a dynamic fellowship of Christians demonstrating that Christ is contemporary and relevant, that the purpose of his incarnation was redemption. God has not left himself without a witness . . . not even in Hollywood!"[46]

"The gradual tempering of Christian attitudes toward the HCG and the recognition that there could be a legitimate Christian witness to the industry probably had something to do with the organization's vigilance about disciplining its membership when deemed appropriate. Such discipline did not originate with Mears or other advisors but from within the leadership itself. The group hoped that stringent self-policing would win over cynical believers and more clearly delineate acceptable values and standards to skeptical (or curious) nonbelievers. No visitors were turned away from the open meetings of the HCG, no matter how notorious their reputations or nefarious their lifestyles. However, the actual members of the association were held to an even stricter standard of behavior than that of some Southern California evangelical churches. In the previously mentioned article containing the "Movie

Religion" diatribe against the group, the author failed to mention that the HCG had unequivocally repudiated the activities of the person accused of misconduct. One couple wanted to attend the Bible study and prayer meetings (closed to all except professing Christians), but was turned away. Another couple also desired entry to these meetings and was told that each of them was most welcome to attend the evangelistic meetings that were open to all but "until their association was fully recognized by society they could not be considered members." In light of this rebuke, one of them had a conversion experience and ended the relationship.[47]

When members were suspected of transgressing the principles set out in the group's "Resolutions," cautious but deliberate action was taken emphasizing repentance and restoration.[48] More trying for the HCG were decisions and behaviors by members that did not cross any boundaries specifically proscribed by the group's standards but still might be construed as detrimental to a reliable Christian witness. Here again, the example of Henrietta Mears is instructive, for it is indicative of the premium she placed on God's grace and the deep importance of relationships. Never was this more evident than at a meeting of the Hollywood Christian Group in the home of popular screen star and recording artist Jane Russell.

Of all the celebrities associated with the formation and early years of the HCG, perhaps none was more enigmatic than Russell. Discovered by Howard Hughes in 1940 and marketed by him as "the girl with the 'intriguing' measurements," Russell's film roles from the 1940s to the mid-1950s ranged from modest and comedic to quite provocative. The blatant sexuality of the publicity poster for her first film *The Outlaw* (1941) generated controversy that followed her for much of her career. Yet Russell's Christian convictions led her to cofound the HCG; perform and record gospel songs with Connie Haines, Beryl Davis, Rhonda Fleming, and Della Russell; support mission work in Africa; and organize the World Adoption International Fund. She built a chapel on her family property in the San Fernando Valley and held informal Friday evening meetings there for anyone wishing to attend. During the production of one of her most successful films, 1953's *Gentlemen Prefer Blondes*, Russell even tried to convert costar Marilyn Monroe, but without success. Monroe accepted her invitation to attend a meeting of the HCG at the home of Haines but decided against further participation.[49]

Russell often hosted open meetings of the HCG in her home, and on one instance in 1949, Billy and Ruth Graham attended as special guests, with Billy slated to bring the evangelistic message.[50] During the course of the evening Russell shared about her Christian walk. But knowing something of her controversial career, Ruth entertained doubts about the authenticity of her faith: "How can this woman, who plays such questionable roles on the screen, talk this way about Christ?"[51] Almost immediately after the thought crossed her mind, Ruth was jolted by the barely audible words spoken by her companion on the sofa, Henrietta Mears. For just as Ruth could not help questioning Russell's integrity, Mears could not contain her pleasure in Russell. In reflecting on this incident Ruth later wrote, "It's a good thing she couldn't hear what I was thinking. . . . And all the time I was thinking little, suspicious, mean thoughts, Miss Mears was muttering, 'Bless her heart! I just love that girl! She is the dearest thing!' . . . Some of us talk about love. Miss Mears loves. No wonder God uses her!"[52] Also present at that meeting was Colleen Townsend, who in recalling Mears's words that evening said, "She could put her arms around Jane Russell and say, 'Isn't she darling?' and not everyone could do that. . . . And I just loved her for that, because I love my friends in the industry and when they got to know her they just loved her."[53] Mears's gracious spirit of acceptance set the tone for others to follow.[54]

Annual meetings of the HCG were occasions to celebrate how the Spirit was moving in Hollywood and to showcase the work of the group. The first one in 1950 drew an estimated one hundred members and guests. Recent convert Roy Rogers shared from his Christian experience and then yielded the podium to the speaker for the evening. Neither Mears nor Orr could attend the second meeting, which included a banquet at the Beverly-Wilshire Hotel for the two hundred attendees. Among them were producers, twenty top-tier film stars from various studios, and celebrities from across the spectrum of popular entertainment. Rogers spoke again but this time as host for the evening. Ronald Reagan, president of the Screen Actors Guild, joined him as cohost and friend of the HCG for a portion of the program. Evangelistic testimonies highlighted the evening, and Mears's pastor, Louis Evans Sr., gave the message.[55]

Throughout the rest of the 1950s, the HCG continued to expand both its influence and its membership. Mears participated as best she could, but by the latter years of the decade other pressing responsibilities and her declining health somewhat limited her involvement in the enterprise—though not her enthusiasm for it. The open meetings quickly outgrew even the largest private homes and in 1952 moved to the Knickerbocker Hotel a few blocks west of First Presbyterian. By the end of 1957 Mears reported up to two hundred enrollees in the group.[56] Eventually, to protect the privacy of its members, the HCG had to issue identification cards. No one could be admitted to the meetings unless in possession of an identity card or in the company of someone who carried one.[57]

Over the course of the 1950s group members used their talents in widely divergent ways. Many pursued their careers in the conventional entertainment world while bearing witness to their faith. Connie Haines continued her vocal career and often incorporated gospel songs into her repertoire. Her gospel-themed engagements with Jane Russell, Beryl Davis, and Rhonda Fleming drew large audiences. Davis persisted in her singing career and her husband, Peter Potter, remained a popular radio disc jockey in Southern California. Tim Spencer also maintained his managerial association with the Sons of the Pioneers and exercised his musical gifts while seeking to enhance the effectiveness of his Christian witness to his colleagues in the industry. He ultimately secured the rights to many popular gospel songs and hymns including "How Great Thou Art," which became the unofficial theme song of Forest Home. Eva Pearson and Ray MacDonald continued to work in mainstream motion pictures as did John Holland and Porter Hall. Jimmie Dodd and his wife, Ruth, also witnessed to their faith by remaining in their professions. Joy Eilers's career bridged the secular entertainment and Christian worlds through heavy involvement in both, including a stint in the office of the HCG.

While these members and many others lived out their calling within the industry, some of their colleagues elected to pursue different options. Colleen Townsend left commercial entertainment and married Louis Evans Jr. She became an accomplished speaker and author and went on to act in Christian films including *Lord of All*, a documentary filmed by Cavalcade Productions. Lois Chartrand also acted for a time in Christian cinema. Eventually she and her husband, Dee Dee, served on the foreign mission field. After her conversion Lee Childs remained a popular figure on stage and in the opera world, but by the mid-1950s she chose to use her talents solely in Christian service. Big band vocalist Louise James, the former wife of band leader Harry James, had already left the business before her conversion in 1949. Early in her Christian walk, she supported the HCG by opening her home to its meetings, but she ultimately moved to Texas in order to raise her two sons and focus on her growth in the faith.

Stuart Hamblen became a featured speaker at Youth for Christ rallies across the country, largely at his own expense. His first YFC rally in Minneapolis drew ten thousand to hear him share his conversion experience. He continued to write music after leaving radio, but with a decidedly Christian message. His most celebrated composition had its genesis in a conversation he had with John Wayne, with whom he had worked extensively before his conversion. Hamblen had actually been Wayne's stand-in for the latter's dangerous fighting and riding scenes in many films. When word reached Wayne that Hamblen had changed his ways, he found it hard to believe. He marveled, "Hell, Stu, you've been drinking so long you're practically embalmed. What's the secret?" Hamblen replied, "It's no secret what God can do." From this brief exchange came the popular hymn, "It Is No Secret (What God Can Do)." The tune shot to the top of the Hit Parade list and sold more than a million copies (sheet music and audio recording).

Western composer Cindy Walker used her composition, vocal, and acting talents for the benefit of Christians. Barbara Watkins initially entered the television industry, then became director of the radio and television ministry of a large Los Angeles church. Charles Turner served as featured vocalist for the "Haven of Rest" religious radio program. Ralph Hoopes, husband of Georgia Lee, completed seminary and ultimately became the pastor of a new Presbyterian church in the San Fernando Valley. Film producer Dick Ross was a founding member of Hoopes's congregation. Don and Jean Harvey remained active members of First Presbyterian and also served the African American congregation of Salem Baptist Church of Val Verde. Malcolm Boyd left his position as a radio and television producer to study for Episcopal Holy Orders. After his ordination as an Episcopal deacon, he advanced his theological education at Oxford University.[58] Redd Harper continued his Armed Forces Radio Service program *Redd Harper's Hollywood Roundup* until October 1952, when he joined the Billy Graham evangelistic team. Other HCG members assisted Graham in his evangelistic ministries. In addition to Stuart Hamblen's contribution to the success of Graham's 1949 Los Angeles evangelistic campaign, Colleen Townsend and her fiancé Louis Evans Jr. also actively participated in the meetings. At Graham's landmark 1954 London Crusade, Roy Rogers, Dale Evans, Henrietta Mears, and Louis and Colleen Townsend Evans all took part.

The multiple, overlapping connections between Henrietta Mears, Billy Graham, J. Edwin Orr, Forest Home, and the HCG led to a creative collaboration that contributed dramatically to the reemergence of filmmaking by Christians after a hiatus of two decades. Dick Ross founded Great Commission Films the same year the HCG organized. By the mid-1950s the production company had worked on films for Billy Graham, Bob Pierce (founder of World Vision and Samaritan's Purse), Child Evangelism Fellowship, Youth for Christ, the Pocket Testament League, and other Christian service organizations. HCG members appeared in many of these films. They also appeared in productions by other firms, such as Cathedral Films, Family Films, Cavalcade Productions, and Sacred Films, as well as in features sponsored by the Missouri Synod of the Lutheran Church.[59]

Henrietta Mears also looked to members of the HCG for assistance with at least two different projects. In December 1948 Forest Home began airing a weekly fifteen-minute evening broadcast of music and inspiration. Charles Turner contributed his vocal talents, and Dick Ross offered to produce the program. Beginning the same year, the conference center initiated an annual commemorative Memorial Day celebration. Mears often turned to group members to assist in the organizing and staging of these ceremonies. Colleen Townsend, for example, was one of the speakers at the 1949 presentation. The following year Roy Rogers, Dale Evans, Tim Spencer, and Stuart Hamblen participated. For the 1953 commemoration Mears asked group member Barbara Hudson Powers to come up with an idea for a theatrical pageant. Powers wrote, directed, and produced "God of the Mountain" for six years. HCG member Harry Woodard depicted Christ in the 1953 program, and Tim Spencer and Stuart Hamblen made return appearances in 1954. The most elaborately staged production occurred in 1955. Richard Halverson and Charles Turner sang, Don Harvey played the Old Testament leader Joshua, and Robert Clarke narrated the entire performance. For this version of the play Powers not only persuaded Billy Graham and California governor Goodwin J. Knight to offer prerecorded remarks to the audience, but she also secured the passage of a bill in Congress allowing military jets to fly over the site in the shape of a cross. Both President Dwight Eisenhower and FBI Director J. Edgar Hoover sent congratulatory telegrams.[60] *(See table 3 on page 283.)*

In April 1959 Henrietta Mears returned to the HCG as its primary speaker. Close to celebrating its ten-year anniversary, the group had come a long way since that first meeting in Mears's home in July 1949. The two hundred in attendance now filled an entire convention room at the Knickerbocker Hotel. *(See table 3 on page 283.)* According to an article by Kenneth Lewis in the *Los Angeles Times,* the group still included Connie Haines, Jane Russell, Dale Evans, and Roy Rogers. Some had left the organization for various reasons, but many more had taken their place. Actor Dick Jones opened the meeting with introductions, which were followed by renditions of "Lonesome Road" and "Use Me Lord" by singer-composer Ruth Dodd, the latter being her own composition. Her husband, Jimmie Dodd, master of ceremonies for television's *Mickey Mouse Club* and current president of the HCG, accompanied her. Between songs Ruth shared with the crowd how she and Jimmie had been converted at an HCG conference at Forest Home. Program Chair Georgia Lee Hoopes then stepped forward to introduce Mears, who spoke on the topic "Does Hollywood Need a God?"—the same topic she addressed nearly ten years earlier. She wryly mused that the size of the audience answered her question. The group had multiplied tenfold from its first meeting even while shunning publicity for fear of its being misinterpreted or misunderstood. But in light of the fact that recent unsolicited exposure had been so misrepresented, members were glad of reporter Lewis's presence. Jimmie Dodd confided to him that the group had initiated plans to air some of the future meetings on television so that both entertainers and the public might be better informed as to the content of the meetings. The small cards members handed out to their friends and colleagues succinctly reaffirmed the purposes of the HCG from ten years prior:

> 1—To inspire men and women in the entertainment industry to commit their lives to the Lord Jesus Christ. 2—To provide Christian fellowship and a means of growth in the grace and the knowledge of God. 3—To encourage an effective Christian witness through our daily life and occupation.[61]

In the decade since the founding of the Hollywood Christian Group, Mears and group members had weathered many storms, and there were more yet to come. But what must have been a courageous step for a nationally recognized evangelical leader like Henrietta Mears to take in 1949—freely and openly associating with members of what most theologically conservative Christians considered a hopelessly corrupt industry—seemed by the dawn of the 1960s to be a natural function of the Christian church at work in the world.

Chapter Nine

Long Shadow Cast

Peter Macky just laughed at his Sunday school teacher. Him, a minister? He must have misunderstood her. After all, the Harvard graduate was a rising star at the Lockheed Corporation and looked toward earning his doctorate in aeronautics at UCLA. But Henrietta Mears believed that God had a different plan for his future, and she told him so. Once he regained his composure, Macky trotted out all the reasons why her disclosure had to be a misreading of the Holy Spirit's guidance. He had school debts to pay and was already halfway through his PhD. Surely she must be mistaken. Mears assured him she was not and persuaded Macky to participate in the church's deputation program. His deputation service experience softened Macky to the possibility of a career change, but he still had loans to repay and no money. Never one to let finances dictate direction, Mears offered to take care of his remaining Harvard debt and pay for a year of seminary at Princeton. Macky never returned to Lockheed or UCLA. He took his seminary degree, became a Rhodes scholar at Oxford (attired in the best that tony Rodeo Drive clothing stores could offer, thanks again to Mears's generosity), and embarked on a storied career as a Presbyterian minister.[1]

Accounts like Macky's, with infinite permutations, could be told by any number of Mears's students over the years. Her seminarians went on to serve churches up and down the West Coast and around the country. Others held foreign and domestic mission assignments for the northern Baptist and Presbyterian churches as well as a wide variety of independent interdenominational agencies. Mears taught hundreds of white collar professionals, media personalities, and civic leaders who brought a vibrant Christian witness to their workplaces. And even in the patriarchal environment of the first two-thirds of the twentieth century she charged women by the score to make a difference in the world.

AS JOEL CARPENTER HAS CLEARLY DEMONSTRATED, in the 1930s and early 1940s theological conservatism may have lost face relative to mainstream American culture, but a transdenominational web of relationships sustained traditional Christian faith. Successful cultivation of its grassroots base, via a burgeoning network of institutions and media outlets, reinvigorated the persuasion.[2] Garth Rosell has described the nationwide "band of brothers" who filled churches and meeting halls, utilized popular electronic media technologies, and led new parachurch organizations, all stumping on behalf of Protestant Christian orthodoxy.[3] Their collaborative efforts prepared theological conservatives to reassert themselves culturally by the late 1940s. What is less acknowledged is the debt the new evangelicals of the 1940s and 1950s—Rosell's band of brothers, if you will—owed to Henrietta Mears. For much of their movement operated out of precedents she had introduced during her years in Minneapolis and had been refining ever since. Mears surfaced as a compelling figure in the vanguard of this emerging breed of Protestant Christians not because she was new to the game but precisely because she was not. Her willingness to engage secular American culture in innovative, sometimes remarkable, ways opened the door for such internationally known leaders as Billy Graham, Bill Bright, and Jim Rayburn, as well a multitude of lesser-known but no less noteworthy evangelicals. By the end of the 1930s she had piled up more than two decades of outstanding achievements that had already begun to reform Protestant America. Ultimately, her ministry would not only raise two generations of evangelicals but also facilitate the ongoing development and training of a swelling band of brothers (and sisters) that would impact American life and culture for the rest of the twentieth century. Individuals, parachurch institutions, and ministry groups that drove the postwar resurgence of the evangelical wing of American Protestantism thrived under her long shadow, whether they knew it or not.

Mears's sway over the midcentury revival exhibited a depth and breadth matched by only a very few of her contemporaries. Many who rose to the pinnacle of evangelical celebrity could trace a lineage back to her or those she trained. Harold John Ockenga, for example, initially "met" Mears through

First Presbyterian's William Blackstone, a fellow student at Princeton Seminary and member of Ockenga's traveling gospel team. Both men left Princeton in the fall of 1929 for Westminster Seminary, where they roomed together. Blackstone participated in Ockenga's wedding in August 1935 before the former's departure for mission service with the China Inland Mission. By the early 1940s Ockenga's awareness of Mears's contributions led to her leadership roles in the NAE, and her appreciation for his service to Protestant orthodoxy resulted in his participation in Forest Home conferences.[4] Ockenga's unsuccessful bid to entice her to Fuller Seminary did not dampen his enthusiasm for her wide-ranging ministry; he readily acknowledged that "her vision encompassed the world and God privileged her to see the fruits of her labors."[5]

Mears often called those who graduated from the College Department her "boys," although plenty of women could just as easily have been called her "girls." There were also dozens who never attended her Sunday school class but saw themselves as adopted into her network as "close relatives." Richard Halverson knew of her through "Mears boy" David Cowie and only later came to be more closely connected to her through First Presbyterian and the Hollywood Christian Group. Robert Munger, among the most celebrated Presbyterian ministers on the West Coast, first encountered Mears through some of her collegians attending a conference at Mount Hermon. He had hoped to take one of the young women he met there to a film but ended up in the second row at the meeting hall listening to Mears speak. After that evening he acknowledged, "I didn't have a chance!" Two years later Munger discovered that two "Mears boys" were to be his fellow seminarians at Princeton. His first pastorate, South Hollywood Presbyterian Church, brought him into sustained contact with Mears and resulted in a fruitful, lifelong association with her. Munger became a fixture at Forest Home College Briefing Conferences, including the 1949 iteration with Billy Graham, David Cowie, J. Edwin Orr, Richard Halverson, Charles Templeton, and of course Henrietta Mears. Munger considered her "my mentor and my guide, one for whom I have often been grateful during the subsequent years of my ministry as pastor and teacher."[6]

Mears's impact on the next generation of evangelicals through her "boys" is perhaps best demonstrated by the essential role Clyde Kennedy played in the life of the Young Life Campaign's founder Jim Rayburn, who began his ministry with students during the darkest days of the Great Depression.[7] In the mid-1930s he and his wife worked in the Southwest as Presbyterian home missionaries. While on a camping trip in Arizona he found a tattered copy of Lewis Sperry Chafer's *He That Is Spiritual.* Confronting Chafer's call to a deeper spiritual life changed Rayburn's perspective on Christianity.[8] The recognition that a conversion experience was only the beginning for Christians altered the course of his life. He enrolled at Dallas Theological Seminary in the autumn of 1936 and almost immediately began developing youth leadership and child evangelism in a Dallas church via the Good News clubs he created and a boys' club ministry that included the soon-to-be Southern Methodist University football star Doak Walker. Two years later his seminary internship assignment brought him into direct contact with Kennedy.

Kennedy's family had moved to Southern California from Nova Scotia in 1924. After his conversion at the First Presbyterian Church of Hollywood, Kennedy sensed a call to the ministry. He spent one year at Chicago's Moody Bible Institute then transferred to UCLA, earning his BA in 1933. As a member of the College Department, Kennedy sat under Mears's teaching and held a variety of departmental posts. The Mount Hermon college conferences Mears took her students to contributed significantly to his spiritual development and introduced him to Munger. In the fall of 1933 Kennedy began his graduate study at Princeton with both Munger and David Cowie. The three Californians joined two Wheaton graduates at Princeton to initiate a much-maligned ministry to distressed and impoverished youth in Trenton, New Jersey. They also established a mission Sunday school and worked to meet some of the physical needs of the children. Within two years, sixty seminarians participated in the work. After graduating from Princeton in 1936, Kennedy briefly held a pastorate in Southern California before accepting a call to the Gainesville Presbyterian Church in Texas.[9]

Kennedy had just begun his duties in Gainesville when Rayburn appeared. Profoundly moved by his encounters with the underprivileged of Trenton, the new pastor charged Rayburn to work with unchurched youths. Kennedy believed that young people already in the pews did not need Rayburn, but those who never darkened the doors of a church did. In so orienting Rayburn, Kennedy gave personal direction to his future ministry. Rayburn's parish turned out to be the local high school. He had a heart for young people but struggled to know how best to approach those beyond the church's grasp. Rayburn sought assistance from books on youth ministry and his seminary professors but received no insight from either quarter. He found the help he needed by way of Kennedy's College Department Sunday school teacher.

The young youth leader had heard about Henrietta Mears's ministry at First Presbyterian just as he began working with young people in 1933. He subsequently devoured anything he could find that she had written and listened intently to anyone who could tell him more about her work, undoubtedly including Kennedy. He later recalled:

> What I heard, chiefly her continual exaltation of the Person and work of Christ, her emphasis of a personal conversion experience, and a vital and dedicated relationship to Him in the Christian walk, these things were so impressive that I tried to incorporate into my work everything I heard about her way of doing things.[10]

Rayburn went on to found what was to become the Young Life Campaign International in June 1940 to reach teenagers not associated with any formal church body.[11] Young Life expanded in 1944 to include the publication of a periodical (*Young Life*) and a camping program at several different sites that Rayburn patterned after what Mears had developed at Forest Home.[12] By 1946 twelve men and eight women comprised the paid staff, assisted by a corps of volunteers. Rayburn himself spoke at one hundred fifty high school assemblies yearly. The ongoing expansion of Young Life staff necessitated the creation of a leadership training course called the Young Life Institute in 1951. Also, in the early 1950s and at least partially in response to Mears's urging, the campaign initiated its international outreach, opening its first European operation in France.[13] As the ministry continued to develop, Rayburn acknowledged that her effect on him meant that she "had a great deal to do with the shaping of the progress and ministry of the Young Life Campaign."[14] "She was my teacher long before she ever heard of me. . . . I tried my best to do things the way she would want them done."[15]

The two shared a mutual admiration for each other's commitment and service. Mears "loved what she saw in Young Life." Rayburn was "her kind of man" and he "considered her as probably the outstanding female leader that he knew." She had Rayburn speak to her College Department members at First Presbyterian and also invited him and other Young Life staffers to Forest Home on numerous occasions to address high schoolers and collegians. In later years Young Life rented the conference center's facilities to host its own camps, often bringing together a thousand teenagers. After the day's activities, Mears would invite Rayburn to the Biltmore for a discussion of matters related to the youth work to which they were both so dedicated. Staff member Robert Mitchell accompanied Rayburn to Forest Home in the early 1950s and remembered the animated ministry-related conversations between the two. That they tended to be direct and frank with each other during these conversations is best illustrated by Mears's challenge to Rayburn about his somewhat skeptical view of the church.[16] As an observer of two of the "greats," as he called them, Mitchell said that "they just were on the same wavelength; they had the same style, and neither of them had an unexpressed thought. . . . They would play off each other; they appreciated each other's humor."[17]

The Young Life emphasis on winning the right to be heard through the forging of authentic relationships, wholesome fun, a call to service after conversion, leadership training programs, bridge building with churches, and the necessity of specialized ministries could all be located in the example Mears began setting for theological conservatives in the 1910s. At one point in his ministry Rayburn said that he adopted Mears's Forest Home model of a personal commitment service for his Young Life camps "solely because Miss Mears did it. I knew it was right, if she did it."[18] He might just as well have said something similar about nearly his entire ministry to unchurched young people, including his practice of spending a great deal of time in prayer.[19] The mutuality of purpose between Mears and Rayburn even after her death is best symbolized by the appointment of Darrell Guder, one of her former College Department leaders, as director of ministry resources for Young Life's Institute of Youth Ministries.[20] When Mitchell assumed the presidency of Young Life, he used Mears as a prime example when pushing the organization toward gender equity in leadership and training.

She could also exert an ambivalent, even negative, initial effect on others which often developed over time into mutual respect and admiration, for Mears called out the best in people and expected the same in return. Such was the case with Dawson Trotman, founder of the Navigators international ministry. Trotman joined the Lomita Presbyterian Church in Southern California at the age of fourteen and had a powerful conversion experience six years later in June 1926, which eventually induced him to quit his job to enroll at the Bible Institute of Los Angeles and seminary. He also began an intense period of Bible memorization and informal ministry. In the early 1930s, Trotman's pastor recommended him to the staff at the First Presbyterian Church of Hollywood as a boys' group leader. At this point the possibility existed that he could be hired by the church as a boys' work minister under Mears. The suggestion, however, drew a strong negative response from her. She believed that Trotman would "never fit in Hollywood." Although she could not give her unqualified support to Trotman at the time, two of Mears's collegians, Hubert Mitchell and Dick Hillis,[21] were among Trotman's dearest friends and closest associates—Hillis meeting with him weekly for years and Mitchell serving as one of his directors in Southern California. Trotman went on to collaborate informally with Mears friend Irwin Moon, fellow Bible Institute student Helen Rittenhouse, and former First Presbyterian minister Milo Jamison to build a ministry focused on caring for recent Christian converts—particularly boys and servicemen. He maintained a strong camp and conference program that emphasized discipline and Christian discipleship. He met Billy Graham during the latter's Wheaton College days, still exhibiting the hard edge that had so concerned Mears ten years earlier.[22]

As Trotman's ministry widened to include boys, girls, businessmen, nurses, and military personnel, he connected with others in Mears's orbit including Jim Rayburn, Bob Munger, Jim Vaus, William Blackstone, Richard Halverson, J. Edwin Orr, Stuart Hamblen, and Bill Bright. By the spring of 1946 Forest Home began hosting West Coast Navigators conferences. A few years later Billy Graham hired Trotman to train counselors for his evangelistic crusades. Now fully supportive of Trotman's work, Mears served as one of his follow-up counselors. His tragic death while saving the life of a young girl in June 1956 powerfully affected her: "The loss is so terrible, because Navigators is Dawson." She believed his death "was just such a blow to everyone." In late June she attended his memorial service at the Navigators Glen Eyrie compound in Colorado with the most noteworthy leaders of the evangelical Protestant world.[23]

Dozens more personal stories could be cited to demonstrate the power Mears exercised over the cause of theological conservatism through the lay and professional Christian leaders she nurtured during her nearly five-decade ministry. Such an exercise, however, would potentially trigger the law of diminishing returns. Still, if this study is to convey the full scope of her impact and to unpack the complex relational associations she facilitated, her substantial imprint on two of the most acclaimed evangelicals of the twentieth century cannot be ignored. Of all those whom Mears inspired, no two individuals played a larger role in the midcentury revival than a pair of southern Williams: William Rohl "Bill" Bright of Oklahoma and William Franklin "Billy" Graham Jr. of North Carolina. While it would be specious to imply that Mears exercised the sole influence on their respective ministries, an examination of their history with her and her extensive associations clearly illustrates the ways in which she touched not only the men but also, through them, so many of the new evangelicals of the mid-twentieth century. It also provides another lens through which to observe the network of mutually edifying interdenominational relationships Mears facilitated and maintained.

Both men readily acknowledged their debt to First Presbyterian's director of Christian education. Billy Graham declared that she

> had a remarkable influence, both directly and indirectly on my life. In fact, I doubt if any other woman outside of my wife and mother has had such a marked influence. Her gracious spirit, her devotional life, her steadfastness for the simple gospel, and her knowledge of the Bible have been a continual inspiration and amazement to me. She is certainly one of the greatest Christians I have ever known![24]

Bill Bright went even further, writing that "apart from my mother no one has influenced my life for Christ so profoundly as has Dr. Henrietta C. Mears."[25] Although Mears knew both men for roughly the same length of time, her more intimate association with Bright in a broader range of contexts provides a richer palette from which to sketch the contours of her effect on them both.

Raised on a ranch in Coweta, Oklahoma, Bright graduated from high school in 1939 and matriculated at Northeastern State College in Tahlequah.[26] After a full collegiate career, he received his education degree in 1943. A high school football injury kept him out of military service so he secured a position as a county field agent, advising local farmers and agricultural students. Bright soon became restless, however, and struck out for California in 1944 hoping the move would result in a successful enlistment in the armed forces. If that failed, the ambitious transplant looked toward a career in the-

Ashley Hall, the Mears family home in East Poultney, Vermont. Left to right: Henrietta Mears's paternal uncle Amos Thompson, her paternal grandmother Dotha Thompson Mears, her paternal aunts Elizabeth and Cornelia Mears, children, and caretaker . *Photograph used by permission from Gospel Light/Regal Books, Ventura, CA 93003.*

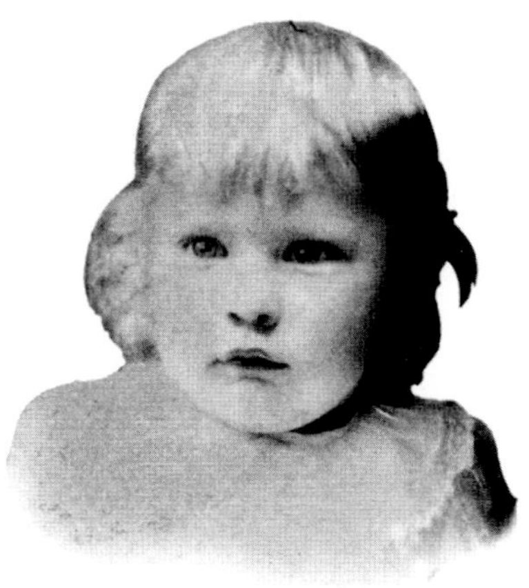

The earliest known photograph of Henrietta Cornelia Mears, probably taken in 1892. *Photograph used by permission from Gospel Light/ Regal Books, Ventura, CA 93003.*

411 13th Street, Fargo, North Dakota, childhood home of Henrietta Mears. *Photograph used by permission from the Institute for Regional Studies, North Dakota State University, Fargo, ND.*

The ruins of downtown Fargo, North Dakota, after the devastating fire of June 7, 1893. The standing arch in the right center of the photo is all that remained of the Mears Block building. *Photograph used by permission from the Institute for Regional Studies, North Dakota State University, Fargo, ND.*

Henrietta Mears at three, just as her family's financial and legal problems began to emerge. *Photograph used by permission from Gospel Light/Regal Books, Ventura, CA 93003.*

Henrietta Mears in her mid-teens. By the time this photograph was taken, her family had moved seven times. *Photograph used by permission from Gospel Light/Regal Books, Ventura, CA 93003.*

Mears and some of her Minneapolis students. *Photograph used by permission from Gospel Light/Regal Books, Ventura, CA 93003.*

The Fidelis Sunday school class of First Baptist, Minneapolis, 1920. Henrietta Mears is seated in the first row, third from the right, with Margaret Mears on her left. *Photograph used by permission from the First Baptist Church of Minneapolis.*

Mears also conducted conferences at Taquitz Pines near Idyllwild in Southern California's San Jacinto Mountains, including this Senior Young People's camp in September 1936. *Photograph used by permission from the First Presbyterian Church of Hollywood.*

First Presbyterian Church of Hollywood staff members soon after Henrietta Mears's arrival in Southern California. She is front and center wearing the fox fur. *Photograph used by permission from Gospel Light/ Regal Books, Ventura, CA 93003.*

The first warehouse of The Gospel Light Press—the Engle garage, 1933. *Photograph used by permission from Gospel Light/Regal Books, Ventura, CA 93003.*

On Thanksgiving Day, 1936, Ethel May Baldwin, Esther Ellinghusen, Stan Engle, and Henrietta Mears celebrated the new location of The Gospel Light Press at 1443 North Vine Street in Hollywood. The location served a dual purpose as the company's headquarters and a retail bookstore. *Photograph used by permission from Gospel Light/Regal Books, Ventura, CA 93003.*

By 1942 the explosive growth of The Gospel Light Press obliged the partners to lease two adjacent spaces on Vine Street to provide additional room for more retail merchandise and stock storage. *Photograph used by permission from Gospel Light/Regal Books, Ventura, CA 93003.*

In 1950 The Gospel Light Press moved to Brand Boulevard in Glendale. *Photograph used by permission from Gospel Light/Regal Books, Ventura, CA 93003.*

The Gospel Light Press Glendale headquarters complex in 1956. *Photograph used by permission from Gospel Light/Regal Books, Ventura, CA 93003.*

Badges produced by The Gospel Light Press supplemented the junior workbooks and would be affixed to long ribbons with the student's name at the top and displayed in the department meeting room. *Photograph used by permission from the First Presbyterian Church of Hollywood.*

The Gospel Light Press display at a mid-century Sunday school conference. *Photograph used by permission from Gospel Light/Regal Books, Ventura, CA 93003.*

Henrietta Mears addressing a conference sponsored by the National Sunday School Association at Moody Memorial Church in Chicago. *Photograph used by permission from Gospel Light/Regal Books, Ventura, CA 93003.*

President of the College Department (1945–1946) Gordon Severance with Henrietta Mears. *Photograph used by permission from the First Presbyterian Church of Hollywood.*

Henrietta and Margaret Mears (third and fourth from the left) at the Arc de Triomphe du Carrousel in Paris, 1947. *Photograph used by permission from Gospel Light/Regal Books, Ventura, CA 93003.*

The Biltmore, Henrietta Mears's cabin at Forest Home. *Photograph used by permission from Forest Home Ministries.*

Leonard Eilers, the "Preachin' Cowboy." *Photograph courtesy of Joy Eilers.*

Detail from the 1949 College Briefing Conference group photograph. Billy Graham is in the first row, third from the left. Mears is fifth from the right. On her right is David Cowie. In the center of the row is Bill Dunlap. *Photograph used by permission from Forest Home Ministries.*

Henrietta Mears "assisting" in the construction of Lakeview Lodge at Forest Home, 1952. *Photograph used by permission from Forest Home Ministries.*

Henrietta Mears and the Book of Remembrance at Victory Circle, Forest Home. *Photograph used by permission from Gospel Light/Regal Books, Ventura, CA 93003.*

Billy Graham speaking at Forest Home in the early 1960s. *Photograph used by permission from Forest Home Ministries.*

Cyrus Nelson looks on as Henrietta Mears attempts to blow the candles out on a cake celebrating the silver anniversary of the founding of Gospel Light and her sixty-eighth birthday in 1958. *Photograph used by permission from Gospel Light/Regal Books, Ventura, CA 93003.*

Under construction in the early 1950s, the Hollywood Freeway barely skirts the First Presbyterian Church campus seen toward the left center in this photograph. As testament to her legendary ability to accomplish the seemingly impossible, many believe to this day that the church was spared only due to the formidable influence of Henrietta Mears. *Photograph used by permission from Gospel Light/Regal Books, Ventura, CA 93003.*

Henrietta Mears shortly before her passing. *Photograph used by permission from Gospel Light/ Regal Books, Ventura, CA 93003.*

ater. The evening Bright arrived in Los Angeles, he noticed a well-scrubbed hitchhiker while stopped at the corner of Sunset Boulevard and Figueroa Street. Bright decided to give him a ride and the hitchhiker, who worked with the Navigators, reciprocated by offering his driver a place to stay, which turned out to be Dawson Trotman's home.[27] At the Trotmans' table that evening other Navigators staff members peppered the conversation with Bible verses and carried on a lively discussion. After dinner Bright's hosts invited him to join them at the residence of Charles and Grace Fuller—founders of radio's *Old Fashioned Revival Hour* program—in honor of their son Dan's birthday. Bright enjoyed the evening and exchanged pleasantries with Dan Fuller, but aside from appreciating the intellectual sophistication of the Christians he met, Bright remained spiritually unmoved and went on his way the next morning.

A short while later he rented an apartment in Hollywood and went to work for a defense contractor who Bright soon realized was defrauding the government. He quit and entered a partnership with a friend producing specialty foods. Bright soon bought him out and advanced his business career as the owner of Bright's Epicurean Delights with an assortment of thirty-two sweets laced generously with brandy.[28] His pricey confections were a hit with the well-heeled, and many high-end department stores carried his products. Bright worked long hours but had enough spare time to study drama at the Hollywood Talent Showcase and host an amateur radio program one afternoon a week. He reveled in his wealth and status, describing himself as "a happy pagan."[29]

His landlords attended the First Presbyterian Church of Hollywood, and they repeatedly invited Bright to visit. On a whim one Sunday after horseback riding in the Hollywood Hills, he slipped into a back pew for the evening service—and slipped out before it ended so "no one else would see me—or smell me."[30] Without his knowledge, his landlords added Bright's name to the visitors list, which led to his first contact with Henrietta Mears indirectly through her well-organized calling program. Soon after his visit, Bright received a telephone call from a College Department young woman who invited him to a party at the ranch of a First Presbyterian film star. The possibility of meeting the caller got the better of him and Bright agreed to go, but he was unprepared for what happened that evening:

> Gathered together in a big, play-barn were three hundred of the sharpest college-age men and women I had ever seen. They were happy, they were having fun, and they obviously loved the Lord. In one evening, my notion that Christianity is appropriate only for women and children was really shaken. I had never met people like these before.[31]

More curious now about the church than before the party, Bright started attending worship services as well as functions sponsored by the College Department and the young professionals group. In the process, he discovered that many of the most eminent business leaders of Southern California also lived as committed Christians associated with the church. Spurred by these unanticipated revelations, Bright began a systematic study of the life of Jesus. The more he studied Scripture, the more he recognized a deficiency in his life.

At this point Henrietta Mears surfaced as the central figure in his quest for spiritual understanding. Like so many others, Bright was drawn to her ebullient personality, authoritative teaching, and graceful manner. At one of her Wednesday evening expressional services in the spring of 1945, Mears challenged her collegians to get down on their knees upon their return home and seek answers to two central questions: Who is God and what does God want of me? Bright recalled that when he got to his apartment, "I realized that I was ready to give my life to God. . . . I knelt beside my bed that night and asked the questions with which Dr. Mears had challenged us. 'Who art Thou, Lord? What wilt Thou have me do?'"[32]

Though not dramatic, Bright's decision to do as Mears directed signaled the first defining moment in his spiritual life. He maintained his commercial interest, but contemplating God's direction for his future loosened the grip material success had played in his life and prepared him for what was to come. For the next year, Bright juggled his expanding candy business with a deepening commitment to Christian service, including a term as president of the College Department. He shadowed Mears, soaking up her biblical teaching and closely watching her live out her faith. As a key member of the department's officer corps, Bright regularly spent time with her praying and planning how most effectively to reach others for Christ. He learned her lessons well and followed her lead in assessing which aspects of contemporary American culture he could support and which he could not. As early as August 1945 he sensed a call to the ministry. After consulting Mears he decided to enroll in the fall of 1946 at Princeton Theological Seminary, where he became reacquainted with fellow student Dan Fuller. He managed his business from the East Coast, but profits eroded drastically by November, motivating him to leave Princeton to try to reverse the trend. Unfortunately, with the end of wartime rationing, consumers rediscovered the joy of chocolate and his brandied sweets lost significant market share. He also experienced turbulent business relationships with some fellow parishioners at First Presbyterian, which probably contributed to a measured disquiet about the nature of his call to ministry.

It was in this state of uncertainty that Bright attended the June 1947 Gospel Light Teacher Training Conference. With Mears, he pledged to become an expendable for Christ. Also with her, Bright signed his name as a charter member of the Fellowship of the Burning Heart. The morning after the Biltmore prayer meeting, Bright was among those who began planning the first College Briefing Conference. That evening Bright, Mears, Jack Franck, Louis Evans Jr., and Richard Halverson returned to Hollywood to share with the collegians what had happened at Forest Home. When Bright exhorted those who wished to surrender completely to God's will as expendables, the entire group of over two hundred stood to make the commitment. He also accompanied Mears and his three other original fellowship members to the previously mentioned Mount Hermon high school conference, which had similar results.[33] As ambitions mounted for the College Briefing Conference, Bright's summer experiences led him to apply to Fuller Theological Seminary, whose inaugural class also included Dan Fuller and fellow College Department member Gary Demarest.

After Bright's term as president of the College Department ended, he assumed at least partial leadership of the deputation programs at First Presbyterian from Mears. It is unclear whether she prompted him to add this responsibility to his seminary studies or whether he did so of his own volition.[34] In any event, Bright coordinated the deputation ministries of the church and expanded them to include college campuses. Much like Mears had done years earlier, Bright and Demarest made it a special point to connect with the student body presidents of UCLA, Occidental College, and the University of Southern California. The USC president not only became a Christian but also invited the pair to speak to his fraternity. Bright's zeal for evangelism, however, did not translate well into the seminary classroom for he much preferred fieldwork to schoolwork. In December 1947 the Fuller faculty placed him on academic probation. He and Demarest contemplated leaving seminary to pursue full-time student ministry, but both decided to stay for the time being. By 1948 Bright, along with Richard Halverson, Louis Evans Jr., and a number of other collegians and young professionals from First Presbyterian participated in regular Christian outreach events at dormitories, sororities, and fraternities scattered throughout Southern California.

The year 1948 also proved to be pivotal in Bright's personal life. He had been engaged to Vonette Zachary for over two years, but she did not share his new enthusiasm for the Christian faith. After her graduation from Texas State College for Women, he persuaded her to come west to attend the College Briefing Conference. He planned to have Zachary spend time with Mears, but Zachary intended "to rescue him from this religious fanaticism or come back without a ring."[35] The students she met at the conference impressed her as much as they had impressed Bright more than four years earlier. But it was her conversations with Mears that proved critical. Zachary felt welcomed, but she was also on her guard as Mears spoke to her about her Christian walk. At first Zachary defended her take on Christianity, but Mears used a scientific analogy that resonated with the chemistry minor. Zachary subsequently committed her life to Christ, but she needed further encouragement when the first days after her conversion failed to meet her unrealistic expectations.[36] Now spiritually on the same page with her fiancé, Zachary married Bright in December 1948.

As they began their life together, the evangelical urgency that first jolted him in June 1947 and manifested itself in his work with the deputation programs at First Presbyterian, burst upon the national consciousness with full force in 1949. Much ink has been spilled studying this midcentury revival, and Mears usually makes a cameo appearance as a bit player in the dramatic events of those years. But when her overlooked connections to the acknowledged leaders of the evangelical awakening are exposed, it becomes obvious that she played much more than just a supporting role to the male cast of characters. As had been the case with Bill Bright's formative years in Southern California, the influence of Henrietta Mears would be instrumental in the life and ministry of Billy Graham, the most prominent evangelical of the era.

Mears most likely first met Graham in early 1946, just over a year after he became a traveling evangelist for Torrey Johnson's Youth for Christ International. William Bell Riley invited Graham to speak at a Bible conference sponsored by his Northwestern Schools in Minneapolis, and he wanted Mears in the audience. He confided to her that he believed Graham would be his successor at First Baptist and at Northwestern. Graham did take the helm of Northwestern Schools in 1948, but continued his work with YFC. Just a few months after this first encounter with Mears, Graham unknowingly had a surrogate second when Cliff Barrows joined his team, for Barrows had become a Christian through the ministry of Mears protégé Dick Hillis at Mount Hermon.[37]

Bill Bright and Billy Graham were not the only ones in Mears's circle who desired to serve college-age young people. J. Edwin Orr of Northern Ireland began holding open-air evangelistic meetings in Belfast before the age of twenty as a prelude to his vocation as an itinerant evangelist. He traveled the world preaching and writing, first visiting the United States in 1936—all forty-eight of them. After serving as a chaplain for the American military during World War II, Orr and his family established a permanent residence in Southern California. He focused on evangelistic work in colleges and universities around the world. While pursuing doctoral study at Oxford, Orr met Graham in late 1946 or early 1947 and most likely became acquainted with Mears's ministry soon thereafter. Orr knew about the revival among the collegians at Forest Home in 1947 and believed that the movement would spread. His return from Oxford brought him into closer contact with Mears. Her success with college-age students at First Presbyterian quickened his incentive to work among young adults as the catalyst to worldwide revival. In early 1949 after consulting with Mears, her student leaders, and Revival Prayer Fellowship founder Armin Gesswein, Orr departed from Southern California for two months of exclusive work with students in Minneapolis. Two members of the Fellowship of the Burning Heart, Jack Franck and Bill Dunlap, drove two thousand miles to join him and do what they could to kindle in the upper Midwest the revival fire that burned so brightly in Southern California in 1947. Just prior to Orr's first meetings in the spring of 1949 at Saint Paul's Bethel College, Franck and Dunlap joined him and Graham for a midnight prayer meeting in the latter's Minneapolis office. The spiritual awakening began almost immediately at Bethel and quickly reached the St. Paul Bible Institute and Graham's own Northwestern Schools. A number of regional colleges and universities including the University of Minnesota sponsored meetings that resulted in further evidence of revival. Two thousand students on six campuses testified to its reality. Orr held eighty meetings in the first month with a reported aggregate attendance of forty thousand students. Dunlap and Franck traveled to Wheaton College in Illinois to share the news about the regional awakening and found students there stirred regarding the need on their own campus. By the time collegians dispersed for summer break, "Christians of Arminian, Calvinist and Lutheran theology agreed unanimously that the student campaign had been an outpouring of the Spirit from start to finish." Mears's contacts in Minneapolis and Saint Paul kept her apprised of the revival as it progressed.[38] Although she had not been physically present, her initiatives emanating outward from First Presbyterian and Forest Home, her personal counsel, and her students played a significant role in the awakening.

Events in the autumn of 1949 played a definitive role in advancing the cause of American evangelicalism. The locus of interest remains Billy Graham's Los Angeles campaign, as well it should. But the preoccupation with it has obscured the magnitude of other developments that both contributed to the success of Graham's landmark crusade and extended the reach of American theological conservatism. Not surprisingly, many of the most momentous of those developments can be traced back to the influence, either directly or indirectly, of the soon-to-be sexagenarian Henrietta Mears. From mid-1949 through the early 1950s, the interrelationships among Mears, Graham, Bright, and Orr demonstrate how pervasive her presence was in the knitting together of a postwar interdenominational evangelical Protestant consensus.

BECAUSE NO PAPER TRAIL EXISTS, it is not possible to know exactly when speakers received invitations to participate in the third College Briefing Conference at Forest Home the week before Labor Day in 1949. Mears most likely approached Graham because of his connections to young people as YFC evangelist and the then-youngest college president in the country. He accepted the invitation (probably offered in early 1948) because he believed it was the latter office that made him attractive to the expected audience.[39] In all likelihood, Mears invited Orr to Forest Home after he spoke to her collegians and attended the College Department Saturday morning prayer meeting at her home in the late winter or early spring of 1949. Other speakers included

Canadian evangelist Charles Templeton, "Dad" Elliott of the YMCA, Louis Evans Sr., and Mears associates David Cowie and Robert Munger. Bill and Vonette Bright attended the conference with roughly five hundred other registrants from a dozen western universities.[40]

The months leading up to the conference signaled a renewed interest in evangelical Protestantism. Orr's March meetings in Southern California in preparation for Graham's crusade in September were enthusiastically received, which augured well for the young evangelist's sojourn in the Southland. April brought the late-night prayer meeting in Graham's office to which Fred Hoffman traced the origin of the midcentury college revival that enveloped the Twin Cities through the spring and rippled outward from there over the next few years.[41]

Graham's experience during those months, however, could not have been further removed from these hopeful signs. The Northwestern Schools enjoyed a banner academic year, but by the spring of 1949 Graham considered taking a sabbatical from the presidency to pursue doctoral study. Disheartened by his exploration of relevant graduate programs, he pondered his future direction. To add to his quandary, the June 12–26 Altoona, Pennsylvania, campaign suffered a series of problems. He later wrote, "if I ever felt I conducted a Campaign that was a flop, *humanly* speaking. Altoona was it!" To make matters worse, his close friend and YFC associate Charles Templeton, who had resigned from his Toronto church to enroll at Princeton Theological Seminary in the fall of 1948, began wrestling with the questions that also plagued Graham as he read Karl Barth and Reinhold Niebuhr in an effort to stay attuned to the latest theological scholarship. For both, the accuracy and authority of Scripture arose as the central issue. As Graham embarked on an intensive study of the subject, his friend began to drift away from orthodoxy.[42] Worn down and discouraged, Graham tried to extricate himself from the Forest Home commitment. Without knowing the extent of Graham's spiritual and mental malaise, Mears and her colleagues reiterated their desire for him to serve as one of the two conference headliners. As a result, the despondent thirty-year-old evangelist found himself a mile high in the San Bernardino Mountains on the last week of August as the featured morning speaker at Forest Home.[43]

Jack Franck and Bill Dunlap helped infuse the conference with an air of great expectations by reporting on the revival they had witnessed a few months earlier. Orr's evening messages hit a responsive chord among the students. Though Graham's morning talks appeared to be similarly effective,[44] during the opening days of the conference he could often be found at the Biltmore praying with Mears and seeking her counsel. Her love for the students, her grasp of biblical truths, her knowledge of modern scholarship, and her unwavering commitment to the veracity of Scripture deeply impressed him. He later reflected that "I was desperate for every insight she could give me."[45] However, Graham also had opportunity to spend time with Templeton, who taunted him for being "fifty years out-of-date," and challenged his now shaky belief in the authority of the Bible. The anguished evangelist felt "Miss Mears stretching me one way and Chuck Templeton stretching me the other."[46]

Finally, on Thursday evening Graham confronted his doubts and faced his future: "With the Los Angeles Campaign galloping toward me, I had to have an answer. If I *could not* trust the Bible, I could not go on. I would have to quit the school presidency. I would have to leave pulpit evangelism."[47] His mind racing, Graham stepped out into the moonlit night and dropped to his knees in the forest, confessing his uncertainties about Scripture and his inability to answer the questions raised by Templeton and others. At this point he believed the Holy Spirit gave him the freedom to call on faith to transcend his doubts and questions. Graham did not ignore what he did not understand, but resolved to believe the Bible was God's inspired word and to act confidently on that belief. A new assurance transformed his ministry, with the results immediately evident to conference participants like Ruth Schnicke, director of Christian education at Tabernacle Presbyterian Church in Indianapolis.[48] Graham returned to Minneapolis after the College Briefing Conference still somewhat anxious about the Los Angeles campaign but free of doubts about the authority of Scripture.

The role that Mears played in Graham's radical about-face is at least partially documented, but the week at Forest Home proved to be only the initial experience that welded the two together for further productive work on behalf of evangelical Protestantism. Soon after his return to Minneapolis, Graham drafted a letter to Mears on September 9 noting his appreciation for the time at Forest Home with her and hinting at future collaborations:

> God has indeed given you a tremendous ministry. You shall be in our daily prayers that He might continue to use you for His glory. Thanks a million for letting me in on it. I shall always treasure those hours in my memory as

> hours spent with the Lord. . . . Really, I feel a definite part of Forest Home and even if I am not going as a speaker, I shall probably be coming to your conferences just for the sheer thrill of it all.

Graham informed her that he would be back in Southern California on September 19, nearly a week before the opening meeting of the campaign. At the College Briefing Conference Colleen Townsend had spoken with him about the possibility of sharing a message with the newly organized Hollywood Christian Group during his time in Los Angeles, and he wanted to be "of service if you need me." He concluded his letter with the hope that an invitation he had extended to Mears to speak in Minneapolis during the coming winter would be accepted because "we want you and need you."[49] Graham seemed to sense instinctively that his relationship with Mears had only just begun, and he looked forward to future collaborative endeavors with her.

What Graham did not know was that Mears had already decided the young college president had a stellar future as an evangelist. During the College Briefing Conference Graham had been completely unaware that four representatives from the Christian Business Men's Committee sat in the audience. They had earlier conferred with Mears in her Forest Home cabin regarding whom they might invite to hold an evangelistic campaign in Los Angeles. Rather than suggesting potential candidates, Mears invited the men to sit in on the conference sessions to determine whether either Billy Graham or Charles Templeton might best serve their purpose. She proposed that on Friday they would meet again at the Biltmore when "the Lord will tell us which one is the one that we should choose for this two week campaign." When the group reconvened at the end of the week, Mears informed the men that she had been in prayer about the matter and "the Lord tells me that it should be Billy Graham." To a person, all in the room were taken aback by her declaration as Templeton appeared the more polished speaker. The little-known, southern-born-and-bred Graham did not seem to them to be the appropriate choice, but they followed her advice, which led directly to Graham's 1951 Hollywood crusade. Merely on the strength of her conversations with him and his morning messages that critical week, Mears discerned Graham's great yet largely unknown gift for evangelism. National recognition of that gift still lay weeks away in a canvas tent erected at the corner of Washington Boulevard and Hill Street in downtown Los Angeles.[50]

By the end of 1949 the scope and number of interdenominational evangelical initiatives bearing Mears's imprimatur was truly staggering. Her personal stake in Graham's Los Angeles campaign went beyond the decisive week at Forest Home as Mears College Department members such as Louis Evans Jr. and Colleen Townsend participated directly in crusade meetings. Over and above the ongoing popularity of Gospel Light curricular materials, annual conventions of the National Sunday School Association as well as state and local Sunday school conferences brought a robust vitality to evangelical Protestant educational programs. (Mears's colleague Cyrus Nelson would cofound the Greater Los Angeles Sunday School Association in 1951.) The first contingent of Mears's student volunteers began preparations for their 1950 World Deputation assignments, and at least a dozen Christian organizations either originated from or greatly expanded their ministries because of the 1949 College Briefing Conference.[51]

The revival among collegians spread at least partially due to the ministrations of Mears associates. From late 1949 into 1950, Orr at California Baptist Seminary, Los Angeles Pacific College, Pasadena College, Seattle Pacific College, the University of Washington, and Baylor University; David Cowie at Spokane's Whitworth College and the University of Washington; Robert Munger at Columbia University; and Billy Graham at the University of Minnesota, all contributed to a growing respect for evangelical Christianity that journalist Stanley Rowland of the *New York Times* recognized by the middle of the decade.[52]

Of all those committed to the evangelization of collegians, however, none had more passion or motivation than one of Mears's most devoted "boys," Bill Bright. He returned from the 1949 College Briefing Conference energized by the "extraordinary student awakening" he sensed at the conference. Bright first met Graham that week and wrote, "I feel a communion of spirit with him because it was here the Lord spoke to many of us, giving us a new challenge for service plus a greater sense of urgency for the lost."[53] Like so many others, he watched with keen interest the progress of Graham's Los Angeles campaign in the fall. Buoyed by the conference and the response to Graham's messages, Bright recentered himself on his ministerial aspirations. Fuller reinstated him, and he returned to his graduate studies.

The inevitable pressures of balancing his evangelistic work on regional campuses with his class schedule, business interests, and Vonette, however, precipitated a series of crucial events by mid-1951. His grades improved in the spring 1950 term, but disagreements with presbytery leaders over his matriculation at the non-Presbyterian seminary ended his quest for ordination in the denomination. Bright continued his coursework but his grades dropped ominously, undermining his prospects for graduation. Added to his disappointment regarding his future in the Presbyterian Church was the disparity he perceived between his dedication to evangelistic ministry and the seminary's insistence on rigorous inquiry. For Bright the study of theology and biblical languages could not hold a candle to the practice of evangelism. So convinced was he that active evangelistic work in the field trumped preparation in the study carrel that he cautioned both fellow Mears protégé Dale Bruner and Dan Fuller that the demands of academic life paled in comparison.[54]

The Brights experienced a serious marital crisis in the spring of 1951. Its successful resolution persuaded him to submit every personal desire and every hope for the future to the lordship of Christ and to wait on his direction. A short week later while studying late at night for a language examination, he received that direction. The next morning he described to Vonette his sense that God called him to "help reach the world for Christ and fulfill the Great Commission in his lifetime" by focusing first on evangelizing the leaders at universities and colleges. The great charge from Mears at the 1947 conference to be persons of destiny had finally crystalized for Bright. After conferring with her, Wilbur Smith (his mentor at Fuller), and Louis Evans Sr., Bright sold his business and withdrew from seminary to begin Campus Crusade for Christ. Members of his initial advisory board included Mears, Smith, Graham, Orr, Halverson, Trotman, and Cyrus Nelson.[55]

Of those board members, Mears proved to be the most significant for the future of the interdenominational evangelistic ministry. Just a few months after Bright's late-night revelation, Mears's sister, companion, and keeper since 1916 was struck down by a cerebral thrombosis on December 18. Margaret died two days later.[56] As Mears dealt with her loss, the work of Campus Crusade began at UCLA. Within a few months, more than 250 students including the school's student body president, the editor of the student newspaper, and top athletes such as all-American linebacker Donn Moomaw converted to Christianity. Bright's efforts melded seamlessly with the ongoing revival of interest in spiritual matters on the nation's college and university campuses.[57]

Following their mother's example, the Mears sisters had always maintained an open home. Although Henrietta hosted a number of houseguests since Margaret's passing, by mid-1952 she found caring for her six-bedroom house increasingly burdensome. Aware of her love for life's finer things and in an attempt to buoy her spirits, a real estate friend offered to show Mears an opulent listing that would soon go on the market closer to UCLA. Located at the intersection of Stone Canyon Road and Sunset Boulevard directly across the street from the campus, the residence resembled a small castle and carried a price tag to match. As she toured it, Mears imagined how ideal the property might be for her collegians—thoroughly surprising her friend, since she had no thought of selling it to Mears. Unfortunately, the house sold while Mears mulled over whether to purchase it. Unperturbed, she continued her work, traveled overseas, and forgot all about the matter until the Brights mentioned that it had been relisted. With the ministry to the UCLA campus expanding, they were looking for a location closer to campus. When Don Tarbell, a College Department alumnus and Southern California real estate agent, showed all three of them the property, they realized that with a spacious common entertainment area and a huge dining room but with separate living quarters, the home could serve the needs of both parties. One of Mears's "boys" offered to buy her other house, allowing her to purchase "the castle," as it came to be known. They moved in the early fall of 1953. The Brights helped out financially, and Vonette managed the household, reprising many of the duties Margaret had borne for so long. In the nearly ten years the Brights spent with Mears and others who joined them, thousands of young people associated with Campus Crusade and First Presbyterian came through their door. Bill Bright recalled that of all the places where Crusade met, "the favorite was always 110 Stone Canyon Road."[58]

Mears's impact, however, went well beyond providing the Brights and Campus Crusade a comfortable home base. She also regularly opened Forest Home to Crusade conferences and was a popular speaker at many Crusade functions. By 1954 Mears had allowed Bright to build a cabin at the conference grounds for the exclusive use of the ministry. Bright adopted her strategy of winning the campus stars to Christ, particularly males, believing they would attract others to the faith. He also stressed the positive, as demonstrated by the first "law" in the organization's primary evangelistic tool ("God loves you and offers a wonderful plan for your life.")[59] The idea of spiritual laws also came from Mears's teaching. Campus Crusade's "action groups," which were small

Bible study and evangelism training units, were built on her practice of breaking up the Wednesday evening meetings into small study groups. Even his use of diagrams and acrostics in Crusade materials may have been borrowed from Mears's longtime practices.[60]

Paralleling Billy Graham's ministry after his Forest Home experience, Bright's grew rapidly through the 1950s. Campus Crusade added nine staff members in addition to Bill and Vonette Bright in 1952. There were forty-four staffers in 1955, and 109 in 1960.[61] The ministries of Bright, Graham, and Orr flourished at least partially because of the overlapping and complementary nature of their labors. While it would be an overstatement to place Mears at the absolute center of these beneficial interrelationships, her dominant role in their cross-fertilization—nationally, but especially on the West Coast—cannot be denied or minimized. And nowhere is it more readily apparent than in her involvement with the Hollywood Christian Group during its formative years. The part she played in the conversion of Redd Harper and Stuart Hamblen best demonstrates how her multilayered influence, both directly and through her associates and friends, affected so many other frontline evangelicals of the time.

After some local radio success in Iowa, Harper moved in the early 1930s to Southern California, where he was able to find similar work.[62] His vocal and instrumental abilities also secured him a position with Jimmie Grier, "the Musical Host of the West Coast." Grier's orchestra had a regular booking at the Biltmore Bowl in the stylish hotel of the same name in downtown Los Angeles playing for VIP parties and Academy Award dinners. Though he met many of the major stars of prewar Hollywood and even had a screen test with 20th Century Fox, Harper remained on the celebrity sidelines. After a disappointing recording session with Benny Goodman, Lionel Hampton, Gene Krupa, and Goodman's vocalist Helen Ward as well as a devastating missed opportunity with Paramount, Harper became somewhat pessimistic about his prospects. His stint with the 11th Naval District Coast Guard Band during the war, however, helped launch *Redd Harper's Hollywood Roundup* radio program after V-J Day. It became his ticket to fame and fortune. He put together a cowboy band, wrote his own scripts, and secured as guests the brightest western stars, such as Stuart Hamblen, Cindy Walker, Roy Rogers, Dale Evans, and the Sons of the Pioneers among many others. He also achieved some screen success in 1947 with an uncredited part in *Under Colorado Skies*. Harper graduated to a feature role in the Gene Autry vehicle *The Strawberry Roan* (1948), but that was the extent of his cinematic resume to 1950.[63]

In January 1950 he assisted Tim Spencer and Cindy Walker in producing the "Western Hall of Fame" benefit performances in the San Francisco Bay area for the Variety Club's boys work. Most of the major Hollywood stars topped the bill and nearly all tipped the bottle to one extent or another, but Harper noticed that neither Spencer nor Roy Rogers or Dale Evans touched a drop. Knowing of Spencer's former addiction, Harper questioned his lack of lubrication. Spencer replied that it was a miracle of God and that he wanted to tell Harper about it when they returned to LA.

Harper flew back the next day and promptly became deathly ill. Harper's wife had learned of Spencer's conversion and called him seeking prayer for her husband. Velma Spencer in turn called Frances Eilers, who contacted members of the Christian sorority she worked with to pray also. In the meantime, Tim Spencer had alerted First Presbyterian of Harper's illness, and the church's prayer group added him to its list. Tim and Velma Spencer arrived at the hospital with Leonard and Frances Eilers to check on his condition, praying together for their ailing friend. Harper later recognized that visit and prayer—from four people Mears had touched personally—as the beginning of his journey toward God.

Shortly after the prayer session in his room, Harper recovered enough from his mysterious illness to leave the hospital. In early February Tim Spencer invited him to a meeting of the Hollywood Christian Group. Harper had never heard of the organization and thought the idea sounded bizarre. But when Spencer explained that he would know a number of the attendees (and when Harper realized it might be an occasion to meet a director or producer in need of his talents), he agreed to go. Jack Franck led the singing, which was followed by a time of sharing by a number of members Harper did not know. But he did recognize Colleen Townsend, Louise James, Joyce Compton, and the Spencers, among others. John Holland introduced the speaker, who expounded on being "born again." Though quite impressed that no collection was taken, Harper remained dumbfounded that anyone could believe what he had heard yet also amazed that so many seemed to be truly affected by the proceedings. Upon returning to his home he told his wife that "crazy Tim Spencer has turned out to be a religious fanatic."[64]

Clearly uninterested in what the HCG offered, Harper had no intention of attending another meeting when Spencer called to invite him—until he heard that Connie Haines would be there. Harper had known Haines for years and worked with her prior to the war. Spencer explained that Haines's fiancé had recently died tragically and the meeting would be in his parents' home. That was enough to pique Harper's interest. He greeted Haines when he arrived but did not know what to make of her. He knew her as an accomplished swing and blues vocalist, but this evening she sang "I'd Rather Have Jesus," composed by George Beverly Shea of the Billy Graham evangelistic team. By the time she concluded the piece Harper was in tears. The line "I'd rather have Jesus than men's applause" was especially meaningful to him sung with integrity by another entertainer he knew and respected. He regained his composure, but Haines's serene faith while facing a traumatic personal loss stayed with him.

By the end of March, Spencer's composition "Room Full of Roses" had begun its rapid rise up the pop charts, and as it did Harper developed more respect for the religious fanatic. Perhaps it originated to some extent from the fact that Spencer had asked Harper to write the manuscripts for some of his new songs. Spencer's enthusiasm centered on "The Sea Walker," a ballad about Jesus walking on the water, but Harper correctly predicted that "Room Full of Roses" would be the hit. Spencer ultimately framed Harper's original manuscript and hung it in his office. Harper was also intrigued that Spencer's first hit record was also the first song he had written after his Christian conversion. When Spencer's publisher advanced him enough money to purchase a new home in the San Fernando Valley, Harper could not help but wonder if God would do the same for him. Success in his chosen profession remained a cherished goal.

The Spencers invited him to attend the dedication party for their new home. Included on the guest list were all the members of the various incarnations of the Sons of the Pioneers and many other western stars, including Rex Allen. Also present were those who were, in Harper's words, "much more important in the life of this old country boy even though, at that time, I certainly did not think so." They included Mears, Orr, Halverson, and Leonard Eilers, along with many Hollywood Christian Group regulars.[65] After plenty of singing and barbecue, the Spencers told the gathered crowd the story of their faith and how their commitment to God's service led to the writing of the song that allowed them to purchase the home. They concluded by asking Halverson to offer a prayer dedicating the home, their possessions, their teenage children, and themselves to Christ. Their actions probably stunned many at the party, but it increased Harper's appreciation and caused him to consider the possibility that the God they spoke about might provide him the peace he could not find elsewhere.

The next meeting of the HCG proved crucial for him. The group met at Mears's home and included recent Christian convert Stuart Hamblen. Harper and Hamblen had a rocky history. *Stuart Hamblen and His Lucky Stars* was already a popular radio program in 1932 when Harper arrived in Hollywood. Hamblen invited him on as a guest artist, and in short order he became a regular performer. He subsequently played saxophone and clarinet with Hamblen's dance band. One evening when Hamblen failed to appear on time, Harper filled in as vocalist. When the intoxicated headliner arrived an hour later, he wrested the microphone from Harper, obviously displeased at Redd's ability to perform in his stead and gave the stand-in his two weeks' notice. Needless to say, he took his leave with a liberal dose of bitterness aimed at his jealous former employer. Now here he was, more than fifteen years later, at a meeting of Christians in the home of a respected Christian teacher facing an old nemesis.

What Harper did not know until that evening at Mears's home was that Hamblen had undergone a powerful conversion to the faith. Until very recently, he only had gone to First Presbyterian infrequently with his wife and children, although they worshipped there regularly.[66] But in 1949 when Henrietta Mears invited Billy Graham to speak at her summer College Briefing Conference, Hamblen's wife, Suzy, and sister Oberia went to hear him. The power of his message deeply moved them both, and Suzy asked many of those she met at Forest Home to pray for her husband's salvation.[67] A short while later Hamblen expressed a desire to go to a prayer meeting with her at First Presbyterian and even asked the group to pray for him. Hamblen then attended one of the early meetings of the HCG. When the time came for questions from the audience, he queried Orr about the unpardonable sin. Orr did not even know that the curious man was Hamblen until Jack Franck informed him. It was only then that he realized this was the man Suzy had asked prayer for at Forest Home. Though not yet a believer, Hamblen attended another HCG meeting with his wife. This time Orr spent a substantial amount of time with him. While the chaplain explained the gospel message, group members Charles Turner, Suzy Hamblen, and Tim and Velma Spencer adjourned to another room to pray, but Hamblen hesitated to make a decision to follow Christ. There the matter lay in late September.[68]

Billy Graham's return to Southern California in late summer to conduct what was supposed to be a three-week evangelistic campaign in Los Angeles included a pre-crusade commitment to Colleen Townsend to address the HCG at Mears's home—the first of his many visits to her residence during the course of the campaign.[69] That Monday evening Hamblen and his wife arrived ninety minutes early, as had Graham. The men took an instant liking to each other. Hamblen described Graham as "truly inspired," and the evangelist returned the compliment: "You're a forward fellow and I like that."[70] Mears and Suzy paired off to allow Hamblen and Graham some time together before the arrival of the others. When the formal meeting got underway Graham gave a gospel message and concluded with a call to follow Christ. Hamblen did not respond but invited the evangelist to dinner after the meeting ended. As Graham spoke with him and Suzy about the coming evangelistic campaign, Hamblen promised to help get the word out. By this time he was the number one radio personality on the West Coast and so could reach a vast audience through his program. He also told Graham he would welcome the evangelist on the broadcast as a guest. Hamblen bragged, only half facetiously according to Graham, that he could fill the tent with his endorsement. Before they parted that evening, Suzy made sure that Graham knew that her husband was not yet a Christian.[71]

Hamblen proved true to his word and encouraged his listeners to "go on down to Billy Graham's tent and hear the preaching," which Graham himself believed had grown stronger since his Forest Home experience.[72] After resolving doubts about appearing on a program sponsored by a tobacco company, the evangelist also accepted Hamblen's invitation.[73] The cowboy star did not initially attend Graham's meetings in person, but after Suzy gently accused him of being something of a hypocrite by endorsing but not appearing at the crusade, Hamblen relented and happily found many of his fans glad to see him. He did not, however, appreciate Graham's message of condemnation aside from a commitment to Christ. Hamblen returned, but as at the previous meeting he thought Graham was speaking right to him. He complained to Suzy: "'You're going to hell' is what he always shouts at me and points directly at me." Hamblen grew so enraged at Graham during one meeting he actually shook his fist at the evangelist as he exited the tent. Though Hamblen bristled at Graham's message, he did tell his wife that he thought he needed to go to church with her.[74]

As the three-week campaign entered its final few days, Hamblen's fury boiled over. He went hunting in the High Sierra to get away from Graham and his own frustrations, but the trip solved nothing and his anger failed to dissipate. He returned to Los Angeles somewhat ill and troubled, yet he accompanied Suzy to one of the last scheduled meetings. Hamblen found fault with every aspect of the service. At its conclusion he stormed out of the tent and went to a nightclub for cocktails, but they did little to dull his senses. Returning home thoroughly frightened, Hamblen made his way to the bedroom and ordered Suzy to get up and pray with him. They prayed in earnest but to no avail from Hamblen's perspective. He suggested that they call Graham, but because it was 3:30 in the morning Suzy tried to dissuade him. He shot back, "He's responsible for all of this. He's torn me up mentally, he's torn me up physically, and I'm going to call him." Hamblen did, and within an hour he and Suzy were in Graham's room at the Langham Hotel, where the most popular radio star in the West surrendered his life to Christ. In the wake of Hamblen's conversion, the Graham team decided to continue the campaign at least another week, believing that "the Lord had unfinished business to do in the lives of people who were just beginning to hear about the meetings and think about the Gospel."[75]

During the first week of the extended campaign, Hamblen shared his Christian conversion experience over the radio. His decision to do so demonstrated the minor but significant role Mears, Orr, Townsend, and the HCG played in his journey to faith. It also brought Billy Graham to national prominence, for it was directly after Hamblen's dramatic radio testimony that newspaper magnate William Randolph Hearst charged his editors to "puff Graham." While it cannot be categorically stated as to why Hearst chose this particular moment to "kiss" the evangelist, as one reporter put it, the role of the players in Hamblen's preconversion narrative should not be disregarded. Without the preparatory events leading up to his radio confession—from Mears's invitation to Graham and the promise Hamblen made at Mears's home to publicize Graham's campaign, to Graham's appearance on his radio program and Hamblen's early morning conversion experience—Hearst probably would never have directed his editors to pay any more attention to Graham than they had over the previous weeks of the campaign. It was only *after* Hamblen's discussion of his conversion experience on the air that Graham considered prolonging the campaign *and* that Hearst's reporters showed up in droves.[76]

It was this Stuart Hamblen who stood before Redd Harper in Mears's living room that evening barely six months later—and Harper was not quite sure what to make of the chastened celebrity. He had heard from Buddy Dooley, a regular on Hamblen's radio show, that he had a religious awakening and was ending the program to preach, but this was the first time he had heard Hamblen's story—and from Hamblen himself in a room full of his colleagues in the industry. Harper was intrigued at the radical change in Hamblen's demeanor from the crude and jealous man he had known earlier. Hamblen stunned him when he shared that his desire for alcohol completely disappeared and that he sold his stable of prized racehorses because of his new faith. Harper even noticed a difference in the quality of Hamblen's voice when he sang "He Bought My Soul at Calvary," a song he wrote soon after that early morning conversion experience in Billy Graham's hotel room. He did not want to believe that Hamblen and others in the HCG were on to something, but he could not dismiss what he witnessed at Mears's home that evening.

Harper ridiculed the idea of personal sinfulness that the speaker at another meeting of the group traced back to Adam and Eve, but even though Harper continued to scorn the work of the HCG, he kept returning to the meetings—and watching the members very closely. He regularly taunted Tim Spencer about his faith and his earlier bout with the bottle. He tried to convince Spencer that he was a good man, certainly a better man than Spencer had been in his preconversion days. After one meeting of the HCG at which Mears's friend Harry Rimmer spoke and Harper actually found himself seriously contemplating Christianity, he flew into a private rage directed primarily at Spencer for his key role getting him involved with the band of religious zealots. A few days later, still infuriated with Spencer, Harper burst into his office and fired off an obscenity-laced tirade against his strangely calm adversary, then turned and stormed out. Not five minutes later, Harper knew he needed to apologize. Instead he swore at his behavior and drove off. It was May 1950. In two weeks the HCG would meet again in the home of Henrietta Mears.

By his own admission Harper rarely went to church unless Tim Spencer or someone else offered to take him, but Sunday, May 19, was different. He went to First Presbyterian alone hoping he could find a friend with whom to sit. He searched but did not see anyone—except Henrietta Mears. She knew Harper from the group meetings and asked if he planned to come to the next one. Sensing indecision in his reply, she pursued him further: "The meeting is at my house, you know. You're coming aren't you?" Pressed by her follow-up query, he nonchalantly assured her that he would be there although he had little real intention of going. But as Harper wrote in his 1957 autobiography, "God had different ideas about my encounter with Miss Mears. He has never let me forget it, even until this very moment."[77]

Monday evening Harper intended to see a new film at the Egyptian Theatre on Hollywood Boulevard, but recoiled at having to pay for parking. The longer he searched in vain for a free parking space, the more irritated he became. Recalling his offhand promise to Mears, he decided to try to find her home even though he had been to only one other meeting of the HCG at her Westwood address. Harper had been quite impressed with Mears and did not want her to think ill of him, so he worked hard to find her residence but to no avail. Just as he made up his mind to give up, a man got out of his car and crossed the street in front of him. It turned out to be Bill Bright, whom he knew from earlier meetings. And the only parking spot on the entire block was right in front of Mears's home. She greeted Harper as he entered and handed him a Bible. Although he did not realize it at the time, this was actually a closed meeting meant only for those who had made a Christian commitment. On this particular evening Mears gave the Bible lesson on John 15:7, taking the theme of abiding in Christ. Her command of related biblical passages and her thoughtful words impressed Harper in a new way. After the Bible study portion of the meeting ended everyone knelt to pray. Mears charged the group to "remember to pray for your enemies as well as your friends. You can hate sin but you can't hate sinners. God hates sin but He loves sinners."[78]

This was a revelation to Harper, for he had despised his father for many years. Mears's words helped him redirect his hatred toward his father's actions and away from his personhood. He later wrote that "my hiding place was suddenly destroyed. I could no longer run, coward that I was, and hide behind this hate because I realized God loved my father no matter what he had done or could do."[79] Mears followed her charge with an invitation to commit to God whatever interfered with spiritual victory. What was left of Harper's resistance to Christianity evaporated in a conversion experience.

That evening he told Velma Spencer and Henrietta Mears of his commitment to Christianity. The following week when the meeting moved to the Spencers' home, Harper was the first to tell the gathering what had happened to him that spring evening at the home and under the teaching of Henrietta Mears.

Nearly four years to the day after Redd Harper's conversion, Billy Graham's epochal Greater London Crusade came to a conclusion with more than 165,000 crowded into White City and Wembley stadiums for the final meetings.[80] Over the course of the previous twelve unprecedented weeks, Graham had received many guests from the spreading network of evangelicals, including his friend and occasional counselor Henrietta Mears. She joined him after a speaking engagement in Philadelphia and a quick visit to her fifteen former College Department members then studying at Princeton Theological Seminary. Donn Moomaw, another College Department member and one of Graham's crusade assistants, met her at the airport along with two other College Department alumni—Louis Evans Jr., who was studying for his doctorate at the University of Edinburgh, and his wife, former film star Colleen Townsend Evans. Upon arriving at the crusade site, Mears greeted many of her longtime friends before ascending the speaker's platform resplendent in a canary yellow coat and watermelon red hat. Making a point to welcome their valued associate were Dawson Trotman; Hubert Mitchell, a missionary to Asia and another former College Department member; Dr. Paul Rees, pastor of the First Covenant Church in Minneapolis; Dr. A. W. Goodwin-Hudson, vicar of London's St. Mary Magdalene Church; and Graham coworkers Cliff Barrows and George Beverly Shea. As a measure of the esteem Graham had for Mears, he made sure that she received an invitation to one of the formal functions planned for the crusade team at the elegant Dorchester Hotel.

Shortly thereafter Mears left London for a visit to Scandinavia and Amsterdam before returning for the last three days of the crusade. After the climactic final meeting, Mears took a side trip to Oxford for tea with C. S. Lewis to invite him to speak at Forest Home, as Goodwin-Hudson had on two previous occasions. Although Lewis showed an interest in the offer, he never took advantage of her open invitation. But the noted English Bible translator and author J. B. Phillips did. Her visit to his home in Redhill after leaving Oxford allowed them to strategize about his upcoming speaking engagements at her conference center.[81]

Mears's warm reception by four of her College Department alumni, a former Youth for Christ evangelist little known before his life-changing experience at Forest Home, two of Great Britain's most renowned Christian writers, a one-time candidate to head a youth ministry under her leadership, and other noted Christian leaders at Graham's Greater London Crusade, epitomized not only the growing influence of the new evangelicalism, but also the decisive role Henrietta Mears played in the interlocking network of theologically conservative individuals and institutions that emerged by the middle of the twentieth century. The collaborative kinship between Mears, her collegians, and many of the foremost figures in the evangelical movement beyond First Presbyterian contributed extensively to the nationwide reformation of Protestantism in the postwar era.

Chapter Ten

Paradoxes and Limitations

Over the decades, when asked about her own personal faith journey, Henrietta Mears always stressed the preeminent significance of her mother and maternal grandmother. However, since she only knew the latter through the perceptions of the former, it was her mother's Christian witness in word and deed that exerted the greatest power over her perspectives on life and ministry. Margaret Burtis Everts Mears lived with a focused intensity that inspired accolades and unreserved tributes wherever she lived. Her devotion to God, care for the neglected, and love for her family gave her life its profound meaning and purpose. But she was also something of a saintly martinet—especially to her children. Although not overly demonstrative, she modeled standards of religious devotion, service to the community, and personal character formation that few could grasp and fewer still could ever hope to emulate. At her memorial service the Rev. William Bell Riley called her the most perfect person he ever knew.[1] It is little wonder that after his charge to Henrietta in the wake of her mother's death, she lapsed into a period of introspection and probably mild depression.

Margaret drew a striking parallel for her children between the passing of time and a free flowing river. Just as water passes any given point only once on its journey to the sea, so also does time pass from our lives. Each person must seize every moment before it disappears, so Margaret made sure her time passed in purposeful work. She had no tolerance for inactivity or ineptitude in any form. Any task begun must be completed, and completed well.[2] Her strong advocacy for living a disciplined (some might say an overly regulated life) helped transform her somewhat pampered daughter into a force to be reckoned with as an adult. As Mears herself recalled, "It seems as if I were but a piece of plastic clay in the skillful fingers of my darling mother's hands to mold and smooth. How yielding I was to her touch, which was gentle yet firm. How often she would say, 'You must learn to obey your mother. Then you must obey your God. All through life your success depends on obedience. When you go to school, you must obey your teachers. In business you must obey those in authority. In laboratory you must obey the laws of God.'"[3] The practice of asking forgiveness from anyone she offended was also part of young Henrietta's learned regimen. Margaret's emphasis on personal responsibility and exemplary conduct not only sustained and deepened Henrietta's Christian faith, it also conditioned her exercise of it. Since Margaret inspired her youngest child to seek God's best in all things, Henrietta required the same aspiration in others—whether they wanted it for themselves or not. Moreover, as Margaret gave strict parental guidance to her sons and daughters, so also did Henrietta wield formidable authority over those she mentored in the faith. The perfectionist tendencies she learned so well from her mother were reinforced by her sister Margaret and placed limitations on her exercise of grace, generating paradoxes that defined her ministry.[4]

Another aspect of her personal heritage that shaped the exercise of her gifts proceeded from her family's checkered history. Over the decades Mears enjoyed telling her audiences that she had been born into privilege but it had been so short-lived that she never really knew what privilege was like.[5] While there is truth to that admission during her younger years, by the time she reached young adulthood the economic insecurity of her girlhood and youth retreated for the rest of her life thanks to the financial success of her siblings and close relatives. As a university student, Mears found one hundred dollar checks from her brother Clarence hidden in books after his visits to Minneapolis. He eventually left his estate to Henrietta and Margaret.[6] Margaret herself owned property in Crow Wing County, Minnesota, and purchased stock in a steel company.[7] She also appears to have secured several parcels of property in her own name after the move to Southern California as well as one with Henrietta.[8] Brothers Will and Norman, cousin Charles Buckbee, and uncle and aunt John Colgate and Henrietta Buckbee most likely contributed to the financial welfare of other members of the family. Because of her familial connections to so many commercial interests, Henrietta may have owned stock at some point in the Bureau of Engraving, the Buckbee-Mears Company, and even the steel company in which Margaret invested. She may also have had a financial arrangement with Will during his career at Paine Webber. The last home she shared with Margaret in Minneapolis on West River Road probably could not have been purchased on the sisters' salaries alone, and the trips Henrietta took in 1927, 1935, and later would have been inconceivable without additional resources.

Aside from Clarence's periodic checks, his subsequent estate conveyance, and Margaret's known investments, only circumstantial evidence exists regarding the exact origin of Henrietta's considerable wealth until 1944 when her sole surviving tax return provides some clarity. Mears declared salaries from both Gospel Light and First Presbyterian that year, but almost double that amount from other income. Royalties from Gospel Light amounted to $4,869.72 while her partnership in the company added $6,571.27 to her income. Of her total adjusted income of $17,440.99, all but $3,525 of it came from Gospel Light.[9] When the partners incorporated The Gospel Light Press in 1947 Mears owned more than fifty percent of the company's stock. By mid-July of the following year, her shares were worth $54,955.63—more than $575,000 in 2019 dollars.[10]

Clearly the Mears sisters left the financial instability of their youth far behind, but they still clipped coupons and shopped the sales. Her older sister modeled frugality for Mears and she learned her lessons well.[11] She and Margaret never forgot that wealth could vanish overnight and reputation with it. The precarious circumstances of their formative years meant that Mears never felt financially secure even though she lived an exceedingly privileged life as an adult.

While aware of where every dollar went, Mears also spent lavishly. Each of the three homes she owned with Margaret in Southern California was a step up from the last. She bought expensive museum quality souvenirs, designer clothing, and accessories during her many travels. She dined at some of the best restaurants but could still enjoy a chocolate ice cream shake. Mears gave generously but cautiously to a wide variety of Christian causes. Some of her collegians believed that she tithed at least fifty percent of her First Presbyterian salary, others thought she gave it all back. Both of these claims belong to the realm of unprovable hypotheses since only one of her tax returns remains, but it is undeniable that many of her "boys" and some of her "girls" were on the receiving end of her largesse.

As surely as night follows day, elevated social status accompanies wealth accumulation, and Mears relished the atmosphere. Her extended family on the East Coast and in the Midwest provided her opportunities to rub shoulders with many of the high society scions of the day, while her international network of theological conservatives operated as a kind of clearinghouse that gave her access to Christian luminaries whom she called upon without hesitation to speak at First Presbyterian or at Forest Home. She moved freely among well-known politicians, media stars, popular athletes, and high-powered business leaders, and she delighted in her ability to do so. At the same time, whether because of the implications of her lived-out faith or as a consequence of her unstable youth, she extended herself to the shy seeker just as easily and as genuinely as she did to the lauded celebrity.

PRIOR TO 1928 ONLY A PROVOCATIVE COMMENT alluding to her relationship with Marie Acomb hinted at any personal conflict during her years in Minneapolis.[12] Once she relocated to Hollywood, however, tension resulting from her exacting nature became apparent almost immediately. Her iron fist in a velvet glove approach to effective ministry served her in good stead but could certainly be off-putting.

The first indication that Mears would not tolerate anything less than the best came shortly after her arrival in Hollywood. During those first few hectic weeks she enlisted the aid of some collegians to publicize an early special event. Several of them toiled nearly all night to prepare an announcement regarding the meeting. The students duplicated the requisite number of copies and presented them to their new teacher. She promptly tossed them in the trash can. Dumbfounded and more than a little vexed, they questioned why she had so summarily rejected their effort. Mears pulled no punches: "See how poorly the job has been done. I would rather they didn't go out at all. People will think that is the standard for all our work. We must be Christ-honoring in all that we do." Chastened but resolute, the students finally completed their task to her satisfaction at three o'clock Sunday morning. Through the years Mears often reiterated the sentiment she so bluntly expressed to the weary collegians. What Christians do must be done exceptionally well and above reproach because it reflects divine agency and purpose. A similar rationale extended to the physical plant of First Presbyterian. Sunday school rooms, Mears said, should be as bright and fresh as possible, so volunteer painting crews were formed, seamstresses recruited, and cleaning parties mobilized. After the makeover, suitably framed pictures hung on lightly colored walls and cut flowers sat on refurbished pianos while new curtains hung over clean windows. There was no room for half-baked endeavors, shabby facilities, or out-of-date dress in Mears's world, for all things reflected a higher purpose.[13]

Even her closest associates could feel the sting of her disapproval. Barbara Hudson Powers contended that she "always demanded perfection and preparation in everything done under her supervision. . . . She has never been able to tolerate inefficiency and has never excused it. . . . She has demanded a vigilant standard of perfection in everything her leaders do." Mears abhorred the tendency of Christians to settle for slipshod or second-rate results of any sort. She often reminded her students, "Never have anything mediocre or good. The good is the greatest enemy of the best. Let your continual challenge be, 'Is this the best we can do? Can we make it better? Is this the biggest, the best, we can make it for the Lord?'" Should these lofty standards not be met, Mears could be "inexorable in her demanding judgment." The fervor with which Mears enforced this dictum proceeded from her running practice of assuming that every person who crossed the threshold to the Hollywood church or to her own home might only be present one time. If that turned out to be the case, all aspects of the experience must fold together to provide the most appealing reflection of Christ possible.[14]

Mears's extraordinary ability to combine such idealism with care for each individual resulted in leaders who simultaneously blossomed under her strong guidance and sometimes chafed under her exacting mentorship. David Cowie, president of the University of Southern California student body and one of the collegians who first heard Mears speak when she visited Hollywood in 1927, early championed her leadership of the College Department. As one of its first presidents, he felt called upon by Mears to exercise responsibilities that he believed were beyond his capacity to perform. When she informed him that if he failed to lead music, no one else would do it, he complained bitterly but fulfilled her wishes. In assessing her impact on his life, Cowie recalled the extent of her devotion to the faith and to individuals: "She expects *everything* for Christ. She has the knack for making you feel that you are the most important person in the whole world. No matter how much she has to do she makes you feel that she has all the time in the world for you." At the same time Cowie recognized that "She puts you on your mettle to produce. You *had* to do it and she wanted you to be able to do it, to feel the sole responsibility, and not to have any feeling that she would do it for you. She literally forced me into being a leader. She *pushed* me into responsibility." As if to clarify the paradox Cowie said, "Teacher ruined my life! It was as though she placed a burr under my saddle and I could never be content with anything unless I tried to do my ultimate best, and strive for perfection. I could never rest or be satisfied with anything less than that. She ruined my life. Of course, I would have it no other way! Nothing is too good for the Lord—or Miss Mears." Bill Dunlap had a similarly paradoxical reflection on his mentor.[15]

Thirty years later, Dale Bruner expressed to Mears the impact of her passion for excellence on him and his contemporaries:

> I rarely left your presence without a sense and a scent of excellence. You hate with a hatred the shoddy, the ill-prepared, the "that will be good enough" approach to Christian work, or indeed, to life. Everything you touch turns to the gold of excellence. Everyone you touch longs to be excellent. Your consumption for Christ, who deserves the excellent, has made you give your life to seeing that as for *you* and *your* house, Sunday School and work, he shall have excellence.[16]

The experiences of Powers, Cowie, Dunlap, and Bruner not only demonstrate the consistency of Mears's commitment to the best. They also serve as representative examples of the powerful relationships she inspired with her collegians over the decades. For so many, she negotiated the narrow ridge between judgment and grace with an almost eerie dexterity that made most whom she chastised redouble their efforts to do better.

Her correspondence with members and officers of the College Department carried a similar double edge. She could be very encouraging to those on the periphery, regularly greeting every person who walked through the door and assuring them of their importance to the class. Her letter to visitors or spotty attenders let them know how much they had been missed.[17] Mears often linked the health of the class to the talents that new members could contribute, which of course stimulated regular attendance.[18] Once the collegian entered the ranks of regular membership or accepted an executive leadership position in the class, however, her tone became rather more clinical and significantly more prescriptive.[19] Her deft blend of gratitude, empathy, and exhortation became decidedly less gracious if executive officers dodged any of their responsibilities. To those leaders who failed to respond appropriately Mears had little sympathy and less compassion:

> You have been chosen in an executive position in our great department and as an executive member you should be a leader. You are not doing a good piece of work unless you are getting others to work. Remember this. Our slogan should be, "Every Member of Our Class Working."
>
> If you have shirked in any way up to this time, begin immediately to do your very finest piece of work. You have been put on the executive because you are able to lead. Now do it![20]

Her forthright, no-holds-barred communication style reflected Mears's impatience with those who allowed themselves to be distracted from the essential goal of completely surrendering their lives to God so they could be used mightily for kingdom purposes. Many of her former collegians remembered the illustrative story of Dale Robertson. On the final evening of each Forest Home conference for young people, campers would come together at Victory Circle for a service of commitment, publicly bearing witness to their desire to live a truly Christian life. As a tangible reminder of their decision, students would speak briefly, throw a small stick into the crackling campfire signifying their dedication, and then sign the Book of Remembrance located at a table near the fire where Mears always sat. Young Robertson had struggled, misrepresenting his military service and picking up some unsavory habits. At the commitment service for the camp he attended, Robertson approached the fire, reached into his pocket, and threw in a pack of cigarettes declaring "I'm giving up my cigarettes for Jesus." Mears bolted out of her seat, nearly knocking over the table in the process. She dashed to the fire and rescued the cigarettes retorting, "Young man, young man, Jesus doesn't want your cigarettes, He wants you!"[21]

Mears adroitly coupled such startling candor with a sincere personal regard to remind preoccupied believers about their first priority no matter what their personal circumstances. Amy Mumford lost her husband in a traffic accident in February 1950 while working for Baptist Publications under Bob Mosier in Denver, Colorado. Over the next few months, Mumford struggled to make sense of the tragedy. Mosier, who had previously served as business manager at Gospel Light and knew Mears quite well, decided to send Mumford and three other employees to a conference at Forest Home later in 1950. Unknown to Mumford, Mosier had asked Mears to connect with her, thinking her advice might be helpful to the grieving young widow. Accordingly, one day during the conference Mears asked Mumford to join her for tea at the Biltmore. Surprised that she had been singled out for such an honor, Mumford approached the meeting with some consternation. She was not particularly taken with Mears's physical presence, noting, as so many did, her thick glasses behind which her eyes blinked constantly. At first Mumford was underwhelmed, but as she later recalled, "You didn't talk to her for five minutes until she was the most beautiful person you ever saw." In short order Mumford opened up to Mears and shared her confusion about her husband's tragic passing. After listening intently, Mears pointed her finger at Mumford and said brusquely, "Amy, stop feeling sorry for yourself. The Lord has something for you to do. Now go home and do it!" And she did, spending thirty-nine years with Baptist Publications and related Sunday school activities.[22]

Mears's discerning spirit could also sense when empathy required a creative nudge rather than a provocative challenge, as in the case of a young woman she took into her home in the late 1950s. She had run away from a severely abusive home and along with the emotional scars she carried, the collegian stammered uncontrollably. A powerful conversion experience soon transformed her life, and Mears hoped she would share her story with others so they might be fortified by it. Understandably sensitive about her speech impediment and quite withdrawn socially, the collegian just could not speak publicly. Mears floated the idea of audiotaping her as they spoke together in the privacy of the church office with the stipulation that the recording would never be made public without her permission. She agreed and the church's media specialist, Bruce Angwin, saw to the details. Though she stammered constantly through the original half hour conversation, Angwin edited out all the repetitive syllables, resulting in a clearly articulated, nine-minute discourse on her life and faith. When Mears played the tape for her, she was so moved upon hearing her own flawless monologue that she broke down in tears and agreed to let Mears release the tape to be played over the radio during the College Department's regular chapel hour program. Within two months not only had the young woman assumed a very active role in departmental activities, she also had not stammered since Mears played the tape for her.[23]

Mears's capacity to give her complete attention to the task of building the larger community of faith while concurrently exhibiting an authentic regard for the real needs of individuals, resulted in a most unlikely fusion of compassion and critique. As Mumford said and many others affirmed, she had "tremendous interest in you as a person. When she talked to you, you felt that you were the only person that she was interested in at that moment, and that she really loved you."[24] Certainly there were those who could not reconcile themselves to her "loving rebukes," but those who did continued to hold her counsel as among the most important encounters of their lives.

Another paradox proceeded from her conviction that two concerns dominated the consciousness of college-age young people—their choice of vocation and spouse.[25] But aside from her teaching on the necessity of total surrender to God's direction in their lives, Mears never pushed an agenda on her students even though some believed that she could be thought of as a feminist or a civil rights advocate in certain contexts.[26] Her central purpose remained calling students to a personal faith commitment to Christ and the church and helping them to mature spiritually. Mears stressed not what one had to do as a Christian, but what the Christian had in Christ.[27] As she famously said, "What you are is God's gift to you. What you can become is your gift to Him."[28] Mears firmly believed that as Christians progressed in the faith, God would reveal to them their field and form of service. That was not her role. She often told her collegians thinking about the formal ministry to "be sure the Lord is calling you. You are not doing this to please me or anybody else. This is because you've got a call that was real." She said this to Bill Craig and others and let them discern their vocation without further counsel.[29] June Loomis sought her advice, but Mears never told her what she should do; she asked clarifying questions that helped Loomis understand the pertinent issues.[30]

Yet, as in the case of Peter Macky, there were those who she firmly believed were called to particular service, and she did not hesitate to inform them of that fact. Gary Demarest, a civil engineering graduate and former student body president at the University of California at Berkeley, had taken a position with the city of Pasadena when Robert Munger invited him to lead singing at a 1947 high school conference at Mount Hermon. Mears was also at the conference and shortly after being introduced to Demarest, she turned to him and announced, "Young man, do you know that God wants you in the ministry?" Initially shocked at her audacity, Demarest nonetheless accepted her invitation to attend the first College Briefing Conference at Forest Home to sing with his gospel quartet. Soon after returning from the conference, Demarest quit his job and enrolled in the inaugural class at Fuller Seminary.[31] He went on to a notable career as executive director of the Fellowship of Christian Athletes and a Presbyterian pastor serving at University Presbyterian Church of Seattle and La Cañada Presbyterian Church in Southern California, among other assignments. Taylor Potter began attending the College Department in 1950 soon after his graduation from Penn State University and in short order received appointment as a member of the executive. Although he did not think of himself as a member of the inner group of department leaders, Mears took a special interest in Potter. He entered San Francisco Theological Seminary by February of the following year.[32] A decade later, Mears called collegian Dick Spencer into her office to encourage him to consider a deputation assignment in Germany. Younger than either Demarest or Potter had been at the time of their first meeting with Mears, Spencer took her suggestion as a directive to go. He knew the decision would change his life, and it did.[33] Newt Russell ran for the California State Legislature at least partially because of Mears's general challenge to Christians to participate fully in the political process.[34] As these examples demonstrate, Mears took a decidedly hands-off approach to pushing her charges into particular vocational choices—except when she did not.

Unlike the measured ambivalence that characterized her approach to the career choices of her collegians, she took a more consistently active role in their romantic lives. As one of her college women put it, "she knew the Holy Spirit was moving when couples were getting engaged. It worried her if there was nobody getting engaged."[35] Mears exhibited such an interest in the relationships of her students it was rumored that she knew who dated whom in the entire College Department, which itself became known as the "match factory" by the 1950s. Her interest extended all the way to the altar, and she did everything in her power to nurture those matches.[36] Her machinations leading to the marriage of Kathy Booth and Dale Bruner are legendary to their contemporaries in the College Department.[37] She also gave cupid more than a little help getting Ardelle and David Cowie, Peggy and Cyrus Nelson, and Edie and Robert Munger together.[38] Doris Seaton first met her future husband, Richard Halverson, in Mears's office at the Hollywood church shortly after he graduated from Princeton Theological Seminary. While Mears did not orchestrate their relationship, she did persuade Seaton to work at Forest

Home one summer—and it just happened to be the summer that Halverson managed the conference center.[39] Gary Demarest spoke to Mears about his intentions toward Marily Evans before he even spoke to her about them.[40]

But it was difficult to stand against Mears's selected partner, as Nancy Macky discovered. Mears matched her to Ken Kroll, a young Harvard surgeon. She knew Teacher was not pleased when she married Peter Macky, but she eventually reconciled herself to the fact.[41] Mears was such an intimidating presence that some of her college women, like Polly Craig, may have wondered what she thought of the men they loved, but they did not dare ask her.[42]

While she amused her students with self-deprecating jests about her own singleness and assured them of her abiding satisfaction with her life, Mears's preoccupation with her students' romantic relationships revealed a certain wistfulness about the single life.[43] As she did with so many other collegians over the decades, Mears took an active interest in potential marriage partners for Rachel Spencer. She first tried to match her with Oregon political leader Mark Hatfield when he visited. Failing in that effort, she hatched other plans to find Spencer a suitable marriage partner. In an intimate conversation, the older woman confessed why she cared so much about locating a godly husband for her friend: "I really worry about you. I don't want you to be like I have been. I don't want you to be alone."[44] Her honesty with the younger woman in this vulnerable moment underscores a truth about her singleness that Mears rarely, if ever, shared with others. She often spoke about the thousands of children that were hers during her decades of service. But in her comment to Spencer, she allowed herself to face her sense of loss of what was not.

Perhaps the most intriguing paradox in the life and ministry of Henrietta Mears was the one she personified—the complex gendered configuration of midcentury evangelicalism. She referred to herself as a teacher of the Bible, not a preacher— except in a single letter to her Fideltians in February 1928. Mears always served under male leaders, but they all gave her significant latitude in creating her own programs and developing her own initiatives. This was typified most evocatively when Louis Evans Sr. proclaimed in mock exasperation, "Lady, who am I to stop *you*?"[45] Her active leadership in directing the success of Gospel Light, Forest Home, and the National Sunday School Association belied the patriarchal tendencies of the wider evangelical Protestant movement, yet Mears acceded to many of those norms, as did the Moody

Bible Institute, Wheaton College, and Fuller Theological Seminary—three institutions that attempted to woo her from her educational church ministry.[46] How might these apparent contradictions be explained?

The starting point must be her baseline principle that Scripture had to be taken seriously and on its own terms. She believed the Bible taught only males should comprise the ordained clergy, and she remained wary of women who assumed religious leadership roles that she thought men should fill.[47] Beyond this bellwether theological belief, Mears accommodated herself to the cultural norms of the time for pragmatic reasons, not doctrinal ones.[48] Given that the gendered inclination evident throughout western culture at the time elevated males above females, it was her cardinal conviction that if men held the top leadership positions in her Sunday school—and specifically in the College Department—women would follow, thereby building a healthy church. And the more charismatic the male leadership, the more people would be drawn to the church. That she would choose female leadership in the Sunday school if a male leader could not be found is borne out by the fact that the first head of her thriving Junior High Department was female. Oddly, only when she moved from the area twelve years later did Mears finally "find" a male to lead the department.[49]

Other grand ironies abounded. It was in her Fidelis Class at First Baptist, Minneapolis, which had only female presidents, that she forged the philosophical and organizational template for her coeducational College Department at First Presbyterian. But Mears refused to allow any of her Hollywood young women to hold the presidency of the College Department per se, even when the nominating committee of collegians thought otherwise. Women did fill practically every other office in the department executive at one time or another, and Connie Haines served as president of the group's Christian Endeavor society during World War II.[50] Mears championed their leadership in these other offices, sometimes even creating positions for females to cultivate their gifts and supporting programs that brought distinguished professionals like Judge Georgia Bullock to speak to them.[51] She fostered the aspirations of countless women in Minneapolis and Hollywood, and as one College Department alumna declared, "She developed the women to be stronger."[52]

Mears of course was the grandest irony of all. She may have believed that merely by speaking from a pulpit on Sunday evening while refusing to do so on Sunday morning constituted a teaching ministry, not a preaching one. Fuller Seminary professor Clarence Roddy failed to recognize the difference when he called her the best preacher in Southern California—and he was not the only one to do so.[53] Perhaps since she had been the prime mover behind the creation of Gospel Light as well as the acquisition of Forest Home, and because they were not actual churches, she felt justified in serving as president and CEO, leading boards composed primarily if not completely of males. She may also have construed her countless addresses, workshop presentations, counseling sessions, and Sunday school lessons offered to thousands of men and women as educational opportunities rather than theological expositions. Conversely, she could have merely lived into the paradox and never given it a second thought, as speculated her second cousin William T. Grieg Jr., the president of Gospel Light.[54]

HOWEVER MEARS MAY HAVE UNDERSTOOD the relationship between males and females, she clearly wanted her students to live authentic lives by thinking for themselves and standing firm in their convictions.[55] "She didn't want 'yes' people around her,"[56] but she could also forcefully oppose them in no uncertain terms. Louis Evans Jr. once approached her with an idea that she rejected out of hand. They went back and forth for some time, but Evans held his own. She finally relented, placing the burden of success squarely on his shoulders. Although she remained skeptical, when she saw that he had been right, she complimented him on a job well done.[57] During his seminary years, Gary Demarest participated in a meeting with Mears dedicated to planning a Bible study. After some discussion, she suggested that the group begin with Genesis. Demonstrating his knowledge of the Old Testament from his graduate classes, Demarest countered that the study should begin with Exodus "because that's where salvation history really begins." Mears shot back, "If Genesis was good enough for Moses, it's good enough for us!" Demarest did not feel slighted by her rejoinder, but he knew the matter had been settled in her favor.[58]

Her oppositional behavior appears to have gotten more pronounced and more strident over the last decade of her life as her health deteriorated. Though one of Mears's most valued collegians in the 1950s, Rachel Spencer experienced her intense opposition on numerous occasions. Mears believed, for example, that Spencer should attend a prestigious East Coast university because Mears believed she was "an East Coast woman." Spencer had to rebuff her repeatedly over this issue and only later realized that Mears wanted her on the East Coast so she could meet and marry an appropriate East Coast man. Spencer was delighted when Mears introduced her to actress Anne Baxter (Mears thought they looked alike), but she was less than enthused when Mears manipulated her into meeting Mark Hatfield against her will. Probably the most severe disagreement came when Spencer and others in leadership positions opposed Mears's choice for the presidency of the College Department. Upon realizing that the executive did not share her enthusiasm, Mears pushed her candidate even harder. They tried to explain why he would not be a good nominee, but she would not listen.[59]

Spencer's younger brother Richard had similar conflicts with the aging Mears a few years later as a member of the department. One of her major concerns had always been securing good leadership for the department so that its success would be ensured for the foreseeable future. Since she could not teach the Sunday school class very often because of poor health in the late 1950s and early 1960s, guest teachers filled in for her. The teacher when Spencer was a junior, a Mears protégé, did not meet her expectations. Though not president of the department at the time, Spencer did occupy an important place on the leadership executive. At the Saturday morning leaders' meeting, Mears took Spencer and the president aside and charged them with the responsibility of informing the teacher he would no longer be needed. He carried out her directive but found it a trying task. When he moved into the presidency in 1961, Spencer had to do much of the organizational planning for the department because Mears could not. But without informing any members of the executive, Mears announced that Bob Edwards would be conducting a discipleship series for the department. Spencer subsequently led a discussion on the matter. As he and some of the leaders expressed their concerns, Mears became indignant: "I know what is good for this department and this is the very kind of thing that we need right now to anchor us properly in the Word. . . . This is what we must do!" Her heated rejoinder took Spencer and the executive by surprise—and she refused to reevaluate her decision. Spencer recalled that "she muscled us. You didn't stand against her. If you weren't going to go along with it, you had to just bail." Her response so disillusioned him that he considered leaving the presidency but thought better of it after conferring with an associate pastor at the church.[60] Mears similarly put a damper on the nomination of at least one prospective president of her Homebuilders class, who subsequently left the class and the church.[61]

A personal characteristic that undergirded Mears's frankness—and her intransigence—was her steadfast belief in the accuracy of her perspective. Because of the nearly mythic status she held among evangelicals, she often exuded a confidence in her assessments that seemed to carry the added authority of the divine. As Ted Cole, one of her closest associates and pastor of the largest American Baptist Church in the country, said, "She could do anything she wanted to do—and she was right. Father, Son, Holy Spirit, and Henrietta Mears."[62] When she believed she was in the right, Mears moved ahead with boldness. It was extremely difficult to persuade her to do otherwise. She did not easily take no for an answer—no matter what the question. Mears's assistant Ethel May Baldwin could often be heard telling her boss, "You can't do that! You just can't do that!" to which Mears would reply, "Oh yes I can." And more often than not, she did.[63] Reflecting on her reputation for unwavering tenacity, Baldwin alleged, "She always ignores what she doesn't want to hear." Barbara Hudson Powers added that "If it is something she doesn't want to hear, then she asks the question [What do you mean?] hoping you will change the facts or just go away."[64]

A significant corollary to the straightforward self-confidence that carried her ministry forward on so many fronts was a decided difficulty in apologizing to those she had wronged in some way. The Bright family had only recently taken up residence in Mears's home when Vonette Bright noticed how hard it was for her to express contrition. As she wrote to a friend shortly after Mears's death, "I only remember one instance of her saying to me she was sorry about something. These words just did not seem to be in her vocabulary. The reason being that she always said something may happen once, but there is no excuse for it to happen a second time." The fact that Mears found it inordinately difficult to *say* the words, did not mean she failed to *act* repentant. Bright noted that "she showed that she was sorry if she had offended an individual by expressing her love for that person, or doing something very, very, nice for them. But the words 'I am sorry' were very seldom, if ever, given."

Bright traced her reluctance to apologize back to her mother and father. Mears often quoted her mother, who said, "If you are a worm in your own eyes, you're going to be a worm in another person's eyes. If you are a butterfly in your eyes, then you'll be a butterfly in the eyes of others." In linking this aphorism with an act of contrition, Mears may have equated words of apology with a negative self-image. With regard to material things, Mears remembered her father's word of caution to those who worked for the family. He warned them that anything they broke, they paid for because "I am sorry does not replace anything." Mears once told Bright that "there is no excuse for breaking a piece of china; it just does not happen." Considering these parental precedents, the reasons for her limited capacity to apologize become more apparent, but knowing the reasons would take none of the sting out of being on the receiving end of one of her nonapologies. Ironically, Mears believed teaching children to say "I am sorry" was of the utmost importance.[65]

DESPITE THE CERTITUDE with which she held her perspectives, by all accounts Mears maintained good relationships with pastoral leadership whether the Rev. Riley or her colleagues in Hollywood. She also sustained cordial relationships with governing board members of the churches she served. In fact, according to a longtime member at First Presbyterian, session members—many of whom were her College Department alumni—"seemed all to be delighted to eat out of her hand."[66] When she did have differences of opinion with her supervisors or colleagues, she dealt with them privately. So scrupulously did Mears hold confidences of this nature that Doris Halverson expressed great surprise upon hearing from an elder of the church about his disagreements with her.[67]

The pastors with whom she worked appreciated her contributions to the cause of Christian education but also expressed some concern about keeping the lines of authority well defined. In a sense she became an unintended victim of her own success. By the late 1930s she had been given the authority to hire some of her seminarians as Christian education assistants during their summer recess. She placed "her boys" in positions that best matched their gifts and proved most beneficial to the overall ministry of the church. Since at least the early 1930s, Mears had been charged with supervision of the weekday programs for boys and girls and viewed those programs as under her purview.[68] But as the church grew, the ministerial staff became more specialized. Enter Walt James. She had only just met the new minister of weekday programs in early 1946 before she left on her trip. When she returned in February 1947 he had mapped out strategies for and relationships with the unchurched young people living near First Presbyterian. She must have tried for nearly four months to define their relationship in the same way she defined her relationship to her summer seminarians, assuming that the weekday programs still fell under her authority.

On the evening of June 13, Mears had an honest conversation with James in which she communicated her sense of their professional relationship. She saw herself as "handicapped" because she had "always had a younger minister" to assist her. It became obvious to James that she indeed believed that he should be functioning the same way. In the same spirit of candor, James drafted a letter to her the next day, gently but decisively reminding her that he "was *not* a younger minister." He also assured Mears that he valued and supported her ministry, but that he and his committee "having properly cleared with the Christian Education Committee, are the ones who must decide" what the "departmental working priorities shall be."[69] When Richard Halverson joined the pastoral staff, Mears repeated her mistaken assumption that he would be her assistant, not the assistant pastor for the entire congregation.[70] In both cases, Mears stood corrected and accepted the fact that though she felt stretched beyond her capacity, it was inappropriate to treat her colleagues as subordinates. Her relationships with both James and Halverson blossomed, both ministers freely recognizing her tremendous contributions to the cause of Christ.[71] All Louis Evans Sr. had to do when collegians filtered into the sanctuary late because Mears's lesson had run a bit long was let her know she needed to finish by 10:55 a.m. He did not have to remind her again.[72]

While the ministerial staff, particularly senior pastors Evans and his successor, Raymond Lindquist, maintained strong connections to the regional and national leadership of the Presbyterian Church, Mears's evangelical ecumenism and Baptist heritage engendered a hesitant if not paradoxical loyalty toward the denomination. She and Margaret formally joined First Presbyterian shortly after their arrival and supported the church fully, but the Hollywood church itself tended to look beyond denominational ties. Much of its lay leadership downplayed the local church's linkage to the greater Presbyterian family. When Polly Craig became a member of the church all she need to affirm was that Jesus was her Lord and Savior.[73] To Mears and many in the congregation, only Christ could claim their primary allegiance. As Warren McClain, one of her seminarians, put it, "If you became a Christian at Hollywood church, you didn't necessarily know you were a Presbyterian. . . . She didn't stress that."[74] What at first blush appeared to be her ambivalent attitude toward the Presbyterian persuasion did not escape notice. Glenn Moore, executive secretary of the Synod of California, Southern Area, once approached Evans about Mears's ministry, which by this time had become the stuff of legend outside the Presbyterian Church. Moore complained to the senior pastor that he just could not have "this Baptist woman running your Christian Education program." Evans, whose commitment to the greater Presbyterian cause was unimpeachable, replied, "You know, there is some concern there, but if you can find me a Presbyterian that can do half of what she can, let me know and we'll do something."[75] Moore never did.

Moore's specific concern regarding Mears probably represented a greater worry among Southern California church leaders about the Hollywood congregation in general, but her ecumenism also made room for a deferential perspective with regard to Presbyterianism. She strongly encouraged her prospective seminarians to attend Princeton, the flagship institution for Presbyterians, and expressed some disappointment when they chose other graduate schools of theology.[76] Of the hundreds of her collegians who went on to seminary, the vast majority found their clerical vocations within the denomination. When Presbyterian authorities criticized the dispensational tenor of her early Gospel Light curriculum, she took it in stride and confessed that it was not her intention to distribute materials that taught against Presbyterian beliefs. During Warren McClain's tenure at San Francisco Theological Seminary in the early 1950s, he enrolled in a Christian education course that surveyed the available Sunday school curricula. The class included a critical analysis of Gospel Light products from a Presbyterian theological perspective. The critique found its way back to Mears. Within three years she made revisions to the materials in light of the concerns raised. The fact that so many Presbyterian churches adopted Gospel Light Sunday school curriculum rather than denominational materials remained a point of contention throughout her career, for although Mears responded positively to the concerns of the Presbyterian Church, the denomination never allowed Gospel Light representatives into its bookstores.[77] The depth of the divide became apparent to Gary Demarest as he prepared for ordination in 1952 when serving Seattle's University Presbyterian Church. The presbytery's ordination committee attempted to link a favorable ruling on his candidacy with the church's rejection of the Gospel Light curriculum and its adoption of the Presbyterian Faith and Life educational program.[78]

In spite of evidence to the contrary, the interdenominational network of evangelicals that Mears helped create continued to threaten the Presbyterian status quo. Her Christian education successes may have been touted nationally by the 1950s, but major texts in the discipline virtually ignored her. For example, Herman James Sweet, director of Christian education, Board of Christian Education for the Presbyterian Synod of California since 1946, did not even mention Mears in his article "The Education of Lay and Professional Religious Education Leaders" for Philip Henry Lotz's 1950 anthology *Orientation in Religious Education*. Marvin Taylor's otherwise ecumenical volume, *An Introduction to Christian Education*, contained numerous chapters that could have benefited from Mears's expertise. Yet the only mention of her anywhere in the nearly four-hundred-page tome is a brief paragraph on her founding of Gospel Light in "Evangelical Christian Education and the Protestant Day School Movement."[79]

Paradoxically, although clearly not supported by the denomination to which she belonged, Mears contributed more to the health and welfare of the Presbyterian Church than any other single individual of her time. With her locus of authority always radiating outward from the campus of First Presbyterian, Mears constructed a formidable network of committed laypersons and professionals that strengthened the church across the country and particularly along the West Coast. By the 1960s, Presbyterian ministers she had trained or deeply influenced had held pastorates in Maryland, Washington, DC, New Jersey, Pennsylvania, New York, Ohio, Minnesota, Kansas, Alabama, Florida, Colorado, and Montana. Bellingham, Richland, Tacoma, Seattle, Bellevue, Ellensburg, and Spokane in Washington and Coalinga, Berkeley, Sacramento, Salinas, Menlo Park, Sonoma, and Walnut Creek in Northern California were only a few of the places "her boys" served. Mears-trained pastors or those trained by them spread all over Southern California from Bel Air to Palm Desert, La Jolla to San Bernardino, Pasadena to La Mesa, Compton to Cathedral City, North Hollywood to Westminster, La Cañada to Laguna Hills, and Pomona to Brentwood. Some of the most vital Reformed churches on the West Coast hired successive generations of her protégés—churches such as First Presbyterian, Hollywood; University Presbyterian, Seattle; Knox Presbyterian in Spokane; First Presbyterian, Berkeley; Bel Air Presbyterian; First Presbyterian, Coalinga; West Side Church in Richland; First Presbyterian, Fresno; Fremont Presbyterian in Sacramento; and La Jolla Presbyterian, among many others. First-generation Mears enthusiasts and ordained Presbyterian ministers Homer Goddard and Robert Munger assumed professorships at Fuller Theological Seminary in their late career years. Missionaries she influenced served with the Presbyterian mission agency and many other mission boards in Europe, Asia, Africa, Australia, and the United States.[80] So many of her former collegians held pastorates in Southern California that to this day many believe the only reason the eighty-four-year-old Presbytery of Los Angeles split into five separate judicatories on January 1, 1968, stemmed from the fear that "Mears boys" exerted too much power in the region. *(See table 4 on page 284.)*

Her commitment to the Presbyterian denomination (as well as its open suspicion of her) must be set against Mears's broad Protestant ecumenism. She may have called herself a "Bapterian," but she cast a much wider net than even that sobriquet implies. She addressed conferences nationwide with speakers and active participants scattered across the spectrum of mid-twentieth century Protestantism, and she drew on the same network for her own conference center in the San Bernardino Mountains. Among the best examples of the breadth of her vision for a reinvigorated Protestantism came when she invited her friends John Mackay, president of Princeton Theological Seminary, and Bob Jones Jr., president of Bob Jones University, to speak at the same Forest Home conference though they represented vastly differing perspectives on Christian practice and American culture. Ardent dispensationalist Robert Thieme; German Lutheran theologian Helmut Thielicke, who was a member of the confessing church in Germany under the Nazi regime; Keswick-oriented Major Ian Thomas, founder of Capernwray Missionary Fellowship of Torchbearers; psychologist Clyde Narramore; philosopher Robert Smith; and of course Billy Graham were but a few among dozens whom Mears wanted her students to hear regarding faithful Christian living in the contemporary world.

A similar ecumenicity characterized her College Department class at First Presbyterian. She invited well-known Presbyterians such as Mackay and Robert E. Speer, secretary of the Presbyterian Board of Foreign Missions and former moderator of the General Assembly of the northern Presbyterian Church. But she also yielded the podium to other prominent Christian notables, such as Isaac Page of the China Inland Mission; Charles Trumbull, editor of the *Sunday School Times*; apologist Harry Rimmer; storyteller and author Ethel Barrett; Berlin pastor Albert Schröder; Corrie Ten Boom; and Marge Saint, the young widow of slain South American missionary Nate Saint, among many others.[81] There was even room in her theological big tent for Seventh-day Adventists, Foursquare Church founder Aimee Semple McPherson, and faith healers Oral Roberts and Agnes Sanford.[82]

While Mears actively recruited respected Christian leaders from across the country and around the world to speak at First Presbyterian or Forest Home, she could also be somewhat protective of her own contributions. Ethel Barrett was not only a popular Christian author and Gospel Light employee but also an engaging speaker and humorist. At one Forest Home conference she had the group in stitches with her "Alphabet Sermon." The sermon consisted entirely of repeating the alphabet using over-the-top vocal inflections, contorted facial expressions, and exaggerated hand motions to drive home important "details." Barrett's hysterical send-up of the classic stump preacher brought down the house. But a crestfallen Mears found Barrett's parody so close to her "Book of Numbers" routine that she feared being upstaged. An eyewitness doubted that Barrett even knew about her rendition, but nothing could take the sting away for Mears, who believed the speaker had intruded onto her territory.[83]

As expansive as her tent might have been for the times, not all gained admission. And even those tentatively admitted could be interrogated to ascertain the propriety of their continued inclusion. Mears rarely, if ever, raised such issues publicly, but did not hesitate to voice her concerns privately in her travel journals. This is particularly true with regard to Roman Catholicism, for although her personal experiences with Catholics—from her North Branch sweetheart and Beardsley's Father Shanahan to the Pope himself—tempered her responses, she nonetheless shared some of the same concerns that animated Protestants of her time to take a much more antagonistic stance than she ever did. According to one of her closest friends, Mears believed that as churches became more tied to sacramental rituals, they became less evangelical—and Catholicism majored in liturgy and ritual.[84]

During her 1940 trip, for example, she entered a Catholic church of indigenous Mexican communicants to observe the worship service, and she was touched by their devotion. She later took the time to meet their German missionary priest.[85] During her 1946–1947 world excursion, Mears exhibited a more enigmatic attitude. She marveled at the grandeur of an ornate shrine in a well-to-do section of Mexico City, remarking that the statues lacked "all the grotesqueness and horror of almost all of the Mexican churches." She also praised the "refinement in the color" and compared its "culture and beauty" to the "grotesque ugliness of Guadeloupe." But she wrote "whether it be grand or lowly, God seems far away. No one can see the churches of Mexico without an aching heart."[86] The following month during a short stay in Taxco, she despaired at the "sad religious life these poor benighted people have." Observing another indigenous worship service Mears confided to her journal that "it is the most depressing sight. They are so sincere and so deluded."[87]

She appears to have been most agitated by the amalgamation of Roman Catholicism with indigenous religious practices in Latin America. Just before Easter she wrote pointedly about how inadequately the native peoples had been Christianized—outwardly appearing Catholic but inwardly remaining committed to traditional spirituality. It is clear that Mears found the native populations appealing, but she faulted them for their pre-Christian religious rituals and faulted the Catholic Church for "holding them in gross ignorance." Reflecting on what she had seen of Roman Catholicism in Latin America over the past few months, Mears wrote in early May, "This trip has made me grateful indeed that I was not born a Catholic. This religion is so binding and blinding! What a little comfort! How much ignorance! I am reminded that our salvation 'is not of works, lest any man should boast.'"[88] Whatever her personal misgivings about Roman Catholicism, Mears kept them to herself, refusing to join the rising chorus of mainline American Protestants and their more theologically conservative compatriots who sallied forth in the postwar years to denounce a perceived threat to Protestant hegemony in the United States.

It should be remembered that Mears could also be critical of Protestant churches that did not meet her expectations. She often attended worship services of other denominations and mission agencies during her travels, reserving her praise for those most closely associated with her own evangelical views and keeping her disapproval for others private. In 1940 she attended Christ Church in Rio de Janeiro and pronounced the worship "cold and formal" but "the sermon was good."[89] She often attended and enjoyed the preaching at the American Methodist Church in Buenos Aires, but on June 2, 1946, found only "one woman in the Bible class and sixty in the Sunday School. The women's teacher had a well-prepared lesson, but so few interested." Later that month she visited St. Andrew's Scots Church, and while she characterized the service as "very formal, but spirited," Mears also found it "strange how no one speaks to you in these churches." She believed that "so much could be done in an evangelistic way here in Argentina, both among English-speaking and Spanish-speaking people. I wish some dynamic 'on fire' person could come here. The churches seem so stiff and formal, and few seem to have any missionary vision." Mears was particularly disturbed by the Union Church in Rio de Janeiro, which she visited many times.[90] During her 1950–1951 trip around the world, Mears wrote dismissively about a Protestant service aboard ship on route to South Asia. Not only did she complain about its heavily liturgical nature, she also took issue with the superficiality of the "sermon," as she put it.[91] Whether Protestant or Roman Catholic, if a church failed, in her appraisal, to uphold the centrality of Christ or teach the Bible as the authoritative Word of God, it earned her private censure.

Mears's perspectives with regard to matters of race and ethnicity are nearly as complex as her thoughts on and behavior regarding other issues discussed in this chapter. Ultimately, they must be extrapolated from random comments and actions as she rarely, if ever, directly addressed the topics in any public context. The one exception to this rule was her well-known support of the Jews, which extended to her support of the state of Israel. Nonetheless, she also exhibited elements of stereotypical thinking with regard to physical and behavioral characteristics of Jewish people in general. In her many travels, Mears often demonstrated a distinctly western bias while almost simultaneously expressing an appreciation for the indigenous cultures with which she interacted. This included her concern for displaced Palestinians in the wake of the UN resolution of 1947 that ended the British mandate in Palestine in May 1948 and resulted in war and the creation of Israel.

As early as June 1946 Mears observed the agitation of Jews for their return to Jerusalem. Given her dispensational proclivities, she found great encouragement in that development. But she qualified her support, noting that "the Bible is quoted in court by the young terrorists, assuring the court that Palestine is promised to them."[92] Nearly five years later, on the way to Bethlehem, Mears got her first glimpse of Palestinian refugee camps and wrote that "some 200,000 are housed in these projects under the most miserable of circumstances." The following day, after passing through several blockades manned by heavily armed Arab policemen, Mears poured her despair onto the pages of her journal: "Our hearts had been heavy often when we passed one refugee camp after another housing their portion of the 200,000 Arabs that are living this way. They have nothing to do all day long, time hangs on their hands. I should think they would go stark mad waiting for their rations from UNRA [United Nations Relief Agency]."[93]

When she returned to the Mideast the following year, her personal interactions with individual Arab residents of the region brought home to her an even greater sense of the geopolitical tragedy they experienced. Her driver, a refugee from Jaffa, had been forcibly separated from his family in Damascus because of the conflict. Her guide took her to his cousin's shop in Jerusalem where she observed, "The streets of Old Jerusalem were dark and deserted. It was not like the old days. We got out of the Damascus gate in time. It was closed at 9:30 because of fear of the Jews." On a visit to John the Baptist's birthplace, Mears recognized that it had been "an Arab village, now [a] flourishing Jewish city." Then, almost clinically she explained how the transformation occurred: "We passed the Arab section of fine homes that had been deserted and were now occupied by the poorest Jews who went in to take possession."[94] While her admiration for Jews and their cause is clearly evident throughout this section of her journal, so also is her compassion for the displaced Palestinians.

Because of her extensive, albeit limited, exposure to world cultures, Mears held a somewhat more sophisticated view of global diversity than most theological conservatives of her day. That more nuanced outlook, however, did not translate very well with regard to American minority populations. Although she seems to have accepted quite readily members of white ethnic groups, she brought stereotypical thinking to Hollywood with her, particularly regarding African Americans. As early as her years with the Fideltians of First Baptist, Minneapolis, Mears allowed her students to perpetuate negative portrayals of blackness, sometimes intertwined with the notion of Christian service. The February 1924 Fidelis class newsletter *The Fid'ler* included "At The Darky Mission," a short recounting of a positive experience Fidelis class members had helping out one Sunday afternoon at the Camp Presbyterian Mission. Misinformed that it was a Jewish mission, the Fideltians were surprised when "seven little Darkies" arrived, but "the beaming faces and broad grins of these children showed they were just as glad to come to Sunday school as any other children would be." When a young boy took the offering, he "nearly jigged for joy" and had a very difficult time relinquishing the money. At the end of the meeting, the children's "eyes almost bulged out of their heads" at the African American minister's offer of Christmas candies. The same issue of the newsletter recounted a racial joke attributed to infamous fundamentalist Frank Norris, complete with slurred southern dialect and the n-word.[95]

Members of her College Department at First Presbyterian, Hollywood drew on similar depictions of African Americans. The department's publications early in her tenure portrayed African Americans with exaggerated physical features. Her collegians sponsored southern-themed banquets that featured blackface entertainment. Mears herself subscribed to racially insensitive myths. Car trouble on the way to the airport in San Jose, Costa Rica, led her to observe "Negro style, our driver lifted up the hood, tinkered with everything he could find, then he pulled on the emergency brake, rattled the gears, turned on the lights and got out the screwdrivers, but no avail!"[96] Vacationing in Rio in 1946, Mears wrote about how charming and hospitable she found the people who, because they had "so much of the negro strain," made for "a carefree, happy folk."[97] When the elevator at her hotel broke down, she had to wait forty-five minutes "until a negro came in leisurely with a kit of tools and fixed it."[98] On a visit to Hawaii a few years later she wrote "the Hawaiian reminds one of the negro, he is so easygoing and happy and loves to sing."[99]

By the later 1940s as racial attitudes began to shift, some of the more obviously insensitive practices waned, but Mears appears to have maintained a tentative ambivalence about matters of race. For example, in a May 1949 letter, John, who may have been one of her collegians, wrote offering constructive criticism (perhaps at her request) of some of her Gospel Light material for high school students. He took issue with a paragraph on Booker T. Washington indicating that "the positive approach to the negro problem would be better." He also objected gently to her use of the phrase "A colored man once said," arguing that "by merely saying colored we are making a distinction. God I don't think does except for his choosed (*sic*) people the Jews. Isn't the saying true if a white man said it?"[100]

Aside from these oblique references, Mears herself seems never to have specifically addressed racial matters in a public context, unlike some of her younger evangelical colleagues. There has even been disagreement among her admirers regarding how open Mears was to African American involvement in the College Department. This uneven assessment could be indicative of her restraint in dealing with contemporary issues overtly, whether racial or political. It could also conceivably delineate discrepancies between her philosophical belief about equity (to which she alluded by noting that a good pianist needs both the black and white keys) and its actual practice. Yet some of her collegians held that had she lived longer Mears would have been a supporter of the civil rights movement and one of her chosen favorites, Japanese American Joe Kinishida, was instrumental in convincing Dale Bruner to attend the 1951 College Briefing Conference, where he committed his life to Christ.[101] Others, however, wondered how welcome African Americans were in the department. The outstanding UCLA track athlete and Olympic decathlon champion Rafer Johnson did visit a few times but really became more involved with the Fellowship of Christian Athletes organization supported by Louis Evans Sr. and Mears protégé Gary Demarest. His status as a world-renowned athlete probably played well to Mears's desire to showcase the most attractive exemplars of Christian living. Perhaps as a reflection of the mission emphasis, international students seem to have fared quite well at the church.[102]

Although her personal racial attitudes are open to speculation, some of those most influenced by Mears focused more on social issues than their teacher. She never taught on civil rights nor exhorted her students to pursue activist goals although there was always an element of that in her deputation programs. Yet in surrendering their lives to the Spirit's leading, as Mears constantly incited them to do, a number of her students felt called to social service, unlike earlier generations of theological conservatives. Recall that Clyde Kennedy, Robert Munger, and David Cowie cofounded an initially disparaged ministry to the dispossessed of Trenton, New Jersey, while they studied at Princeton. College Department member Lillian Barnhart spoke out specifically against racial prejudice and narrow-mindedness in the department periodical. She and Constance Wheeler assisted local Chinese students with their studies and incited other department colleagues to join them. Ralph Hamburger and the dozens of other College Department members who served as World Deputation volunteers certainly took to heart the injunction to put their faith to work among those in need. Louis Evans Jr. and Colleen Townsend Evans joined the fair housing fight in San Diego County as did Robert Munger in King County, Washington.[103] David Cowie and Ron Frase also realized the importance of giving voice to the voiceless. Another College Department alumna, Harriet Prichard, founded Alternative Gifts International and set up the Haitian National Coalition for the Environment, which together raised in excess of twenty-seven million dollars for people in crisis and environmental causes.[104] These and others like them helped recover the practice of doing earthly good that had so characterized evangelicals prior to the Civil War. In many ways they functioned as the advance guard of new evangelicals who believed that the gospel committed believers to evangelism *and* social justice. But it was not in Mears's nature to tell them so. She never allowed any cause, no matter how valuable, to supplant the importance of evangelism and obedience to the Bible. She left it to the moving of the Spirit in the individual lives of her students to direct their postconversion avenues of service and supported them regardless of where the Spirit so led them.[105]

That Mears had "favorites," and yet valued and encouraged all comers is perhaps best illustrated by a group interview conducted with a number of College Department alumni, most of whom were retired Presbyterian ministers and their spouses. Fairly soon after the interview began, it became obvious that only one had been a "Mears boy" in the specially favored sense, but none of the others bore a hint of jealousy and all spoke of her positive impact on them. They had not the slightest awareness that she treated Peter Macky any differently than she treated any of them. They all acknowledged that Mears perceived intuitively who the best leaders would be and worked to develop their skills, but they also knew she simultaneously cherished each of them.[106]

Virginia resident and former College Department member Charles King recognized that Mears's "deep concern and interest extended even to the quiet, bashful types who sneaked into the services of the College Department and sat in the back rows." As a result, even after twenty years, he hesitated "to say that you won't remember me." King, a military veteran, university professor, US Information Agency officer, and US Office of Education employee, had just attended an especially poignant men's conference on the East Coast led by Richard Halverson. There he reconnected with Halverson and fellow College Department member and naval officer Johnny Johnson. King wrote to catch her up on one of her quiet collegians, assuring her that she "had such a tremendous influence on thousands of lives, and whether you remember me is not the least bit important. I just wanted you to know that here I am at age 40 . . . just as certain of Christ's reality" as he had been as a camper at Forest Home. He concluded by expressing his personal appreciation for her ministry: "To say, 'Thank you' sounds so hollow and inadequate." He believed that her influence on him "will last through all eternity," for "you shared God with me, and thousands more like me."[107] As with many of the other paradoxes Mears embodied, there were some who must have been puzzled, even hurt, by the leadership culture Mears cultivated, but because she could make anyone feel cared for no matter what their role in the department, those like Charles King appear to have been by far in the majority.

FOR HENRIETTA MEARS the limits of grace appeared most clearly when juxtaposed with matters of faith or family. And when she faced a circumstance in which both were in play simultaneously, she was most liable to contravene the charity she so often exemplified. Perhaps more than any other association, her rocky relationship with Jim Vaus provides the best example.[108] Vaus was raised in a middle-class Christian family that attended the theologically conservative Church of the Open Door in downtown Los Angeles. In the autumn of 1937 he registered for classes at the Bible Institute of Los Angeles, where his father, a Baptist minister and founder with his Jewish wife of the Los Angeles Hebrew Mission, taught for twenty-five years.[109] Finding the environment too confining, Vaus transferred first to a local community college and then to Wheaton College, where he roomed with Carl F. H. Henry and Richard Halverson. He lasted only one semester before dropping out and reenrolling at LA's Bible Institute. His growing interest in electronics enabled him to set up a vindictive wiretap of a female student's room. That incident and financial impropriety as an institute fundraiser got him expelled. Close on the heels of his expulsion Vaus spent time in jail for attempted robbery, incarcerated at the same institution as the LA mob boss Bugsy Siegel. While serving his time he organized a choir and taught the men some of his favorite hymns.

Upon his release, Vaus began attending the College Department Sunday school class and other church meetings at First Presbyterian. Always on the lookout for captivating leaders, Henrietta Mears facilitated his rise to the presidency of the department (1942–1943) and entertained hopes that Vaus would attend Princeton Theological Seminary. He began dating her niece Peggy Grieg, but his termination of their relationship devastated Mears, driving the first wedge between them.[110] By this time Vaus had joined the Army and further honed his expertise in electronics. Unfortunately he thought nothing of misappropriating government property and faced a court martial that ended a brief engagement to Lauralil Evans, daughter of the senior pastor. While awaiting his trial in the fall of 1944 Vaus attended a church hymn-singing event where he became acquainted with teenager Alice Park. Subsequently tried and declared guilty, Vaus faced jail again but because of his skills found a measure of redemption, which led to an honorable discharge in December 1946.

A short time later he started his own electronics consulting business in Hollywood, eventually counting the likes of J. Paul Getty, Errol Flynn, Dick Haymes, Xavier Cugat, and Mickey Rooney—as well as the vice squad of the Los Angeles Police Department—among his wealthy and well-placed clients.[111] As his reputation in the electronics industry grew, Vaus straddled two worlds. On the one hand he relished the Hollywood high life; on the other he continued to value his church connections. By the time he married Park in 1947, however, his checkered personal history at First Presbyterian led them away from that congregation to join South Hollywood Presbyterian Church and assist with its youth ministry. Over the next two years his life spun out of control. He had provided wiretapping services prior to this time, but in the late 1940s he worked in this capacity for the Los Angeles Police Department *and* for LA's most notorious crime figure, Mickey Cohen, Bugsy Siegel's former lieutenant.

At the height of his wealth and influence in late 1949 Vaus turned on his radio one Saturday in November only to hear western personality Stuart Hamblen testify to his newfound faith in Christ. He had also been aware of the conversion experiences of others at the Billy Graham crusade. A recent death in the family and a reminder of his own duplicitous life from an unexpected source led Vaus to Graham's tent. Vaus steeled himself against the urge to make a genuine Christian commitment because he knew the decision would have life-changing ramifications, but his resistance melted away and he went forward to commit his life to Christ.[112]

Word about Jim Vaus's conversion spread nearly as quickly as it did for Hamblen's and probably contributed to the further extension of the Graham meetings. Two days after his conversion, the evangelist welcomed Vaus back to speak about what had happened to him. A few days later he told Mickey Cohen of his new Christian commitment. As the Los Angeles crusade drew to a close in mid-November 1949, Graham invited Vaus along with Hamblen, film star Harvey Fritts, and Olympian and war hero Louis Zamperini (who also became connected to Mears's education program) to share their conversion experiences with five hundred pastors at the Alexandria Hotel.[113] Soon after this appearance with his fellow high profile converts the Hollywood Christian Business Men's Committee became one of the first organizations outside of the Graham team to ask Vaus to talk about his newfound faith.

These occasions were only the first of countless opportunities that came to

Jim Vaus over the ensuing years to express his faith in Christ. In addition to his speaking engagements across the United States and in foreign nations, Vaus started ministry groups including the Jim Vaus Evangelistic Association, the Missionary Communication Service, and Youth Development Incorporated. He also established a camp ministry somewhat like Forest Home. Mears and Vaus shared many influential evangelical friends and collaborators, such as Mark Hatfield, Dawson Trotman, Billy Graham, Cliff Barrows, and George Beverly Shea.

But no matter who endorsed him, how consistently he lived his faith, or under which conditions he and Mears appeared together, she never reconciled with Vaus. How much of her animosity sprang from his repudiation of Grieg, his inability to live a consistent Christian life throughout the early and mid-1940s, or her belief that he abused her trust in him will never be known. The sense of betrayal she felt after such trust vanished must have been palpable and certainly played a major role in the irreparable breach.[114] What is known is that she never believed that his 1949 conversion had been sincere. Upon hearing of it she responded with obvious skepticism: "Oh, he's done that before." A short while after his conversion both Mears and Vaus appeared at the same meeting of Christian leaders, but she refused even to acknowledge him. Decades later at a conference in Charlotte, North Carolina, Vaus spoke with a colleague who had also known Mears about how the animus she carried to her grave had severely wounded him. Their conversation reduced Vaus to tears. The friend to both believers conceded, "Well, she could be that way."[115] Vaus was perhaps the most well known of those who failed to live up to Mears's expectations, but he was not alone. When she believed that God led her to select and then groom individuals for leadership in the church, her disappointment could be dramatic and unrelenting.

In March 2012 clinical psychologist Tom Brunner explained why so many of those who have the capacity to make a significant mark in the world fail to do so. He argued that any number of individuals may have the character traits necessary for the achievement of great things, but failure to manage constructively even a few personality "thorns" or annoying habits derails their potential by stifling "the personal and professional maturity process." From Brunner's perspective "insightfully managing" personality "thorns" can clear the way for greatness to happen.[116]

In reflecting on the perplexing paradoxes and limitations in the life and ministry of Henrietta Mears, what remains so intriguing is the inescapable conclusion that even her thorns drew people to her. Some of her collegians and colleagues may have gotten scratched in the process, but if they remained in relationship with her they became stronger for the effort. There are certainly those, like Harriet Prichard, Dale Vree, or Van Harvey, who dropped away either because of Mears's forthright assessments and proclamations or because of a theological parting of the ways, but even they sometimes acknowledged her role in their lives.[117] She drove others hard, but she drove herself harder because although the limited grace she communicated to others revealed the boundaries around her own understanding of the term, that same limitation generated a twentieth-century American Protestant renaissance whose effects continue to reverberate into our own time.

Brunner's "thorns" are the polar opposite of grace, for its most common definition centers on the concept of favor or goodness communicated by one party to an undeserving other. In putting others before self, the graceful person must surrender her initiative and perspectives if those initiatives and perspectives in any way impede the conveyance of unmediated favor. Yet if Mears incarnated grace to that extent, she clearly would never have risen to take an honored place in the pantheon of evangelical Christian leaders who together transformed midcentury American Protestantism. She herself characterized grace as "neither treating a person as he deserves, nor treating a person better than he deserves; it is treating a person graciously without the slightest reference to his deserts."[118] Earlier chapters of this volume have demonstrated the many ways that Henrietta Mears lived into an ecumenical and reliable grace that attracted so many to the faith. The greatest paradox of her distinguished career might be that even in the rough-edged limitations of that grace she probably attracted just as many.

Chapter Eleven

Expended

In 1950, *The Christian Century* polled a hundred thousand ministers nationwide to choose which church should be profiled by the popular religious journal as the most successful in the twelve-state American Southwest. The First Presbyterian Church of Hollywood surfaced as the clear choice.[1] The resulting article surveyed various ministries of the church and devoted approximately an entire page of its six and a half page text to senior pastor Louis Evans Sr. The five other ordained pastors and two renowned music ministry professionals on the staff collectively merited three paragraphs. Henrietta Mears received as much coverage as did Evans. The page-long description of her ministry included discussions of her Sunday school, her work with the College Department, and her Gospel Light curriculum. The article attempted to tease out her reputation in the greater Los Angeles ecclesiastical community, noting that "naturally, a woman who has accomplished as much as this director of Christian education is a subject for much discussion throughout the churches of the area." The consensus opinion placed her in the fundamentalist camp, but the periodical discovered

> in the Hollywood congregation few stop to ask whether or not the director of Christian education is a fundamentalist. Her driving but inspiring personality makes the question seem of minor importance. She can stir the interest and compel the affectionate loyalty of all kinds and conditions of people, including hundreds at an age when church ties frequently dissolve or snap.[2]

Although Mears could not be personally interviewed because of prior speaking commitments elsewhere, the reporter observed that "she was an unseen presence, an offstage voice, felt and heard at every turning. 'Miss Mears says . . .' 'If Miss Mears were here . . .' 'The way Miss Mears handles a problem like this . . .'" The writer concluded that he "became so accustomed to replies of this sort that he finally grew to feel as well-acquainted with this woman as with any member of the Hollywood staff whom he met in person. She must be a human dynamo."[3]

When the article appeared in September 1950, Mears was barely a month removed from her sixtieth birthday but showed no signs of slowing down. Over the next ten years her Sunday school enrollment would jump from 3,958 in 1951 to 6,102 in 1960. The education buildings constructed in the 1950s barely contained enough room for all her students. Mears also kept up a nearly constant conference speaking schedule until late in the decade. The Hollywood Christian Group experienced its greatest growth and influence during the 1950s and the church's deputation programs continued to expand. Gospel Light materials enjoyed such ongoing favor both domestically and internationally that the staff quintupled between 1948 and 1958. Millions of copies of the seven hundred individual items shipped annually from the Gospel Light facilities to more than eighty different countries. By the early 1960s major distribution centers for its materials had opened in London, Tokyo, Auckland, Johannesburg, Sydney, and Toronto. Well-attended banquets at venues such as the Hollywood Palladium on Sunset Boulevard brought guests like governors Arthur Langlie of Washington and Mark Hatfield of Oregon in addition to Charles Fuller of *The Old Fashioned Revival Hour* radio program; Billy Graham; former UCLA football great and Presbyterian minister Donn Moomaw; and Bob Pierce, founder of World Vision to help raise money for ongoing improvements at Forest Home, which hosted thousands of conferees of all ages and denominational backgrounds each year. In the 1940s and 1950s the prestige and reputation of the conference center led to her critical involvement in an international consortium of Christian retreat facilities that incorporated as the Christian Camp and Conference Association International in 1963. After her 1954 visit with Lillian Dickson who served homeless orphans and lepers in Taiwan through a network of hospitals, schools, and hospitality compounds, Mears helped spread the news about her ministry. Alongside several of her associates she played an instrumental role in the formation of the Mustard Seed Incorporated, the entity by which Dickson's work "became known to hundreds of thousands of American friends."[4]

And still Henrietta Mears dreamed bigger dreams. Her many travels in the 1950s took her to places rife with literature advocating communist solutions to the world's problems. She also heard from missionaries across the globe desperate for Christian educational materials in the languages of the people to whom they ministered, for only the rare mission board had enough money to produce such literature. Mears believed that in order to train national leaders and root new converts solidly in the faith, the Bible had to be taught more diligently on the world's mission fields.[5] When she saw children in Hong Kong reading communist comic books, students in Tokyo carrying communist literature, and other such scenes around the globe, Mears vowed, "I must do something."[6] In 1961 she established GLINT (Gospel Light International), a nonprofit foundation dedicated to assisting mission groups worldwide in the adaptation, translation, and distribution of biblical Christian education literature in the languages of the world's indigenous peoples. Gifts from contributors were channeled through GLINT to deliver support to mission causes backing these objectives. Her longtime associate Cyrus Nelson assumed the presidency while Mears served on the board of directors.[7] She believed that the foundation could be the vehicle to spread systematic, biblically based teaching curricula that would "give lasting depth to evangelistic missionary efforts, to train national churches, and Bible-teaching groups that would be able to carry on without outside assistance."[8]

Mears planned a formal luncheon at the stylish Statler Hilton Hotel in downtown Los Angeles for the official launch of her newest project, but just a few days before the event, her doctor ordered her to undergo tests at the Mayo Clinic. Instead of cancelling the affair, Nelson took her place as the master of ceremonies—and Mears addressed the two hundred guests via telephone from her hospital room.[9] Upon hearing of her global enterprise, one correspondent wrote expressing a sentiment no doubt shared by others:

> The work of promoting Sunday Schools in foreign lands has staggering possibilities. And you! Henrietta C. Mears! You fill us with awe. You have given a life of enthusiasm and work toward raising the standards of American Sunday Schools. . . .

> You have surely sipped from some eternal spring of energy and enthusiasm for service to Christ and his children of this world. You have been an inspiration to all your friends! . . . May GLINT meet with the great success it deserves.[10]

At her last GLINT board meeting just a few days before her death, Mears delighted in the news that significant aid was already being provided by the two-year-old organization to countries in Africa and Latin America as well as to Japan, Korea, India, Vietnam, and Greece. In response to such heartening news, she shared with fellow board members, "I just want to be God's helper."[11] With the creation of GLINT, Henrietta Mears validated the necessity of training native-born leaders to ensure a healthy worldwide church, long before Christians in the West began to think about the globalization of the Christian movement. By 1972 GLINT was supplying funds to distribute biblically based educational materials in eighty languages. Its reach extended to five nations in Africa (Egypt, Ethiopia, Kenya, Burundi, South Africa), eight in Asia (India, Indonesia, Malaysia, Vietnam, the Philippines, Hong Kong, Japan, Korea), two in Latin America (Mexico, Brazil), and seven in Europe (Italy, Greece, Sweden, Norway, Finland, Poland, Russia).[12]

Though her vision broadened again as she passed seventy, the cumulative loss of family and friends coupled with the infirmities of age cast longer shadows across her life. Her beloved brother Will passed away in 1945, followed by Margaret in 1951. In 1957 Mears not only lost the last of her siblings to the heart disease that ran in her family, she also had to endure the accidental death of a dear nephew.[13]

As early as 1946, Mears began to recognize the benefits of slowing down the hectic pace of her life. While vacationing in Buenos Aires she wrote:

> It is strange to be such a lady of leisure. But I guess it is a good thing once in a while. I'm afraid I have been burning the candle at both ends for too long a time. Our human machinery must slow down, and we ourselves must "come apart and rest awhile." Activity does not always mean accomplishment, neither does rest mean idleness.

Less than two weeks later she confessed "it seems as if I've rushed all my life. Even when I have taken trips, I have run against time." In August her delight in relaxing with no commitments was obvious: "I like to just idle along and let my motor rest. It's wonderful not to be trying to meet engagements or to feel you have to do anything."[14] Unfortunately, once she returned to Hollywood her calendar immediately refilled to overflowing. The daily struggle to meet all her commitments began to weigh on Mears as the years slipped by.

Her eyesight, always her most apparent physical ailment, had been one of the main reasons that she often spoke without notes, committing to memory what she wanted her audiences to hear. After a period of relatively stable vision, Mears became more intentional about caring for her eyes by the mid-1940s. She consulted a popular book on eye care and wrote four pages of notes on practices designed to mitigate her condition. In August of 1946 she undertook a serious regimen of ocular exercises. Later, on at least one occasion she asked Oral Roberts to pray for her healing, without apparent results.[15] By the 1950s her eyes watered frequently, requiring the constant use of a handkerchief. Poor eyesight also affected how she walked, obliging Mears to look down often for safety's sake.[16] On a South Pacific cruise with friends in 1957 she experienced further deterioration and increasing pain, particularly in the eye on which she most depended. Immediately upon her arrival in Australia Mears consulted a doctor who diagnosed her with an ophthalmic rupture and urged her to return home. Back in Hollywood her eye care specialist admitted he could do nothing for her professionally, "but as a Christian, I suggest you pray and ask others to pray with you." Her eye condition stabilized, but she had to relinquish her driving privileges.[17]

Except for this 1957 incident, Mears's health issues on her many trips abroad tended to be relatively minor, although it appears that she remained quite susceptible to intestinal complaints compounded by colds and bouts of influenza. Shortly after returning from her 1950–1951 trip around the world, however, Mears collapsed while addressing a women's group at First Presbyterian. She was hospitalized and subjected to a battery of tests, but doctors could find no physical cause for Mears's episode. Her longtime assistant Ethel May Baldwin believed that the unsettling incident was a consequence of her aging body's struggle to meet the continuous demands on her time and talents.[18] After a spring and summer filled with her regular activities, a visit to Minnesota, and speaking engagements in Cincinnati, Detroit, Toronto, and Chicago, Mears was packed off to the hospital in an ambulance in late August 1953. A team of four doctors vetoed any involvement with the College Briefing Conference while she battled viral pneumonia.[19] By late 1957 her ailments made it increasingly difficult for her to sustain the frenetic weekly schedule that had been her modus operandi since her early twenties, although her eighteen-page annual performance report provides no indication that either her responsibilities or her vitality waned.[20] Mears did rely more and more on guest teachers such as Bernard Ramm and her seminarians such as David Benson and Dale Bruner to help teach the College Department classes after the mid-1950s.[21] Her physician's diagnosis of arteriosclerosis in 1960 and her unplanned visit to the Mayo Clinic in 1961 clarified the unstable nature of her health and may help explain the reason for her increased perspiration, mounting inflexibility, and tendency to repeat herself, which became evident by the late 1950s.[22]

Recognizing the declining condition of their director of Christian education, the First Presbyterian Church of Hollywood planned a celebration of her prolific ministry at the church during the spring of 1961. The ruse of a dinner honoring Senior Pastor Raymond Lindquist ensured Mears's attendance. Her closest friends ushered her down the stairs to Fellowship Hall on the evening of April 21 to the applause of the capacity crowd gathered to pay her tribute. Those who could not attend, such as Billy Graham and Dwight Eisenhower, sent congratulatory messages. Nearly one hundred such letters and telegrams arrived, with another forty audiotaped communiqués received from around the world. Over the ensuing five and a half hours former collegians, church members, and national leaders of a rejuvenated evangelical Christian movement alternately lauded, parodied, and paid homage to their thoroughly surprised seventy-year-old doyenne. Although she retired to a cot in the ladies' powder room after dinner because of her limited physical condition, speakers piped the entire program directly to her.[23]

In April 1962, Mears attended the first meeting of what would become the Forest Home Auxiliary, an organization founded by professional harpist and former College Department member Martha Mortenson and devoted to the care and maintenance of the conference center. A month later Mears hosted a tea for the nearly three hundred women who had expressed an interest in its purpose. Thrilled at the prospect of what the auxiliary could accomplish, she called Mortenson almost daily for a time, always asking how much money the women had raised in the last twenty-four hours. The group would eventually include twelve hundred women who raised countless thousands to maintain and upgrade the conference center that played an essential part in the renewal of evangelical Protestantism.[24]

During the summer of 1962 Don Williams from nearby Glendale Presbyterian Church took the summer off from his studies at Princeton to intern at the Hollywood church, with primary responsibility for the College Department. Well-received by the collegians and with the support of Mears, Williams accepted a call to serve as the college pastor upon the completion of his doctoral degree in the spring of 1963.[25] With Williams ready to step into his position in June, a well-trained Sunday school staff in the hundreds, a growing patronage base for Forest Home, and a number of her former College Department members capably shepherding other aspects of the Christian Education program at the church under her guidance, Mears anticipated a future full of promise and planned accordingly.

Early in 1963 Mears spotted a pianist friend at a garden party sponsored by the women of First Presbyterian. Mears greeted her warmly and asked if she would play for the group. Caught somewhat off guard, her friend declined but promised to play for her sometime during the coming year. Mears's disappointment went further than her friend and most in attendance knew, for only those closest to her heard her whisper, "I'll not be here next year."[26] In February she and Ethel May Baldwin visited former Fideltian Kay Sewall, who noticed how slim Mears had become—too thin from her perspective. Mears, however, informed Sewall that her latest medical tests showed no problems and her kidneys and heart were functioning properly. Before her guests left, Sewall arranged to stay with her in the early fall. Shortly thereafter in early March Mears attended the annual Forest Home banquet celebrating the silver anniversary of its acquisition.[27]

She had spoken repeatedly about her desire to purchase a still fairly rare electronic technology that included a key component invented by her nephew in 1950.[28] So on Monday, March 18, she and Ethel May finally settled on the model and placed the order for a new color television set. Baldwin drove her out to the San Fernando Valley, where they noticed new construction sites. The women spoke expectantly about the implications of Southern California's continuing growth on the ministry they had shared for more than three decades. A few days earlier, Mears and Baldwin had looked at carpet samples for the rooms formerly occupied by the Bright family. Since the Brights had recently moved out of her Stone Canyon home to the new headquarters of

Campus Crusade for Christ at the former Arrowhead Springs Hotel in the San Bernardino Mountains, Mears thought it an opportune moment to recarpet before her new housemate moved in. She had just reached an agreement with her friend Louise James, who planned to relocate from New York and move into the refurbished rooms in June. On Tuesday evening, Mears had a long telephone conversation about Forest Home's future with Jack Franck, her former collegian and current director of operations at the conference center. She spent time studying for an Ambassadors lesson she was to present on Sunday and reviewed her notes for an upcoming teacher training session. She also looked ahead to the Easter breakfast for her College Department on April 14.[29]

Sometime in the morning of March 20 Mears experienced discomfort and appears to have called or had her housekeeper call her physician, who rushed to the home. It is unclear whether he examined her and then left or whether she momentarily excused herself during the examination to go into the bathroom. In any event, as she stood in front of the bathroom sink Mears suffered a massive heart attack and died at 10:30 a.m.[30] Word spread quickly of her death, and condolence letters poured into Hollywood from across the country and around the world. So many wished to pay their respects that friends planned two memorial services—one at First Presbyterian, Hollywood, on Saturday, March 23, and another at First Baptist, Minneapolis, on Sunday, April 28.[31] In writing about her passing Larry Ward, director of the Evangelical Press News Service, expressed what many believed: "'Teacher' dead? Don't you believe it. She'll live this Sunday in the thousands of classes where her lessons are taught . . . in the hundreds of pulpits across the United States and around the world where one of 'Miss Mears boys' stands up to preach . . . and in every heart like mine where she has had a ministry."[32] When news of Mears's death reached Billy Graham in Hawaii, he sent a cablegram to those in mourning. Toward the end of his message, Graham indicated what he believed constituted the most the fitting testament to her life's work. The now world-renowned evangelist wrote, "If you would see anything that we could erect as a memorial to her faithful years of service, look about you and see the lives that she has helped to lead into the knowledge of Jesus Christ as Savior and Lord."[33] His choice of words in the final phrase is particularly instructive. For Mears and others moved by the Keswick emphasis on complete surrender of the will to God, salvation served only as the prelude to a lifetime of self-reflection and spiritual growth as believers submitted themselves to Christ's lordship over all aspects of their lives. Her great gift, as Graham suggested, had always been in both evangelizing those outside the faith and nurturing the faithful across denominational lines to greater maturity.

The pews at First Presbyterian filled with nearly two thousand mourners for the Hollywood memorial service. Hundreds in the audience had been led to the Christian faith or a deeper experience of faith by Mears personally and went on to serve the church as dedicated laypersons as well as ordained ministers and missionaries. Clothed in a dark blue chiffon dress she had only recently purchased, with a simple string of pearls, a white orchid pinned to her shoulder and her hands clasping her treasured red leather-covered Bible, Mears's body lay in an open casket at the front of the sanctuary.[34] Raymond Lindquist, David Cowie, Richard Halverson, Cyrus Nelson, and Louis Evans Jr. offered eulogies, and another of her "boys" sang "How Great Thou Art." Luther's hymn "A Mighty Fortress Is Our God" paid homage to Mears's unshakable faith in God's majesty. As the service ended with the choir's rendering of Handel's "Hallelujah Chorus," one participant whispered reverently, "Dear Teacher! Even in her death she pointed us to Christ."[35] In recalling the challenge that William Riley left with Mears at her mother's service more than fifty years earlier, her biographers Ethel May Baldwin and David Benson asked, "I wonder upon whom her mantle may fall?" But they answered their own question, "her mantle already lay on the shoulders of thousands upon thousands who have been directed to Christ by her life."[36]

A graveside service at Forest Lawn in nearby Glendale followed. With a procession of 180 automobiles and an estimated nineteen hundred in attendance, only one other person's rites, held nearly two decades earlier, drew a comparable audience, according to cemetery officials.[37] Pallbearers carried Mears's casket up the slope where her body was interred under an evergreen tree beside Margaret with a simple bronze plaque that read "A Willing Instrument in the Hands of an Almighty God." Ironically, from the vantage point of her burial site, mourners could look across the cemetery's Vale of Memory to the lavish marble crypt of the only other twentieth-century Protestant woman whose influence (and burial service) rivaled Mears's—Aimee Semple McPherson, founder of the International Church of the Foursquare Gospel.

In death Mears continued to care for those individuals and institutions most dear to her. She left separate bequests of between $1,000 and $2,000 to at least eight family members. She gave David Cowie, Dale Bruner, Bill and Vonette Bright, and her housekeeper, Lura Shearer, each $1,000. To each of the Bright's sons, Mears bequeathed $500. Ethel May Baldwin—her assistant since 1928, Gospel Light partner, and sometime traveling companion—received $12,500. As a token of her esteem, in addition to all the money Mears had contributed to the ministry of the First Presbyterian Church of Hollywood over the years, she gave the church an additional $2,000. Mears donated the remainder of her sizable estate to Forest Home. Excluding the unknown amount of her much larger bequest to the conference center, her posthumous gifts totaled $31,500—well over $260,000 in 2019 dollars. The value of personal property that she willed to family and friends, often by writing their names on the individual items, is indeterminable.[38]

A letter from the Davis family of Portland, Oregon, written to Cyrus Nelson a week after her passing, summed up what so many felt about the life and ministry of Henrietta Mears:

> We all feel that one of our own family has been taken from this earthly scene. For Miss Mears had the ability to make you know we are all one in Christ, that we are all members of His body and members of one family. Through her gracious spirit she drew us to her and to Christ.[39]

Conclusion

No Ordinary Life

Toward the end of her life, Henrietta Mears paid a final visit to friends and former associates in Washington, DC. By this time, Richard Halverson had left the Hollywood church to take a position with International Christian Leadership soon to be followed by a pastorate at Fourth Presbyterian Church in Bethesda, Maryland, and the Senate chaplaincy. The Halversons accompanied Mears to a dinner engagement where she sat with Methodist clergyman Abraham Vereide, the ICL director who began the Presidential Prayer Breakfast movement in 1953. Over the course of their conversation, Vereide asked Mears what she would do differently if she had her life to live over again. Without a moment's hesitation, Mears replied matter-of-factly, "I would trust God more."[1] Probably no one in her worldwide circle of mentees, colleagues, friends, and admirers would have guessed that to be her answer, for the remarkable results of her unstinting faith in a loving God were obvious wherever evangelicals labored.

Even in her own day, Mears cut an improbable figure. So short she often stood on risers to be seen over the speaker's podium, she was built as one of her devotees put it, "like a fireplug." Rather stocky with thick glasses and husky voice, she did not often leave her home without a fur draped over her shoulders and a hat perched jauntily atop her neatly coiffed hair. Nothing about her physical presence would lead a casual observer to view her as anything more than a rather well-to-do middle-aged Southern California matron out for a drive down Sunset Boulevard on a sunny Sunday morning. But once she turned left onto Gower Street, parked the car, and made her way to the College Department hall in the lower level of the First Presbyterian Church of

Hollywood's original sanctuary, that impression melted away when she began her lesson. Her clipped, rapid-fire delivery utilized every inflected nuance of a powerful voice that commanded attention. She exposited the biblical text with confidence, pacing the front of the room, punctuating her main points with dramatic pauses and rarely, if ever, consulting her notes. Interjecting seemingly tangential stream-of-consciousness asides that somehow wound their way back to the central narrative every single time at just the right moment, she seemed to grow in physical stature as the significance of her words turned more trenchant and the force of her arguments more persuasive. By the end of the hour every person in the room knew that this formidable presence was no ordinary Bible teacher.

The Protestant world had also learned that about Henrietta Mears. For since the second decade of the twentieth century she had been in the advance guard of those who worked to recast orthodox Christianity. Though committed primarily to the educational welfare of those under her authority, initially at First Baptist, Minneapolis, and then at First Presbyterian, Hollywood, her local endeavors became the springboard for imaginative thinking and inspired action whose effects rippled far beyond Minneapolis and Hollywood. To appropriate a phrase in current usage, Mears always acted locally but thought globally about the church. As a direct consequence of her creation of evangelically oriented programs and institutions that arose from her local responsibilities, and her cultivation of a rich network of mutually beneficial relationships across boundaries many chose not to cross, Henrietta Mears could justifiably be considered a foremost architect of the twentieth-century reformation of Protestant America.

Had we the chance to sit under Mears's teaching in her six-thousand-plus member Sunday school at the First Presbyterian Church of Hollywood, she would inevitably remind us of the preeminent necessity to foster the inner life of faith, for she declared that "the inner life is all the life we have as Christians." With bespectacled eyes riveted on her audience, Teacher would lean over the podium and, as if telling us for the first time, reiterate that "the Christian life is not 'trying to be good,' or 'trying to be like Jesus.' It is seeking to have a deeper experience of fellowship with Christ."[2] For her the gospel had to stand pure and unadulterated by other causes or concerns, however just and honorable they might be. Throughout her years as an educator and administrator Mears never deviated from a Christ-centered ministry intent on producing spiritually mature Christians who could lead others with integrity and wisdom. How often her staff and students heard her proclaim prophetically, "If He is not Lord *of* all, He is not Lord *at* all," over the years is anyone's guess.

Over the course of more than five dozen interviews conducted with those who knew her well, one of the questions I asked repeatedly concerned her teaching on political and social topics. Many could tell me where she stood politically, but not one could remember a time when she taught directly on these potentially divisive subjects. For example, while more than a few Protestant leaders of the post–World War II church preached entire sermons or offered conference seminars regarding the threat of communism, Mears kept a discreet distance from ideology in her teaching, although on a few occasions she apparently allowed some introduction of political perspectives among her teachers.[3] She often used the intense dedication to Marxism unmistakable in the postwar world as a powerful illustration to provoke Christians to take their faith development more seriously just as she utilized statistics from social, economic, and other political issues to drive home the importance of total commitment to God. But she persistently refused to politicize the gospel. According to Betsy Cox, who wrote a thesis on her in 1961, Mears believed "that the field of Christian Education should first introduce men, women, and children to Christ as Savior and Lord and then train them in the Word of God." While she drew extensively upon stories or aphorisms of a political or social nature to energize her text and enliven her message, she constantly affirmed that "Christ should be the center and circumference of the Christian Education program."[4] Mears never forgot that the purpose grounding her decades of service was "to know Christ and to make Him known," as the motto of her College Department made clear. Any other activity paled in comparison to building the kingdom.

This single-minded devotion to evangelism and discipleship, of course, meant that her deafening silence on contemporary issues could be heard from coast to coast. Her refusal to take a public stand with respect to anti-Semitic or anti-Catholic rhetoric or California's Rumford Fair Housing Act, to name a few hot-button issues of her day, could certainly be perceived as complicity in perpetuating an unjust status quo. Yet it would be helpful to remember the tightrope she believed she had to walk as a bridge-building evangelical female at a time when there were precious few of them and the span was still under construction. If she faced censure in some quarters of the interdenominational network she did so much to enrich because of her attachment to the Hollywood Christian Group, how much more might her work be threatened if she gave public voice to her inward convictions on these and other matters?

At the same time, she refused to devalue the importance of active participation in and service to a world both broken and blessed. If the inner life is all the life Christians have, Mears believed that "the outer life is that expression of life that makes Christ known to others."[5] Though insistent on a laser-like focus on matters of faith and spiritual growth in the Christian education work of the church, Mears believed just as intensely that personal piety must have tangible public consequences. Her charge to "Live the Gospel first! Tell about it afterward!" motivated generations of theological conservatives to pursue redemptive work in the world as the Spirit gave guidance.[6] For to Mears making a faith commitment meant entering a life of service to those both within and outside the walls of the church just as it had for past generations of her family. Her devotion to service only broadened the longer she lived as her support for the work projects of the World Deputation program, Lillian Dickson's holistic Mustard Seed ministry, and the social activism of her friends and associates demonstrates. Like her grandmother and mother before her, Mears reaffirmed that the supreme need for humanity remained spiritual regeneration, but she also recognized that Christ called the church to sustain and enrich the material and emotional lives of all those for whom he died as the Holy Spirit gave direction.

If Christians are to serve those beyond the church effectively, Mears believed, they must participate actively in the wider secular world that surrounds them, for to speak into the culture it must be understood. She modeled a willingness to wear theological orthodoxy proudly while dancing with prudence and grace in often less than hospitable circumstances. Even as her home church pastor at First Baptist, Minneapolis, led the fundamentalist cause, Mears already took her first steps away from much of what fundamentalists of the 1920s held dear, including a virulent antagonism toward American popular and intellectual culture. One might argue that her professional positions in North Branch and Beardsley, funded as they were by public dollars, dictated her acceptance of conventional cultural patterns, but her selective embrace of popular culture continued when she returned to Minneapolis in 1916 and contributed to her success as the teacher of her cherished Fideltians. Mears's astonishing ability to blend an evangelical Christian faith with modern sensibilities kept the Fideltians and College Department members coming back week after week, year after year.

She personally felt more constrained by other believers than by her own sense of God's guidance in these matters. Mears felt no trepidation, for example, about wearing the latest hairstyle or enjoying a good film. But even in her later years she feared that some churches would not allow her to speak if they knew she used popular beauty aids, observing that "if some church people knew I ever wore lipstick or nail polish, they wouldn't let me inside of their churches to talk about Jesus Christ."[7] And one can only imagine what detractors might have said about her use of sex education materials from the public school film library, or her invitation to psychologists and philosophers to address her collegians.

To Mears, however, if such engagement furthered the central Christian mission to evangelize the unconverted, helped Christians mature in their faith, and resulted in opportunities to serve others, she had no qualms about suffusing the profane with divine purpose. Nor did she major on directly proscribing activities for her young people. She once put it this way in an address she gave after the Second World War:

> If I would get up in Hollywood and tell people that they shouldn't go to movies and they shouldn't do this and they shouldn't do that, and all that sort of thing, do you know I wouldn't have any following at all? . . . But do you know what I can do? I can go before that group of young men and women and boys and girls, and I can tell them, say this. "Young people, God demands everything. If Christ is not Lord of all then He is not Lord at all. And He wants you to give Him absolutely everything you have. Put Him first. . . ." When you put the cross where it belongs and you let young people bow there and not merely give up a lot of superficial things in life, those things fall away. Definitely. If they're absolutely where God wants them to be, and the cross is right in the very dead center of life.[8]

Roger Arnebergh, former member of her College Department and city attorney for Los Angeles in the early 1960s, learned from Mears that "Christianity did not force us to give up other things, but Christianity crowded out the things that were inconsistent with being a Christian, [offering] much better things, things that made a happier and a fuller and a richer life."[9] Since at least the days of early church leader Tertullian, Christians have struggled to maintain an appropriate relationship between faith and culture. Mears balanced an unwavering fidelity to the essential tenets of Christianity and a cautious convergence with aspects of modern American life. She thus effected an appealing synergy between participation in the culture while concurrently standing apart from it that struck a responsive chord.[10] Her novel approach to pinpointing suitable intersections between the sacred and the secular as early as the 1910s contributed significantly to the reformation of evangelical Protestantism in the decades after World War II.

Mears believed that a deepening faith commitment would lead to a life of service, which in turn required thoughtful interaction with the surrounding culture. A substantial portion of that thoughtful interaction should come from cultivating the life of the mind. She often spoke unequivocally about the absolute importance of the intellectual virtues for believers. She looked out at her audience at a 1959 leadership conference and thundered:

> I want you to grow intellectually. Christians by and large are apt to be stupid and ignorant. . . . I always tell young men and women in college not to dare to speak out in college against anything that's taught them unless they are an "A" student. . . . God put no premium on ignorance. And if we are to become teachers and leaders of this age . . . we must keep abreast.[11]

Mears often said that students raised in the church did not lose their faith during their university studies because they had no faith to lose. And she laid that onus directly on the church.[12] In an address at a Chicago conference ten years earlier Mears pulled no punches in her negative assessment of church leadership, nor the reasons for its ineptitude:

> We haven't given young people, really, a reason for their faith. And so instead of having it built, wisdom being the very foundation of it, we discover that they meet a little more the intellectual power as far as the world is concerned, and then there becomes intellectual frustration, and here we are left, and our leadership is in the hands so often of men and women who know not God.[13]

Mears often despaired of the church's educational programs for college-age students, calling some of them "an intellectual disgrace."[14] She countered the rampant anti-intellectualism of so many theological conservatives with a genuine admiration for scholarship and the academic life. Her conspicuous pro-intellectualism proceeded directly from her own educational journey and reflected her steadfast conviction that students appropriately educated in the church had nothing to fear from any teaching they received outside its walls.

Finally, Mears modeled an ecumenicity missing from many of her evangelical contemporaries because she believed passionately that to meet the challenges of modern life, the church needed the concerted effort of all its members as well as courteous relationships with those outside the faith. Mears seems not to have shared the deep suspicion of Roman Catholics that characterized so many Protestants in the decades before Vatican II, although it is hard to determine just how far her ecumenism went in this regard. That she exhibited a more expansive practice of grace than many of her era is perhaps most clearly demonstrated by her 1954 nomination for the Mary Margaret McBride Project, a cooperative venture of the United Church Women, the National Council of Catholic Women, and the National Council of Jewish Women to select local women across the country who contribute most generously to the vitality of their communities.[15]

Her founding of The Gospel Light Press in 1933, her acquisition in 1938 of what would become Forest Home Christian Conference Center, her multifaceted contributions to the National Association of Evangelicals beginning in the early 1940s, her decisive role in the formation of the Hollywood Christian Group in 1949, her involvement with the Christian Camp and Conference Association International during its formative years, and her creation of GLINT in 1961—these pursuits confirmed that she always implemented a big-tent ministry strategy. All of these organizations were interdenominational from their inception and nourished the decentralized "horizontal, weblike, informal lines of leadership and organization" so characteristic of the neoevangelical movement.[16] Mears extended friendship and hospitality to those not universally appreciated by the wider church—including Aimee Semple McPherson, with whom she kept a cordial relationship prior to her death in 1944, controversial faith healer Oral Roberts, whom she hosted in her home, and like-minded Agnes Sanford, at whose residence her collegians held many an evening song fest. Mears's private library contained a number of well-used volumes written by some who would have been considered suspect at the time by many in the evangelical movement.[17] As historian Amber Thomas recently observed, "Mears drew upon multiple, sometimes divergent, theological streams: She was a dispensationalist but not a cessationist; a Presbyterian but not a rigid Calvinist; a proto-charismatic but not a full Pentecostal."[18] Certainly not all found a place in her evangelical tent, but it tended to be much larger and more accommodating than most.

In a 1949 speaking engagement she noted the diversity of participants in her college group, mentioning particularly "twelve young Jewish students who are brilliant, three of them went to seminary this year" and a Catholic young woman who decided to join the fellowship. Mears explained to her audience that "we don't proselyte [*sic*] in that sense at all. We merely preach, it's all positive. It's nothing negative. We don't dig at anybody else. We just talk about Christ. And if they want to join Him, why, they join us, and we have great fellowship one with the other."[19] A few years later in a lecture at Fuller Seminary Mears elaborated on her strategy: "You want to orient men and women into the church. Not because you want to make them Presbyterians or Baptists or whatever it is—that's not it at all. But you want to really get their roots into the church—we want college men and women for leaders of tomorrow! And if you don't get them there, you'll never get them."[20] She lived her life convinced that the call to discipleship demanded passion for a larger kingdom membership than others might acknowledge.

If the above examples constitute the frame upon which Mears constructed her vision of a transformed Protestantism, she poured the foundation with a generous measure of grace. Perhaps she could dispense so much grace in such a contentious time because she found herself so often in need of it. As a young woman, challenged by William Bell Riley to fill her mother's unfillable shoes and bereft of both parents before the age of twenty-two, Paul Rader's sermons brought home the absolute necessity of appropriating God's grace, which assured her of God's love and care no matter what her accomplishments. But she also needed to call on it in day-to-day life, for her opponents could be numerous and implacable. Most likely speaking out of her own experience, when counseling one of her former collegians about how to address a criticism, Mears advised him to "forget about it; for every fire you put out they'll light ten more."[21] In a candid moment she once told a confidant: "It's so much easier to be swallowed by a whale than to be picked at by minnows."[22] Her colorful metaphors paint a clear picture of the constant harassment she faced from those who disagreed with her. Without a graceful spirit (and a healthy ego), she could not have thrived for nearly fifty years, even with all her successes. Just as her ecumenical tent could not hold all comers, her ability to confer grace had definite limits—especially with those she believed had wronged her or her family. But on a comparative scale for those of her era, her capacity to take criticism and her willingness to forgive and move on provide a commendable example of graceful living.

Mears brought that sense of grace with her to the far West along with her Baptist-bred, Keswick-oriented Christian faith. The unique configuration of her personal spiritual heritage played a profound role in shaping the contours of American evangelicalism in general and within the Presbyterian Church specifically from the 1920s well into the twenty-first century.

In the spring of 1955 American Presbyterians from across the country met for their annual General Assembly in Los Angeles for the first time since 1903—the same year that the small village of Hollywood incorporated and the town's First Presbyterian Church organized. At the dawn of the new century the Presbytery of Los Angeles contained fifty-three churches with 7,639 members. As the diverse metroplex of Greater LA prepared to welcome the delegates in 1955, the presbytery had grown as much as Southern California itself with 162 congregations and more than a hundred thousand members. It was a vastly different Los Angeles and an appreciably different presbytery. When the Rev. William Meyer greeted his fellow Presbyterians from across the nation, he hoped that the commissioners would "catch the vibrant, forward-looking spirit of West Coast Presbyterianism" and that they would "sense the challenge which the rest of us feel here."[23] It is unknown whether Meyer had more in mind than a geographic region when he invited the delegates to catch that forward-looking spirit, but over the half century since the national conclave of Presbyterians had last convened in Southern California, there had developed something more intrinsically distinctive to the exercise of Presbyterianism on the Pacific shore than merely geography, and the ministry of Henrietta Mears had a great deal to do with it.

Decades later, Fuller Theological Seminary professor and former pastor Tod Bolsinger identified what he called the "Western Stream" of American Presbyterianism. According to Bolsinger,

> In the Western Stream, local iconic and innovative congregations and notable preachers are more important than seminaries or camps or conferences. It's the Stream of Hollywood Pres, and University Pres, and Berkeley Pres. And the "Pres" part was the brand that proudly indicated to others that we were more educated, more socially involved, more inclusive, more open-minded and more Reformed than our other evangelical and even fundamentalist neighbors. . . . In this Stream, the DENOMINATION as BRAND was most important. Our relationships are more with our friends from seminary. . . . Churches [in the Western Stream] are like local coffee shops who decided to become "Starbucks" and now the managers just hope the "Corporate Office" doesn't do anything to make the customers mad.[24]

While Mears might quibble with aspects of Bolsinger's analysis, she could take much of the credit for the recognition that there was, in fact, such an entity. After all, each of the three churches he cited called successive generations of Mears-inspired pastors to their pulpits. Because she had developed such a strong following over three and a half decades, many of her evangelical perspectives reproduced themselves in Presbyterian pulpits and ministries from San Diego to Seattle, from Sacramento to Spokane, and dozens upon dozens of other Reformed parishes along the way. She had sent so many evangelicals to Princeton Theological Seminary by the mid-1950s that they were perceived as a breed apart and tagged "West Coast Presbyterians." So pervasive was their presence that at least until the late twentieth century the seminary's student directory was better known colloquially as the "fundy finder."[25] Like Mears, the evangelical wing of Presbyterians in the Far West tends to be suspicious of sacramental ritual and programmed liturgical worship. Biblical literacy takes precedence over catechetical instruction. Personal reflection and penitence trumps homage to creeds or confessions. Expository preaching concentrates on calls to repentance and victorious living rather than denominational theological subtleties.

As a direct consequence, many West Coast Presbyterians even today may reach maturity virtually oblivious to any coherent notion of what it means to be a Presbyterian but deeply cognizant of the imperative to live a life fully honoring to God and actively serving others. Some have not heard of the five points of Reformed theology or the Westminster Confession but remain on the cutting edge of the evangelical ecumenism that marked Mears's entire career. They may not be particularly fond of the interlocking, hierarchical structure of the Presbyterian Church, but they inhabit their own networks of like-minded congregations—both within and beyond the Presbyterian fold—which often take precedence over their official positions as constituent members of the denomination. Perhaps most telling in the eyes of Presbyterian loyalists was the rapid acceptance up and down the coast of Gospel Light Sunday school curriculum over the denomination's own Faith and Life series.

It would be stretching the truth to claim that the seminal and wide-ranging impact of Henrietta Mears was the only factor pulling Presbyterians in these directions, but it was the most influential one in shaping the less formal and more affective variant that coalesced along the western seaboard. George Marsden recognized clearly not only that Presbyterians in the far West were (and are) a different breed from their counterparts in other sections of the country, but also that probably more than any other person Henrietta Mears conformed them to her image.[26]

For a theologically conservative female to exert such power seems to fly in the face of conventional wisdom regarding the role of women in the twentieth-century church. It had been assumed that once they lost control of gendered denominational mission agencies by the 1920s, male leadership among theological conservatives mounted an enthusiastic campaign to relegate female communicants to a subordinate position.[27] But scholars have found that a number of theologically conservative males vigorously defended female leadership within the church as long as it did not include formal ordination to the gospel ministry. Such support from the theological right actually outpaced the protofeminism of progressives in the years immediately preceding the Second World War.[28] The unqualified backing Mears received from MacLennan prior to the war, and from Evans and Lindquist during and after the conflict, clearly demonstrates the validity of this perspective in the case of First Presbyterian.

Many early historians of women's experience assumed a mutual exclusivity between religion and feminism, but more recent research has uncovered "a heroic role for religion in conferring a gospel freedom upon women." Ultimately, however, the relationship tended to be rather more complex than either of these staked positions might allow—religion operating in either way depending on the context.[29] As revealed by studies of the spiritually conservative women's Aglow movement, female involvement in politically conservative movements in postwar Southern California, and the Fascinating Womanhood Movement, women found ways to operate as agents of significant change within the gendered constructions of the 1940s and 1950s.[30] Mears's reticence to call herself a preacher, her practice of relegating female collegians to leadership responsibilities other than the presidency of the College Department, and her opposition until late in her career to the formal ordination of females were her only concessions to convention. Her manifold accomplishments illustrated convincingly just how far the right woman in the right place at the right time could go even within a systemically patriarchal culture. Perhaps Colleen Townsend Evans put it best when she reflected that Mears "didn't talk feminist talk, she just modeled it."[31]

HISTORIANS ARE FOND OF STAKING OUT precedents and drawing parallels, so I would like to conclude with a personal nod to both in turn. My profession has been inestimably enriched by historians who have opened up many new avenues of inquiry over the past few decades. Among them are a coterie of scholars committed to exploring the vast subject of American religious history on its own terms. Like historians in every field, sometimes they reaffirm the validity of past interpretations and sometimes they prompt us to question them. The life and ministry of Henrietta Mears provides something of an experimental laboratory—or as close as historians can get to one—to test new appraisals of twentieth-century American evangelicalism.

In *American Apocalypse: A History of Modern Evangelicalism*, Matthew Sutton suggests a revised paradigm for understanding theologically conservative believers. Unlike earlier analysts, he contends that they remained socially engaged and intent on influencing the broader culture rather than withdrawing after the Scopes trial.[32] In some ways, building a parallel case for the continued vibrancy of theological conservatism throughout the twentieth century, Michael Hamilton dissects what has traditionally been recognized as a singular movement of "fundamentalists" into three constituent orthodox groups. Reappropriating Joel Carpenter's conception of an "interdenominational revivalist network" that coalesced around D. L. Moody in the late nineteenth century,[33] Hamilton deconstructs major myths regarding theological conservatism after 1920s by focusing his attention on the Moody-inspired coalition. This "interdenominational evangelicalism," Hamilton writes, "was a genuine popular movement, institutionally grounded in the network of parachurch organizations and autonomous urban churches. It was antimodernist in its beliefs but not militant in behavior."[34] Mears never forgot her meeting with Moody as a young girl and seems to fit, at least to some extent, Hamilton's depiction of that particular brand of theological conservative although she could hardly be construed as antimodernist. While there is more to Sutton's and Hamilton's nuanced arguments than this, the broad scope of Mears's strategic objectives and labors over the entire span of her adult life lends at least partial credence to the assertions of both scholars.

Likewise, Molly Worthen's intellectual history of modern evangelicalism also challenges prevailing assumptions about American theological conservatives. Taking issue with earlier portrayals of them, Worthen argues that they are "far more thoughtful and diverse . . . than most critics—and even most evangelicals themselves—usually realize." She acknowledges the strain of anti-intellectualism that runs through the persuasion, but locates it not primarily in authoritarian predispositions as earlier historians have. Instead she finds it nestled ominously in the paradoxes with which theological conservatives live out their Christian experience—the reconciliation of "reason with revelation, heart with head, and private piety with the public square."[35] Worthen's study is far more intricate than this basic contention. But again, as with Sutton's and Hamilton's conjectures, Mears's ongoing commitment to champion intellectual rigor in herself and in her students presents a promising case study with regard to how some evangelicals resolved the crisis of authority that Worthen parses.

Finally, scholars such as Timothy Gloege and Darren Dochuk have brought our attention to basic, some would argue causal, intersections between democratic capitalism and the American expressions of Christianity.[36] But because their thought-provoking macro-level interpretations rely so extensively on evidence gleaned from dominant males, they must be probed further. Here again, Mears's example can be instructive. She, for instance, could be considered a member of a middling economic elite and has some commonalities with Dochuk's "wildcat Christianity." I would contend, however, that the lines he draws around this manifestation of theological conservatism are unable to enclose the scope of her achievements. By the same token, she freely utilized the language of the Christian entrepreneurial class described by Gloege;

she spoke often about the "big business" of the Sunday school and Christian "work." If there was anyone more attuned to the need for efficiency and maximized return on financial (or relational) investment, it was Mears. But unlike Gloege's "corporate evangelicals," her theological absolutes never changed to fit the time, and relationships trumped individualist inclinations. She valued education across disciplines at all levels and remained subject to the authority of her denomination. Finally, because of her own miraculous encounters with healing, Mears continued to believe in that controversial practice. In all these matters it is obvious that Mears, like so many other evangelicals of her day, drank from more than one font. Certainly the bureaucratization and rationalization of modern mass culture provided one source, but so also did the drive to promulgate an activist and culturally engaged theological conservatism. Perhaps more than anything else when attempting to comprehend the phenomenon of American evangelicalism, Mears's contributions attest to the necessity of thinking more about "both/and" and less about "either/or" when it comes to interpretive frameworks.

In closing, I cannot help but draw parallels between Mears's time and our own. Her life spanned a volatile period in American history. Born just prior to the chaos generated by the depression of 1893–1897, she reached maturity on the cusp of World War I and found her first significant success in formal ministry while serving at the First Baptist Church of Minneapolis under fundamentalist firebrand William Bell Riley. She arrived in Hollywood as sound pictures initiated a cinematic revolution and barely a year before the Great Crash of 1929 would lead to the worst economic collapse Americans have ever suffered with its attendant dislocations and reassessments. The arc of her success began in those years and transcended both the Second World War and the years of postwar prosperity in the midst of global Cold War tensions. She arguably wielded her greatest influence through the hundreds she trained and those whom they in turn mentored in all manner of evangelical Christian ministries. That she lived and flourished in perilous times is obvious.

Henrietta Mears modeled a needed charity in that earlier era, one not that dissimilar to our own rancorous time. Between the 1910s and 1960s she remained on the frontline of Protestant Christians willing to engage secular American culture in ways that set her apart from those who advocated a bellicose separatism between true Christians and everyone else. She veered off the path taken by her iconoclastic contemporaries toward a gentler but no less orthodox expression of Christianity. Rather than erect barriers meant to separate, Mears fashioned bridges to connect in innovative, sometimes startling ways, and she did so with a generosity of spirit largely absent from the greater theologically conservative American Protestant community. In so doing, Henrietta Mears championed evangelical orthodoxy while simultaneously defending the necessity of intellectual vitality, embracing domestic and international social service, eschewing inflammatory rhetoric, and forging alliances with those quite different from herself. Twenty-first-century Americans, whether people of faith or not, could do worse than emulate her uncommon grace in troubling and uncertain times.

Bibliographic Note

As this book goes to press, Azusa Pacific University has assumed responsibility for the largest trove of records pertaining to Henrietta Mears. Formerly housed at Gospel Light headquarters in Ventura, California, the archive includes family photographs and audio recordings as well as Mears's library, letters, notes, journals, Gospel Light documents, and memorabilia related to all aspects of her life. Second in import are the records housed at the First Baptist Church of Minneapolis and the First Presbyterian Church of Hollywood. In addition to their collections of official church reports, the archive room at both institutions includes an array of photographs and ephemera linked to Mears's ministry. The Forest Home Christian Conference Center archive provides the best collection of written and audio sources related to the campground's crucial role in Mears's multipronged ministry.

As one might imagine, much has been written about Henrietta Mears. She has been the subject of short essays in numerous religious publications over the years, but they have tended to repeat similar details with minor glosses here and there tailored to the particular audiences for which they were written. All find their genesis in the two previous biographies of Mears, authored by her close associates during the Southern California years. Both studies relied heavily on personal memory as their primary source and emphasize the second half of Mears's life. Taken together, Barbara Hudson Powers's *The Henrietta Mears Story*, with an introduction by Billy Graham (Westwood, NJ: Revell, 1957), and Ethel May Baldwin and David V. Benson's *Henrietta Mears and How She Did It!* (Glendale, CA: Gospel Light Publications, 1966) provide the most complete picture of Mears to date. Two more recent studies, one by editor Earl O. Roe, *Dream Big: The Henrietta Mears Story* (Ventura, CA: Regal Books, 1990), and the other by Marcus Brotherton, *"teacher": The Henrietta Mears Story* (Ventura, CA: Regal Books, 2006), primarily retell the same stories found in the first two biographies with a few new details. None of them spend much time on the first thirty-eight years of her life in the Midwest.

For those seeking a somewhat more scholarly approach, two articles and three master's theses would be worth consulting: Richard J. Leyda, "Henrietta C. Mears: Evangelical Entrepreneur," *Christian Education Journal*, 3rd ser., 1, no. 1 (fall 2003): 54–65; John G. Turner, "The Power Behind the Throne: Henrietta Mears and Post–World War II Evangelicalism," *Journal of Presbyterian History* 83, no. 2 (fall/winter 2005): 141–57; Betsy Cox, "Henrietta Mears as a Christian Education Director" (master's thesis, Fuller Theological Seminary, 1961); Andrea V. B. Madden, "Henrietta C. Mears: 1890–1963, Her Life and Influence" (master's thesis, Gordon-Conwell Theological Seminary, 1997); and Laura E. Range, "The 'Grandmother of Modern Evangelicalism': The Life and Work of Henrietta Mears" (master's thesis, Gordon-Conwell Theological Seminary, 2008).

Melissa Ortiz Berry's "Evangelical Orthodoxy: Henrietta Mears and the Boundary Lines of Modern American Evangelicalism" (PhD diss., The Claremont Graduate University, 2018) is the most recent treatment of Mears. While not a biography of her as such, Amber R. Thomas's PhD dissertation "'God Has a Plan for Your Life': Personalized Life Providence (PLP) in Postwar American Evangelicalism" (PhD diss., University of Edinburgh, 2018) contextualizes Mears's ministry alongside those of her colleagues Bill Bright, Billy Graham, and Richard Halverson.

Appendix

Tables

***Table 1.** Membership Statistics for the First Presbyterian Church of Hollywood, 1904–1938**

	Members added by examination/ confession of faith	**Members added by certificate of transfer**	**Total communicant membership†**	**Total Sunday school enrollment‡**
1904	1	29	30	25
1905	2	10	35	45
1906	2	20	56	n/a
1907	0	18	65	80
1908	2	24	85	103
1909	12	30	123	140
1910	27	40	174	182
1911	28	29	193	268
1912	4	47	253	304
1913	16	108	379	365
1914	12	58	378	410
1915	17	67	428	380
1916	37	58	495	382
1917	17	69	536	431
1918	44	76	626	538

* Compiled from GAM, 1904–1938.

† Does not include losses due to death, suspension, or dismissal.

‡ Includes teachers and officers.

	Members added by examination/ confession of faith	Members added by certificate of transfer	Total communicant membership	Total Sunday school enrollment
1919	20	51	661	300
1920	18	84	651	350
1921	21	68	626	377
1922	25	100	710	500
1923	74	140	877	565
1924	45	126	1019	675
1925	102	235	1311	1053
1926	149	272	1687	1287
1927	42	184	1814	1536
1928	152	211	2104	1624
1929	144	233	2220	1875
1930	126	216	2370	2440
1931	195	189	2547	3562
1932	200	154	2701	4131
1933	127	107	2458	4167
1934	287	179	2686	3765
1935	248	123	2802	4107
1936	142	110	2871	3637
1937	120	54	2668	3315
1938	161	109	2627	3477

***Table 2.** Membership Statistics for the First Presbyterian Church of Hollywood, 1939–1963**

	Members added by examination/ confession of faith	Members added by certificate of transfer	Total communicant membership†	Total Sunday school enrollment‡
1939	127	89	2411	3398
1940	113	67	2444	209§
1941	42	56	2378	2673
1942	323	302	2904	2930
1943	236	231	3244	2781
1944	240	209	3598	2791
1945	231	200	3930	2933
1946	206	243	4230	3140
1947	305	333	4677	3783
1948	219	231	4971	3605
1949	281	276	5290	4214
1950	289	252	5601	4228
1951	297	253	5822	3958
1952	308	306	6153	4272
1953	301	303	5836	5122
1954	348	328	6085	5465
1955	294	248	6357	5556
1956	362	243	6611	5898
1957	253	269	6818	5626
1958¶	371**	337	7228	5929

* Compiled from GAM, 1939–1963.

† Does not include losses due to death, suspension, or dismissal.

‡ Includes teachers and officers.

§ Due to a reporting error, this figure refers only to Sunday school teachers and officers. No students are included.

¶ Denominational merger of northern and southern Presbyterians formed the United Presbyterian Church in the United States of America.

** Beginning in 1958 members restored to fellowship were included in the enumeration of members received through examination and confession of faith.

	Members added by examination/ confession of faith	Members added by certificate of transfer	Total communicant membership	Total Sunday school enrollment
1959	311	281	7478	6076
1960	276	284	7726	6102
1961	248	279	7949	6065
1962	219	270	8136	6073
1963	212	202	8221	6024

***Table 3.** Partial List of Hollywood Christian Group Members and Associates**

Nick Adams
Beverly Adland
Rue Barclay
David Benson
Pat Boone
Malcolm Boyd
Bill Bright
Barbara Britton
George Chandler
Lois Chartrand (Harvey)
Robert Cherry
Lee Childs (Carver)
Robert Clarke
Nudie, Bobbie, and Barbara Cohn
Joyce Compton
Beryl Davis
Jimmie Dodd
Ruth Dodd
Buddy, Hazel (Abigail), and Beverly Dooley
George Eastman
Leonard, Frances, and Joy Eilers
Dale Evans (Rogers)
Rhonda Fleming
Mickey Finn
Jack Franck
Connie Haines
John Hall
Porter Hall
Richard Halverson
Stuart and Suzy Hamblen
Ty Hardin
Redd Harper
Don and Jean Harvey
John Holland
Luther Hoobyar
Ralph Hoopes
Louise James
Darlene Janzen
Walter Jolley
Dick Jones
Alexander Kuzichev
Georgia Lee (Hoopes)
Jimmy Lloyd
Virginia Mayo
Ray MacDonald
Gordon and Sheila McRae
Henrietta Mears
Kristine Miller
Dennis Morgan
Hugh O'Brien
Donald O'Connor
J. Edwin Orr
Bonnie Parker
Eva Pearson
Peter Potter
Paul Power
Barbara Hudson Powers
Marjorie Rambeau
Hal Riddle
Roy Rogers
Dick Ross
Jane Russell
Bill Schuyler
George Slocum
Tim and Velma Spencer
Elaine Stewart
Gale Storm
Darlene Jenkins Swanson
Robert B. Thieme, Jr.
Colleen Townsend (Evans)
Theron Triplett
Charles Turner
Gregory Walcott
Cindy Walker
Barbara Watkins
Dick West
Marie Wilson
Ralph Wolsey
Harry Woodard

* Compiled from sources cited in chapter 8 and related *Los Angeles Times* articles, First Presbyterian Church of Hollywood archival documents, personal interviews, and Cobina Wright's essay in the Gospel Light archive (Catalog A—Box 21).

Table 4. Partial List of Students Intending to Pursue Full-Time Christian Service Vocations during Henrietta Mears's Tenure at the First Presbyterian Church of Hollywood Spring 1928–January 1965†*

George Francis Abdo
Jane Adams
Karsten F. Adison
Carl Ahlfedt
Harold Alexander
Helen Alexander
John Alsup
Richard V. Anderson
William A. Anderson
Peter Bowley Angier
Bill Antablin
James F. Armstrong
Jean Armstrong
David Peter Arnold
James Arnold
Ned Ayarian
Jeannette Babikian
Ann Baker
Ethel May Baldwin
John Baird Barnes
Michael L. Barnes
Jack Barnhart
Kenneth Conrad Bealo
Kelly Bennett
David Benson
Daniel Bernstein
Margaret Bertram
Stanley Howard Bigelow
Robert T. S. Bircsak
Don Blackie
Barbara Blackstone
Betty (Beth) Blackstone
Bob Blackstone
Jean Blackstone
Jim Blackstone
Margaret E. Blackstone
William Blackstone
Jack Blendinger
Clarence Boehm
Jack Bourguin
Ruth Boyce
Kenny Boyd
Leonard Boyd
Bill Bright
Don Broadbent
Hubert Brom
Mary Brom
Dale Bruner
Kathy Bruner
Byron Lee Buck
Jon Cecil Bullock
Bob Burns
Margaret Burns
Linda Burton
Robert R. Byrd
Diane Byron
Donald Camphouse
Peggy T. Cantwell
Glenn Chester Carlson
Steen Carlson
William Dewey Case Jr.
Pasquale Allen Castellano
Nancy Charles
Vern A. Clark
Ross Cleland
Don Cole
Leland G. Cole
Robert Cole
Ted Cole
William Cole
Bethel Coloneus
William Colt
Bobbie Connelly

* Compiled from First Presbyterian's Session and Board of Directors Minutes, Christian Education Department Annual Reports, College Department publications, Life Work Recruit notebook, related church documents, and personal interviews.

† This enumeration includes very few who pursued Christian service vocations outside the Presbyterian denomination, affiliated with independent mission agencies, or assumed staff positions with interdenominational parachurch organizations.

Kenneth Cook
Fern Cover
L. David Cowie
Paul Cox
Maxine Craig
William H. Craig
Gladys Dartford
Gary Demarest
Mildred D. Dodd
Foster Donaldson
Dorothy Drew
William A. Dunlap
Anne S. Edwards
Don Edwards
Paul R. Edwards
Frances Eilers
Leonard Eilers
Dean Charles Ellern
Douglas Elliott
Joseph Elliott
Bob Evans
Colleen (Townsend) Evans
Evan Lloyd Evans
Louis Evans Jr.
Marily Evans (Demarest)
Melba Dunkelberger Evans
William Evans
Jim Ferguson
Robert R. Ferguson
Frances Nelson Finley
David E. Fischer
James Fisk
Paul R. Fiske
Gregory W. Foster
Beverly L. Fox
Pauline Fraas
John Louis Franck
Edward Frisius
Marjorie Frisius
Marian Gay
David Gileson
Sandra Adele Gillis
Dudley Girod
Rena Girod
Homer Goddard
James E. Goff
William L. Goff
Dorothy Goodner
Jane Goodner
Marguerite Goodner
Paul J. Goodwin
Alex Gould
Dorthea Gould
Joanne Grace
Harold Graham
Wilimena Graham
Carol Grant
Kenny Grant
Donald F. Groth
John Grund
Darrell Likens Guder
Clarence George Hagman
Ann Page Haire
Douglas Hall
Ralph Hamburger
Fannie Lee Hancock
Samuel M. Hankins
Willard Hanson
Arnold C. Harms Jr.
Roland Harr
Dick Harris
Hugh Scott Harris
Phyllis Harris
DeDe Harvey
Van Harvey
Frank Havens
Walter D. Hawk Jr.
Margaret Heacock
Dee Hendricks
Phoebe Herrin
Carl Hildebrandt
Lon Hitchcock
Anthony L. Hite
Paul Hittson
Margaret Hixson
Joseph C. Holbrook
Ezra Hollister
Ronald Holmes
Ruth M. Holmes
Ralph M. Hoopes
Art Hudson
Rena Hudson
Traff Huteson
Edith Inglis
Roy Inglis
Richard L. Jacobson
Beth James
Jeanette B. Jeanes
Gordon D. Johnson
William Johnson
Mary Elizabeth Jones
Shirley Jones
Frank Jordan
Garrett Kamerling

Clyde J. Kennedy
Earl William Kennedy
Fred C. Kennedy
Mary Kestner
Ralph R. Kimbrough
Earl King
Edith King
Leroy King
Rob King
Kent W. Kinney
Allen Dean Koehn
Bruce A. Kurrle
Richard M. La Deene
Richard P. Langford
Douglas Lasher
Charles Donald Latourette
Stephen H. Lawhorn
Lester Lee
Lewis Lee
Betty Linday
Gladys Lindsay
Richard Logan
Carroll Londoner
June Marilyn Loomis
Flora Loughead
Bernice Ludlow
J. Wyman Ludlow
Mary Lyons
Mel Lyons
Noel Lyons
John Macadam
Peter Macky
Ed MacLennan
Robert Stewart MacLennan
William A. MacPherson
Warren C. McClain
John Brice McCluskey
David McCullouch
Gill McCusker
Roger Merriweather
Catherine Miller
C. O. Miller
Lindsey Paul Miller
Bob Mitchell
Kay Mitchell
Donn Moomaw
Lardner Moore
Erwin Moradian
Ann Mortenson
Freddit Nation
Kenneth Nelson
Donald W. Neubauer
Gordon R. Nicholson
Ted S. Nissen Jr.
Vincent Nubling
James Whitehead Oates
Gary Orrick
Dean Osterberg
Marian Parish
Paul R. Pearson
Taylor Potter
Harriet C. Pritchard
Stephen D. Pritchard
Julius Raplee
Ruth Raplee
Richard Redfield
Teresa Redman
Audrey Reed
Aileen Reinhart
Edwin G. Reitz
Ronald W. Richardson
Brandon Rimmer
Sheryl Robb
Vernon V. Robertson
Dale Robinson
Ev Robinson
Peggy Robinson
Edwin P. Rogers
Mark B. Rohloff
John Rose
Betty L. Ross
Bill Ruddick
Esther Russell
Don Safstrom
Stephen V. Schneider
Robert Lee Schwenck
Cameron W. Seitz
Gordon Simpson
William David Simpson
David Skarin
Louise Skarin
Helen Skilling
Barry D. Smith
Elizabeth Smith
Emily Smith
Esther Smith
Gene M. Smith
Grace Smith
Ira Smith
Jean Smith
Mike Smith
Rexford Smith
James Aden Snow
Jane Snyder
Milton Snyder
Richard Harvey Spears

Rachel Joan Spencer
Richard LeRoy Spencer
Bill Stahl
Robert K. Staley
John H. Stevens
Jean Stokes
John Stokes
Barbara Sturgis
William R. Sweat
Jack Swift
Tillie Paul Tamaree
Bill Thomas
Roe Thomas
Thelma Thornton
Naomi Tingley
Patrick James Thyne Jr.
Patricia VandeCarr
Frank M. Vanderhoff
David Van Meter
Hank Vigeveno
Lynne Wade
Ula Wade
Mary Waldschmidt
Wayne Walker
William A. Walmsley
William Ward
Charles H. Washburn
Emma Washburn
Marilyn Smith Webster
Stanley Webster
Constance Wheeler
Henry M. White Jr.
C. B. Whitewell
Ann Williams
Eleanor Blackstone Wilson
Frank Wilson
Kenneth Wilson
Bob Winter
Ula Winter
Dean Wolf
E. C. Wood
Frank Woods
James Woollett
H. Norman Wright
Charles Yoder
Margaret Yoder
Paul H. Young Jr.
Glenn Zachary
Vern Zook

Notes

Introduction

1. Ted Cole interview with the author, August 3, 2007.

2. Wilbur M. Smith, "Foreword," in Henrietta C. Mears, *God's Plan: Finding Yourself in His Grand Design* (Ventura, CA: Regal Books, 2008), 6.

3. George M. Marsden, *Reforming Fundamentalism: Fuller Seminary and the New Evangelicalism*, paperback edition (Grand Rapids: Eerdmans, 1995), 89; Margaret Lamberts Bendroth, *Fundamentalism and Gender, 1875 to the Present* (New Haven: Yale University Press, 1993), 86–87.

4. D. G. Hart, *Deconstructing Evangelicalism: Conservative Protestantism in the Age of Billy Graham* (Grand Rapids: Baker Academic, 2004), 21; Barry Hankins, *American Evangelicals: A Contemporary History of a Mainstream Religious Movement* (Lanham, MD: Rowman and Littlefield, 2008), 14.

5. Hart, *Deconstructing Evangelicalism*, 23–25; Hankins, *American Evangelicals*, 37.

6. David W. Bebbington, *Evangelicalism in Modern Britain: A History from the 1730s to the 1980s* (London: Routledge, 1993), 2–3; Hankins, *American Evangelicals*, 1, 30.

7. Alister McGrath, *Evangelicalism and the Future of Christianity* (Downers Grove, IL: InterVarsity Press, 1995), 55–56.

8. Note particularly Timothy E. W. Gloege, *Guaranteed Pure: The Moody Bible Institute, Business, and the Making of Modern Evangelicalism* (Chapel Hill: UNC Press, 2015), and Darren Dochuk, *Anointed with Oil: How Christianity and Crude Made Modern America* (New York: Basic Books, 2019). See also Kathryn Lofton, *Consuming Religion* (Chicago: University of Chicago Press, 2017); Kevin Kruse, *One Nation Under God: How Corporate America Invented Christian America* (New York: Basic Books, 2015); Darren Grem, *The Blessings of Business: How Corporations Shaped Conservative Christianity* (New York: Oxford University Press, 2016); and Bethany

Moreton, *To Serve God and Wal-Mart: The Making of Christian Free Enterprise* (Cambridge, MA: Harvard University Press, 2010).

9. Hankins, *American Evangelicals*, 35.

10. Joel A. Carpenter, *Revive Us Again: The Reawakening of American Fundamentalism* (New York: Oxford University Press, 1997); Matthew Avery Sutton, *American Apocalypse: A History of Modern Evangelicalism* (Cambridge, MA: Harvard University Press, 2014).

11. Edith L. Blumhofer, *Aimee Semple McPherson: Everybody's Sister* (Grand Rapids: Eerdmans, 1993); Daniel Mark Epstein, *Sister Aimee: The Life of Aimee Semple McPherson* (New York: Harcourt, 1993); Matthew Avery Sutton, *Aimee Semple McPherson and the Resurrection of Christian America* (Cambridge, MA: Harvard University Press, 2007); Amy Collier Artman, *The Miracle Lady: Kathryn Kuhlman and the Transformation of Charismatic Christianity* (Grand Rapids: Eerdmans, 2019); Dale E. Soden, *The Reverend Mark Matthews: An Activist in the Progressive Era* (Seattle: University of Washington Press, 2001); Darren Dochuk, "Fighting for the Fundamentals: Lyman Stewart and the Protestant Politics of Oil," in *Faithful Republic: Religion and Politics in Modern America,* ed. Andrew Preston, Bruce Schulman, and Julian Zelizer (Philadelphia: University of Pennsylvania Press, 2015), 41–55; B. M. Pietsch, "Lyman Stewart and Early Fundamentalism," *Church History: Studies in Christianity and Culture* 82, no. 3 (September 2013): 617–46.

12. Barbara Hudson, "Hats, Hearts----and Henrietta!: The Henrietta Mears Story—Revised," (incomplete manuscript), Catalog B—Box 33, GL, 35.

Chapter One

1. Details for this and the previous paragraph are from various telephone conversations between the author and Barbara Hudson in 2007 as well as Hudson's "Hats, Hearts----and Henrietta!: The Henrietta Mears Story—Revised," incomplete manuscript, Catalog B—Box 33, GL; and Henrietta Mears's interview with Barbara Hudson Powers, 1956, GL. See also Barbara Hudson Powers, *The Henrietta Mears Story* (Westwood, NJ: Revell, 1957).

2. Much of the following discussion here and in the first few pages of the next chapter appeared in somewhat altered form in Arlin C. Migliazzo, "Progress of a Young Pilgrim: Henrietta Mears on the Northern Plains, 1890–1913," *The Journal of Presbyterian History* 94, no. 1 (spring/summer 2016): 16–28 and is reproduced by permission.

3. United States Internal Revenue Service Tax Assessment Lists, 1862–1918, State of Illinois, October-December 1863; no author, *A Church in Lowertown: The First Baptist Church of Saint Paul, the Congregation 1849–1974, the Building 1875–1975*

(Saint Paul: Mason Publishing, 1975), 44; Powers, *Mears Story*, 91-92; T. M. Halpin, comp., *Halpin and Bailey's Chicago City Directory for the Year 1862–1863* (Chicago: Halpin and Bailey, 1862), 271; Halpin, comp., *Halpin's Seventh Annual Edition Chicago City Directory, 1864–1865* (Chicago: Halpin, 1864), 365; Halpin, comp., *Halpin's Eighth Annual Edition Chicago City Directory, 1865–1866* (Chicago: Halpin, 1865), 450; John C. W. Bailey, *Chicago City Directory for the Year 1865–1866* (Chicago: Bailey, 1865), 446; Mears interview.

4. The following discussion of Mears's maternal lineage is adapted from E. E. Wrenn, *Christian Womanhood: Life of Mrs. M. K. Everts with an Introduction* (Chicago: Church and Goodman, 1867), and W. W. Everts, *The Life of Rev. W. W. Everts, D.D. by His Son* (Philadelphia: Louis H. Everts, 1891).

5. Wrenn, *Christian Womanhood*, 74 (quotation), 76.

6. Wrenn, *Christian Womanhood*, 256.

7. Mears interview.

8. *History of the First Baptist Church of Chicago with the Articles of Faith and Covenant and a Catalog of Its Members, December 1889* (Chicago: R. R. Donnelley & Sons, 1889), 42–43n25.

9. First Baptist Church of Chicago Membership Ledger, 1834-1884, register numbers 90, 1328, 1789, 1790, Archives of the Chicago Historical Society, Chicago; *History of the First Baptist Church, Chicago with the Articles of Faith and Covenant and a Catalogue of Its Members, June 15, 1866* (Chicago: Church & Goodman, 1866), 38; Marvyn Wittelle, *28 Miles North: The Story of Highwood* (Highwood, IL: The Highwood History Foundation, 1953), 24–26.

10. Powers, *Mears Story*, 91.

11. Ashley to Margaret, June 13, 1869, Catalog B—Box 14, GL; Certificate of Marriage, W. W. Everts and Naomi Townsend, May 18, 1869, Catalog B—Box 52, GL; Powers, *Mears Story*, 90–91.

12. Will Everts Jr. to Margaret Mears, August 2, 1878, Catalog B—Box 14, GL; U.S. Bureau of the Census, Federal Census of 1880, Inhabitants of Jersey City, Hudson County, New Jersey, 48; Everts, *Life of Everts*, 117.

13. Mother to My Dear Children, 10 o'clock (August 22, 1882) and Father to Ashley and Maggie, September 1, 1882, Catalog B—Box 14, GL.

14. Father to Ashley, June 24–25, 1883, Catalog B—Box 14, GL.

15. *Ipswich: Home of the Yellowstone Trail, 1883–1958*, 75th Anniversary Book (Ipswich, South Dakota, 1958), 16, 17; Forrest Daniel, "E. Ashley Mears: Boomer Banker in North Dakota," *North Dakota History: Journal of the Northern Plains* 57, no. 1 (winter 1990): 5–7; Dakota Territorial Census of 1885, Inhabitants of Ipswich, Edmunds County, (South) Dakota, B12.

16. *Minot Years Ago* and M. L. Berg, *Buffalo Wallows and Bayous: A History of Minot, Dakota Territory, 1886–1889* (Minot: North American Heritage Press, 2008), 10, 22, 44–45, 56-57, 71–72, 76, 78, 82, 89, 98, 134, 139, 208–9; Daniel, "Boomer Banker," 7–8.

17. Much of the information in this paragraph comes from Daniel's overview of Mears's career. See also Samuel Torgerson, "Early Banking in North Dakota," *The Quarterly Journal of the University of North Dakota* 13 (1922–1923): 287–88.

18. Berg, *Buffalo Wallows*, 56–57.

19. "Corridor Chat," *Minneapolis Tribune*, November 1, 1891, 4; Daniel, "Boomer Banker," 12.

20. *Bismarck (ND) Daily Tribune*, October 9, 1891, and January 31, 1893; *Fargo (ND) Forum*, May 29, 1893, and June 7, 1893; *Daily Huronite (SD)*, November 15, 1893, and November 27, 1895; Powers, *Mears Story*, 97; Index of Divorce and Civil Court Cases, Cass County, North Dakota, Institute for Regional Studies and University Archives, North Dakota State University, Fargo, ND; Chelsea D. Chamberlain, "The Boom and Bust of Western Speculative Banking: E. A. Mears' Flight from Failure" (unpublished research paper, Whitworth University, 2012), 11.

21. "Buckbee Rites to Be Wednesday Afternoon," unknown Minneapolis newspaper article, Catalog B—Box 14, GL; Chronological Register of Church Members, First Baptist Church of Minneapolis Church Records, vol. 2, 1889–1903, FBCM; *R. L. Polk and Company's Duluth Directory, 1893–1894* (Duluth: R. L. Polk & Co., 1893), hereafter cited as *Duluth Directory; Duluth Directory, 1894–1895; Duluth Directory 1895–1896*, 445; *Duluth Directory, 1896–1897*, 364; *Duluth Directory, 1897–1898*, 349; Minnesota State Census of 1895, Inhabitants of Duluth, St. Louis County, 591; *Davison's Minneapolis City Directory Volume 26, 1898* (Minneapolis: Minneapolis Directory Company, 1897), 841, hereafter cited as *Minneapolis Directory*. The Fargo city directory for 1894 is missing but the directory for 1895–1896 published in 1894 contains no listing for William Mears. See *Fargo and Moorhead Directory* (Fargo, ND: C. C. Beckwith, 1894).

22. *Minneapolis Directory Volume 26, 1898*, 841; *Minneapolis Directory Volume 27, 1899*, 874; *Minneapolis Directory Volume 28, 1900*, 940; *Minneapolis Directory Volume 29, 1901*, 909; *Minneapolis Directory Volume 30, 1902*, 1031; *Minneapolis Directory Volume 31, 1903*, 1101; *Minneapolis Directory Volume 32, 1904*, 1145; *Minneapolis Directory Volume 33, 1905*, 1197; *Minneapolis Directory Volume 38, 1910*, 1175; *Minneapolis Directory Volume 39, 1911*, 1210; *Minneapolis Directory Volume 40, 1912*, 1278; Daniel, "Boomer Banker," 17–18; *Nebraska State Journal* (Lincoln), January 25, 1910; Death Certificate of Elisha Ashley Mears, MHC.

23. Testimony of Christine C. Thomson, *A. D. Blair v. E. Ashley Mears and Margaret B. Mears* (1896), 7971, Cass County, North Dakota Civil Case Files (MS 339), IRS.

24. Henrietta Mears to William Mears, June 10, 1903, and undated (quotation), Catalog B—Box 48, GL.

25. Undated letter, William Mears to Henrietta Mears, Catalog B—Box 14, GL.

26. Henrietta Mears to William Mears, June 10, 1903, Catalog B—Box 48, GL. See also Mears interview with Powers.

27. Henrietta Mears to William Mears, undated, Catalog B—Box 48, GL.

28. Henrietta Mears to William Mears, June 10, 1903, Catalog B—Box 48, GL; William Mears to Margaret Everts Mears and Margaret Burtis Mears, undated letter, Catalog B—Box 14, GL. See also Mears interview.

29. Deposition of Margaret Mears (daughter) and testimony of Margaret B. Mears, *A. D. Blair v. E. Ashley Mears and Margaret B. Mears* (1896), 7971, Cass County, North Dakota Civil Case Files (MS 339), IRS.

30. Ethel May Baldwin and David V. Benson, *Henrietta Mears and How She Did It!* (Glendale, CA: Gospel Light Publications, 1966), 37; Death Certificates of Margaret Burtis (Everts) Mears and Elisha Ashley Mears, MHC.

31. Mears interview.

32. Norman Cobb Mears interview with the author, July 14, 2010.

33. Angelo Cohn, *Norman B. Mears: The Man Behind the Shadow Mask* (Minneapolis: T. S. Denison, 1972), 40–41, 213; Earl O. Roe, ed., *Dream Big: The Henrietta Mears Story* (Ventura, CA: Regal Books, 1990), 70n9.

34. Baldwin and Benson, *Henrietta Mears*, 36-37; Powers, *Mears Story*, 99–100, quotation from page 100; Marcus Brotherton, *"teacher": The Henrietta Mears Story* (Ventura, CA: Regal Books, 2006), 39.

35. W. H. Bayliss, *Finer Than Fine Gold: The Faith and Fellowship of South Dakota Baptists* (South Dakota Baptist Convention, 1956), 65; Margaret Mears to Will, undated letter from Ipswich, Catalog B—Box 14, GL.

36. Ernest Johnson to Henrietta Mears, May 8, 1950, and "History of First Baptist Church of Minot, North Dakota," 1–3, Catalog B—Box 32, GL; Berg, *Buffalo Wallows*, 72, 80, 209. Quotations from the *Minot Journal* and the *Nelson County News* cited in Daniel, "Boomer Banker," 7.

37. Testimonies of Homer Cook and Herbert L. Loomis, *A. D. Blair v. E. Ashley Mears and Margaret B. Mears* (1896), 7971, Cass County, North Dakota Civil Case Files (MS 339), IRS; testimonies of M. B. Mears and Jennie A. Benedict, *Will S. Sigmund v. Ashley Mears and M. B. Mears* (1896), 8044, Cass County, North Dakota Civil Case Files (MS 339), IRS; inscribed Bible presented to Margaret Mears, December 25, 1894, Young People's Class, First Baptist Church, Fargo, North Dakota,

Catalog B—Box 48, GL; "100 Years in His Service, 1879–1979: History of First Baptist Church, Fargo, North Dakota, 1879–1979," centennial pamphlet, FBCF; Women's Baptist Home Mission Secretary's Book, January 1894–October 1902, minutes of July 20, 1898, FBCM.

38. Deacon's Minute Book, 1890–1913, minutes of November 22, 1897, FBCM.

39. Chronological Register of Church Members, First Baptist Church of Minneapolis, Church Records, vol. 2, 1889–1903, FBCM.

40. The following discussion is taken from the Women's Baptist Home Mission Secretary's Book, January 1894–October 1902, FBCM, and other sources as cited.

41. Women's Baptist Home Mission Secretary's Book, January 1894–October 1902, minutes of March 16, April 20 (quotation), July 20, 1898, and May 17, 1899, FBCM.

42. Manual of the First Baptist Church, Minneapolis, 1904–1905, FBCM; Women's Baptist Home Mission Secretary's Book, January 1894–October 1902, minutes of July 20, 1898, December 20, 1899 (quotation), and December 19, 1900, FBCM.

43. Manual of the First Baptist Church, Minneapolis, 1901–1902, 1903–1904, 1904–1905, FBCM.

44. Deacon's Minute Book, 1890–1913, minutes of February 14, 1903, FBCM.

45. Church Records, vol. 2, 1889–1903, FBCM; Deacon's Minute Book, 1890–1913, minutes of December 23, 1903, FBCM. See also Mears interview.

46. Mears interview; quotation from Powers, *Mears Story*, 93. See also Roe, *Dream Big*, 63. The following discussion of Henrietta Mears's early spiritual life is adapted from Powers, *Mears Story*, 92–114, and other sources as cited.

47. Mears interview.

48. Roe, *Dream Big*, 65.

49. Mears interview.

50. "Piano Recital Given by the Pupils of Miss Grace D. Feltus Assisted by Miss Mabel Lee Violinist and Miss Margaret Mckercher Soprano, May 28, 1901," program, Catalog A—Box 22, GL.

51. Baldwin and Benson, *Henrietta Mears*, 33–34.

52. Baldwin and Benson, *Henrietta Mears*, 33; Powers, *Mears Story*, 94.

53. Women's Baptist Home Mission Secretary's Book, January 1894–October 1902, minutes of July (no date given), 1899, FBCM; Chronological Register of Church Members, First Baptist Church of Minneapolis, Church Records, vol. 2, 1889–1903, FBCM.

54. Deacon's Minute Book, 1890–1913, minutes of May 6, 1900, FBCM; Chronological Register of Church Members, First Baptist Church of Minneapolis, Church Records, vol. 2, 1889–1903, FBCM.

55. William Vance Trollinger Jr., *God's Empire: William Bell Riley and Midwestern Fundamentalism* (Madison: University of Wisconsin Press, 1990).

56. Powers, *Mears Story*, 100.

57. Notes from Dr. Riley's remarks at the funeral service of Mrs. M. B. Mears, Catalog B—Box 32, GL; Powers, *Mears Story*, first quotation, page 109, second and third quotations, page 111.

58. Quoted in Roe, *Dream Big*, 74. See also Powers, *Mears Story*, 112–14.

59. See Steven Barabas, *So Great a Salvation: The History and Message of the Keswick Convention* (London: Marshall, Morgan and Scott, 1952), and J. C. Pollock, *The Keswick Story: The Authorized History of the Keswick Convention* (London: Hodder and Stoughton, 1964).

60. Mears interview; Manual of the First Baptist Church, Minneapolis, 1912, 1913, FBCM; Minutes and Record Book, YPSCE, book 2 (April 1, 1910–October 1, 1919), executive committee meeting minutes of September 27, 1912, and November 24, 1912, FBCM; Church Records and Minutes, vol. 4, 1910–1919, minutes of April 24, 1913, FBCM.

61. Student Government Association of the University of Minnesota, "The Shevlin Record" (February 1, 1911), UMA.

62. The *Minnesota Daily*, October 21, 1911.

63. *The Gopher*, vol. 26, Annual of the University of Minnesota, published by the junior class, 1913.

Chapter Two

1. Henrietta Mears interview with Barbara Hudson Powers, 1956, GL.

2. Student Records, Office of the Registrar, University of Minnesota, Minneapolis campus; *The Hesperian*, Annual of West High School 1909, Minneapolis, MHC; High School Diploma, Henrietta Cornelia Mears, June 11, 1909, Catalog B—Box 11, GL; "The Annual Register, 1913–1914," *Bulletin of the University of Minnesota* 16, no. 2A (March 1915): 43.

3. "The Annual Register, 1913–1914," *Bulletin of the University of Minnesota* 16, no. 2A (March 1915): 88; *North Branch Review*, supplement, June 5, 1913.

4. "The Town Crier of Forest Home," College Conference (July 1938): 2, 7, FPCH.

5. "The School of Chemistry, 1913–1914," *Bulletin of the University of Minnesota* 16, no. 12 (June 1913): 19; "The Annual Register, 1913–1914," *Bulletin of the University of Minnesota* 16, no. 2A (March 1915): 28; Ethel May Baldwin and David V. Benson, *Henrietta Mears and How She Did It!* (Glendale, CA: Gospel Light Publications, 1966), 37–38.

6. Max Malmquist, *From Prairie Chickens and Potatoes . . . to Houses*, vol. 2 (North

Branch, MN: R. D. Rascal, 2007), 228-3.4, 387-3.8a, 395-3.8a, 404-3.8a, 408-3.8a, 413-3.8a–415-3.8a, 421-3.8a; *North Branch Review*, September 11, 1913.

7. School Board of Directors Meeting Minutes, Records of School District # 32, North Branch, Minnesota, July 20, 1899–July 21, 1923, District Office, North Branch, MN. Minutes of 1913: March 18, May 20, June 2, July 16, August 18 (quotation, author's brackets).

8. *Thoughts for All Seasons from the Notes of Henrietta C. Mears* (Glendale, CA: G/L Publications, 1973), 13.

9. School Board of Directors Meeting Minutes, Records of School District # 32, North Branch, MN, July 20, 1899–July 21, 1923. Minutes of September 13, 1913.

10. *North Branch Review*, November 20, 1913 and December 25, 1913.

11. *North Branch Review*, December 25, 1913.

12. *North Branch Review*, May 14 and 21, 1914.

13. *North Branch Review*, May 28, 19.14

14. Much of the content of the following paragraphs on Everett Alvin comes from Barbara Hudson Powers, *The Henrietta Mears Story* (Westwood, NJ: Revell, 1957), 116–17 and other sources as noted.

15. Malmquist, *Prairie Chickens*, vol. 1, 298-1.7–308-1.7

16. Powers, *Mears Story*, 117.

17. *North Branch Review*, September 18, 1913, October 2, 1913 (quotations), December 4, 1913, June 4, 1914.

18. Mears interview.

19. Mears interview.

20. Quotations from Mears interview and Powers, *Mears Story*, 115–16.

21. *Beardsley News*, August 27, 1914, October 22, 1914, March 25, 1915, August 19, 1915, September 9 and 16, 1915; Big Stone County Teacher's Certificate and Examination Record Cards, Henrietta Mears, MHC.

22. *Beardsley News*, August 27, 1914, November 12 and 26, 1914, January 14, 1915, August 19, 1915 (quotation); Big Stone County Superintendent's Record Book, vol. 2: Teacher Examination Record, 1902–1934, entries of June 12, 1913 and September 17, 1915, MHC.

23. Powers, *Mears Story*, 117.

24. *Beardsley News*, October 22, 1914, November 5 and 12, 1914, November 26, 1914, January 14, 1915 (first quotation), October 28, 1915 (second quotation).

25. *Beardsley News*, October 22, 1914 (quotation), November 5, 1914.

26. *Beardsley News*, May 13 and 20, 1915, December 16, 1915, May 4 and 18, 1916.

27. *Beardsley, Minnesota Centennial, 1880–1980* (Beardsley, MN: Beardsley Senior Citizen Centennial Book Committee, 1980), 46.

28. *Beardsley News*, October 8, 1914, October 22 and 29, 1914, April 22, 1915, December 23, 1915; Powers, *Mears Story*, 118; *Beardsley Centennial*, 46.

29. *Beardsley News*, October 29, 1914 (quotations), February 17, 1916.

30. Eleanor L. Doan, comp., *431 Quotes from the Notes of Henrietta C. Mears* (Glendale, CA: G/L Publications, 1970), 46.

31. *Beardsley News*, October 29, 1914, October 7, 14, and 28, 1915, November 11, 1915, April 13, 1916.

32. *Beardsley News*, January 14, 1915, February 18, 1915, May 20, 1915, February 24, 1916, April 27, 1916, May 11, 18, 25, 1916; Malmquist, *Prairie Chickens*, vol. 2, 430-3.8a.

33. *Beardsley News*, November 19, 1914, February 18, 1915.

34. *Beardsley News*, September 17, 1914, October 29, 1914, November 5 and 12, 1914, January 28, 1915, October 7 and 28, 1915, November 11, 1915, March 9, 16, and 23, 1916.

35. *Beardsley News*, November 26, 1914, December 24, 1914, April 1, 1915, May 27, 1915, November 11 and 25, 1915, February 17 and 24, 1916, May 11 and 25, 1916, June 1, 1916.

36. *Beardsley News*, November 26, 1914, December 24, 1914, January 28, 1915, February 11, 1915.

37. *Beardsley News*, October 29, 1914.

38. Sources for this and the preceding two paragraphs are Official Class Book for the Sunday School Teachers, 1915, and Sunday School Secretary Record Books, 1912–1915 and 1916–1919, BMC; *Beardsley News*, February 10, May 4, and June 1, 1916.

39. *Beardsley News*, January 27, 1916, March 16, 1916, April 13, 1916, and May 25, 1916.

40. *Beardsley Centennial*, 21; *Beardsley News*, November 15, 1915, and March 2, 1916; Powers, *Mears Story*, 118–19.

41. *Beardsley News*, March 9, 1916.

42. *Beardsley Centennial*, 19, 23–24; *Beardsley News*, September 10, 1914, November 26, 1914; Powers, *Mears Story*, 119.

43. Powers, *Mears Story*, 119–20.

44. Letter of recommendation, J. L. Fitzgerald for Henrietta Mears, April 2, 1916, Catalog B—Box 31, GL.

45. Powers, *Mears Story*, 121.

Chapter Three

1. *Directory Minneapolis Public Schools, 1917–1918* (Minneapolis: Minneapolis Public Schools District Office, 1917), 132, *1918–1919*, 115; Barbara Hudson Powers, *The Henrietta Mears Story* (Westwood, NJ: Revell, 1957), 121–22.

2. *Central High School Red and Blue Handbook 1925*, 9, MHC. Hereafter cited as *Handbook* with the appropriate year. See also *Centralian 1918*, 16; Powers, *Mears Story*, 122.

3. Powers, *Mears Story*, 122.

4. *Centralian 1922*, 151; *Central High News*, October 19, 1922; Senior class advisor lists, *Centralian 1921–1927*.

5. *Central High News*, February 23, 1921, January 15, 1925.

6. *Central High News*, April 23, 1919, May 12, 1920, October 30, 1924.

7. *Central High News*, March 26, 1925.

8. *Central High News*, April 27, 1927.

9. *Central High News*, October 27, 1920, March 19, 1925, March 16, 1927.

10. *Central High News*, October 29, 1919; Margaret Atwood interview with the author, July 4, 2008.

11. *Central High News*, November 10, 1922 (quotation); *Handbook 1924*, 25; *Handbook 1925*, 24.

12. Powers, *Mears Story*, 122–23; *Centralian 1921*; *Central High News*, February 5, 12, and 26, 1925.

13. *Central High News*, January 19, 1921.

14. *Central High News*, March 1, 1923.

15. *Central High News*, April 13, 1923, December 20, 1923, February 7 and 14, 1924, February 5, 1925, March 2, 1927, May 18, 1927.

16. *Handbook 1925*, 77; *Central High News*, March 26, 1925, April 23 and 30, 1925, April 23, 1926, May 4, 1926.

17. Atwood interview (quotation); Powers, *Mears Story*, 122–23.

18. *Centralian 1921*, 148; *Centralian 1924*, joke pages section; *Central High News*, December 15, 1920, November 23, 1922, May 14, 1925, May 4, 1927.

19. *The Centralian 1927*, 46; *Central High News*, March 16, 1927, May 4, 1927.

20. Prospectus of the City Temple and artist rendering of "the proposed City Temple and Bible School," FBCM.

21. "Dedication of First Baptist Church of Minneapolis," Dedication Week booklet, January 6, 1924, FBCM.

22. Minutes and Record Book, YPSCE, book 2 (April 1, 1910–October 1, 1919), minutes of the Executive Committee, March 21, 1915, and minutes of the semi-annual business meeting and banquet, September 21, 1916, FBCM.

23. Church Records and Minutes, vol. 5 (1918–1924), October 28, 1920, meeting and annual report, April 16, 1925; "Five Ministers Respond to Toasts at Dinner in Honor of Dr. W. B. Riley," *Minneapolis Morning Tribune*, March 4, 1922; H. B. O.

Phillpotts to unknown, April 20, 1963 (quotation); Henrietta Mears interview with Barbara Hudson Powers, 1956, GL.

24. The following discussion on the formation of the Fidelis class is drawn from *The Fid'ler* (June–July 1924), 2, FBCM; Dedication Week booklet, FBCM; Powers, *Mears Story*, 123; and other sources as cited.

25. *The Fid'ler* (June–July 1924), 2, FBCM; "Sunday School Classes at First Baptist," n.d., FBCM; "Fidelis Class 1920–1921," FBCM; Alta Attwater to Mr. Stixrood, April 23, 1963, Catalog B—Box 16, GL.

26. Membership information from these paragraphs is taken from: the annual Sunday school reports ending March 31 of each year; "First Baptist Church Bulletin," March 3, 1918; first quotation from "The Booster," vol. 1, no. 5 (July 14, 1918); "Baptist Beacon," vol. 1, no. 2 (March 7, 1920) and vol. 1, no. 8 (November 1920): 47, second quotation; "Fidelis Class 1920–1921"; "The Bellman," vol. 1, no. 7 (April 18, 1926): 4. All sources from FBCM. See also Powers, *Mears Story*, 123.

27. Henrietta Mears to My dear Fidelis Member, November 24, 1920, FBCM.

28. Miss H. C. Mears to My dear Girls, January 6, 1920, FBCM.

29. W. B. Riley, "What Our Sunday School Did for Our Church," *"Baptist,"* vol. 1, no. 7 (July 1924): 8, 12, FBCM.

30. Henrietta C. Mears to My dear Mabel, February 23, FBCM.

31. Minutes of the Advisory Board, April 12, 1920, December 29, 1920, February 14, 1921, April 1, 1921, October 31, 1921, March 6, 1922; Jackson Hall Dedication announcement; Dedication Week booklet; "Today's Sunday School Attendance," October 11, 1925; all sources FBMC. Transcript of Curtis Akenson interview with James Fogerty, March 21, 2000, MHC.

32. "Where the Secret Lies," *The Fid'ler*, September 1929, FBCM.

33. Gene Fornell to Mr. Stixrood, April 25, 1963. Other quotations from Alta Attwater to Mr. Stixrood, April 23, 1963; Harriet C. Blank to unknown, n.d.; Adabelle Christensen to Mr. Stixrood, April 22, 1963; Ann Kludt (Thompson), "A Loving Tribute to Miss Henrietta Mears," n.d. All sources Catalog B—Box 16, GL.

34. Antoinette Abernathy Lamoreaux, "The I Wills for Teachers of Girls," reprint, First Baptist Sunday School, Minneapolis, Minnesota, n.d., Catalog B—Box 52, GL; Henrietta C. Mears, "A Teacher's Ten Commandments," *Teach* (fall 1963): inside front cover.

35. Fornell to Stixrood.

36. Fornell to Stixrood.

37. Kludt, "Loving Tribute"; Agnes E. Olson to Mr. Stixrood, April 21, 1963, Catalog B—Box 16, GL.

38. Details for this and the following paragraphs on the structure and function of the Fidelis class are taken from two undated documents, "Organization of the Fidelis Class" and "The Fidelis Class," FBCM, and other sources as cited.

39. Fornell to Stixrood; Kludt, "Loving Tribute"; Rachel Larsen (Gustafson), "In Memory of Miss Mears," April 25, 1963, Catalog B—Box 16, GL; Mears interview.

40. Fornell to Stixrood; Olson to Stixrood; Mrs. James Cummings to Mr. Stixrood, April 22, 1963, Catalog B—Box 16, GL; Miss Mears to My dear Girls, December 20, 1920, FBCM.

41. Nell Peterson to Mr. O. L. Stixrood, April 23, 1963, Catalog B—Box 16, GL.

42. Minutes of the Advisory Committee, February 14, 1921; *The Fid'ler*, September 1929; undated, unknown newspaper photo and caption. All sources, FBCM.

43. "Fidelis Class 1920–1921"; *Fidelis Tatler*, May 13, 1923; "First Baptist Church Bulletin," March 9, 1924, and "Fidelis Glee Club Concert Program," March 10, 1924. All sources, FBCM.

44. "Fidelis Class Program," September 1925–December 1925, January–June 1926, November 1926–June 1927; "Fidelis Class 1920–1921"; "Fidelis Songs," FBCM.

45. "Spending 28 Birthdays in Bed Only Brightens Smile and Eyes of Invalid," *Minnesota Journal*, February 22, 1925.

46. *The Fid'ler*, September 1929, FBCM; YPSCE, Record Book Two, minutes of semi-annual business meeting, March 31, 1919, FBCM; Powers, *Mears Story*, 124; Ethel May Baldwin and David V. Benson, *Henrietta Mears and How She Did It!* (Glendale, CA: Gospel Light Publications, 1966), 47.

47. Kludt, "Loving Tribute."

48. *The Fid'ler*, September 1929, FBCM; Olson to Stixrood.

49. Quoted in Powers, *Mears Story*, 123–24 (author's parentheses).

50. Henrietta Mears to "My own dear little girl," n.d., Catalog B—Box 32, GL.

51. Dedication Day booklet, FBCM.

52. Report of the Clerk of Session, April 4, 1923, FPCH.

53. Source for this and the previous paragraph is Powers, *Mears Story*, 125–26; Angelo Cohn, *Norman B. Mears: The Man Behind the Shadow Mask* (Minneapolis: T. S. Denison, 1972), 11.

54. Henrietta Mears to Margaret Mears, July 20, 1925, Catalog A—Box 17, GL.

55. Barry Hankins, "The (Worst) Year of the Evangelical: 1926 and the Demise of American Fundamentalism," *Fides et Historia* 43, no. 1 (winter/spring 2011): 1–14.

56. Akenson interview.

57. Mears interview.

58. *Central High News*, March 16, 1927, April 27, 1927, and May 4, 1927.

59. Mears interview; "Clarence Mears Dead: Prominent Grain Man Here," *Duluth News Tribune*, September 2, 1926.

60. *Central High News*, May 4, 1927, June 1, 1927, and October 12, 1927; "Henrietta Mears 1927 Travel Diary," June 17, Catalog B—Box 51, GL.

61. For examples of these conversations see "1927 Travel Diary," June 25, June 29, July 3, July 9.

62. Henrietta C. Mears to the Fidelis class, n.d., FBCM.

63. "1927 Travel Diary," July 14, July 21 and 22 (quotation).

64. "1927 Travel Diary," July 11.

65. "1927 Travel Diary," August 9.

66. "1927 Travel Diary," July 30, August 12; Henrietta to "Dearest," n.d., Mears Letters in Oversize Binder, GL, quotation; collection of postcards from the Cabaret du Néant, Catalog B—Box 21, GL; "1927 Travel Diary," July 30.

67. *Central High News*, October 12, 1927; Fidelis Class Tenth Anniversary Announcement, FBCM.

68. Henrietta C. Mears to the Fidelis Class, February 1928, Catalog B—Box 32, GL.

69. Daniel Fuller interview with the author, May 27, 2011.

70. Mears to Fidelis Class.

71. Henrietta Mears to My Dearest Mabel, August 15, 1928, Mears Letters in Oversize Binder, GL.

72. The following discussion of Mears's decision to leave Minneapolis is adapted from Baldwin and Benson, *Henrietta Mears*, 48–50, and other sources as noted.

73. Mears to Mabel.

Chapter Four

1. Erwin G. Gudde, *California Place Names*, 4th edition revised and enlarged by William Bright (Berkeley: University of California Press, 1998), 168; Carey McWilliams, *Southern California: An Island on the Land* (Salt Lake City: Gibbs-Smith, 2010), 332; Val Toms, *First Presbyterian Church of Hollywood: A Seventy-Five Year Photographic Retrospective* (Hollywood: First Presbyterian Church of Hollywood, 1978), 2, 6.

2. Minutes of the General Assembly of the Presbyterian Church in the United States of America, new series, vol. X, no. 2 (Philadelphia: Office of the General Assembly, 1910), 479; Toms, *First Presbyterian*, 11.

3. Robert M. Fogelson, *Fragmented Metropolis: Los Angeles, 1850–1930* (Berkeley:

University of California Press, 1993), 122, 124, 127, 133; McWilliams, *Island on the Land*, 332–33.

4. GAM, new series, XX: 485, third series, IV: 591, and third series, VII: 178. Sunday school enrollments include teachers. Session Minutes, December 1, 1926, and March 21, 1939, FPCH. Quotations from Report of the Clerk of Session, April 4, 1923, FPCH. See also Marc Wanamaker and Robert W. Nudelman, *Early Hollywood* (Charleston, SC: Arcadia Publishing, 2007), 96.

5. Annual Report, Department of Christian Education, 1927–1928, FPCH.

6. Report of the Clerk of Session, April 4, 1923, FPCH.

7. Information for this and the next paragraph was taken from Session Minutes, vol. April 12, 1925–December 1930, FPCH and other sources as cited.

8. Session Minutes, September 19, 1927, and March 20, 1928, FPCH.

9. Annual Report, Department of Christian Education, fiscal 1927–1928, FPCH.

10. Barbara Hudson Powers, *The Henrietta Mears Story* (Westwood, NJ: Revell, 1957), 136–37.

11. Annual Report, Christian Education Department, April 1936–March 1937, FPCH.

12. Margaret Lamberts Bendroth, *Growing Up Protestant: Parents, Children, and Mainline Churches* (New Brunswick, NJ: Rutgers University Press, 2002), 9, 64, 66, 70–72, 75–76.

13. Powers, *Mears Story*, 130.

14. Powers, *Mears Story*, 131,

15. Annual Sunday School Report, April 9, 1930, FPCH; Powers, *Mears Story*, 130–31.

16. The following discussion is drawn from an analysis of Sunday School Cabinet and Teachers' and Officers' Meetings (agendas), Sunday School Treasurer's Reports spanning the period from January 23, 1929, to March 30, 1930, and Mears's Sunday School Reports of April 7 and 9, 1930, FPCH and other sources as cited.

17. Eleanor L. Doan, comp., *431 Quotes from the Notes of Henrietta C. Mears* (Glendale, CA: G/L Publications, 1970), 45.

18. Annual Sunday School Report for fiscal 1931–1932, FPCH.

19. Dorothy C. Haskin, "Henrietta C. Mears, L.H.D.: Teacher, Writer, Christian," pamphlet n.d., GL. Quotations from Powers, *Mears Story*, 147.

20. Quoted in Ethel May Baldwin and David V. Benson, *Henrietta Mears and How She Did It!* (Glendale, CA: Gospel Light Publications, 1966), 61. See also page 60.

21. See Teachers' and Officers' Meeting agendas for spring 1930 and Mears, informal notes on church attendance card, FPCH.

22. Baldwin and Benson, *Henrietta Mears*, 60.

23. Powers, *Mears Story*, 147.

24. "The Gospel Light Story," in the *Gospel Light Handbook*, 2, manuscript, Catalog B—Box 27, GL.

25. Baldwin and Benson, *Henrietta Mears*, 61.

26. Baldwin and Benson, *Henrietta Mears*, 61.

27. Baldwin and Benson, *Henrietta Mears*, 62, 63 (first quotation), 64; "The Gospel Light Story," 1, 2 (second and third quotations), 3.

28. Baldwin and Benson, *Henrietta Mears*, 62–64.

29. Annual Sunday School Report, April 9, 1931, FPCH.

30. Teachers' and Officers' meeting agenda, September 4, 1930, FPCH.

31. Peggy Cantwell interview with the author, March 11, 2010.

32. See "Outline for Sunday School Course" and "Do You Know That" newsletter in the fall 1932 Teachers' and Officers' Meeting agendas, FPCH.

33. GAM, 1928, 1930, 1932; Powers, *Mears Story*, 148–49; Baldwin and Benson, *Henrietta Mears*, 64.

34. Bendroth, *Growing Up Protestant*, 53, 55, 63, 70, 73, 75–76.

35. Lamoreaux, "The I Wills for Teachers of Girls"; Annual Sunday School Report, April 9, 1930, FPCH.

36. Announcement of the proposed young people's council, n.d., coverless black teachers' meeting book, 1933–1935, FPCH.

37. The following discussion is taken from an analysis of Mears's Annual Reports from fiscal 1929–1930 to 1938–1939 as well as her agendas, newsletters, and reports of Cabinet and Teachers' and Officers' meetings from January 1929 through December 1935, FPCH.

38. The history of Forest Home and its acquisition by Mears is most completely told by Barbara Becerra, *One Mile Nearer Heaven: An Early History of Forest Home* (Fairway Press, 2001). Unless otherwise noted, the following discussion is taken from Becerra's text.

39. Quotation from Becerra, *One Mile Nearer Heaven*, 84.

40. Becerra, *One Mile Nearer Heaven*, 97.

41. Mears quoted in Baldwin and Benson, *Henrietta Mears*, 197. See also Becerra, *One Mile Nearer Heaven*, 98.

42. Mears quoted in Becerra, *One Mile Nearer Heaven*, 99.

43. Mears quoted in Baldwin and Benson, *Henrietta Mears*, 198.

44. Baldwin and Benson, *Henrietta Mears*, 198.

45. Quotation from Becerra, *One Mile Nearer Heaven*, 103. See also Baldwin and Benson, *Henrietta Mears*, 199; Powers, *Mears Story*, 176.

46. Becerra, *One Mile Nearer Heaven*, 104, 105 (quotation).

47. Mears quoted in Becerra, *One Mile Nearer Heaven*, 107. See also Powers, *Mears Story*, 176; Baldwin and Benson, *Henrietta Mears*, 200.

Chapter Five

1. William Vance Trollinger Jr., *God's Empire: William Bell Riley and Midwestern Fundamentalism* (Madison, WI: University of Wisconsin Press, 1990), 17–22.

2. Much of the following discussion is a modified version of Arlin C. Migliazzo, "The Education of Henrietta Mears: A Fundamentalist in Transition," *Baptist History and Heritage*, vol. 46, no. 2 (summer 2011): 65–76 and is reproduced by permission.

3. Trollinger, *God's Empire*, 63, 67–68; "A Diary of the Travels of Henrietta C. Mears, 1940," file cabinet, drawer one, GL.

4. W. B. Riley, quoted in Trollinger, *God's Empire*, 70.

5. Trollinger, *God's Empire*, 68–75.

6. Trollinger, *God's Empire*, 69–71, 75–77; Timothy P. Weber, *Living in the Shadow of the Second Coming: American Premillennialism, 1875–1982* (Grand Rapids: Zondervan, 1983).

7. David A. Rausch, *Zionism within Early American Fundamentalism, 1878–1918: A Convergence of Two Traditions* (New York: Edwin Mellen Press, 1979).

8. Henrietta Mears, *Highlights of Scripture—Part 2: God's Great Covenants* (Hollywood: The Gospel Light Press, 1937), first quotation, 23; second and third quotations, 34. Hereafter page references from this work will be given in parentheses in the text.

9. Annual Sunday School Report for fiscal 1931–1932, FPCH.

10. *The Fid'ler* (June–July 1924): 6, FBCM.

11. Annual Sunday School Report, 1931–1932, FPCH; Ethel May Baldwin and David V. Benson, *Henrietta Mears and How She Did It!* (Glendale, CA: Gospel Light Publications, 1966), 191–95; Robert Bruce Young Jr. scrapbook, November 1928–November 1929, FPCH; Henrietta Mears 1946–1947 Travel Diary, October 11, 1946, Catalog B—Box 51, GL; Nancy Macky interview with the author, January 25, 2009; *The Quest* (June 1929): 5, FPCH; Barbara Hudson Powers, *The Henrietta Mears Story* (Westwood, NJ: Revell, 1957), 17.

12. Annual Sunday School Report, 1931–1932, FPCH; last sentence quotations from the *Christian Collegian* (January 1938): 2.

13. Henrietta Mears, transcript of untitled address from 1958, 21, Catalog B—Box 47, GL.

14. Henrietta Mears, "The Calling of the Sunday School Teacher," recording of a conference address given in the 1950s, Atlanta, GA, personal library of Andrea Van Boven (Madden).

15. George M. Marsden, *Understanding Fundamentalism and Evangelicalism* (Grand Rapids: Eerdmans, 1991), 1.

16. *The Fid'ler* (June–July 1924): 5, FBCM.

17. *The Fid'ler* (February 1924): 7–8, FBCM.

18. Both quotations from Powers, *Mears Story*, 114.

19. Mears quoted in Baldwin and Benson, *Henrietta Mears*, 110–11; Macky interview with the author, January 25, 2009; "Fidelis Reminiscences," *The Fid'ler* (September 29, 1929): 10.

20. *The Fid'ler* (June–July 1924): 8–9, FBCM.

21. Robert Bruce Young Jr. Scrapbook, December 1929–November 1930, FPCH.

22. The following discussion is drawn from an analysis of the publications of her College Department: the "Y.P.D. Newsletter" (1929), the *Quest* (1929–1931), and the *Christian Collegian* (1936–1938), FPCH and other sources as noted.

23. George M. Marsden, "Evangelicals and the Scientific Culture: An Overview," pp. 23–48 in Michael J. Lacey, ed., *Religion and Twentieth-Century American Intellectual Life* (Cambridge: Cambridge University and the Woodrow Wilson International Center for Scholars, 1989).

24. Baldwin and Benson, *Henrietta Mears*, 184–85.

25. Teaching notes, "The Bible Confirmed by Science," Catalog B—Box 13, GL.

26. James H. Moorhead, *Princeton Seminary in American Religion and Culture* (Grand Rapids: Eerdmans, 2012), 218–24. On the Galileo connection, see William E. Carroll, "Galileo, Science and the Bible," *Acta Philosophica* 6 (1997): 5–37, and Owen Gingerich, "How Galileo Changed the Rules of Science," *Sky and Telescope* 85 (March 1993): 32–36.

27. Henrietta Mears, "College Age (18-)," transcript of undated address, 6–7, Catalog B—Box 47, GL.

28. *The Quest* (September and October 1929).

29. *The Quest* (October 13, 1929): 4.

30. "Did You Know," newsletter, March 1930, FPCH; Teaching notes, "The Seven Dispensations," Catalog B—Box 25, GL; *The Quest* (May 1933): 4–5; Dale and Kathy Bruner interview with the author, September 1, 2007.

31. *The Quest* (October 13, 1929): 1–2.

32. "Gospel Light Believes," Catalog A—Box 19, GL; Barbara Becerra, *One Mile Nearer Heaven: An Early History of Forest Home* (Fairway Press, 2001), 107–8.

33. Henrietta Mears, "How to Build a College Department," transcript of a lecture presented to the Presbyterian Fellowship at Fuller Theological Seminary, Fall 1954, p. 4, Catalog B—Box 47, GL. Hereafter page references from this work will be given in parentheses in the text.

34. Session Minutes, vol. 1925–1930, September 25, 1928, FPCH.

35. *Christian Collegian* (March 1938): 1; Louis Evans Jr. interview with Andrea

Van Boven (Madden), December 18, 1996; Colleen Townsend Evans interview with the author, July 31, 2007.

36. *The Quest* (May 1931): 8.

37. *The Quest* (September 8, 1929): 9.

38. *The Quest* (June 9, 1929): 2.

39. *The Quest* (November 23, 1930): 4 and (December 1930): 10, 14.

40. *The Quest* (April 1929): 1 (quotation); *The Quest* (September 8, 1929): 10.

41. *The Quest* (September 8, 1929): 9.

42. *The Quest* (June 9, 1929): 2.

43. *The Quest* (September 8, 1929): 9.

44. No front cover black Teachers' Meetings binder, FPCH.

45. *The Quest* (April 20, 1930): 16.

46. Celtic Cross tract, Green Binder 10, Catalog B—Box 25, GL.

Chapter Six

1. Buswell to Mears, January 22, 1936, Presbyterian Church in America Historical Center, St. Louis, MO.

2. Wire, Buswell to Mears, March 10, 1936, and telegram, Mears to Buswell, March 12, 1936, PCAHC.

3. Buswell to Mears, March 13, 1936, PCAHC.

4. Mears to Buswell, March 25, 1936, PCAHC.

5. "The Gospel Light Story," in the *Gospel Light Handbook*, 3, Catalog B—Box 27, GL; Barbara Hudson Powers, *The Henrietta Mears Story* (Westwood, NJ: Revell, 1957), 148. Quotations from Ethel May Baldwin and David V. Benson, *Henrietta Mears and How She Did It!* (Glendale, CA: Gospel Light Publications, 1966), 64–65.

6. Powers, *Mears Story*, 150–51; Baldwin and Benson, *Henrietta Mears*, 66.

7. Powers, *Mears Story*, 150; Baldwin and Benson, *Henrietta Mears*, 66–68. Quotation from "Gospel Light Story," 4.

8. Powers, *Mears Story*, 150; Baldwin and Benson, *Henrietta Mears*, 67–68; "Gospel Light Story," 4.

9. Minutes of the Meeting of the Directors of the Church, April 3, 1934, Board of Trustees Minute Book, September 1929–April 1934, FPCH.

10. "Gospel Light Story," 4–5; Baldwin and Benson, *Henrietta Mears*, 68, 70.

11. Sources for this and the previous paragraph are "Gospel Light Story," 5–6; Powers, *Mears Story*, 150–51; Baldwin and Benson, *Henrietta Mears*, 69-70.

12. Special Meetings of the Board of Directors, May 13, 1949, and June 6, 1950, The Gospel Light Minute Book, 1947–1964, GL.

13. Marriage Register, FBCM.

14. Catalog B—Box 33, GL.

15. The following discussion of the progress of The Gospel Light Press is excerpted from "Gospel Light Story" and other sources as noted.

16. Lyda Mosier (July 9, 2007), Amy Mumford (July 11, 2007), and Joann J. Johnson (July 13, 2007) interviews with the author; Board of Directors Meeting, April 22, 1948, GL Minute Book.

17. Gospel Light stationery stock used for the letter of D. Stanley Engle to William T. Greig, December 7, 1937, Catalog B—Box 33, GL.

18. There is a lack of agreement in the sources on exactly when Nelson rejoined the firm. "The Gospel Light Story," in the *Gospel Light Handbook,* lists 1948 as the year that he returned as executive director, but he is not listed in the May 13, 1949, Minutes of Special Meeting of the Board of Directors. He does not appear as a director of the corporation until the minutes of June 6, 1950.

19. Special Meeting of the Board of Directors, May 13, 1949, GL Minute Book.

20. Source for this paragraph is Special Meeting of the Board of Directors, June 6, 1950, GL Minute Book and other sources as noted.

21. Memorandum for Attachment to Minutes of Directors Meeting, June 20, 1950, GL Minute Book.

22. Christian Education Department Annual Report, 1940–1941, FPCH.

23. Eleanor L. Doan, comp., *431 Quotes from the Notes of Henrietta C. Mears* (Glendale, CA: G/L Publications, 1970), 41–42.

24. Mears quoted in Val Toms, *First Presbyterian Church of Hollywood: A Seventy-Five Year Photographic Retrospective* (Hollywood: First Presbyterian Church of Hollywood, 1978), 177.

25. Doan, *431 Quotes*, 42.

26. Annual Sunday School Report, April 3, 1938–March 26, 1939, FPCH.

27. Christian Education Department Annual Report, 1938–1939, FPCH.

28. Christian Education Department Annual Reports for 1940–1941, 1941–1942, 1942–1943, 1943–1944, 1944–1945, 1945–1946, FPCH. See also Annual Sunday School Report, April 6, 1941–March 29, 1942, FPCH.

29. Christian Education Department Annual Reports for 1946–1947, 1949, 1951, 1958, FPCH.

30. General Assembly Report of the First Presbyterian Church of Hollywood for 1957, FPCH.

31. Christian Education Department Annual Report, 1937–1938 (quotation), 1941–1942, FPCH.

32. Christian Education Department Annual Report, 1938–1939, 1939–1940, 1941–1942, 1943–1944, 1944–1945, 1948, 1956, FPCH.

33. Christian Education Department Annual Report, 1948, 1949, 1952, 1956, FPCH.

34. Christian Education Department Annual Report, 1944–1945, 1957, FPCH.

35. Christian Education Department Annual Report, 1941–1942, 1955, FPCH.

36. Christian Education Department Annual Report, 1939–1940, 1940–1941, 1941–1942, 1946–1947, 1948, FPCH.

37. Christian Education Department Annual Report, 1941–1942, FPCH.

38. Christian Education Department Annual Report, 1941–1942, 1946–1947, 1949, 1959, FPCH.

39. Henrietta Mears, "Who Are the Young People You Teach?" transcript of an undated address in Baldwin and Benson, *Henrietta Mears*, 309.

40. Christian Education Department Annual Report, 1937–1938, FPCH.

41. Christian Education Department Annual Report, 1951, FPCH.

42. Joel A. Carpenter, *Revive Us Again: The Reawakening of American Fundamentalism* (New York: Oxford University Press, 1997), 258n64.

43. Christian Education Department Annual Reports, 1928–1958, and Annual Sunday School Report, April 6, 1930–March 29, 1931, FPCH.

44. Christian Education Department Annual Report, 1956, FPCH.

45. Christian Education Department Annual Report, 1937–1938, 1940–1941, 1941–1942, 1942–1943, 1948, 1949, 1956, 1959, FPCH.

46. Christian Education Department Annual Report for 1938–1939, 1940–1941, 1941–1942, 1942–1943, 1947–1948, 1949–1952, 1955, 1956, FPCH.

47. Christian Education Department Annual Report, 1940–1941, FPCH.

48. Christian Education Department Annual Report, 1949, FPCH.

49. Christian Education Department Annual Report, 1950, FPCH.

50. Mears 1946–1947 Travel Diary, July 21, 1946, Catalog B—Box 51, GL.

51. *Christian Collegian* (January 1938): 2; Baldwin and Benson, *Henrietta Mears*, 70–71.

52. Minutes of the Committee for United Action Among Evangelicals, October 27-28, 1941, Moody Memorial Church, Chicago, Illinois, NAE Records, Collection SC-113, Box 1, WCA; Letter to the "Signers of the Call," January 30, 1942, Taylor Papers, Collection 20, Box 65, BGCA. Quotations from the Conference for United Action Among Evangelicals program, St. Louis, MO, April 7-9, 1942, Taylor Papers, Collection 20, Box 65, BGCA.

53. Transcript of the business session, Second National Convention, National Association of Evangelicals, April 17, 1944, NAE Records, Collection SC-113, Box 139, WCA.

54. James DeForest Murch to V. E. Cory, December 18, 1944, NAE Records, Collection SC-113, Box 138, WCA.

55. Annual Report, Commission on Church Schools, NAE Records, Collection SC-113, Box 139, WCA; James DeForest Murch to V. E. Cory, April 6, 1945, NAE Records, Collection SC-113, Box 138, WCA; "Convention Plans to Revitalize Sunday School," undated press release, NAE Records, Collection SC-113, Box 138, WCA.

56. Minutes of the Conference of Sunday School Leaders, Stevens Hotel, Chicago, IL, April 30, 1945, NAE Records, Collection SC-113, Box 139, WCA.

57. Minutes of the First Meeting of the Executive Committee of the National Sunday School Association, May 1, 1945, NAE Records, SC-113, Box 139, WCA; Letter of C. V. Egemeier, Executive Secretary, NSSA, December 12, 1945, NAE Records, SC-113, Box 139, WCA.

58. Polly Craig interview with the author, January 25, 2009.

59. Sources for this and the preceding paragraph are the 2003 interview with Howard Hendricks cited in Marlene LeFever, "Clate A. Risley," in "Christian Educators of the Twentieth Century," website maintained by the Talbot School of Theology at http://www2.talbot.edu/ce20/educators/view.cfm?n=clate_risley; NSSA national and regional conference flyers, programs, announcements, and workshop outlines, NEA Records, Collection SC-113, Boxes 138, 139, 188, WCA; Taylor Papers, Collection 20, Box 66, 67, BGCA; *Chicago Daily Tribune*, September 18, 1948, and September 28, 1951. See also the Reports of the Executive Secretary, NSSA, April 15–June 20, 1947, January 1–April 30, 1948, Results of the Executive Committee Meeting Board of Directors, NSSA, December 2, 1947, NAE Records, Collection SC-113, Box 139; *The Church of God Evangel* 41, Issue 41 (December 16, 1950): 12, 42, Issue 38 (November 24, 1951): 2, 43, Issue 25 (August 16, 1952): 5, 44, Issue 27 (September 5, 1953): 13, 45, Issue 29 (September 25, 1954): 10, 46, Issue 40 (December 3, 1955): 15 (quotation).

60. Gertrude D. Clark to H. J. Taylor, May 5, 1950, Taylor Papers, Collection 20, Box 67, BGCA; J. Elwin Wright, "World Evangelicals Gather in Rhode Island," undated report, Taylor Papers, Collection 20, Box 67; J. Elwin Wright to Herbert J. Taylor, October 22, 1956, April 30, 1958, and June 17, 1958, Taylor Papers, Collection 20, Box 67, BGCA.

Chapter Seven

1. The following discussion is based on the transcript of Mears's Travel Diary, 1946–1947, Catalog B—Box 51, GL, and other sources as cited. Subsequent reference to this source will include only entry dates.

2. See for example her entries for May 30, June 12, 15, 18–19, 21, 25, July 1, 3, 23–24, August 7, September 4, 13, 18, 22, 25, 28, October 18–19, 1946.

3. August 31, 1946.

4. August 13, 1946.

5. Henrietta Mears interview with Barbara Hudson Powers, 1956, GL; October 11, 12, 14, 15 (quotation), 1946.

6. Ethel May Baldwin and David V. Benson, *Henrietta Mears and How She Did It!* (Glendale, CA: Gospel Light Publications, 1966), 225.

7. Baldwin and Benson, *Henrietta Mears*, 230–31.

8. Baldwin and Benson, *Henrietta Mears*, 231.

9. Doris Halverson interview with the author, September 1, 2007; Michael Richardson, *Amazing Faith: The Authorized Biography of Bill Bright* (Colorado Springs: Waterbrook Press, 2000), 35–37; John G. Turner, *Bill Bright and Campus Crusade for Christ: The Renewal of Evangelicalism in Postwar America* (Chapel Hill: UNC Press, 2008), 26–27; Barbara Hudson Powers, *The Henrietta Mears Story* (Westwood, NJ: Revell, 1957), 181–82; Baldwin and Benson, *Henrietta Mears*, 232–47.

10. Richard Halverson quoted in Powers, *Mears Story*, 181.

11. Bill Bright quoted in Richardson, *Amazing Faith*, 36.

12. Louis Evans Jr. quoted in Turner, *Bill Bright*, 27.

13. Henrietta Mears to Don, August 13, 1947, FPCH.

14. Joel A. Carpenter, *Revive Us Again: The Reawakening of American Fundamentalism* (New York: Oxford University Press, 1997), 216, 222; Baldwin and Benson, *Henrietta Mears*, 235.

15. Baldwin and Benson, *Henrietta Mears*, 237. Richardson attributes this text to Bill Bright. See Richardson, *Amazing Faith*, 39.

16. Powers, *Mears Story*, 181.

17. Baldwin and Benson, *Henrietta Mears*, 240–41.

18. Fellowship of the Burning Heart binder, Catalog B—Box 8, GL; Doris Halverson interview.

19. Mears quoted in Walter E. James with Christy Hawes Zatkin, *Tumbling Walls: A True Story of Ordinary People Bringing Reconciliation in Extraordinary Ways to an Alienated World* (La Jolla, CA: The Diaspora Foundation, 1990), 10.

20. Minutes of the Meeting of the Board of Directors, January 18, 1946, FPCH; James, *Tumbling Walls*, 217–21. Quotation from page 221.

21. James, *Tumbling Walls*, 10–21.

22. Ralph Hamburger interview with the author, January 25, 2009. See also James, *Tumbling Walls*, 20–21.

23. Hamburger interview.

24. Ralph Hamburger to Miss Mears, September 17, 1947, Catalog A—Box 22, GL.

25. Hamburger interview.

26. James, *Tumbling Walls*, 22.

27. Hamburger interview (author's brackets).

28. Papers in the personal library of Ralph Hamburger shared with the author, July 29, 2007.

29. "Foreword" by Richard Halverson, in James, *Tumbling Walls*, 3 (author's brackets).

30. Corrie Ten Boom quoted in James, *Tumbling Walls*, 26.

31. James, *Tumbling Walls*, 23–24, 26.

32. James, *Tumbling Walls*, 67; Ralph Hamburger, "Excerpts from a paper on Ecumenics," Princeton Theological Seminary, 6; Hamburger interview.

33. Hamburger, "Excerpts," 6; quotation from Hamburger interview.

34. J. B. Phillips, "Preface to the American Edition," in *The Church Under the Cross* (New York: Macmillan, 1956).

35. See the 1989–1990 letters from East Germans excerpted in James, *Tumbling Walls*, 5.

36. Alfred Schröder to Ralph Hamburger, April 16, 1956, and announcement of Pastor Schröder's visit, private papers of Ralph Hamburger; Dan L. Thrapp, "Berlin Pastor Gives Sidelight on War," *Los Angeles Times* (April 7, 1957), part IA, 2.

37. Hamburger interview (author's brackets).

38. The following discussion is adapted from Arlin C. Migliazzo, "'She Must Be a Proper Exception': Females, Fuller Seminary, and the Limits of Gender Equity among Southern California Evangelicals, 1947–1952," *Fides et Historia* 45, no. 2 (summer/fall 2013): 1–19 and reproduced with permission.

39. Harold Lindsell, *Park Street Prophet: A Life of Harold John Ockenga* (Wheaton, IL: Van Kampen Press, 1951), 128–31; George M. Marsden, *Reforming Fundamentalism: Fuller Seminary and the New Evangelicalism* (Grand Rapids: Eerdmans, 1987; paperback edition, 1995), 24–27.

40. Fuller Theological Seminary Faculty Minutes, June 28 and September 13, 1950, FTS. Hereafter cited as Faculty minutes. Marsden, *Reforming Fundamentalism*, 127.

41. Faculty minutes, June 28, 1950.

42. Ockenga to Lindsell, December 8, 1950, FTS.

43. Faculty minutes, December 13, 1950 (first quotation); Lindsell to Ockenga, December 15, 1950 (second quotation), FTS.

44. Lindsell to Ockenga, December 15 and 27, 1950, FTS.

45. Faculty minutes, December 21, 1950, FTS; Lindsell to Ockenga, December 27, 1950, FTS (all quotations).

46. Ockenga to Mears, December 29, 1950, Catalog B—Box 48, GL.

47. Faculty minutes, January 10, 1951, FTS.

48. Lindsell to Ockenga, January 12, 1951, FTS.

49. Faculty minutes, March 2, 1951; Ockenga to Lindsell, March 28, 1951; Lindsell to Ockenga, April 2, 1951, all FTS. Quotations from Ockenga to Mears, March 5, 1951, Catalog A—Box 22, GL.

50. Ockenga to Mears, April 20, 1951, Catalog A—Box 22, GL.

51. Ockenga to Lindsell, April 9, 1951, FTS.

52. Lindsell to Ockenga, April 17, 1951, and April 18, 1951; Ockenga to Lindsell, April 23, 1951, all FTS.

53. Ockenga to Mears, April 20, 1951, Catalog A—Box 22, GL.

54. Dale Bruner, "Tribute to Henrietta C. Mears, April 21, 1961," First Presbyterian Church of Hollywood, recorded by Bruce Angwin, cassette in the personal library of Andrea Van Boven (Madden).

Chapter Eight

1. Carey McWilliams, *Southern California: An Island on the Land* (Salt Lake City: Gibbs-Smith, 2010), 332; Marc Wanamaker and Robert W. Nudelman, *Early Hollywood* (Charleston, SC: Arcadia Publishing, 2007), 31, 32, 35, 41; Paul Zollo, *Hollywood Remembered: An Oral History of Its Golden Age* (New York: Cooper Square Press, 2002), 316.

2. Richard B. Jewell, *The Golden Age of Hollywood, 1929–1945* (Malden, MA: Blackwell, 2007), 115 (quotation); McWilliams, *Island on the Land*, 333.

3. Information and unreferenced quotations for the following paragraphs are taken from Mears's three-page typewritten manuscript "Description of Beginnings of Hollywood Christian Group," Catalog B—Box 24, GL and other sources as noted.

4. Colleen Townsend Evans quoted in Andrea V. B. Madden, "Henrietta C. Mears: 1890–1963, Her Life and Influence" (master's thesis, Gordon-Conwell Theological Seminary, 1997), 105.

5. Doris Halverson interview with the author, September 1, 2007.

6. Sources for this and the previous paragraph are *The Quest* (June 9, 1929): 2 and (April 20, 1930): 14, FCPH; Pledges to Benevolences for Year of 1932–1933, FPCH; *The Christian Collegian* (December 1936): 11, (February 1937): 5–6, (March 1937): 4, 7, (June 1937): 2, 5, 11, (October 3, 1937): 4, (November 7, 1937): 8, 10–11, (January 1938): 6, (March 1938): 4, (October 1938): 10, (November 1938): 12, 15, FPCH; Joy Eilers interview with the author, June 26, 2009.

7. J. Edwin Orr, *The Inside Story of the Hollywood Christian Group* (Grand Rapids: Zondervan, 1955), 15-16, 133; *Life*, vol. 26, no. 2 (January 10, 1949): 80; Eilers interview with the author, June 26, 2009.

8. Orr, *Inside Story*, 17–18.

9. Ethel May Baldwin and David V. Benson, *Henrietta Mears and How She Did It!* (Glendale, CA: Gospel Light Publications, 1966), 251–52.

10. Connie Haines, "Tribute to Henrietta C. Mears, April 21, 1961," First Presbyterian Church of Hollywood, recorded by Bruce Angwin, cassette in the personal library of Andrea Van Boven (Madden); Orr, *Inside Story*, 19.

11. Mears quoted in Barbara Hudson Powers, *The Henrietta Mears Story* (Westwood, NJ: Revell, 1957), 169.

12. Orr, *Inside Story*, 19.

13. Orr, *Inside Story*, 20.

14. Dale Evans Rogers quoted in Powers, *Mears Story*, 169.

15. Orr, *Inside Story*, 20–21, 52–53, 64, 71, 74, 77–78, 117–18, 132–33; Bill Bright, "The Truth About Hollywood," *Christian Life* (July 1950): 11.

16. Quoted in Bill Bright, "The Truth About Hollywood," *Christian Life* (July 1950): 12. See also Orr, *Inside Story*, 55, 133.

17. Colleen Townsend Evans quoted in Madden, "Henrietta C. Mears," 104.

18. Orr, *Inside Story*, 55, 63.

19. Redd Harper, *I Walk the Glory Road* (Westwood, NJ: Revell, 1957), 38.

20. The following discussion is taken from "Resolutions of the Hollywood Christian Group," n.d., Catalog B—Box 32, GL, and other sources as cited.

21. See Bright, "The Truth About Hollywood," 12.

22. Orr, *Inside Story*, 54–55.

23. Orr, *Inside Story*, 16; Powers, *Mears Story*, 169.

24. *The Quest* (June 9, 1929): 2, FPCH; Dale Evans Rogers, *In the Hands of the Potter* (Nashville: Thomas Nelson, 1994), vii, 37–38; "Do You Know That," newsletter, fall 1930, FPCH; Christian Education Report, 1936–1937, FPCH. *The Quest* (April 20, 1930): 16, (May 11, 1930): 8, and (November 23, 1930): 14, FPCH. First and third quotations from Orr, *Inside Story*, 112–13, second from Harper, *Glory Road*, 23, fourth from Eilers interview with the author, June 15, 2009.

25. Velma Spencer, *How to Have a Happy Christian Home* (Grand Rapids: Zondervan, 1957), 8. See also Orr, *Inside Story*, 35–36; Spencer, *Christian Home*, 6–7, 12.

26. Eilers interview with the author, June 11, 2011; Harper, *Glory Road*, 23.

27. Orr, *Inside Story*, 37–39; quotation from Spencer, *Christian Home*, 12. See also pages 8–9, 11, 13.

28. Catalog B—Box 34, GL; Eilers interview with the author, June 26, 2009.

29. Richard C. Halverson, "Any Good—from Hollywood?" *Christianity Today*, vol. 11, no. 6 (December 23, 1957): 9; Bright, "The Truth About Hollywood," 40; Orr, *Inside Story*, 24–25, 44, 62, 76–78, 83–84, 88–93, 117–21. Quotation from page 40. See also Harper, *Glory Road*, 71.

30. Bright, "The Truth About Hollywood," 12.

31. Quoted in Orr, *Inside Story*, 29. See also pages 26–27.

32. Orr, *Inside Story*, 56–57, 60–61.

33. Harper, *Glory Road*, 56. See also Harper, *Glory Road*, 55; Orr, *Inside Story*, 79.

34. Hamblen quoted in Lewis W. Gillenson, *Billy Graham and Seven Who Were Saved* (New York: Trident Press, 1967), 189.

35. Hamblen quoted in Orr, *Inside Story*, 111.

36. Gillenson, *Seven Who Were Saved*, 189.

37. First and third quotations from Gillenson, *Seven Who Were Saved*, 189–90; second quotation from Oberia Hamblen, *My Brother Stuart Hamblen* (Los Angeles: Cowman, 1950), 128.

38. Eilers interviews with the author, June 19, 2009, and June 11, 2011.

39. Harper, *Glory Road*, 69.

40. Bright, "The Truth About Hollywood," 10–12, 40, 42, quotation from page 12; John G. Turner, *Bill Bright and Campus Crusade for Christ: The Renewal of Evangelicalism in Postwar America* (Chapel Hill: UNC Press, 2008), 36.

41. Orr, *Inside Story*, 55–56, 94–99.

42. Dick Phebus to Teacher, no date, Catalog B—Box 14, GL.

43. Eilers interviews with the author, June 26, 2009, and June 11, 2011; Orr, *Inside Story*, 19, 45, 79.

44. Bright, "The Truth About Hollywood," 42; Phil Kerr, "Hollywood's Spiritual Awakening," *Christian Life* (July 1954): 16–17, 50, 52.

45. Halverson, "Any Good—from Hollywood?," 8, 9 (quotation, author's brackets).

46. Quotations from Halverson, "Any Good—from Hollywood?," 9–10.

47. Orr, *Inside Story*, 57 (quotation), 58, 95.

48. Orr, *Inside Story*, 58.

49. Orr, *Inside Story*, 100–101; Jane Russell, *My Path and Detours: An Autobiography* (New York: Franklin Watts, 1985), 106–7, 143. See also "Buxom Actress Jane Russell Dead at 89," *Entertainment News* (February 28, 2011), http://www.reuters.com/article/2011/03/01/us-janerussell-idUSTRE72001620110301/.

50. Ruth Bell Graham to Barbara, December 12, 1956, Catalog B—Box 48, GL.

51. Baldwin and Benson, *Henrietta Mears*, 104; second quotation, Ruth Bell Graham to Barbara, December 12, 1956, Catalog B—Box 48, GL.

52. Graham to Barbara.

53. Colleen Townsend Evans quoted in Madden, "Henrietta C. Mears," 107.

54. Orr, *Inside Story*, 100–101.

55. Orr, *Inside Story*, 44, 59–60.

56. Christian Education Department Annual Report for 1957, FPCH; Richard

Quebedeaux, *By What Authority: The Rise of Personality Cults in American Christianity* (San Francisco: Harper and Row, 1982), 39.

57. Madden, "Henrietta C. Mears," 107; Earl O. Roe, ed., *Dream Big: The Henrietta Mears Story* (Ventura, CA: Regal Books, 1990), 301.

58. Orr, *Inside Story*, 85–86.

59. Madden, "Henrietta Mears," 107; Graham, *Just As I Am: The Autobiography of Billy Graham* (Carmel, NY: Guideposts, 1997), 174–75.

60. Barbara Becerra, *One Mile Nearer Heaven: An Early History of Forest Home* (Fairway Press, 2001), 170–74.

61. Kenneth Lewis, "Hollywood Film Group Spreading Christianity," *Los Angeles Times*, April 6, 1959, III, 32.

Chapter Nine

1. Nancy Macky interview with the author, January 25, 2009.

2. Joel A. Carpenter, *Revive Us Again: The Reawakening of American Fundamentalism* (New York: Oxford University Press, 1997).

3. Garth Rosell, *The Surprising Work of God: Harold John Ockenga, Billy Graham, and the Rebirth of Evangelicalism* (Grand Rapids: Baker Academic, 2008), 118.

4. Rosell, *The Surprising Work of God*, 56n92, 59, 59n108, 71n163, 130n18. See also Harold Lindsell, *Park Street Prophet: A Life of Harold John Ockenga* (Wheaton, IL: Van Kampen Press, 1951), 30, 32, 61–62.

5. Ockenga quoted in Val Toms, *First Presbyterian Church of Hollywood: A Seventy-Five Year Photographic Retrospective* (Hollywood: First Presbyterian Church, 1978), 35.

6. Robert Boyd Munger with Robert C. Larson, *Leading from the Heart: Lifetime Reflections on Spiritual Development* (Downers Grove, IL: InterVarsity Press, 1995), 24–25, 58. Quotation from page 14.

7. The following brief biography of Jim Rayburn and history of the Young Life Campaign is drawn from Emile Caillet, *Young Life* (New York: Harper & Row, 1963), 8–32 and other sources as cited.

8. Caillet, *Young Life*, 9.

9. Howard Carlson, "Clyde Johnstone Kennedy: Casting a Long Shadow for the Cause of Christ," *Redeeming the Time*, online journal, vol. 4, no. 4 (fall 2012): 2–5, 15, http://www.rttpublications.org/files/issues/2012_Fall.pdf/; Bill Kennedy email to the author, April 14, 2014; *The Quest* (January 1930): 2, (March 1930): 8, (April 1930): 16; Munger and Larson, *Leading from the Heart*, 14, 24–25.

10. Jim Rayburn quoted in Barbara Hudson Powers, *The Henrietta Mears Story* (Westwood, NJ: Revell, 1957), 178.

11. Jim Rayburn III, *From Bondage to Liberty: Dance, Children, Dance* (Colorado Springs: Morningstar Press, 2000), 43.

12. Jim Rayburn quoted in Powers, *Mears Story*, 178.

13. Robert Mitchell interview with the author, February 19, 2008; Caillet, *Young Life*, 106–7.

14. Jim Rayburn quoted in Powers, *Mears Story*, 178.

15. Jim Rayburn quoted in Earl O. Roe, ed., *Dream Big: The Henrietta Mears Story* (Ventura, CA: Regal Books, 1990), front matter.

16. Rayburn, *From Bondage to Liberty*, 55–56. See also Jim Rayburn III, *Dance, Children, Dance* (Wheaton, IL: Tyndale House, 1984), 61–64.

17. Mitchell interview. All quotations are from this interview.

18. Jim Rayburn quoted in Powers, *Mears Story*, 178.

19. Jim Rayburn journal entries, 1941–1944, quoted in Rayburn, *From Bondage to Liberty*, 47–50.

20. "The Vision Grows," Gospel Light Publications, 1983, 9, Box 27, GL.

21. Powers, *Mears Story*, 56.

22. Betty Lee Skinner, *Daws: The Story of Dawson Trotman Founder of the Navigators* (Grand Rapids: Zondervan, 1974), 24, 31, 44, 52–54, 60, 69, 70–73, 76–77, 86, 94–95, 98, 106, 135, 139, 141, 143, 166, 182, 188–89, 241. Quotation from page 69.

23. Skinner, *Daws*, 133, 208–12, 241–42, 271, 284, 316, 325, 329, 339, 345, 350, 354, 356, 382–83; quotations from Henrietta Mears interview with Barbara Hudson Powers, 1956, GL.

24. Quoted in Powers, "Introduction," *Mears Story*, 7. See also Billy Graham's cablegram from Hawaii, March 1963, Catalog B—Box 16, GL.

25. Typed statement of Bill Bright, Catalog B—Box 33, GL.

26. Biographical details of Bright's life are taken from John G. Turner, *Bill Bright and Campus Crusade for Christ: The Renewal of Evangelicalism in Postwar America* (Chapel Hill: UNC Press, 2008), 1–39; Michael Richardson, *Amazing Faith: The Authorized Biography of Bill Bright* (Colorado Springs: Waterbrook Press, 2000), 5–65 and other sources as cited.

27. Skinner, *Daws*, 190.

28. Richardson, *Amazing Faith*, 18.

29. Richardson, *Amazing Faith*, 18.

30. Bill Bright quoted in Richardson, *Amazing Faith*, 19.

31. Richardson, *Amazing Faith*, 19–20.

32. Richardson, *Amazing Faith*, 22–23.

33. Ethel May Baldwin and David V. Benson, *Henrietta Mears and How She Did It!* (Glendale, CA: Gospel Light Publications, 1966), 232–35.

34. Vonette Bright to David Benson, n.d., Catalog B—Box 33, GL; Turner, *Bill Bright and Campus Crusade for Christ,* 30, 34.

35. Vonette Bright quoted in Richardson, *Amazing Faith*, 41.

36. "The Influence of Henrietta Mears on the Lives of Bill and Vonette Bright," Catalog B—Box 33, GL.

37. Skinner, *Daws*, 182; Billy Graham, *Just As I Am: The Autobiography of Billy Graham* (Carmel, NY: Guideposts, 1997), 101.

38. J. Edwin Orr, *Good News in Bad Times: Signs of Revival* (Grand Rapids: Zondervan, 1953), 56–61, 74. Quotation from page 61. See also Graham, *Just As I Am,* 98–108; J. Edwin Orr, *Campus Aflame: A History of Evangelical Awakenings in Collegiate Communities*, new and revised edition, edited by Richard Owen Roberts (Wheaton, IL: International Awakening Press, 1994), 171–72.

39. Graham, *Just As I Am*, 137.

40. Orr, *Campus Aflame*, 126, 173; Turner, *Bill Bright and Campus Crusade for Christ*, 36.

41. Fred W. Hoffman, *Revival Times in America* (Holliston, MA: W. A. Wilde, 1956), 163–64.

42. Graham, *Just As I Am*, 134–36. Quotation from page 134.

43. Orr, *Good News in Bad Times,* 62.

44. Orr, *Good News in Bad Times,* 61–62.

45. Graham, *Just As I Am*, 138.

46. Graham, *Just As I Am*, 138.

47. Graham, *Just As I Am*, 138–39.

48. Graham, *Just As I Am*, 139; Ruth Schnicke interview with the author, August 3, 2007.

49. Billy Graham to Miss Mears, September 9, 1949, Catalog A—Box 22, GL.

50. Esther Brinkley interview with the author, July 14, 2007.

51. Graham, *Just As I Am*, 146; Joann Johnson interview with the author, July 13, 2007; Orr, *Campus Aflame*, 174; Lyda Mosier interview with the author, July 9, 2007.

52. Orr, *Good News in Bad Times*, 65–66, 69, 73–74, 82–83; Orr, *Campus Aflame*, 185–87, 195.

53. Bright quoted in Turner, *Bill Bright and Campus Crusade for Christ,* 35.

54. Turner, *Bill Bright and Campus Crusade for Christ,* 34–37.

55. Orr, *Campus Aflame*, 188; Richardson, *Amazing Faith*, 64.

56. Death Certificate of Margaret Burtis Mears, Los Angeles County Hall of Records, Los Angeles and Norwalk, CA.

57. Turner, *Bill Bright and Campus Crusade for Christ,* 46–47, 49; Richardson, *Amazing Faith*, 64–65.

58. Baldwin and Benson, *Henrietta Mears*, 261–63; Group interview with the author, January 25, 2009; Henrietta Mears 1953 Diary, September 20, 1953, Catalogue B—Box 28, GL. Quotation from "The Influence of Henrietta Mears on the Lives of Bill and Vonette Bright," GL.

59. Richardson, *Amazing Faith*, 72–76.

60. "Campus Crusade Cabin at Forest Home Result of Vision and Prayer," *Campus Crusade Communique* (August 1954): 3; Earl Palmer interview with the author, July 12, 2007.

61. Orr, *Campus Aflame*, 190.

62. The following discussion is taken primarily from Redd Harper, *I Walk the Glory Road* (Westwood, NJ: Revell, 1957) and other sources as cited.

63. Harper quoted in Orr, *Inside Story*, 118–21; http://www.wheaton.edu/bgc/archives/GUIDES/235.html/, accessed June 8, 2011.

64. Harper, *Glory Road*, 38.

65. Harper, *Glory Road*, 69–70.

66. See Lewis W. Gillenson, *Billy Graham and Seven Who Were Saved* (New York: Trident Press, 1967), 184.

67. See Orr, *Inside Story*, 104.

68. Oberia Hamblen, *My Brother Stuart Hamblen* (Los Angeles: Cowman, 1950), 84–85; Orr, *Inside Story*, 104–6.

69. Graham, *Just As I Am*, 145–46.

70. Hamblen, *My Brother*, 93–94.

71. Orr, *Inside Story*, 22, 106–7; Graham, *Just As I Am*, 145; Hamblen, *My Brother*, 94.

72. Graham, *Just As I Am*, 147.

73. Gillenson, *Seven Who Were Saved*, 186; Graham, *Just As I Am*, 147.

74. Hamblen, *My Brother*, 86 (quotation), 87; Graham, *Just As I Am*, 147.

75. Hamblen quoted in Hamblen, *My Brother*, 105. See also 98–100, 103–7, 113; Graham, *Just As I Am*, 148 (quotation); Orr, *Inside Story*, 108–10.

76. Graham, *Just As I Am*, 147–49.

77. Mears quoted in Harper, *Glory Road*, 149.

78. Mears quoted in Harper, *Glory Road*, 154.

79. Harper, *Glory Road*, 155.

80. Blog post "Crusade City Spotlight: London," https://billygrahamlibrary.org/crusade-city-spotlight-london/, The Billy Graham Library.

81. Sources for this and the preceding paragraph are Powers, *Mears Story*, 17–21, 68–69; Graham, *Just As I Am*, 211, 214, 218, 231; "Pres-By-Tell," High School Depart-

ment newsletter (August 1954), 4, FPCH; "News from Miss Mears, 1954," private papers of the Rev. Ralph Hamburger.

Chapter Ten

1. Henrietta Mears interview with Barbara Hudson Powers, 1956, GL.

2. Barbara Hudson Powers, *The Henrietta Mears Story* (Westwood, NJ: Revell, 1957), 103, 105, 110.

3. Mears interview.

4. Mears interview.

5. Powers, *Mears Story*, 93.

6. Mears interview; George E. Robson to Miss Henrietta Mears, April 7, 1930, Catalog B—Box 52, GL.

7. H. F. Salyards to Miss Margaret Mears, July 18, 1929, Catalog B—Box 52, GL.

8. Book 13382, 366, Book 13400, 346–48, Book 18527, 51–53, Los Angeles County Hall of Records, Los Angeles and Norwalk, CA.

9. 1944 Tax Return of Henrietta C. Mears, Catalog B—Box 52, GL.

10. "Bill of Sale" dated January 8, 1948, and "Special Minutes," March 15, 1950, The Gospel Light Press Board of Directors Minutes Book, 1947–1964, GL.

11. Mears interview.

12. James Fogerty interview with Curtis Akenson, March 21, 2000, MHC, transcript, FBMC.

13. Amy Mumford interview with the author, July 11, 2007; Mears quoted in Powers, *Mears Story*, 51, 131–33.

14. Powers, *Mears Story*, 164–67, 189. First quotation, 165, second quotation, 166, third quotation, 189.

15. First two quotations from Powers, *Mears Story*, 160, third quotation from Powers, "The Henrietta Mears Story—Epilogue, January 1, 2005," http://www.ccel.us/mears.epi.html/; Reflection of William Dunlap, Catalog B—Box 15, GL.

16. Dale (Bruner) to Dearest Teacher, April 21, 1961, Catalog B—Box 14, GL.

17. Form letter I from Mears, FPCH.

18. Undated form letter from Mears, FPCH.

19. Undated form letter from Mears to My dear Group Leader, FPCH.

20. Form letter from Mears to executive members, October 29, 1931, FPCH.

21. Gary and Marily Demarest interview with the author, July 20, 2007.

22. Special Meeting of the Board of Directors, May 30, 1949, The Gospel Light Press Minute Book, 1947–1964, GL; Mumford interview.

23. Bruce Angwin, "Remembering Teacher," audiotaped presentation, May 27, 1995, from the personal library of Andrea Van Boven (Madden).

24. Mumford interview.

25. Powers, *Mears Story*, 134.

26. Demarest interview; Esther Brinkley interview with the author, July 14, 2007.

27. Dale Bruner interview with Andrea Van Boven (Madden), December 12, 1996.

28. Eleanor L. Doan, comp., *431 Quotes from the Notes of Henrietta C. Mears* (Glendale, CA: G/L Publications, 1970), 6.

29. Bill Craig interview with the author, January 25, 2009.

30. June Loomis Jewett interview with the author, July 10, 2007.

31. Demarest interview; Bill Grieg Jr. interview with Andrea Van Boven (Madden), October 16, 1996.

32. Taylor Potter interview with the author, January 25, 2009.

33. Richard Spencer interview with the author, July 8, 2007.

34. Jack and Anna Kerr interview with Andrea Van Boven (Madden), October 18, 1996.

35. Polly Craig interview with the author, January 25, 2009.

36. Nancy Macky interview with the author, January 25, 2009; Liela Jean Botsford interview with the author, August 29, 2009.

37. Dale and Kathy Bruner interview with the author, September 1, 2007; Bruner interview with Madden.

38. "Reminisces of Henrietta Mears (Henrietta Mears Night)," May 1988, Catalog B—Box 9, GL.

39. Doris Halverson interview with the author, September 1, 2007.

40. Demarest interview.

41. Macky interview.

42. Craig interview.

43. Powers, *Mears Story*, 114.

44. Rachel Osborn interview with the author, July 9, 2007.

45. Louis Evans Sr. quoted in Powers, *Mears Story*, 138.

46. Moody Bible Institute reference from Bruner interview with Madden.

47. Bruner interview with Madden.

48. Grieg interview with Madden.

49. Powers, *Mears Story*, 135–36.

50. Angwin, "Remembering Teacher."

51. *Christian Collegian* (November 1938): 9, FPCH; Jewett interview.

52. Osborn interview. See also Grieg interview with Madden.

53. George M. Marsden, *Reforming Fundamentalism: Fuller Seminary and the New Evangelicalism*, paperback edition (Grand Rapids: Eerdmans, 1995), 89; John G.

Turner, "The Power Behind the Throne: Henrietta Mears and Post–World War II Evangelicalism," *Journal of Presbyterian History* 83, no. 2 (fall/winter 2005): 151.

54. Grieg interview with Madden.

55. Powers, *Mears Story*, 49.

56. Vonette Bright to Mr. David Benson, n.d., Catalog B—Box 33, GL.

57. Louis Evans Jr. interview with Andrea Van Boven (Madden), December 18, 1996.

58. Demarest interview.

59. Osborn interview.

60. Spencer interview with the author, July 8, 2007.

61. Marjorie Sutton interview with the author, August 1, 2007.

62. Ted Cole interview with the author, August 3, 2007.

63. Halverson interview.

64. Powers, *Mears Story,* 105 (first quotation), 131, 180 (second quotation, author's brackets).

65. The source for this and the previous paragraph is Bright to Benson.

66. Anna Kerr interview with John Turner, cited in Turner, "The Power Behind the Throne," 151.

67. Halverson interview.

68. Recommendation of the Special Committee of the Trustees, Board of Trustees minutes, September 1929–April 1934, FPCH.

69. Walter E. James to Miss Mears, June 14, 1947, Catalog B—Box 14, GL.

70. Halverson interview.

71. Walter E. James to My Dear Miss Mears, April 26, 1961, Catalog B—Box 14, GL; Doris Halverson interview with the author, September 1, 2007.

72. John Holland, "Reminisces of Henrietta Mears," transcription of Henrietta Mears Night program, May 1988, First Presbyterian Church of Hollywood, 14, Catalog B—Box 9, GL.

73. Polly Craig interview.

74. Warren McClain interview with the author, January 25, 2009.

75. Potter interview.

76. Bill Craig interview.

77. McClain interview; Grieg interview with Madden.

78. Demarest interview.

79. Philip Henry Lotz, ed., *Orientation in Religious Education* (New York: Abingdon-Cokesbury, 1950); Marvin J. Taylor, ed., *An Introduction to Christian Education* (Nashville: Abingdon, 1966).

80. Powers, *Mears Story*, 28–29.

81. *The Quest* (March 1930): 7, 13, FCPH, (June 1930): 7; Group interview with Ralph Hamburger, Taylor Potter, Jack and Anna Kerr, William and Polly Craig, Nancy Macky, and Warren McClain, January 25, 2009.

82. John G. Turner, *Bill Bright and Campus Crusade for Christ: The Renewal of Evangelicalism in Postwar America* (Chapel Hill: UNC Press, 2008), 21; Halverson interview; Henrietta Mears 1940 Travel Diary, October 20, 1940, File Cabinet, Drawer 1, GL; Grieg interview with Madden; Bill Kennedy interview with the author, February 25, 2014.

83. Halverson interview.

84. Bruner interview with Madden.

85. Henrietta Mears 1940 Travel Diary, October 20, 1940, File Cabinet, Drawer 1, GL.

86. Henrietta Mears 1946–1947 Travel Diary, February 21, 1946, Catalog B—Box 51, GL.

87. Mears 1946–1947 Diary, March 6, 1946 (first quotation), March 28, 1946 (second quotation).

88. Mears 1946–1947 Diary, March 31, 1946, April 2, 1946 (first quotation), May 9, 1946 (second quotation).

89. Mears 1940 Diary, November 17, 1940.

90. Mears 1946–1947 Diary, June 2, 1946 (first quotation), June 23, 1946 (second set of quotations), June 27, 1946 (third quotation). See also July 7, 1946.

91. Henrietta Mears 1950–1951 Travel Diary, January 21, 1951, Catalog B—Box 28, GL.

92. Mears 1946–1947 Diary, June 26, 1946.

93. Mears 1950–1951 Diary, February 22, 23, 1951, author's brackets.

94. Henrietta Mears 1952 Travel Diary, October 6, 8 (quotation), 10 (author's brackets), 1952, Catalog B—Box 28, GL.

95. *The Fid'ler* (February 1924): 10–11, FBCM.

96. Mears 1940 Diary, October 26, 1940.

97. Mears 1946–1947 Diary, July 16, 1946.

98. Mears 1946–1947 Diary, July 20, 1946.

99. Mears 1950–1951 Diary, December 27, 1950.

100. John (Essick) to Miss Mears, late May, 1949, Catalog B—Box 14, GL.

101. Demarest interview; Dale Bruner, "Tribute to Henrietta C. Mears, April 21, 1961," First Presbyterian Church of Hollywood, recorded by Bruce Angwin, cassette in the personal library of Andrea Van Boven (Madden).

102. Group interview.

103. *Christian Collegian* (November 1938): 3–4, FPCH; Colleen Townsend Evans,

interview with the author, July 31 and August 8, 2007; Ron Frase interview with the author, February 12, 2008.

104. Ron Frase interview with the author, February 12, 2008; https://www.alternativegifts.org/userfiles/Harriet%20Prichard2.pdf/.

105. Colleen Townsend Evans interview.

106. Group interview.

107. Charles L. King to Miss Mears, September 23, 1962, Catalog B—Box 14, GL.

108. The following biographical sketch is based on Will Vaus, *My Father Was a Gangster: The Jim Vaus Story* (Washington, DC: Believe Books, 2007), and other sources as cited.

109. Mrs. Jim (Alice) Vaus as told to Dorothy C. Haskin, *They Called My Husband a Gangster*, 3rd ed. (Wheaton, IL: Van Kampen Press, 1952), 30.

110. "The Best Years of Our Lives with Miss Mears," College Department Alumni Banquet Program, 1947, Catalog B—Box 15, GL; Alice Vaus interview with the author, July 31, 2007.

111. Jim Vaus, *Why I Quit Syndicated Crime* (Wheaton, IL: Van Kampen Press, 1951), 10–15, 23, 25; Vaus, *They Called My Husband a Gangster*, 80; L. W. Gillenson, *Billy Graham and Seven Who Were Saved* (New York: Trident Press, 1967), 98–99.

112. Vaus, *Syndicated Crime*, 57–60. See also Vaus, *They Called My Husband a Gangster*, 60–61,

113. Billy Graham, *Just As I Am: The Autobiography of Billy Graham* (Carmel, NY: Guideposts, 1997), 157.

114. Powers, *Mears Story*, 49.

115. Vaus interview; Betty Lee Skinner, *Daws: The Story of Dawson Trotman Founder of the Navigators* (Grand Rapids: Zondervan, 1974), 329.

116. Tom Brunner, "10 Character Flaws That Can Derail Even Good People," blog post, March 1, 2012, http://www.doctorbrunner.com/10-character-flaws-that-can-derail-even-good-people/.

117. Colleen Townsend Evans interview; Van Harvey to Miss Mears, September 21, 1949, Catalog A—Box 22, GL.

118. Henrietta C. Mears, *Thoughts for All Seasons from the Notes of Henrietta C. Mears* (Glendale, CA: G/L Publications, 1973), 16.

Chapter Eleven

1. "Great Churches of America: VIII, First Presbyterian Church, Hollywood, California," *The Christian Century* (September 20, 1950): 1098–1105.

2. Both quotations from "Great Churches," 1104.

3. Both quotations from "Great Churches," 1104.

4. Bob Pierce to Henrietta Mears, December 12, 1961, Catalog B—Box 48, GL; Liela Jean Botsford interview with the author, August 29, 2009; Ethel May Baldwin and David V. Benson, *Henrietta Mears and How She Did It!* (Glendale, CA: Gospel Light Publications, 1966), 271, 273 (quotation).

5. "The Sun Never Sets on Teacher's Influence for Christ," undated GLINT flyer, Catalog A—Box 27, GL.

6. Baldwin and Benson, *Henrietta Mears*, 273.

7. Baldwin and Benson, *Henrietta Mears*, 273–74; quotation from "The Sun Never Sets."

8. "The Sun Never Sets."

9. Undated newspaper article, FBCM.

10. Cary Griffin to Miss Mears, May 1, 1962, Catalog B—Box 14, GL.

11. "The Sun Never Sets."

12. 1972 GLINT support letter from Paul R. Fretz, Executive Secretary, Catalog A—Box 1, GL.

13. Death Certificate of Norman T. Mears, MHC; "Physician's Death Caused by Choking," unidentified Northfield, Minnesota, newspaper, August 29, 1957.

14. Henrietta Mears 1946–1947 Travel Diary, June 17, 27, August 21, 1946, Catalog B—Box 51, GL.

15. John A. Ross and Lowell Rehner, *How to Get and Keep Good Eyesight: The Ross-Rehner Method of Strengthening Defective Eyes by Exercise and Care Including a Complete Eye Testing Kit* (no city, MI: Hall Publishing, 1943); Eye exercise notes, Catalog A—Box 22, GL; Mears 1946–1947 Diary, August 6, 7, 9, October 12, 28, November 2, 4, 1946, GL; Bill Grieg Jr. interview with Andrea Van Boven (Madden), October 16, 1996.

16. Richard Spencer interview with the author, July 8, 2007.

17. Baldwin and Benson, *Henrietta Mears*, 275.

18. Barbara Hudson Powers, *The Henrietta Mears Story* (Westwood, NJ: Revell, 1957), 35; Baldwin and Benson, *Henrietta Mears*, 274.

19. Henrietta Mears 1953 Diary, August 29, 30, 1953, Catalog B—Box 28, GL.

20. Henrietta Mears 1957 Performance Review, Catalog B—Box 25, GL.

21. Polly Craig interview with the author, January 25, 2009.

22. Death Certificate of Henrietta C. Mears, Los Angeles County Hall of Records, Los Angeles and Norwalk, CA; Richard Spencer interview with the author, July 8, 2007; Rachel Osborn interview with the author, July 9, 2007.

23. Bruce Angwin, "Remembering Teacher," Homebuilders Annual Conference, May 27, 1995, audiotape from the personal library of Andrea Van Boven (Madden).

24. Martha Mortenson interview with the author, July 17, 2007.

25. Audiotape of Raymond Lindquist speaking at the first Teachers and Officers Meeting after Mears's passing, April 1963, GL.

26. Baldwin and Benson, *Henrietta Mears*, 276.

27. Kay Sewall to Mabel Norberg, April 21, 1963, Catalog B—Box 16, GL.

28. Angelo Cohn, *Norman B. Mears: The Man Behind the Shadow Mask* (Minneapolis: T. S. Denison, 1972), 163–91.

29. Baldwin and Benson, *Henrietta Mears*, 277; audiotape of Ethel May Baldwin speaking at the first Teachers and Officers Meeting after Mears's passing, April 1963, GL.

30. Mortenson interview; Death Certificate of Henrietta C. Mears, LACHR.

31. Cy Nelson to Mabel Norberg, April 8, 1963, Catalog B—Box 16, GL.

32. Larry Ward, "Teacher is Dead," E P News Service, March 25, 1963, Catalog B—Box 16, GL.

33. Billy Graham cablegram from Honolulu, Hawaii, March 1963, Catalog B—Box 16, GL.

34. Kay Sewall to Mabel Norberg, April 21, 1963, Catalog B—Box 16, GL.

35. Baldwin and Benson, *Henrietta Mears*, 278–79, 280–81 (quotation).

36. Baldwin and Benson, *Henrietta Mears*, 280.

37. Ethel May Baldwin speaking at the first Teachers and Officers Meeting at the First Presbyterian Church of Hollywood after Mears's passing, spring 1963, GL.

38. Last Will and Testament of Henrietta C. Mears, LACHR; Botsford interview with the author, August 29, 2009.

39. The Davis family to Cy Nelson, March 27, 1963, Catalog B—Box 16, GL.

Conclusion

1. Doris Halverson interview with the author, September 1, 2007.

2. Henrietta C. Mears, *Thoughts for All Seasons* (Glendale, CA: Gospel Light Publications, 1973), 18, 64.

3. Dale Vree, *From Berkeley to East Berlin and Back* (Nashville: Thomas Nelson, 1985), 48. She did allow one brief class with regard to communism to be taught.

4. Betsy Cox, "Henrietta Mears as a Christian Education Director" (master's thesis, Fuller Theological Seminary, 1961), 29–30.

5. Mears, *Thoughts*, 18.

6. "Bulletin and Sign Quotes by Henrietta C. Mears," Catalog B—Box 32, GL.

7. Mears quoted in Barbara Hudson, "Hats, Hearts----and Henrietta!: The Henrietta Mears Story—Revised," 7, incomplete manuscript, Catalog B—Box 33, GL.

8. Transcript of an untitled talk by Henrietta Mears, September 24, 1949, 40–41, Catalog B—Box 47, GL.

9. "Tribute to Henrietta C. Mears, April 21, 1961," First Presbyterian Church of Hollywood, recorded by Bruce Angwin, cassette in the personal library of Andrea Van Boven (Madden).

10. Amber Thomas characterizes this relationship as a balance between self-denial and self-fulfillment. See Amber R. Thomas, "'God Has a Plan for Your Life': Personalized Life Providence (PLP) in Postwar American Evangelicalism" (PhD diss., University of Edinburgh, 2018), 142.

11. Henrietta Mears, "A Challenge to Christian Maturity," audiotape of a 1959 address at the Gospel Light Leadership Conference, GL.

12. Henrietta Mears, "The Romance of the Sunday School," transcript of an undated lecture in Baldwin and Benson, *Henrietta Mears*, 286–87.

13. Henrietta Mears, transcript of untitled address given in Chicago, September 24, 1949, 5, Catalog B—Box 47, GL.

14. Henrietta Mears, "How to Build a College Department," transcript of an address given at Fuller Theological Seminary, fall 1954, 7, Catalog B—Box 47, GL.

15. Estella H. Karn to Dr. Henrietta C. Mears, March 9, 1954, Catalog B—Box 14, GL.

16. Joel A. Carpenter, *Revive Us Again: The Reawakening of American Fundamentalism* (New York: Oxford University Press, 1997), 16.

17. William Greig Jr. interview with Andrea Van Boven (Madden), October 16, 1996; Bill Kennedy interview with the author, February 25, 2014; Thomas, "'God Has a Plan for Your Life,'" 120–21.

18. Thomas, "'God Has a Plan for Your Life,'" 121.

19. Transcript of untitled speech by Henrietta Mears, September 24, 1949, 42–43, GL—Catalog B, Box 47.

20. Mears, "How to Build a College Department"."

21. Gary Demarest interview with the author, July 20, 2007.

22. Martha Mortenson interview with the author, July 17, 2007.

23. William S. Meyer and Raymond I. Lindquist, "Host Churches Welcome General Assembly," *Southern California Presbyterian* 20, no. 5 (May 1955): 12–13.

24. Tod Bolsinger, "One Source, Many Streams: On Being Presbyterian in a Parched World," paper prepared as Moderator of the Middle Governing Body Commission, Presbyterian Church in the United States of America, August 10, 2011, attached to an email to the author, July 21, 2014.

25. Joy Eilers interview with the author, June 19, 26, 2009; Ron Frase interview with the author, February 12, 2008.

26. George M. Marsden, *Reforming Fundamentalism: Fuller Seminary and the New Evangelicalism* (Grand Rapids: Eerdmans, 1987; paperback edition, 1995), 90.

27. Note especially Betty A. DeBerg, *Ungodly Women: Gender and the First Wave of American Fundamentalism* (Minneapolis: Fortress Press, 1990; new edition Macon: Mercer University Press, 2000), and Marty Nesselbush Green, "From Sainthood to Submission: Gender Images in Conservative Protestantism, 1900–1940," *The Historian* 58 (spring 1996): 539–56.

28. Janette Hassey, *No Time for Silence: Evangelical Women in Public Ministry Around the Turn of the Century* (Grand Rapids: Academie Books, 1986); Michael S. Hamilton, "Women, Public Ministry, and American Fundamentalism, 1920–1950," *Religion and American Culture: A Journal of Interpretation* 3, no. 2 (summer 1993): 171–96.

29. Margaret Lamberts Bendroth and Virginia Lieson Brereton, "Introduction," pp. xi–xv in Margaret Lamberts Bendroth and Virginia Lieson Brereton, eds., *Women and Twentieth Century Protestantism* (Urbana, IL: University of Illinois Press, 2002), xiii; Janet Wilson James, "Women in American Religious History: An Overview," pp. 1–25 in Janet Wilson James, ed., *Women in American Religion* (Philadelphia: University of Pennsylvania Press, 1980; second printing, 1982), 2.

30. R. Marie Griffith, *God's Daughters: Evangelical Women and the Power of Submission* (Berkeley: University of California Press, 1997); Michelle M. Nickerson, *Mothers of Conservatism: Women and the Postwar Right* (Princeton, NJ: Princeton University Press, 2012); Julie Debra Neuffer, *Helen Andelin and the Fascinating Womanhood Movement* (Salt Lake City: University of Utah Press, 2014).

31. Colleen Townsend Evans interview with the author, July 31, 2007.

32. Matthew Avery Sutton, *American Apocalypse: A History of Modern Evangelicalism* (Cambridge, MA: Belknap, 2014), xiii.

33. Carpenter, *Revive Us Again*, 16.

34. Michael S. Hamilton, "The Interdenominational Evangelicalism of D. L. Moody and the Problem of Fundamentalism" pp. 230–80 in Darren Dochuk, Thomas S. Kidd, and Kurt W. Peterson, eds., *American Evangelicalism: George Marsden and the State of American Religious History* (Notre Dame, IN: University of Notre Dame Press, 2014). Quotation from page 264.

35. Molly Worthen, *Apostles of Reason: The Crisis of Authority in American Evangelicalism* (New York: Oxford University Press, 2014), 2 (both quotations).

36. Timothy E. W. Gloege, *Guaranteed Pure: The Moody Bible Institute, Business, and the Making of Modern Evangelicalism* (Chapel Hill: UNC Press, 2015), and Darren Dochuk, *Anointed with Oil: How Christianity and Crude Made Modern America* (New York: Basic Books, 2019). See also note 8 in the introduction.

Index

Titles published in the

LIBRARY OF RELIGIOUS BIOGRAPHY SERIES

***Orestes A. Brownson**: American Religious Weathervane*
by Patrick W. Carey

*The Puritan as Yankee: A Life of **Horace Bushnell***
by Robert Bruce Mullin

*A Life of **Alexander Campbell***
by Douglas A. Foster

*Emblem of Faith Untouched: A Short Life of **Thomas Cranmer***
by Leslie Williams

*Her Heart Can See: The Life and Hymns of **Fanny J. Crosby***
by Edith L. Blumhofer

***Emily Dickinson** and the Art of Belief*
by Roger Lundin

*A Short Life of **Jonathan Edwards***
by George M. Marsden

***Charles G. Finney** and the Spirit of American Evangelicalism*
by Charles E. Hambrick-Stowe

***William Ewart Gladstone**: Faith and Politics in Victorian Britain*
by David Bebbington

*One Soul at a Time: The Story of **Billy Graham***
by Grant Wacker

*A Heart Lost in Wonder: The Life and Faith of **Gerard Manley Hopkins***
by Catharine Randall

*Sworn on the Altar of God: A Religious Biography of **Thomas Jefferson***
by Edwin S. Gaustad

*The Miracle Lady: **Katherine Kuhlman** and the Transformation of Charismatic Christianity* by Amy Collier Artman

***Abraham Kuyper**: Modern Calvinist, Christian Democrat*
by James D. Bratt

*The Religious Life of **Robert E. Lee***
by R. David Cox

Abraham Lincoln: *Redeemer President*
by Allen C. Guelzo

The First American Evangelical: A Short Life of ***Cotton Mather***
by Rick Kennedy

Aimee Semple McPherson: *Everybody's Sister*
by Edith L. Blumhofer

Mother of Modern Evangelicalism: The Life and Legacy of ***Henrietta Mears***
by Arlin C. Migliazzo

Damning Words: The Life and Religious Times of ***H. L. Mencken***
by D. G. Hart

Thomas Merton *and the Monastic Vision*
by Lawrence S. Cunningham

God's Strange Work: ***William Miller*** *and the End of the World*
by David L. Rowe

Blaise Pascal: *Reasons of the Heart*
by Marvin R. O'Connell

Occupy Until I Come: ***A. T. Pierson*** *and the Evangelization of the World*
by Dana L. Robert

The Kingdom Is Always but Coming: A Life of ***Walter Rauschenbusch***
by Christopher H. Evans

A Christian and a Democrat: A Religious Life of ***Franklin D. Roosevelt***
by John F. Woolverton with James D. Bratt

Francis Schaeffer *and the Shaping of Evangelical America*
by Barry Hankins

Harriet Beecher Stowe: *A Spiritual Life*
by Nancy Koester

Billy Sunday *and the Redemption of Urban America*
by Lyle W. Dorsett

Howard Thurman *and the Disinherited: A Religious Biography*
by Paul Harvey

Assist Me to Proclaim: The Life and Hymns of ***Charles Wesley***
by John R. Tyson

Prophetess of Health: A Study of ***Ellen G. White***
by Ronald L. Numbers

George ***Whitefield****: Evangelist for God and Empire*
by Peter Y. Choi

The Divine Dramatist: ***George Whitefield*** *and the Rise of Modern Evangelicalism*
by Harry S. Stout

Liberty of Conscience: ***Roger Williams*** *in America*
by Edwin S. Gaustad